THE FOURTH GREAT AWAKENING
& THE FUTURE OF EGALITARIANISM

209 – recommends a ch–ch. like program
to publicly fund religiously run nursery
schools
   – big flaw in his analysis: the people +
     cities most likely to *do* the stuff
      fostering spiritual ~~capital~~/presences are
not those he identifies as carrying the
"4th Awakening."
   – A suspect this is true ⊕ for the
    other awakenings also, but even
    it's true for "4th"
   – perhaps could include this in book?

THE FOURTH GREAT

AWAKENING

& THE FUTURE OF EGALITARIANISM

ROBERT WILLIAM FOGEL

The University of Chicago Press
Chicago and London

The University of Chicago Press, Chicago 60637
The University of Chicago Press, Ltd., London
© 2000 by The University of Chicago
All rights reserved. Published 2000
Printed in the United States of America

09 08 07 06 05 04 03 02 01 00   1 2 3 4 5
ISBN 0-226-25662-6 (cloth)

Library of Congress Cataloging-in-Publication Data

Fogel, Robert William.
    The fourth great awakening & the future of egalitarianism / Robert William Fogel.
        p.   cm.
    Includes bibliographical references and index.
    ISBN 0-226-25662-6 (cloth : alk. paper)
        1. Equality—United States.   2. Evangelicalism—United States.   I. Title: Fourth great
    awakening and the future of egalitarianism.   II. Title.
    JC575.F64 2000
    305'.0973—dc21   99-089987

⊚ The paper used in this publication meets the minimum requirements of the American
National Standard for Information Sciences—Permanence of Paper for Printed Library
Materials, ANSI Z39.48-1992.

To Lisa, Andrew, and Rachel
and to all the other grandchildren
who will inherit the twenty-first century

CONTENTS

INTRODUCTION

The Egalitarian Creed in America

Why have moral issues again surged to the forefront in both business and politics? Why is the tradition of dedication to increasing social, political, and economic equality once again in jeopardy? What light can historical experience shed on the social, economic, and cultural aspects of the new egalitarian crisis?

As an economist, I am particularly concerned with America's economic prospects. At the dawn of the new millennium, the critical issues are no longer whether we can manage business cycles or whether the economy is likely to continue to grow at a satisfactory rate. It is not even whether we can grow without sacrificing the egalitarian advances of the past century. Although the consolidation of past gains cannot be ignored, the future of egalitarianism in America turns on the nation's ability to combine continued economic growth with an entirely new set of egalitarian reforms that address the urgent spiritual needs of our age, secular as well as sacred. Spiritual (or immaterial) inequity is now as great a problem as material inequity, perhaps even greater.

Economists and others who worry about egalitarian issues tend to think about distribution in terms of such material goods as food, clothing, and shelter, which used to constitute over 80 percent of the consumption of households. To be poor in the decades before World War I was to be deprived of these tangible essentials of life and to be vulnerable to disease and early death. In that age, things that you could see, count, weigh, or otherwise directly measure constituted the overwhelming output of an economy.

Similarly, the investments of the last third of the nineteenth century and the first third of the twentieth, the investments that embodied the new technologies that drove the economy down the path of rapid economic growth, were also massively physical: railroads, oil refineries, integrated steel furnaces and rolling mills, motor-vehicle-manufacturing plants, power plants to generate electricity and the grids to distribute it, and the whole array of factories that produced the new machines and consumer products made possible by electricity.

During the last six or so decades of the twentieth century, the domination of output by material products began to be eroded at an increasing rate. The rise to dominance of immaterial commodities is symbolized by the growth of such professional occupations as physicians, mathematicians, natural scientists, lawyers, teachers, and engineers, from barely 4 percent of the labor force in 1900 to over 30 percent today.[1] Similarly, the main form of capital today is not buildings, machines, or electric grids but labor skills, what economists call *human capital* or *knowledge capital*. Both for individuals and for businesses, it is the size and quality of these immaterial assets that determine success in competitive markets and conditions of life for ordinary people.

The agenda for egalitarian policies that has dominated reform movements for most of the past century—what I call the *modernist* egalitarian agenda—was based on material redistribution. The critical aspect of a *postmodern* egalitarian agenda is not the distribution of money income, or food, or shelter, or consumer durables. Although there are still glaring inadequacies in the distribution of material commodities that must be addressed, the most intractable maldistributions in rich countries such as the United States are in the realm of spiritual or immaterial assets. These are the critical assets in the struggle for self-realization.

A good place to begin a consideration of the content of a postmodern egalitarian agenda is with Socrates' question, What is the good life? That was a crucial question not only for the sons of rich Athenians but for the sons of the landed rich throughout history. Freed of the need to work in order to satisfy their material needs, they sought self-realization in public service, military adventures, philanthropy, the arts, theology, ethics, and moral philosophy. Their preoccupation with immaterial commodities led Adam Smith to argue that the landed aristocracy ignored their property and lacked interest in advancing methods of cultivation: "The situation of such a person," he wrote, "naturally disposes him to attend rather to ornament which pleases his fancy, than to profit for which he has so little occasion."[2]

In a world in which all but a small percentage are lacking in adequate nutrition and other necessities of life, self-realization may indeed seem like mere ornament, but not in a country where even the poor are rich by past or Third World standards. That is the case in America today since the poverty line is at a level of real income that was attained a century ago only by those in the top 10 percent of the income distribution. Technophysio evolution (the interaction of technological progress and physiological improvement) has made it possible to extend the quest for self-realization from a minute fraction of the population to almost the whole of it.

Some proponents of egalitarianism insist on characterizing the *material* level of the poor today as being harsh. They confound current and past conditions of living. Failure to recognize the enormous *material* gains of the last century, even for the poor, impedes rather than advances the struggle in rich nations against chronic poverty, whose principal characteristic is the *spiritual estrangement* from the mainstream society of those so afflicted. Although material assistance is an important element in the struggle to overcome spiritual estrangement, such assistance will not be properly targeted if one assumes that improvement in material conditions naturally leads to spiritual improvement.

The proposition that material improvement would ennoble the masses, so widely embraced by modernist reformers, did more to promote the consumerism of the 1920s and 1930s than to produce spiritual regeneration. The middle and working classes became preoccupied with the acquisition of automobiles and those household appliances made possible by electricity: irons, lamps, telephones, toasters, refrigerators, radios, and washing machines. Moreover, whatever their virtues in elucidating past issues, the economist's traditional measures of income inequality are now inadequate. They focus on a variable—money income—that currently accounts for less than half of real consumption and that in a generation may account for just a quarter of real consumption. Such measures shed little light on the most intractable forms of poverty (those related to the unequal distribution of spiritual resources). Nor do they bear on the capacity of individuals to overcome the social estrangement that undermines their quality of life.

Realization of the potential of an individual is not something that can be legislated by the state, nor can it be provided to the weak by the strong. It is something that must develop within each individual on the basis of a succession of choices. The emphasis on individual choice does not mean that other individuals and institutions play no role. Quite the contrary, the quality of the choices and the range of opportunity depend critically on how well endowed an individual is with spiritual resources.

The quest for spiritual equity thus turns not so much on money as on access to spiritual assets, most of which are transferred and developed privately rather than through the market. Moreover, some of the most critical spiritual assets, such as a sense of purpose, self-esteem, a sense of discipline, a vision of opportunity, and a thirst for knowledge, are transferred at very young ages.

The reforms required to achieve spiritual equity overlap with, but are not identical to, those required to achieve material equity. Shaping a new, broader program of egalitarian reforms, while continuing to pursue the unrealized objectives of the program for material equity, will not be easy. One of the main obstacles to the expansion of egalitarian reforms in the United States is the attempt to equate the egalitarian ethic with one or another party. Egalitarianism is a national ethic. Or, to put it more precisely, the rise of an egalitarian ethic was one of the major factors that turned the separate American colonies into a nation and eventually led to the establishment of egalitarianism as a national creed.

As a result, the United States has made progress toward increasing egalitarianism under each of the two main parties, despite their differences in interpretation of the creed. For example, elimination of property qualifications for voting during the first six decades of the nineteenth century took place in states governed both by the Democratic Party and its predecessors (most often called the Democratic Republican Party), who trace their roots back to Thomas Jefferson, and by the Republican Party and its predecessors (principally the Federalists and the Whigs), who trace their roots back to John Adams and Alexander Hamilton, secretary of the Treasury under George Washington.

The parties did differ, however, on which issues were key to egalitarian progress in the past and on what role the federal government ought to play. For most of the period prior to the Civil War, the Democrats, North and South, depicted themselves as champions of the laboring classes and of proprietors of small businesses, but they defended slavery; they favored universal male suffrage, but not for blacks; they advocated the free (or virtually free) distribution of land in the national domain to workers; and they wanted to restrict government intervention in the economy. On the other hand, the Republicans and their Whig predecessors denounced the laissez-faire policies of the Democrats, emphasized the obligation of the federal government to promote economic progress, sought to restrict the territorial expansion of slavery, and often championed the extension of the franchise to free blacks in the North—but also tended to favor the resettlement of all blacks in Africa (a policy called *colonization*).

Toward the end of the nineteenth century, the Republicans were ahead of the Democrats on such issues as the regulation of railroads, the use of personal income taxes to finance government welfare programs, and the municipal ownership or control of public utilities. However, the Democrats, especially during Woodrow Wilson's administration (1913–21), soon caught up with the Republicans on these issues and were more sympathetic to labor unions than the Republicans had been. However, they were not yet more sympathetic to blacks; it was not until the 1930s that the Democrats began to address the plight of blacks seriously. This, together with the Republican attempt to court white support in the South, shifted black allegiance from the Republicans to the Democrats.

Over the course of American history, two major principles have emerged as touchstones for egalitarian progress. During the eighteenth century and the first three-quarters of the nineteenth, the prevailing principle was equality of opportunity. That principle accepted the inequality of income and other circumstances of life as natural but held that persons of low social rank could raise themselves—by industry, perseverance, talent, and righteous behavior—to the top of the economic and social order. The "great principle" that kept the Union together so long, said Abraham Lincoln, shortly before his first inauguration, was the promise that "*all* should have an equal chance."[3]

That principle was appropriate for a predominantly agricultural society in which an empire of land was still unexploited and parcels could still be obtained at modest prices. It was appropriate also because most nonagricultural enterprises were still small scale and apprentices and journeymen could reasonably expect that they would eventually become masters of their own modest enterprises.

During the last third of the nineteenth century, new technologies and larger markets promoted a rapid increase in the scale of business, particularly in the railroad, steel, and petroleum industries. This led to the loss of jobs in smaller enterprises that could not compete effectively with the new industrial giants. Beginning workers at the Carnegie Iron and Steel Company could no longer expect that, by dint of hard labor, they would become masters of their own steelworks. Even worse, the new giant corporations took advantage of excess labor supplies, created by huge waves of immigration, to cut wages, and they employed private police and federal troops to break the strikes of unions that sought to resist wage cuts. Nor could urban workers easily escape the misery of their conditions by fleeing to the countryside. By the 1890s, the frontier was declared closed, and an agricultural depression sent millions of farmworkers to the cities in search of employment. Equality of opportunity seemed to be a false promise to workers and reformers alike.

These circumstances gave rise to a new ethic whose touchstone was equality of condition rather than equality of opportunity. Greater equality of condition was to be achieved primarily by government programs aimed at raising wages by reducing the supply of labor (through laws that reduced work hours, ended unrestricted immigration, and prohibited women and children from performing some types of labor) and by supporting union efforts to raise wages and improve working conditions. Income was also to be transferred from the rich to the poor by imposing income taxes on the rich and using the revenue to finance welfare programs for the poor, such as the pension program for elderly veterans of the Union army and their widows and dependent children. The level of taxes and of payments in these welfare programs was initially quite low, but, over the course of the twentieth century, taxes and transfers were substantially expanded both in amount and in the scope of coverage. By the mid-1970s, the modern welfare system was in place, and, by the 1990s, close to 20 percent of the income of the richest fifth of U.S. households was being transferred to those in the lower part of the income distribution.[4]

In recent years, the principle of equality of opportunity has begun to assume its former primacy. This return to the old touchstone is due partly to the upsurge of enthusiastic religion (religion characterized by spiritual intensity linked to conversions), which emphasizes individual responsibility. It is also due partly to the success of the entitlement programs, which have significantly improved the living conditions of the elderly and the incapacitated. Moreover, most of the remaining unresolved egalitarian issues, such as the barriers to occupational and educational access, including the glass ceilings that block the upward career paths of women, blacks, and other minorities, are issues more of opportunity than of income transfer. Additional income alone will not ensure the elimination of inequities. It is, however, the newly emerging equity issues—pension rights, access to medical care, expanded educational opportunity, the accessibility of leisure-time activities, labor flexibility, and the ability to combine careers with a full family life—that do the most to elevate the principle of equal opportunity to the fore.

It is not possible to deal with the future of egalitarianism in America without considering the role of religious movements, particularly those

arising from evangelical Protestant churches or others that practice enthusiastic religion. We know from experience that black churches have played
a key role in the continuing struggle for civil rights and that they received
substantial support from many of the mainline white churches. The leadership role that churches played in the civil rights struggle was not an iso-
lated incident. American churches and the lay movements they generated
were in the forefront of earlier social reforms, such as the right of trade
unions to strike, the use of state and federal fiscal policy to redistribute
income from the rich to the poor, the right of women to vote, Prohibition,
and the provision of universal primary education. The greatest of all the
reform movements in American history, the abolition of slavery, was for
decades almost exclusively a religious movement until a number of religiously inspired Northern politicians developed brilliant tactics and strategies necessary to create a winning antislavery coalition.

The role of American evangelical churches in promoting popular
democracy, radical social reform, and new political alignments stands in
sharp contrast to that of European churches. The main European
churches are state churches: their leaders are formally confirmed, their
clergy paid, and their schools subsidized by the state. These churches are
fundamentally hierarchical in structure. Religious doctrine is laid down by
leaders—the pope, cardinals, and bishops in the Catholic Church—and
the clergy's duty is to inculcate the members of the congregations in
church dogma. Despite important differences in history, doctrine, and administration, the Anglican, Catholic, Lutheran, and Orthodox Churches
of Europe have generally legitimated the governments in power and rallied
popular support for their wars, laws, and other enterprises.[5]

Not only have American evangelical churches been independent of
the state and represented the majority of Protestant churchgoers, but they
have often served as critics of state policy and as advocates of individual
rights. They played a leading role in ending aristocratic privilege in the
United States and were principal vehicles through which the common
people have been drawn into the process of shaping American society.
Evangelical churches promoted popular democracy partly because they
were based on the principle that the congregation rather than the hierarchy
was the pivot of church government. As a result, the local minister was
employed by the congregation rather than the church hierarchy. This principle also meant that the influence of the national church organizations
over a given congregation was limited to what the congregation was willing to accept. Moreover, evangelical churches emphasized the responsibility of each individual to study and interpret the Bible, guided by a personal

struggle to be cleansed of sin and become "born again"; they rejected the idea that only church leaders were able to interpret the Bible. Popular democracy was also promoted by evangelical revivals, beginning with a period known as the First Great Awakening (1730–60), since many of the revivalist clergy encouraged their followers to put their own struggle for salvation above allegiance to ecclesiastical authority.[6]

When considering the future of egalitarianism in America, it is necessary to take account of the "realignment synthesis." This synthesis holds that American politics has been characterized by "critical elections" during which political realignment occurs and a dominant coalition ushers in an extended era of interrelated legislative reforms. The eras of major reforms in public policy generally last several decades. Among the most influential of the political realignments was the Republican Party control of the federal government that followed the election of Abraham Lincoln in 1860 and that led to two generations of Republican-led economic, social, and political reforms. Of similar magnitude was the Democratic coalition shaped by Franklin D. Roosevelt, which captured the federal government in 1932 and, under the banners of the New Deal and Lyndon B. Johnson's Great Society, ushered in half a century of reform.

There is a link between the egalitarian reform movements promoted by the evangelical churches and the legislative reforms that have followed political realignments. The periodic theological crises that have led the churches to reconsider their ethical values and social policies have been central features of the electoral crises that have produced the political realignments. Both the theological and the political crises have been byproducts of the extraordinary pace of technological change and economic transformation that has changed human beings both culturally and physiologically.

An unprecedented series of breakthroughs since 1700 in agriculture, trade, manufacturing, communication, energy production, leisure-time activity, and medical services have made it possible for human beings nearly to double their life spans and greatly to improve the robustness and capacity of their vital organ systems. The process of technophysio evolution has led to an increase in the world's population during the last century alone that is far greater than any that occurred during the whole previous history of humankind.

While economic growth since 1700 has been relatively steady and technological change has accelerated, there has been a recurring lag between the vast technological transformations and the human adjustments to those transformations. It is this lag that has provoked the crises that periodically usher in profound reconsiderations of ethical values, that produce new agendas for ethical and social reform, and that give rise to political movements that champion the new agendas.

This book weaves together themes that are often treated separately—technological change, economic growth, cultural crisis, religious crisis, and political crisis—into a new analysis of the difficult social and economic issues that currently confront the nation and the even more complex issues likely to confront our children and grandchildren. The analysis rests on a synthesis of major new bodies of research in history, economics, political science, medicine, and physiology, much of which is still known only to specialists in each of these fields. This research in these various disciplines is the key to determining which reforms did the most to promote egalitarianism and how much of the progress toward egalitarian outcomes resulted from the reforms rather than from economic and technological changes beyond the reach of the reforms.

As was suggested above, political realignments are set in motion by the lag between new technologies and the human capacity to cope with the ethical and practical complexities that those new technologies entail. The response to profoundly disturbing problems ranging from the urban crisis and the domination of small business by large-scale industry to the numerous adjustments entailed by the Information Revolution has been both religious and political. The religious response has been more rapid because of the high degree of independence of specific evangelical congregations from hierarchical control and from the restraints imposed on political parties, which must often trim their policies to maintain coalitions. Like-minded congregations are free to join with each other on particular issues, often cutting across denominations (as in the campaigns against slavery, for prohibition, and for extending the franchise to women), with the aim of promoting new, often destabilizing political coalitions that will enact their program of reforms. Hence the close identification between populism and evangelical religion.

Chapter 1 sketches a new analytic framework for analyzing these religious-political movements and defines the four overlapping cycles in religion and politics (the four "Great Awakenings") that have shaped the struggle for egalitarianism in America. These Great Awakenings are reform movements with an ethical/programmatic phase followed by a legislative/political phase, both of which arise out of the lag between technological change and institutional adjustment. Each Awakening lasts about one hundred years, including a declining phase during which exponents of one Great Awakening clash with those of the next. The First Great

Awakening began in the 1730s and ripened into the American Revolution against the British Crown. The Second Great Awakening began about 1800 and produced the crusade against slavery that eventuated in the Civil War. The Third Great Awakening arose at the end of the nineteenth century and led to the rise of the welfare state and policies to promote diversity. The Fourth Great Awakening, which began about 1960, has recently entered its political phase and is focused on spiritual reform. The chapter briefly surveys principal aspects of these cycles and the reforms that they ushered in. I give a somewhat more extended treatment of the current religious-political cycle, the Fourth Great Awakening. I also briefly introduce both old and new issues of egalitarianism that are likely to dominate debates over social policy for a generation or more. The chapter ends with a series of caveats on the limitations of the analytic framework and some guides to its proper uses.

Chapter 2 deals with the dual nature of technological change, which provided the foundation for the remarkable economic growth of the past three centuries and was indispensable to the egalitarian achievements of the twentieth century. But rapid technological change has also been highly disruptive of the existing social fabric. Time and again, technological change created problems for which society was ethically, politically, and socially unprepared. Technological advances in distilling reduced the cost of spirits and made it possible for the urban poor to afford immoderate amounts of alcohol. Reductions in the cost of ocean transportation brought huge waves of immigrants into American labor markets, lowering wages and promoting unemployment. Economies of scale in steel and other manufacturing industries undermined small-scale businesses, brought ruin to many middle-class families, and undermined the belief that every journeyman could eventually become his own master. Advances in surgical techniques and the development of antibiotics made it possible to extend lives through organ transplants before we as a society had fashioned adequate ethical guidelines for harvesting organs or distributing them.

Chapter 2 also shows how the accelerating rate of change in the economy and society since 1760 has periodically touched off powerful religious and political protest movements that undermine existing political coalitions, produce a new agenda for egalitarian reforms, and precipitate political realignments capable of realizing these agendas.

Chapter 3 describes the emergence of the "modern egalitarian ethic," which raised equality of condition over equality of opportunity. This change hinged on the belief that society would be better off if income were transferred from the rich to the poor and that the state was the proper instrument to effect such a redistribution. Government efforts in England and France between 1525 and 1800 to cope with periodic and devastating famines provided the seedbed for the egalitarian state. The English policy began in the 1750s by taxing the rich to ensure inventories of grain that could be provided to the poor in periods of scarcity and culminated in the early 1790s with regular allowances in aid of wages sufficient to maintain an adequate supply of food for a worker and his family by the standards of the day.

Nonetheless, down to the middle of the nineteenth century, a fifth of the English population was too malnourished for regular work. There were, however, relatively few paupers in the North American colonies, and hunger was not a major concern. Consequently, the egalitarians of the religious upsurge in America that historians call the Second Great Awakening (beginning about 1800) focused their efforts on a sweeping reform agenda that aimed to eliminate all barriers to equal opportunity. Among the campaigns that they initiated were justice for indigenous Americans, women's rights, temperance, the provision of universal public education, urban reform, the abolition of slavery, and the extension of the franchise to blacks and women. The grassroots movements that they promoted were so powerful that they resulted in seven constitutional amendments and numerous laws at the federal, state, and local levels.

The reform program of the Second Great Awakening was well suited to a rural society of farmers and small businesses based largely on craft labor. With an empire of cheap land, and with the modest capital requirements of handicraft businesses, upward economic and social mobility over a lifetime for hardworking, frugal employees was not an impossible dream. But the march of technology over the decades transformed the structure of the economy. In one industry after another, the optimal size of the firm became very large. Industries in which new technologies required large plant sizes to function efficiently included steel and petroleum refining, food production, transportation equipment, machinery, and chemicals. The small-scale producers that once dominated these industries were driven out of business, paving the way for bitter, bloody confrontations between "robber barons," on the one side, and workers and small proprietors, on the other.

Because individuals could not effectively challenge corporate power, the "new lights" of the Third Great Awakening (which began about 1890) challenged theological doctrines that placed the onus of poverty on individual corruption. They veered away from a belief in the inherent sinfulness of humankind and substituted a belief in the innocence of the newborn. They argued that social reform was prior to, and a necessary condition for, the personal salvation of those in the grip of poverty.

The reform programs promoted by the leaders of the Third Great Awakening included a vast expansion of secondary and higher education, the institution of income taxes and government entitlement programs to redistribute income from the rich to the poor, the regulation of big businesses, the protection of the right of workers to form unions and to strike, and the reduction of the supply of workers (in order to increase the level of wages) by restricting immigration and child labor and by regulating the working conditions of women. The initial focus on economic egalitarianism by the pioneers of the Third Great Awakening was eventually extended to cultural egalitarianism by their successors, who attacked religious and racial barriers to equal opportunity and still later attacked all gender-based assumptions about behavior, demanded the legalization of abortion, and campaigned to end discrimination based on sexual orientation.

Chapter 4 evaluates the contribution of the reforms of the Third Great Awakening to the egalitarian objectives that prompted them. It deals with the extent, timing, and causes of reductions in inequality. The chapter also explains problems in measuring the costs and benefits of programs and describes and interprets the difference in economic and biomedical indices of inequality. A number of policy conundrums are explored, including the proposition that economic growth and egalitarianism are conflicting goals, and a balance sheet of policy outcomes is presented that includes several remarkable successes and one glaring failure. The chapter closes with a discussion of difficulties in anticipating the effect of certain government policies. The difficulties stem partly from the speed with which technology is changing, partly from the long lags between the adoption of certain policies and their payoffs, and partly from the rigidities of political processes.

Chapter 5 is the climax of the book. It shows that the egalitarian agenda of the Third Great Awakening has been largely accomplished and that further progress requires a new agenda focused on new issues, some of which have arisen from the incredible technological advances of the past century, others of which stem from the successes and failures of previous reforms. The initiative in the shaping of this new agenda has, to a large extent, passed to the disciples of the Fourth Great Awakening, who have focused on issues of spiritual (immaterial) equity. This proposition may surprise those who oppose the ideology of the religious Right.[7] However, it is the substance of the proposals, not the rhetoric, that is germane. The issue is whether these reforms are likely to contribute to greater equity in the distribution of the spiritual assets that have such large effects on both the quest for self-realization and economic success in the marketplace.

Chapter 5 defines the new egalitarian issues and explores avenues along which solutions may lie, including a vast expansion of new forms of education. Much of the analysis focuses on the changes in the structure of consumption, the new uses of time, and the potential for spending 45 percent of a long adult life span in healthy, productive, and fulfilling post-retirement activities. To achieve this potential, however, it is necessary to overcome severe misallocations of immaterial resources. Chapter 5 discusses the nature of these immaterial resources, the problems involved in correcting their maldistribution, and possible divisions of reforms among government, business, and compassionate voluntary organizations. Central to the new reforms is a vast expansion of higher education and a variety of new educational forms geared to the needs of alienated young people and the elderly.

Not all the egalitarian agenda established by the Third Great Awakening, however, has been realized. The issues that still remain vital to the progress of egalitarianism, including the problems wrought by globalization and inequality in the international distribution of income, are also considered in chapter 5, as are the policies most likely to lead to their speedy resolution. Although the main focus of this book is on economic, social, and political developments within the United States, these issues cannot be adequately understood without considering experiences elsewhere in the world. Moreover, the rapid economic growth of East Asian societies, with cultures different from those that have prevailed in the United States, requires consideration of the East Asian road to egalitarianism.

The afterword explains why we should not be afraid of the future, although it poses formidable challenges, perhaps even more formidable challenges than those our generation has faced because of the increasing intrusion of science on the mystery of life. Despite the increasing complexities of social life, the profound new ethical challenges, and the potential for disaster, my predictions for the next six decades include longer and healthier lives, more abundant food supplies, improved housing and environments, higher levels of education for larger numbers of people, the narrowing of both material and spiritual inequality (not only within the country but internationally), better-paying and more flexible jobs, more time for parenting, stronger families that spend more leisure time together, lower rates of crime and corruption, and greater ethnic and racial harmony.

This vision is based, not on divine revelation, but on an analysis of available evidence of long-term trends in science, technology, human physiology, education, and economic and social behavior. Forecasting is an art, not a science, and many forecasts, no matter how carefully designed, turn out to be far off the mark because of incorrect assumptions and overlooked considerations. Nevertheless, decisions based on long-term forecasts are made every day by businesses contemplating heavy investments that will take many years to repay and will be amortized over several decades. Parents also have a heavy investment in the future—our children and grandchildren. Hence, we should try to develop the best forecasts that art and science permit.

For readers who want elaboration of the more controversial findings reported in this book, there are appendices keyed to the relevant parts of the text, including appendix 5E, written by Chulhee Lee of Seoul National University.

Readers should be forewarned that I write as a secular child of the Third Great Awakening and that all my life I have accepted its basic ethics and the basic thrust of its reforms. My task as a social scientist, however, is to study society with as much objectivity as I can muster and to report the empirical findings without extenuating those that seem to cut across my most cherished values. Readers will judge for themselves how well I have succeeded in that task.

ONE

The Fourth Great Awakening,
the Political Realignment of the 1990s,
and the Potential for Egalitarian Reform

Americans are more deeply divided and angry with each other today than at any time since the 1850s. Now, as then, distrust of leaders and institutions is widespread, and charges of conspiracy by one group against the liberty, livelihood, or principles of another pour out in torrents of speeches and news stories. Some of the issues are different, but the hatreds and fears are equally intense. Now, as then, there are racial and ethnic clashes in the cities, terrorist confrontations, a fracturing of parties, and charges of corruption everywhere: in government, in churches, in businesses, and in bedrooms. At the heart of the turmoil, now, as then, are three factors: a new technological revolution, a cultural crisis precipitated by technologically induced change in the structure of the economy, and two powerful social and political movements confronting each other across an ideological and ethical chasm, threatening to undermine the great egalitarian reforms of the twentieth century.

The political crisis of the 1850s was set in motion by a powerful religious upsurge that, for reasons explained in the next section, historians refer to as *the Second Great Awakening*. This religious movement produced new and highly controversial ethical and reform programs that first fractured the largest Protestant denominations and then fractured the major parties. The result was a political realignment that precipitated the Civil War and led to Republican domination of the federal government for more than half a century.

The harbinger of the political realignment of the 1850s was the increasing tendency of the evangelical agenda to push aside the economic issues that had been predominant in American politics during the quarter century following the 1828 election of Andrew Jackson as president. Such issues as the tariff, the regulation of banks, land policy, and federal promotion of internal improvements (roads, railroads, and waterways) were superseded by issues initially considered important only to a handful of "religious cranks": emancipation, temperance, the teaching of the King James Bible in the schools, the regulation of immigration, and the restriction of voting by immigrants. These new issues were brought to the forefront by the technological changes that produced the Cotton Kingdom, the first wave of rapid urbanization, massive immigration, the rise of the factory system, and regional dislocation in farming.

The political crisis of the 1990s was also set in motion by a powerful religious upsurge. As was true of the revival during the Jacksonian era, the current revival has produced a new, culturally oriented political agenda and has mobilized a zealous reform movement, often called *the religious Right,* behind that agenda. Galvanized by the charisma of Ronald Reagan, the new movement entered national politics first at the presidential level, although it had been evident in county politics as far back as the early 1970s. Scorned by the liberal leadership of the Democratic Party, the religious Right nevertheless began to exert a distinct influence on presidential elections as early as 1984 but had only a relatively small effect on congressional elections until 1994.

The shift of a major category of deeply religious voters from the Democrats to the Republicans is most clearly evident in the off-year congressional elections. Polls taken during or shortly after the midterm congressional elections of the 1980s revealed that about one-third of adults identified themselves as evangelical or other believers in enthusiastic religion—religion that is characterized by spiritual intensity linked to conversion. Such individuals split their vote fairly evenly between Democratic and Republican candidates in 1982, but, by 1994, they had shifted their allegiance to the Republicans. In 1994, only 26 percent continued to vote Democratic, while 74 percent voted Republican. A shift of this magnitude for a typical presidential election is equivalent to a loss of about 7 percent of the Democratic constituency and a gain of the same amount for the Republicans (i.e., a fourteen-point spread in favor of the Republicans).[1] In addition to this shifting allegiance, the share of ballots cast by believers in enthusiastic religion had increased, which, of course, further increased their influence.

If consolidated, this realignment could make the Republicans the

dominant party for a generation or more. In the American political context, the term *dominant* does not mean that a party wins election after
election by a large margin. Electoral history shows that margins between
the major parties are close even during eras in which one party is dominant, as was the case between the elections of 1868 and 1930, when the
Republicans controlled the presidency 75 percent of the time (the corresponding figures for the Senate and the House were 84 and 59 percent,
respectively). *Dominance* means rather that a particular party wins most
national elections by narrow margins. Hence, although the size of a party's
core constituency has a large influence on the outcome of an election, this
advantage can be offset in any particular campaign by a host of contingent
factors, including economic recession, international crisis, a lackluster
ticket, scandal, voter turnout, poor organization, and intraparty splits.[2]

Election statistics from the 1980s and 1990s indicate that we are in a
process of political change that is to a large extent produced by trends in
American religiousness. One cannot understand current political and ethical trends, or properly forecast future economic developments, without
understanding the cycles in religious feeling in American history and the
social, economic, and political reform movements that they have generated.

RELIGIOUS-POLITICAL CYCLES (GREAT AWAKENINGS) IN AMERICAN HISTORY

Upsurges in religious enthusiasm in America have tended to run in cycles
lasting about one hundred years. Each cycle consists of three phases, each
about a generation long, beginning with a phase of religious revival that
intensifies religious beliefs and ushers in new or reinvigorated ethics and
theological principles. The phase of religious revival is followed by a phase
in which the new ethics precipitates powerful political programs and
movements. Each cycle ends with a phase in which the ethics and politics
fostered by the religious revival are challenged and the political coalition
promoted by that revival goes into decline. These cycles overlap, the end
of one cycle coinciding with the beginning of the next.

Those who directly identify with the new principles of a religious revival are usually a minority of the population, even if a large minority, but
what they lack in numbers they make up in enthusiasm and in an energy
derived from a sense of the righteousness of their cause. They have been
able to extend their political influence far beyond their numbers by build-

ing coalitions on single issues, as in the case of the movements against slavery and for prohibition.

Historians of religion refer to such periods of religious revival as *Great Awakenings*. They generally recognize that the United States has experienced three Great Awakenings. I contend that the United States is currently experiencing its Fourth, which began about 1960. The new religious revival is fueled by a revulsion with what believers see as the corruption of contemporary society. Believers in the new religious revival are against sexual debauchery, against indulgence in alcohol, tobacco, gambling, and drugs, against gluttony, and against all other forms of self-indulgence that titillate the senses and destroy the soul. The leaders of the revival advocate piety and an ethic that extols individual responsibility, hard work, a simple life, and dedication to the family. They emphasize that, in order to resist the corruptions promoted by Satan and abetted by many persons in business and political life, individuals must dedicate themselves to God by embracing an unrelenting struggle for self-purification. They call on their adherents to strive for a mystical experience that will cleanse them of sin and lead to spiritual rebirth. Spiritual rebirth is not just an intellectual concept; it is a profoundly felt, sensuous experience. The religious excitement generated by the current revival has energized a number of movements, such as the assault on smoking and the campaigns against violence in the media and against sexual harassment in the workplace, that have a large, direct effect on political and business life.

It should not be assumed that everyone who experiences religious revival during a Great Awakening embraces the same set of new theological principles and moral precepts. Quite the contrary: every Great Awakening has produced splits within religious circles. Those who have been called *new light, new side,* or *new theology* revivalists have typically embraced the ideas and reforms that became predominant during the phase of political ascendancy. They have usually been opposed by a group of nearly equal strength, at least during the early stages of the revival, that continued to embrace orthodox theology and moral viewpoints. In other words, the characterizations of the revival and ascendancy phases of each cycle are not independent of each other since they take account of which side eventually becomes predominant.

It should also be noted that religious revivals are not confined merely to the years designated *the revival phase*. Revivals have been more or less continuous since the early eighteenth century, although some periods have a higher incidence of conversions than others. What identifies the revival phase, however, is not merely the great number of conversions but the emergence of a distinctive set of theological and ethical principles and a coherent program of reform undergirded by zealous reform movements.

THE FOUR GREAT AWAKENINGS AND THEIR SOCIAL AND POLITICAL EFFECT

To understand fully the meaning of the Fourth Great Awakening, it is necessary to review briefly the effect of the three previous religious-political cycles (Great Awakenings) on social and economic policy. America was from its beginning a deeply religious society. Until 1790, about 80 percent of Americans (90 percent of the free population) were of British descent and were attached primarily to the dissenting British churches: Congregationalists, Presbyterians, Baptists, Quakers, and Methodists. Another 5 percent were pietistic Germans or Scandinavians whose religious creeds and ethics were similar to those of the dissenting British churches. The New England strain of these denominations was particularly strong in America because of favorable demographic conditions that produced both unusually high birth- and unusually low death rates. Consequently, Puritans made up just 5 percent of all the Europeans who migrated into the United States before 1820, but, because of the highly favorable birth- and death rates, the census of 1820 indicates that the descendants of the Puritans represented about 80 percent of the Northern and about 20 percent of the Southern population.[3]

The First Great Awakening

Although the Puritan founders of New England were deeply dedicated to their religious principles, their children and grandchildren were more equivocal. Religious enthusiasm waned until the early eighteenth century, when a new surge of religious feeling became evident. One of the most inspirational figures of what came to be known as *the First Great Awakening* was George Whitefield, an itinerant minister from England who was influenced by both Methodism and Calvinism. From 1738 to 1740, Whitefield evangelized in both Northern and Southern colonies with an explosive emotional power that deeply moved those who heard him preach. Whitefield, who returned to America many times, inspired other ministers and lay itinerants to take up the task of extending the revival to every corner of the British colonies. Jonathan Edwards, a Congregational minister to a venerable church in Northampton, Massachusetts, was the leader of the revival in New England and the most influential theologian of the era. Edwards held out hope that unregenerate sinners might yet be saved through conversion.

The main theological features of the First Great Awakening were the justification of public, emotional revival meetings, the emphasis on "new birth" (conversion) as the central objective of the revivals, the emergence of the ethic of benevolence as an aspect of new birth, and the modification of the Calvinist doctrine of predestination, which held that only those designated before birth by God would be saved. The way in which the advocates of the new theology promoted their views often undermined the authority of church leaders, in that revivalists called on people to trust their own experience and not depend on the authority of church officials. Revivalist leaders accused orthodox leaders of corrupting the church by their pursuit of power and luxury. Although the challenge to Calvinist doctrine by the new lights of the First Great Awakening may be appropriately described as latent, incipient, or muted, it laid the basis for the frontal assault on orthodoxy that emerged during the Second Great Awakening.

The First Great Awakening's phase of political ascendancy ran from 1760 through 1790. It was marked by attacks on British moral and political corruption and by charges that this corruption was being foisted on the American colonies, where it threatened the attainment of spiritual and political virtue. Considering that the new light religion provided much of the popular ideological foundation for the Revolution by questioning the legitimacy of established authority, eroding colonial boundaries, and promoting popular discontent, it is ironic that many of the political leaders of the Revolution were deists, individuals who believed that, although God had set the world into motion, he did not play an active role in human affairs. Steeped in the rationalism of the Enlightenment, and harboring suspicions of the established churches, the leaders of the Revolution tended to view all political issues through the prism of natural rights rather than divine revelation.[4]

The Revolution thus served to weaken rather than enhance religion. Several of the denominations—the Friends, the Anglicans, and the Methodists—were in disrepute for failing to back the Revolution. Other denominations suffered from the spread of rationalism and from the migration of many members to the frontier, both of which led to a decline in church attendance. Moreover, the overriding urgency, during and after the Revolution, of military and political issues sapped the vitality of religion. During the last phase of the First Great Awakening, which extended from 1790 to 1820, the revolutionary coalition of evangelicals, deists, farmers, artisans, and slaveholders broke apart along ideological and partisan lines, and the influence of the churches was at its lowest point in American history, owing in some measure to the effect of the secular ideology popularized by the leaders of the Revolution.

The Second Great Awakening

The Second Great Awakening began about 1800, and its revival phase lasted until 1840. It was during this time that the camp meeting, a vehicle for mass conversion in rural areas, emerged. In the North, the doctrine of predestination was further weakened, and a new theology, reflecting Methodist influence, arose that held that anyone was capable of achieving saving grace through a determined inner and outer struggle against sin.[5] Those who sought a state of grace were told to guide themselves by the principles of disinterested benevolence. They were assured that, if they achieved grace, they would be healthy and prosperous because God rewarded virtue. Those who were condemned would be visited by economic and other catastrophes. Lurking in this view was the belief that poverty was the wages of sin, a doctrine that gained in strength after the Civil War.

Leaders of the Second Great Awakening also preached that the American mission was to build God's kingdom on earth. Belief in the imminence of the millennium promoted a zealous quest not only for personal but also for social perfection. An array of reform movements sought to make America a fit place for the Second Coming of Christ. These included the temperance movement, which at first sought to convince individuals to cease drinking alcoholic beverages voluntarily, the abolitionist movement, which initially hoped to persuade slave owners to free their slaves voluntarily, and the nativist movement, which aimed either to curtail the large number of Catholics entering the country or to convert them to Protestantism.

During the political phase of the Second Great Awakening (1840–70), the temperance movement succeeded in getting many state and local governments to license the sale of alcoholic beverages. The high point of this campaign was reached between 1846 and 1855, when thirteen Northern states, led by Maine, prohibited the sale of all alcoholic drinks. The Second Great Awakening also focused on such urban reforms as getting rid of graft-ridden city governments and protecting children through establishing compulsory education and setting limits on child labor. It was during the Second Great Awakening that the women's suffrage movement also emerged.

Militant abolitionists such as William Lloyd Garrison initially focused their campaign not on the state but on the denominations. They wanted their churches to condemn slavery as an extraordinary sin that infected every aspect of life and created an insurmountable barrier to personal and national salvation. Although that creed gradually gained numerous adherents, it remained a minority doctrine even within the Northern churches.

A fraction of these radicals decided to go over the heads of church leaders by shifting the struggle to the political arena. That decision diluted the benevolent content of the antislavery appeal but greatly broadened the antislavery coalition and eventually led to the formation of the Republican Party.[6] Republicans continued to appeal to the benevolence of voters, especially in New England and in the Yankee diaspora (areas to which New Englanders and their descendants migrated west of the Hudson River and north of the Mason-Dixon Line). However, they increasingly urged the Northern electorate to vote for them not because it was their Christian duty to free the slaves but in order to prevent slaveholders from seizing land in the territories that rightly belonged to Northern whites, to prevent slaveholders from reducing the wages of Northern workers by inundating Northern labor markets with slaves, and to prevent the "slave power," in an alleged alliance with the "papal power" and operating through the Democratic Party, from seizing control of the American government.[7]

The fate of slavery was decided by the Civil War. Despite the passage of the Thirteenth Amendment (abolishing slavery), the Fourteenth Amendment (extending citizenship to former slaves), and the Fifteenth Amendment (establishing the right of former slaves to vote), however, the deep hostility of Southern whites and the ambivalent support of Northern whites compromised the struggle for the civil equality of ex-slaves. By the end of the 1880s, most of the abolitionist leaders were dead or had retired, and their places in the Northern evangelical movement were taken by men and women who were preoccupied with a different set of issues, especially Darwinism and the growing urban crisis.[8]

The Third Great Awakening

The Third Great Awakening began about 1890, and the religious revival phase extended to 1930. It was marked by a major theological split among the principal evangelical churches, with the winning faction rejecting the proposition that poverty was the wages of sin. This split was, to a large extent, precipitated by the urban crisis, which is discussed in chapter 2. Evangelicals were divided on how to reform the cities, which were growing at alarming rates and were viewed as centers of corruption, crime, drunkenness, prostitution, and graft that threatened to infect the entire society.

Darwinism was another issue that promoted splits on ethics and creed. Charles Darwin's theories, especially his theory of evolution, did not just challenge the biblical account of creation. By describing nature as amoral and purposeless, they also challenged the millennial goal of the nation, the building of God's kingdom on earth.

Increasing labor conflict, and how to cope with it, was a third problem that faced the reformers of the Third Great Awakening. In an agrarian world populated by property owners who abhorred any infringement on property rights, it had been relatively easy to make strikes illegal and to use troops to suppress them under state anticonspiracy laws. But, in the new urban world, the great majority of the laboring population owned relatively little property and were thought to be open to anarchistic and syndicalist notions imported from Europe. In such a world, old methods of containing labor strife seemed inadequate.

Debate over these issues produced two camps. The conservatives wanted to stand fast on creedal issues and continued to emphasize the centrality of personal conversion and morality. The most uncompromising of the old lights came to be called *fundamentalists* because of their insistence on the inerrancy of the Bible. Some, like William Jennings Bryan, the Democratic candidate for the presidency in 1896, 1900, and 1908, supported the whole panoply of progressive labor reforms, but the majority hewed close to the urban reform program of the Second Great Awakening. The fundamentalists were initially strong in all regions of the country, in the cities as well as the countryside.

The winning camp of the Third Great Awakening has come to be called *modernist* or *liberal*. Modernists applied scientific principles to the study of the Bible, on the assumption that it was a historical document written by men who were trying to understand God's will within the context of their own times and civilizations. Modernists also believed that evolutionary theory was consistent with biblical thought because the world was evolving, not only toward human beings as the highest form of life, but also toward ever more perfected human beings. In this view, the laws of nature were God's laws, and scientists were the ones who would discover and explain them. As theologians were needed to interpret the Bible, scientists were needed to interpret nature.

The millennialist dream of the Second Great Awakening thus became transformed by the modernists. Disciples of the Second Great Awakening had the wrong theory of how the millennium would arrive, the modernists believed. The new theory emphasized, instead of the Second Coming of Christ, a new, more secular optimism about perfecting American society. In the place of divine revelation, there now stood the revelations of science. Since most of the problems were not physical or biological but social, a new breed of social scientists was required who understood the problems of the cities and who knew how to reconstruct them in a way that would alleviate the social crises of the age.

A radical wing of the modernist camp came to be called *the Social Gospel movement.* Its leading figures argued that, if America was to revitalize itself, it would have to change not only its creed, its theory of man's relationship to God, but also its ethics. It would have to make poverty, not a personal failure, but a failure of society, and evil would have to be seen, not as a personal sin, but as a sin of society. According to these radicals, it was the obligation of the state to improve the economic condition of the poor by favoring labor and redistributing income, reforms necessary to put an end to urban corruption.[9]

During most of the revival phase, it was the conservatives who were in control of the church hierarchies and related organizations, and the reforms that they promoted were those left over from the Second Great Awakening, such as the reform of graft-ridden city governments, the protection of children through compulsory education and limits on child labor, the prohibition of alcoholic beverages, and the extension of the franchise to women. It was not until well into the New Deal era that the political reforms of the Third Great Awakening, including the establishment of the welfare state, moved to the top of the legislative agenda. Indeed, down into the 1920s, it was the theological conservatives who were on the offensive, seeking to limit the influence of the modernists and Social Gospelers within denominational circles, if not to bar them entirely.

Champions of the modernist cause were discovered in an unexpected place. During the nineteenth century and into the early twentieth, colleges and universities were religious institutions and focal points for revivals. Their presidents were usually ordained ministers who taught required courses in moral philosophy or natural theology. However, during the Third Great Awakening, modernist and Social Gospel theories were widely embraced by university teachers, who taught them to their students. Moreover, for reasons that had more to do with technology than with ideology, the student bodies of the colleges and universities began to expand at a remarkable rate. By World War I, universities were producing far more secular than sacred writers. Journalists, essayists, historians, social scientists, novelists, and dramatists who embraced modernist ideology were turned out by the tens of thousands. They became entrenched in the new mass media—low-cost daily newspapers, glossy magazines, inexpensive books, popular theater, vaudeville, and movies—which they used to attack conservative religionists. These attacks were so successful that they drove the fundamentalists out of their denominational offices and into sanctuaries sheltered from such public criticism. The victory of the modernists and Social Gospelers laid the basis for the welfare state, providing both the ideological foundation and the political drive for the labor reforms of the 1930s, 1940s, and 1950s, for the civil rights reforms of the 1950s and 1960s, and for the new feminist programs of the late 1960s and early 1970s.

The Fourth Great Awakening

This sketch of the three previous Great Awakenings suggests some of the complex connections between religious revival and political realignment.[10] I now return to the Fourth Great Awakening and the political realignment of the 1990s. The phase of religious intensification began in the late 1950s and early 1960s, when church membership began to grow across all denominations. However, from the mid-1960s on, only the enthusiastic religions grew rapidly, cutting deeply into the normal membership of the mainline churches, and also drawing many unchurched persons into the fold. Over the past three decades, membership in the principal mainline Protestant churches of America has declined by 25 percent, while membership in enthusiastic churches (such as Pentecostal, Adventist, and neo-fundamentalist) has nearly doubled. In the case of certain enthusiastic denominations, such as the Mormons, membership has quadrupled.[11]

By the end of the 1980s, enthusiastic religion had about 60 million adherents, representing about one-third of the electorate. Although often identified with the rapidly growing neoevangelical, fundamentalist, Pentecostal, and Protestant charismatic denominations, the movement is far wider. It includes about 20 million persons in the churches of the mainline Protestant denominations, 6 million Catholics who reported a born-again experience, and nearly 5 million Mormons. Some mainline churches have responded to the demand for a more passionate religion by embracing Pentecostalism—even the Roman Catholic Church has launched its own charismatic movement.[12]

Single-issue movements began to emerge about halfway through the religious phase: the right-to-life movement emerged during the mid-1970s, tax revolts exploded in the late 1970s, and the movement to reform the media followed early in the 1980s. These developments are comparable to the temperance, nativist, and abolitionist movements of the 1830s and early 1840s, which, despite considerable success, were viewed as zealous minority efforts far from the mainstream of political life.

In 1979, the Moral Majority emerged with a bid to become the vehicle through which believers in enthusiastic religion could unite on a national program of political restructuring that included opposition to abortion, reestablishing prayer in the schools, and the elimination of pornography. Although it had significant success in shifting intensely religious voters from the Democratic to the Republican column during the 1984 elections, the Moral Majority was, like the branch of the abolitionist movement of the 1840s led by William Lloyd Garrison, too rigid theologically, undecided whether the denominational churches or the broader political electorate was its main concern, and too focused on the abortion issue. Tarred by the televangelist scandals of the mid-1980s, the Moral Majority collapsed in 1989, its place taken in 1990 by a broader movement called the Christian Coalition.

The Christian Coalition differs from the Moral Majority in that it is more clearly focused on politics, is more willing to compromise on key issues in the interest of extending the coalition, is theologically more flexible, and has better connections among enthusiastic religionists in the mainline churches. As an example of its willingness to appeal to a broad base, the Christian Coalition has raised the traditional family above abortion as a coalition issue.[13] The Christian Coalition has also reached out to economic conservatives by integrating tax reductions and smaller government into their social program, linking these issues to their principles regarding individual responsibility. This move to a less dogmatic, more issue-oriented basis for institutional change recalls the compromises made by such politically skillful abolitionists as Salmon P. Chase, senator from and later governor of Ohio, when he joined with former adversaries in the 1840s and 1850s in creating the Free Soil Party and then the Republican Party on a minimalist antislavery program.

The persistence of the forces of the Fourth Great Awakening through the political ups and downs of the 1980s and 1990s, the increased flexibility of its tactics, the broadening of its coalition to include more members of mainline churches, Jews, and blacks, and the increasing responsiveness of the Democratic Party to aspects of its program indicate that the effect of the Fourth Great Awakening will continue to be widespread and massive.

In years to come, it will be impossible to understand political and ethical trends or economic developments without understanding the movement centered on enthusiastic religions.

This judgment was confirmed by the outcome of the 1996 and 1998 elections. Not only did the Republicans maintain their control of both houses of Congress, but President William J. Clinton and Vice-President Albert A. Gore changed both their rhetoric and certain policies to increase their appeal to born-again Christians (as in their welfare reform proposals and their criticism of violence in the media). Clinton's effort to reach out to this part of the electorate calls attention to the complexity of the political realignments spawned by the religious-inspired reform movements of previous Great Awakenings. For example, although the Republican Party was the principal vehicle for promoting the reform agenda of the Third Great Awakening during its early decades, many progressive evangelicals shifted their allegiance to the Democratic Party when Woodrow Wilson (president from 1913 to 1921) combined evangelical appeals with a vigorous pursuit of policies previously identified with Republicans. This shift of supporters of the Third Great Awakening from the Republicans was too modest to keep the Democrats in power during the 1920s, but the shift continued, culminating in the 1930s with the presidency of Democrat Franklin D. Roosevelt. The lesson is that coalitions spawned by religious movements are more ideological than partisan.

The resistance of the majority of Democrats in Congress to Clinton's strategy of courting white evangelicals suggests that ideological considerations within the Democratic Party are stronger than purely partisan considerations. Consequently, for the foreseeable future, the Republican Party is likely to continue as the principal vehicle for the political reforms sought by leaders of the Fourth Great Awakening. Nevertheless, the flexibility shown by Clinton, Gore, and a significant minority of the Democrats calls attention to the fact that there are many issues stemming from the ethics of the Fourth Great Awakening that are also embraced in the ethics of the Third Great Awakening. For example, "sexual harassment" may have originated as a radical slogan of the feminist movement, but its content may be seen as Victorian, and the setting of limits on sexual aggression may be seen as conforming with the wish to see a return to traditional family values. Other reforms that unite large parts of both ethical camps include promoting education, curtailing pornography and violence in the media, abolishing state-sponsored gambling, and controlling or suppressing illegal drug trafficking and use.

Table 1.1 Phases of the Four Great Awakenings in the United States

	Phase of Religious Revival	Phase of Rising Political Effect	Phase of Increasing Challenge to Dominance of the Political Program
First Great Awakening, 1730–1830	1730–60: Weakening of predestination doctrine; recognition that many sinners may be predestined for salvation; rise of ethic of benevolence	1760–90: Attack on British corruption; American Revolution	1790–1820: Breakup of revolutionary coalition
Second Great Awakening, 1800–1920	1800–1840: Rise of belief that anyone can achieve saving grace through inner and outer struggle against sin; widespread adoption of ethic of benevolence; upsurge of millennialism	1840–70: Rise of abolitionist, temperance, and nativist movements; attack on corruption of South; Civil War; women's suffrage	1870–1920: Replacement of prewar evangelical leaders; Darwinian crisis; urban crisis
Third Great Awakening, 1890–?	1890–1930: Shift from emphasis on personal to social sin; shift to more secular interpretation of Bible and creed	1930–70: Attack on corruption of big business and the rich; labor reforms; civil rights and women's rights movements	1970–?: Attack on liberal reforms; defeat of Equal Rights Amendment; rise of tax revolt; rise of Christian Coalition and other political groups of the religious Right
Fourth Great Awakening, 1960–?	1960–?: Return to sensuous religion and reassertion of experiential content of Bible; reassertion of concept of personal sin	1990–?: Attack on materialist corruption; rise of prolife, profamily, and media reform movements; campaign for more values-oriented school curriculum; expansion of tax revolt; attack on entitlements	?:

THEORIES OF RELIGIOUS-POLITICAL CYCLES IN AMERICAN HISTORY

Readers familiar with the work of the eminent historian of religion William McLoughlin, and particularly with his 1978 *Revivals, Awakenings, and Reform,* will recognize my indebtedness to him. However, table 1.1 and the discussion in this chapter are more than an attempt to represent his *Great Awakening* construct, which was widely debated by historians of religion during the 1980s. Table 1.1 reflects my effort to integrate Great Awakening constructs with "political realignment theory," quantitative analysis of congressional and popular voting behavior, the history of technological change (including its effect on economic growth, institutional change, and cultural change), and the evolving insights of biodemography.[14]

This effort at integration led me to conceive of overlapping religious and political cycles and to break each cycle into three overlapping phases. In my view, there is not only more dynamic interaction between political and religious developments than McLoughlin allowed but also critically important synergism. Hence, the phases of religious intensification and of political ascendancy cannot be defined independently of each other, only in the light of each other. Moreover, contingent factors play such a large role in each of the phases of a given cycle that the phases and their interactions can be adequately defined only after the fact. In other words, the model of century-long religious-political cycles sketched in table 1.1 and elaborated in the balance of the book is best thought of as a descriptive model of what happened rather than as a forecasting model. Nevertheless, when used cautiously, this model, as with other empirical models, may provide a rough guide to some aspects of future developments.[15]

Great Awakening constructs have played an increasingly important role in American historiography since World War II. Those that have received the most attention are the First and the Second. Bernard Bailyn, winner of the Pulitzer Prize for his work in American colonial history, called the First Great Awakening "the central event in the history of religion in America in the eighteenth century." This movement aroused a spirit of humanitarianism, encouraged the notion of equal rights, and stimulated feelings of democracy.[16] Richard Bushman, a leading American historian at Columbia University, described the colonial Awakening as an instrument that transformed Puritans into Yankees, helped unify New England, and gave the region a larger role in the Revolution than warranted by numbers alone.[17] Gordon Wood, perhaps the most influential authority on the American Revolution and the early years of nationhood, links the Second Great Awakening more closely to the promotion of egalitarianism than the First but argues that, during the eighteenth century, religion played a central role in "the rise of ordinary people into dominance," a phrase that he calls a "one-sentence summary" of his book *The Radicalism of the American Revolution*.[18]

Numerous writers have drawn the connection between the Second Great Awakening and the emergence of the "evangelical united front," including such radical reform movements as temperance, feminism, urban reform, and abolitionism.[19] The radical reform agenda of the Second Great Awakening was implemented through numerous laws at the local, state, and national levels and resulted in seven constitutional amendments: the Thirteenth (outlawing slavery), the Fourteenth (due process), the Fifteenth (black male suffrage), the Sixteenth (federal income taxes), the Seventeenth (popular election of senators), the Eighteenth (Prohibition), and the Nineteenth (women suffrage).

The Third Great Awakening has a more ambiguous status. McLoughlin cogently argued for calling the religious revivals of 1890–1920 a Third Great Awakening.[20] He identified the Social Gospel movement as the core of the new lights and included as old lights such urban revivalists as Dwight Moody and Billy Sunday as well as the orthodox Calvinists who came to be called *fundamentalists*.[21]

Although Moody and Sunday placed their principal emphasis on saving souls through struggle against inner corruption and vigorously opposed Darwinism and other modernist theories, they continued to champion the reform programs of the Second Great Awakening, including the promotion of education, the pursuit of prohibition, and urban political reforms. As with the First and Second Great Awakenings, however, it is the new lights, especially as represented by the Social Gospel movement, that McLoughlin saw as the main bearers of a new theology, a new ethic, and a new set of reforms. Social Gospelers rejected the pessimism of Moody's premillennialism, emphasized the remarkable advances in the natural sciences and their implications for building God's kingdom on earth in the immediate future, and worked out a set of reforms that, if implemented, would solve the cultural crisis caused by large-scale industrialization and urbanization.

Recognition of a Fourth Great Awakening emerged toward the end of the 1970s, when the growth of the religious Right first began to receive wide notice and a variety of commentators began to debate the scope and significance of the movement. Such concerns were reflected in the focus on born-again Christians in the Princeton-Gallup religious surveys of 1978, 1982, and 1988. Some historians of religion tended to identify the Fourth Awakening more with religious innovators on the Left than with those on the Right, emphasizing theologies that seemed to provide an ideological foundation for the civil rights, peace, and women's rights protest movements of the 1960s and 1970s.[22] The rising popularity of Zen Buddhism, the various meditation cults, civil religion, naturalistic religions, and postmodernist literary theory all gave testimony to a loss of faith in the progressive modernism of the Third Great Awakening and the desire for alternative faiths.[23]

By the early 1980s, however, after Ronald Reagan's election as president, but especially after 1984, when the Moral Majority began to emerge as a religious and political juggernaut, the religious Right became the central focus in discussions of the new revivalism. Both scholars of religion and the media began publishing extensive analyses, documenting the stagnation of the mainline churches as well as the vigorous growth of neoevangelicalism.[24] The spectacular successes of enthusiastic religionists throughout Latin America, but especially in Mexico, Guatemala, Brazil, Chile, and Argentina, where between 10 and 40 percent of the population had converted to enthusiastic Protestantism, also helped promote confidence among the evangelists in North America's cities.[25]

The criticisms of Great Awakening constructs fall into three categories. First are those that question the discontinuity in religious enthusiasm implied by the selection of discrete periods that are arbitrarily separated from other years in which revivals were also strong. Second are those that question the link between religious revivals and the political and social reforms that are attributed to them. There are also grave doubts that religious development is cyclic. Many historians of religion and analysts of religious history think that the progress of religious beliefs and reform movements is linear, that is, continuously moving in the same direction. Finally, some hold that the linking of one Great Awakening to another provides a stronger thread of continuity in American history than is warranted. Moreover, the structuring of American history implied by the Great Awakening construct appears to challenge all existing periodizations, tying political history far more closely to religion than some historians consider warranted.

It would be surprising if the participants in any debate over a topic so broadly conceived as the main periods of, the underlying structure of, or the dynamic forces in American history put all virtue on one side and nothing but errors on the other side. Attempts at the periodization or structuring of American history are best described by such terms as *useful, illuminating, misleading,* or *obfuscating.* I found McLoughlin's Great Awakenings structure useful, although I recognize the relevance of many of the criticisms that have been made of the structure as a whole or of particular aspects of the connection between religion and politics in each of the four religious-political cycles. I have sought to take these criticisms into account in my framing of the Great Awakenings construct. I believe that the Great Awakenings construct helps illuminate the lines of continuity in the three-century-long struggle to fulfill the millennialist aspirations of the founders and heirs of the American nation and to win not only the whole national population but the whole world to the egalitarian creed that is at the core of American political culture.

I agree with those who argue that revivals have been continuous in the United States since the late seventeenth century or the early eighteenth.[26] However, not every stretch of years in which there were revivals had the same long-term effect on ideology or politics. Some periods of revival led to major new theological principles, ethics, and demands for social reform. My structuring of the religious-political cycles and the definitions of their three phases takes into account the effect of new theologies and moral precepts on the politics of the middle phase. In other words, one must take account of the nature of the period of political ascendancy in order properly to define a Great Awakening and to distinguish it from other years of revival. As McLoughlin pointed out, effective as the urban revivals of Dwight Moody and Ira Sankey during the 1870s and 1880s were, they did not have the ideological gravity to constitute the revival phase of a new Awakening.[27]

The strength of the connection between the ideology and reform programs of the revival phase and the politics of the two succeeding phases varies from one Great Awakening to another. Several outstanding studies, including the pioneering application of social analysis to religious history by Whitney Cross, *The Burned-Over District*, reveal the strong links between the revival phase of the Second Great Awakening and the politics of its ascendancy phase.[28] These and other studies have revealed the steps by which theologians and lay leaders of the Second Great Awakening designed and implemented a variety of movements. Many campaigns were conceived in the study of Ebenezer Porter, president of Andover Seminary. Some were hatched in the Washington boardinghouse room of Theodore Weld, disciple of the charismatic evangelist of the Burned-Over District, Charles G. Finney, and legislative assistant to the so-called Select Committee on Slavery. Others were drawn up in the homes of the Tappan brothers, among the most dedicated of the lay princes of the evangelical movement.[29] Equally direct links between the religious beliefs and the political reforms of the Third Great Awakening can be traced out in the biographies and autobiographies of such figures as Richard T. Ely, the founding father of the American Economic Association; John R. Commons, a leading economist and labor historian at the University of Wisconsin; Robert M. La Follette, progressive Republican governor of, then senator from, Wisconsin; and William Jennings Bryan, three-time Democratic Party candidate for president of the United States.[30] The volume of recent reports on the effect of the Christian Coalition and other organizations of the Fourth Great Awakening on the programs and rhetoric of the Republican and Democratic Parties obviates an extended recitation here.

Recent thoughtful critiques, and insightful replies, regarding the role of the First Great Awakening and its effect on the nationalization of the colonies and on the coming of the Revolution have promoted an excellent discussion of the pertinent issues.[31] Wood has recently provided a revealing description of the links between religion, the Revolution, and the transformation of American society, providing new insights into the process that transformed the highly stratified aristocratic society of the prerevolutionary colonies into a much more egalitarian society. He delineates the roles of the First Great Awakening, the Revolution, and the Second Great Awakening, with the story carried down to the end of Jackson's second term.[32]

I understand the reservations that some historians have of treating the Third Great Awakening on a par with the others, especially when the Social Gospel movement is made to be the centerpiece of that Awakening. In my view, however, the Social Gospel movement retained strong connections with the theology and morality of the Second Great Awakening. Urban reformers such as Washington Gladden, Josiah Strong, and Walter Rauschenbusch, the principal theologian of the Social Gospel movement, remained committed to regeneration and atonement. As Yale theologian H. Richard Niebuhr wrote, they distinguished themselves "by keeping relatively close to evangelical notions of the sovereignty of God, of the reign of Christ and of the coming Kingdom. In Rauschenbusch especially the revolutionary element remained pronounced; the reign of Christ required conversion and the coming Kingdom was crisis, judgment as well as promise."[33] The full secular flowering of the modernist movement came well after Rauschenbusch's death and was associated with the temporary withdrawal of the fundamentalists from the field of battle. As explained more fully in chapters 2 and 3 below, the fundamentalists were driven out, not by liberal theologians, but by secularists in the new mass media who spearheaded the militant campaign to secularize the reform movements of the Third Great Awakening after 1930.

Political Eras and Political Realignments

Some analysts prefer to divide the American political experience into a series of political eras, each of which is dominated by two main opposing political coalitions. Between these political eras are elections that bring about substantial changes in the makeup of the principal opposing coalitions. These are the "critical elections" that produce the "political realignments" that usher in the next political era.[34]

Although developed by different sets of scholars, Great Awakening and realignment constructs overlap. Great Awakening constructs have been fashioned primarily by intellectual, religious, and political historians whose evidence is primarily qualitative (newspaper stories, church records, sermons, political and religious tracts, theological essays, congressional debates, party platforms, autobiographies, letters, diaries, and oral histories). These scholars are more empirical than theoretical. By contrast, the realignment model has been fashioned primarily by political scientists and historians, who make extensive use of social science theories and quantitative evidence. Much of this work hinges on statistical analysis of popular voting behavior at local and national levels. Patterns of votes in Congress and in state legislatures on a wide variety of issues have been extensively analyzed. For the period since World War II, much use has been made of surveys of attitudes among various sectors of the electorate. Not only do these constructs reinforce each other, but the synergism of the different types of evidence and the analytic techniques employed in developing them enhances explanatory power. Together, Great Awakening and realignment constructs provide a revealing analysis of religious-political cycles in American life.

Realignment studies seek to identify critical elections and the political eras they initiate. Underlying much of this research is the proposition that political realignments are predictable events, whose occurrence can be discerned through analysis of election statistics. The breakdown of the reigning coalition is evident in voting behavior in local elections that precede the critical presidential elections. It has also been argued that critical elections arise with surprising regularity, occurring once a generation—a periodicity attributed to cultural exhaustion and generational change. Walter D. Burnham, a political scientist and the most eminent of the realignment theorists, has designated as critical the six presidential elections of 1800, 1828, 1860, 1896, 1932, and 1968.[35] However, there is considerable disagreement over which presidential elections actually initiated a new political era.

The debate over whether 1968 was a critical election has been particularly intense. Some argue that a sixth political era began about 1968 and extended down to 1994, with the Democrats usually in control of Congress and the Republicans usually in control of the White House. The first two decades of this period were marked by a weakening of party identification among the electorate, as indicated by the increase in ticket splitting. Another feature was a shift from economic to social issues as the battleground of legislative struggles. However, the shift in the focus of issues led to renewed intensification of partisan loyalties. The bitterness of the ideological rift between the parties became pronounced with the election of Ronald Reagan in 1980. It has also been argued that, although 1994 was not a presidential election year, it may have been the beginning of a new alignment, not only because of the bolt of white evangelicals from the Democratic to the Republican Party, but also because of the changing geographic base of electoral support for the Republicans, who, for the first time since the Civil War, now receive more of their votes from Southerners than from Northerners.

One of the leading realignment theorists, Everett Carll Ladd, a political scientist at the University of Connecticut and executive director of the Roper Center for Public Opinion Research, has called the era since 1968 the *postindustrial party system*. He believes that this era is distinguished by a philosophical realignment based on an electorate that is considerably more conservative than it was before 1968 and far less inclined to equate more government with more progress. He also believes that the rise of television as the principle medium of campaigning gives media commentators a powerful influence over the rhetoric of campaigns and increases the volatility of the electorate with respect to partisan loyalties. The social groups that now provide the foundation for partisan coalitions are far different from those of the New Deal era, he argues, because the postindustrial economy is different.[36]

Ladd has redefined the set of political eras to suggest that there were only four. The first is the Jefferson/Jackson party system, extending from 1800 to the end of the Civil War. The second, which extended from the 1870s to the beginning of the 1930s, covers the adjustment of society to the emergence of a Northern urban-industrial complex, dominated by large-scale industry, the adjustment to which was led by the Northern-based Republican Party. Ladd's third era extends from Franklin D. Roosevelt's 1932 victory to the end of the 1960s, and it produced the welfare state. Adopting the analytic framework and terminology of Harvard sociologist Daniel Bell, Ladd argues that, in the fourth and current era, politics is shaped by the dispersion and decentralization of economic activity in much the same way as the politics of the preceding era was shaped by increasing scale and centralization.

This summary of realignment theory indicates the many ways in which it overlaps with the theory of religious-political cycles, and I have incorporated many of the insights provided by statistical analysis of voting behavior and attitude change into the Great Awakenings construct. On balance, the model of religious-political cycles is more germane to the issues with which this book deals because it more effectively incorporates the role of evangelical churches in leading populist protest.[37] Moreover, if, as some realignment theorists argue, critical elections are only those elections in which the domination of the federal government leads to rapid and radical policy reforms, only two realignments prior to 1980 qualify: the political realignment of the 1850s and the New Deal in the 1930s, which correspond to the political ascendancy phases of the Second and Third Great Awakenings.[38]

THE POTENTIAL FOR CONTINUING EGALITARIAN REFORM

The potential for continuing egalitarian reform remains considerable, even if the coalitions of the Fourth Great Awakening continue to dominate national politics. It is a mistake to assume that these forces will necessarily seek to turn back the clock on race relations, universal education, equal opportunity for women, religious freedom, and the other great social reforms of the twentieth century. The emerging black elite, which has relatively conservative views on economic and social issues, has become a potential constituency for the Republican Party. Moreover, the demographic changes that will take place in the electorate over the next several decades will mean that the Republicans can remain the majority party only by vigorously pursuing black, Hispanic, and Asian voters and expanding their base among women. In the future, commitment to diversity is essential to any party that aspires to govern, and the Republican Party is already in the process of becoming competitive among ethnic groups it once neglected. In addition, a growing number of well-to-do persons from ethnic minorities who are open to conservative programs have become part of the movement for enthusiastic religion. However, the most important change is the vigor with which churches long identified as conservative on ethnic issues (such as the Mormons and various primarily white Pentecostal and charismatic churches) have been proselytizing in African American, Hispanic, and Asian communities. The recent collaboration of black and white Pentecostal churches in forming a common umbrella organization, the Pentecostal/Charismatic Churches of North America (PCCNA), suggests that, unlike in the past, enthusiastic religion may serve to promote racial and ethnic unity rather than thwart it.[39]

It might appear that economic issues represent an unbridgeable ideological chasm between the Third and the Fourth Great Awakenings. There is no denying that the social and cultural issues that propel the current revival often lead to conservative economic positions. However, many disciples of the Third Great Awakening are reconsidering long-held theories about economic advancement and morality, especially the theory that moral crises can be resolved by raising income. Although the average real income of the bottom fifth of the population has multiplied by some twentyfold since 1890, several times more than the gain realized by the rest of the population, the national cultural crisis that precipitated the Social Gospel movement remains largely unresolved.[40]

The problems precipitated by industrialization and urbanization that were of great concern to Social Gospelers, such as drug addiction, pregnancy among single teenage girls, rape, the physical abuse of women and children, broken families, and violent teenage death, all of which were indicative of the cultural/moral crisis of the age, are more severe today than they were a century ago.[41] As a consequence, not only members of enthusiastic churches but many in the mainline churches have become convinced that cultural reform must be pursued primarily at the individual rather than the societal level. This reemergence of confidence in the power of personal engagement as the basis for social transformation contributes to the new populism and a demand to return power to the people.[42]

Despite their economic conservatism, evangelicals can be enlisted in support of the unrealized agenda of the Third Great Awakening, which includes such objectives as increasing economic opportunity for the poor and dismantling glass ceilings. The share of the population that completes high school and goes on to college is a key issue that can bridge the ideological divisions between followers of the Third and Fourth Great Awakenings. Not only are there strong ethical and social incentives for legislation designed to promote educational advancement, but economic and technological forces are also at work. The competitive pressures of globalization and the substitution of computers for labor in many lower-level service occupations mean that full employment and continued high rates of economic growth in the United States will require a further expansion of the share of the labor force in technical and professional occupations. Given that nothing has done more to redistribute income in favor of the poor and middle classes over the past century than the subsidization of higher education, and given the long record of evangelicals in promoting education at all levels, this issue offers an excellent opportunity for a successful egalitarian coalition.

Tax reform can also promote egalitarian goals if it is coupled with appropriate programs to reform education, minister to the needs of alienated adolescents and young adults, expand technical and higher education for the young, and promote self-realization (the achievement of a moral and satisfying life) for the middle-aged, the elderly, women, and ethnic minorities whose quest for self-realization has been hampered by discrimination. The tax revolt is not a conspiracy of the superrich, many of whom are quite prepared to live with the current fiscal regimen. It is a genuine, broadly based populist movement, encouraged partly by the new emphasis on personal responsibility and partly by changes in the nature of the households (now mainly dual earner) that are represented in the upper part of the income distribution.

Tax reform is long overdue. The U.S. tax system grew topsy-turvy, with many decisions made to address concerns (such as shoring up the railroads) that, logical as they were at the time, have long ceased to be relevant. Moreover, much of what are called *taxes* are nothing of the sort. Despite appearances, "taxes" such as social security and Medicare are actually forms of forced saving that rearrange personal expenditure patterns over the life cycle. Although these savings are used to provide services that are deeply desired by most working adults—education for children, medical care for their families, and annuities (monthly income payments) to support them when they retire—the role that the government currently plays in the process is so obscure that it provokes social and political tension. Current procedures sometimes also promote inefficiency and corruption (such as fraudulent medical claims) and unnecessarily divert funds to support questionable programs and excessive bureaucratic structures (such as those involved with means testing).[43]

So far I have focused mainly on how the new dominant coalition is likely to react to the unresolved egalitarian issues and reforms previously defined by the Third Great Awakening. However, in the future, the main struggle for egalitarian reform will revolve around a set of issues that have just begun to emerge and that have not yet been adequately defined. It is still not clear how these issues of spiritual or immaterial equity may best be advanced or how responsibility for implementation might best be apportioned among federal, state, and local governments, private businesses, and compassionate voluntary organizations. Because of the novelty of the issues of spiritual equity, positions on them have not yet hardened along partisan or ideological lines, so opportunities to forge broad coalitions for egalitarian solutions are promising. It is the new issues of equity, not the old ones, that will be at the center of the struggle for egalitarian reform during the next generation.

CAVEATS

This chapter has introduced a framework for analyzing the religious-political movements that shaped the egalitarian creed in America. The framework is synthetic. It is based on recent bodies of research in a number of fields and is designed to illuminate how the evangelical churches and political parties responded to periodic crises in the individual and collective sense of well-being among a significant section of the population, crises too urgent and insistent to be ignored by religious and political leaders. These periodic crises split theologians and politicians into factions according to their willingness to reconsider received doctrine or overthrow prevailing institutions.

As set forth here, the Great Awakenings are not merely, or primarily, religious phenomena. They are primarily political phenomena in which the evangelical churches represent the leading edge of an ideological and political response to accumulated technological, economic, and social changes that undermined the received culture. This is not to say that all religious revivals are essentially political but to point out that this book is focused on those religious revivals that promoted egalitarianism through political processes. Although I have drawn on previous research into Great Awakenings, I have placed a heavier emphasis on the political aspects of these phenomena than some other scholars have done. This is partly because of my attempt to call attention to the link between evangelical religious movements and political realignments.

This chapter is only an introduction to the more detailed and critical analysis presented in the balance of the book, so many important issues, particularly the conflict between the increasing mastery of the physical environment and the increasing complexity of the human environment, are set forth only briefly. The limitations of this overview are magnified by the attempt to represent the overview schematically in table 1.1. The table presents only some highlights of the past religious-political movements that have transformed the egalitarian creed during four major eras in

American history. It is designed to introduce a historical perspective on the current struggle to modify the egalitarian creed by outlining the relevant previous history.

The proposition that religion and politics in America have a cyclic component does not mean that cycles have been the dominant characteristic of life over the past three centuries. Quite the contrary: the dominant characteristic has been a relatively steady and rapid growth in the economy based on an accelerating pace of technological change that has drastically transformed life within living memory. What has been cyclic is the tendency of these technological advances to outpace the development both of ethical guidelines for their utilization and of human institutions to control them. It is the lag between technological transformation and the human capacity to cope with change that has repeatedly provoked the crises that usher in profound reconsiderations of ethical values, that produce new agendas for ethical and social reform, and that give rise to political movements to implement these agendas.[44]

Ethical views are not static. Earlier doctrines are revisited not just for inspiration but often because they provide a means of advancing new ideas that transform the original doctrines. The phrase *traditional family values* is a case in point. That phrase is applicable to such diverse cultures as those of the British gentry in the Elizabethan age, the Puritan family of early New England, the pietistic German family of prerevolutionary Pennsylvania, the working-class Irish Catholic families of the Midwest during the age of Lincoln, the slave family of the late antebellum era, the early twentieth-century families from Eastern and Southern Europe, the *House and Garden* families of the post–World War II years (my era of parenting), and the families of recent immigrants from Latin America and Asia. The family cultures differed with respect to who was included within the family, the relationships among individuals within the families, the control over economic resources, and moral standards. Descendants of these numerous family cultures find a legacy that, although modified for present circumstances of work and leisure, is useful as a guide to life. Moreover, despite the differences in the heritages on which they draw, there is a common core of values that might be characterized as follows: A traditional family is a union with the intent of procreating and rearing children to maturity and beyond. Rearing involves the obligation not only to nurse, feed, clothe, train, and prepare children for an occupation and other adult responsibilities. It also involves inculcating in children the ethical and spiritual values to which the parents are committed. In this age in which marriages across religions and cultures have become common and in which remarriage is frequent, the spiritual legacies of families are often modified by altered contexts, but the rearing obligation usually survives custody agreements and is often reinforced by stepparents.

The dedication of American society to the egalitarian creed has not waxed and waned; it has steadily intensified. However, conflicts over the interpretation of the creed and the manner of reform needed to protect and extend it have varied with the nature of the struggle to bring ethics and social institutions into accord with the new conditions of life. In the past, the more far-reaching the technological change, the more sweeping the attendant changes in economic and social institutions have been, and the more highly charged has been the battle over appropriate reform. The nature of the struggle to bring the egalitarian creed into conformity with altered circumstances is heavily influenced by contingent circumstances. Because surprises are normal, past experience and trends are imperfect, often incorrect, guides to the future. Hence, even if the religious-political cycles described in this chapter give us a reasonably accurate picture of the past, it does not follow that the Fourth Great Awakening will necessarily unfold along the lines of previous religious-political cycles.

The Great Awakenings have not usually originated from the top; generally, they welled up from below and have often been given voice by ministers and novice leaders on the fringes of the establishment. The protests that their followers have expressed have been popular responses to perceived threats. Among the developments that provoked one or more groups of citizens to protest have been unjust taxes and graft by corrupt and tyrannical governments, waves of immigrants whose cultures and religions seemed to threaten prevailing habits, new technologies that undermined the jobs, markets, and ways of life of traditional producers, and seemingly secret conspiracies poised to seize control of the government either by economic alliances (bankers, slaveholders, railroad magnates, monopolists, the liquor and tobacco interests) or by political groups (lobbies, the media, the religious Right, unions).

New light religious leaders have responded to these concerns, reaching out to the discontented, reconsidering received theologies, and fashioning new theologies consistent with the changed conditions that provoked the crises. They have also formulated public policy programs aimed at alleviating grievances, and they have built a variety of single-issue organizations coordinated by ministers and lay leaders, as well as federations of organizations, to rally popular support for the new programs.

I have focused on the role of the evangelical churches in the unfolding of religious-political cycles in the United States because they spearheaded the struggle for the adoption of egalitarianism as a national creed and for its extension as conditions warranted. Recognition of their role does not imply that other factors, other religious groups, and secular impulses did not also contribute to the promotion of egalitarianism, both domestically and internationally. The relatively high standard of living in prerevolutionary North America made its colonies an ideal spawning ground for egalitarian doctrine. Property qualifications for voting, which limited the franchise to the wealthiest 15 percent of the English male population, permitted more than half the adult men in the colonies to vote.[45] Instead of a population of landless tenants, America was a country of relatively prosperous landowners, almost entirely lacking in the class of beggars that made up a fifth of the population of West European nations. Landowning farmers shunned traditional ideas of subordination and dependency and felt fit to participate in self-government.

Leaders of the American Revolution were also influenced by the secular egalitarianism of the French Enlightenment. Thomas Jefferson and other leaders saw themselves as more civilized and humane than the British because they had substituted benevolent republican principles for slavish monarchical subservience. Theirs was a secular benevolence that prompted penal reform, civility in relations between all free people, and a hierarchy based on natural ability rather than inherited position. Their egalitarianism emphasized equality of opportunity rather than of condition. They hoped thereby to spur talent and virtue and to destroy kinship and patronage as the basis of position in society. Since position would not be perpetuated from one generation to another, equality of opportunity would promote equality of condition.[46]

Protestant egalitarian ideals have been promoted worldwide partly because of the powerful proselytizing movements of Protestant churches. The most influential of these movements in recent decades have been the Pentecostal and charismatic waves, which have converted more than a quarter of a billion individuals worldwide since 1970. Only Western Europe has remained largely untouched by them.[47] However, the secular institutions of the United States, including the media and government, have promoted the secularized version of the egalitarian creed among those people who remain obdurately secular.

Protestants are not the only religious sources of egalitarianism; radical egalitarianism has been a central tenet of Islam. Like Judaism and most evangelical Protestant denominations, Islam preaches the moral equality of all the faithful, allowing no hierarchy to intervene between the individual Muslim and God. Even hierarchical churches such as the Roman

Catholic have spawned radical egalitarian movements, as embodied in liberation theology, in the U.S. Catholic workers' movement, in some papal encyclicals, and in the recent documents of the American bishops. Comparable egalitarian influences have found expression in upsurges of New Age religions and in Hindu and Buddhist movements.[48]

Nevertheless, the evangelical churches have been the central institution in the elaboration of the egalitarian creed in America, imposing that creed on federal, state, and local governments, and shaping reform programs needed to alter the creed to take account of changes in technology and cultural crises. Recognition of their strategic role is not meant to diminish other contributions to the promotion of egalitarianism either in the United States or abroad. But it is intended to highlight the powerful influence of evangelical churches on the major political realignments in American history.

I have sought in this chapter to put the Fourth Great Awakening into historical perspective. The political realignment now in progress is neither sui generis nor a carbon copy of the previous political realignments that have marked American politics. I believe that it is best understood as the most recent manifestation of the recurring effort to bring human institutions into some reasonable balance with the massive technological changes that periodically destabilize the prevailing culture. The analytic framework that I have employed is not of my invention. It has been richly developed by a number of outstanding scholars of religious, social, political, intellectual, and economic history. I have, however, modified that analysis by bringing the Great Awakenings framework of historians of religion into somewhat closer conjunction with the political eras framework of political scientists and historians and with the technological perspectives of the economic historians and biodemographers. It is now necessary to consider in more detail the clash produced by the most recent wave of changes in productive technology, the extremely severe jolt it has imparted to the prevailing culture, and the great difficulty in designing an adequate institutional response.

TWO

Technological Change, Cultural Transformations, and Political Crises

The ethical crises, religious upsurge, and programmatic demands that heralded the opening decades of the Fourth Great Awakening were precipitated by a series of major technological breakthroughs that destabilized prevailing culture. Some of those unsettling advances were in energy production (particularly nuclear energy), information retrieval, and communications. The unprecedented extension of control of human biology, particularly in the fields of reproductive technology and organ transplantation, also provoked widespread concern. The new technological breakthroughs raised profoundly difficult ethical and practical issues, including many that had never been considered previously, such as how to dispose of large quantities of radioactive waste. Among those who worried about these issues, some became alarmed that humanity was heading toward disaster, led by corrupt or mindless scientists and business leaders.

This turn in perceptions was not immediately obvious to those of us who inhabited the world of science. In our classes, we still sought to find ways that would make the great technological and economic accomplishments of the Industrial Revolution meaningful to students. And so, on a day in the mid-1970s, David Landes, doyen of economic historians at Harvard University, lectured to over a thousand students in Economics 10, the highly popular introductory course in undergraduate economics. "Look to the left of you and to the right of you," he said. "If it were not for the Industrial Revolution, two out of every three of you would not be alive."[1]

It was a striking point that caught the attention of drowsy students. It drove home one of the great benefits of modern economic growth: the enormous increase in life expectancy during the previous two hundred years that had been made possible by the advances in scientific knowledge and by new economic and biomedical technologies associated with the Industrial Revolution.

The post–World War II enthusiasm for technological change was still close to its peak in the 1970s. Not only had the advanced productive technology of the United States made it possible to defeat the evil war machines of the Axis powers, Germany, Italy, and Japan, but the new technologies of the postwar era touched off a period of such unprecedented economic growth that it obliterated fear that Europe and the United States would be plunged back into the destitution of the Great Depression of the 1930s.

After the war, it was difficult initially for Americans to shake off the memories of the depression, particularly the millions of unemployed, up to a third of the labor force.[2] Those memories made it hard for Americans to have faith in the viability of free enterprise systems. But, as the years of prosperity rolled on through the 1950s and the 1960s and into the 1970s, optimism replaced pessimism, and it was widely believed that we had entered a golden age that W. W. Rostow, an economist at MIT and later national security adviser to President Lyndon Johnson, called *the age of high mass consumption*. This was the age in which Herbert Hoover's failed promise—a chicken in every pot, a car in every garage—was finally realized. Most homes in the United States had electricity; radios, refrigerators, vacuum cleaners, washing machines, and dishwashers had become commonplace; and television, a dream before World War II, was by the late 1950s found in nearly 90 percent of homes.[3]

Products considered luxuries a decade earlier became necessities, seemingly overnight. Gone were the endless hours scrubbing clothes on a washboard. By the mid-1970s, not only the rich but virtually everyone in the middle and many at the lower end of the income distribution owned a washing machine or had access to one. Gone was the long ritual of washing and rewashing spinach. All one had to do was pop a package of frozen spinach into a microwave or a pot of boiling water and, voilà, instant cooked spinach. These and numerous other new consumer products liberated many women from the drudgery of household work and permitted millions to enter the labor force. Henry A. Wallace, vice president during Franklin D. Roosevelt's third term (1941–45), courted incredulity when he promised 60 million peacetime jobs. During the postwar boom, however, employment not only swept past 60 million but rushed toward the 100 million mark, a figure that was exceeded during the 1970s.[4]

In such heady circumstances, it was easy to herald technological change and the economic growth that it induced as the saviors of the economy. To many economists, business leaders, and politicians, technological change was transparently good and beneficial to virtually everyone. It was an incoming tide that raised all ships.

THE WANING OF ENTHUSIASM FOR TECHNOLOGICAL CHANGE

Disenchantment with technological change began to emerge during the 1960s. As the former Axis powers and our European allies recovered from the devastation of World War II, they emerged as serious competitors in the U.S. market. With state-of-the-art technologies in newly reconstructed industries, and with labor costs that were a fraction of those in the United States, foreign competitors began to conquer markets that during the first half of the postwar boom seemed secure from outside competition.

Textiles and steel were among the first industries to be undermined. Many small and medium-sized apparel firms in the United States were forced out of business during the late 1950s and early 1960s because the Japanese were delivering ready-made clothes that were less expensive than the cloth that American suppliers sold to domestic producers. Steel began to suffer from Japanese competition in the 1970s. German cars provided the most serious competition to Detroit during the 1960s, but, after the "oil shock" of 1973, small Japanese cars flooded the American market.

Disillusionment with the virtues of technological change was symbolized by the publication of Rachel Carson's *Silent Spring* in 1962. *Silent Spring* poignantly described the devastation of robins by the pesticide DDT, overlooking the fact that its use lowered food cost and saved millions of human lives (by controlling insect populations) during the worldwide campaign to eradicate malaria during the 1950s and the 1960s, especially in Asia.

Even science came under increasing assault. As Edward Shils, an acclaimed sociologist who taught at both Cambridge University and the University of Chicago, put it, the "adulatory enthusiasm for the potentialities of science," so widespread in the late 1940s, "has now [1974] turned a little sour."[5] The mounting attack on science came, not from its old adversaries, the theologians, but from secular critics, who called into question the "value-free, objective, and rational ethic commonly thought to be inherent in . . . modern science."[6] During the 1960s and 1970s, an increasing corps of critics saw scientists as "selfish," as "rushing wherever money is to be had," and as "elitists" whose "claim that they need autonomy is only a demand for privilege."[7]

The most dramatic symbol of the growing disenchantment with science and technology was the rise of the movement against nuclear energy. During the 1960s and early 1970s, nuclear energy was so enthusiastically embraced as a new, clean, limitless source of energy that, by 1975, an eighth of all electricity in the United States was generated in nuclear plants. Nevertheless, the growing fear of nuclear war, the growing sense that this source of energy had been conceived in the sin of Hiroshima and Nagasaki, and the testimony of some scientists that nuclear energy posed enormous potential hazards to life and health produced a movement so powerful that it brought further construction of nuclear energy plants to a screeching halt and even led to the abandonment of some facilities that had already been completed.[8]

Economic and social historians were not surprised by this turn of events. They knew that the history of modern technological change was replete with widespread protest movements. Some were sparked by workers displaced by the new technologies, as in the case of British hand-loom weavers, who were devastated by the introduction of the power loom. That drama was repeated in traditional societies, such as India, when cheap British cloth produced by means of modern technology penetrated their markets, undermining indigenous handicraft production.

In other cases, the protests were sparked by citizens who were alarmed by the threat to the prevailing culture posed by the new technologies. The railroads, for example, were fiercely and deeply resisted when they were first introduced. They were denounced not only as products of Satan and threats to civilization but also, as we shall see below, as threats to health and life. Much the same was said of airplanes by those who thought that, "if God had intended people to fly, he would have given them wings."

It has been argued that such crackpot movements of the past cannot be compared to the modern revolt against technology: whereas the movement against, say, nuclear energy is based on weighty scientific evidence, the opposition to railroads and airplanes was based on prejudice and superstition. However, scientific arguments were as hefty a weapon in the opposition to railroads in the 1820s and 1830s as they have been in the opposition to nuclear energy in our time. Fearful that the new technology would inundate their pastoral communities with unwanted commodities, people, and habits, opponents of the railroad freely employed scientific arguments. Railroads, they said, were great dangers to life and property because of exploding engines and the innumerable fires that would be caused by the sparks of engines even in normal operation. They feared that the noisy monsters would sicken cattle and poison cow's milk. Even more threatening was thought to be the long-term biological danger to persons who traveled at speeds of thirty miles per hour or more for sustained periods of time.[9] Many of these dangers were far from theoretical: thousands of individuals were maimed and killed by exploding boilers on trains and in collisions.[10]

These arguments are similar to those advanced by opponents of nuclear energy, who stress the theoretical hazards of radiation contamination associated with accidents at nuclear installations and with the disposal of nuclear waste. Many centuries will have to pass before the evidence needed to prove or disprove contentions that the danger to life posed by the use of nuclear power exceeds that posed by the use of other forms of energy. The fact is, we cannot disprove, even today, the theory that traveling at speeds of thirty miles per hour for sustained periods of time is producing subtle, long-term genetic damage. The argument has lost vigor, not because it has been disproved scientifically, but because few people care to pursue it. Speeds of thirty miles per hour have lost their capacity to cause ethical conflict because our culture accepts such speeds as normal, even slow, and because no credible evidence of genetic damage has emerged as yet. So, too, with nuclear energy in France, where nuclear reactors are widely accepted as a safe and inexpensive source of energy and today provide over 80 percent of France's electricity.[11]

Ethical movements against intrusions associated with rapid technological change are a modern phenomenon because rapid technological change is a modern phenomenon. Indeed, rapid technological change is confined to a tiny fraction of the 200,000 years that have elapsed since the emergence of our species. For most of its existence, Homo sapiens lived in far-flung hunting-and-gathering communities, each of which was quite small and barely able to reproduce itself. Life expectancy at birth was hardly twenty-five years on average, and those persons who survived childhood often died violently, in combat with other hunters, at relatively young ages. As late as 9000 B.C., the total population of the world was only about 7 million—less than half the population of Mexico City today. The population of all of Great Britain was barely ten thousand.[12]

Technical advances during the previous 190,000 years were very lim-

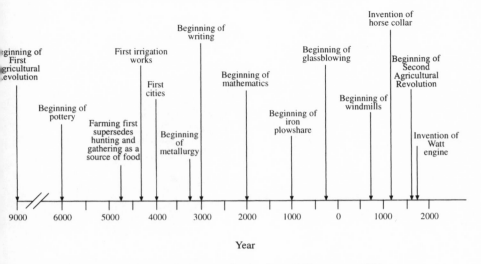

Figure 2.1 Some major events in the history of technology, 9000 B.C.–A.D. 1790.

SOURCES: McNeill (1971); Cipolla (1974); Clark (1971); Bronowski (1973); Derry and Williams (1960); Piggott (1965); Oates and Oates (1976); Trewartha (1969); Bishop (1936); Fagan (1977); and Slicher von Bath (1963). See also Allen (1992, 1994) and Wrigley (1987, chap. 7).

ited. Over the ages, humankind discovered that, once controlled, fire could be used to provide warmth and for cooking. Crude implements, first sticks and later simple tools laboriously crafted from stone, were developed for hunting and processing food. Such new technologies were developed and diffused so slowly that little change could be noticed from one generation to another.

The discovery of agriculture about eleven thousand years ago (ca. 9000 B.C.) broke the tight constraint on the food supply imposed by the previous hunting-and-gathering technology, making it possible to release about 10 percent of the labor force from the direct production of food, and also giving rise to the first cities. However, even these processes developed very slowly by current standards. As figure 2.1 shows, it took about four thousand years after its discovery for agriculture to supersede hunting and gathering as the main source of food, five thousand years for the first cities to emerge, six thousand years to develop writing, and seven thousand years to invent mathematics. Nevertheless, the new technology of food production was so superior to the old one that it was possible to support a much higher rate of population increase.

The slowness with which technology evolved during the agricultural era is illustrated by figure 2.2, which shows the evolution of the plow during the past six thousand years. Two of the principal changes during that

49

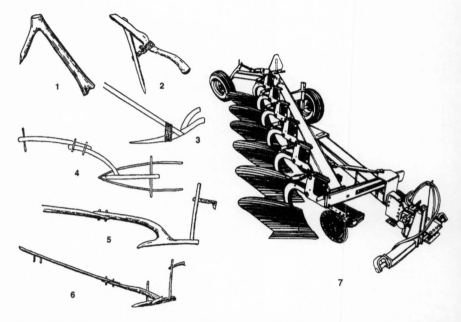

Figure 2.2   The evolution of the plow, 4000 B.C.–A.D. 1979: (1) a primitive hoe, made from a forked branch; (2) an Egyptian hoe, made of wood; (3) an Egyptian plow, apparently derived from a hoe (note the two handles); (4) a Sumerian crook plow with "ears," no stilt visible; (5) general type of primitive Greek crook plow; (6) modern Cypriote crook plow; and (7) modern gangplow. Note joined beams in nos. 4, 5, and 6.

NOTE: Plows 1 and 2 were pulled by humans. Plows 3–6 could in theory have been attached to either an ox or a horse, but the horse collar was not invented until ca. A.D. 1100 (see the text).

SOURCES: Curwen (1953, 69, 70) and Bishop (1936). Illustration no. 7 was provided by Deere & Co.

time were, first, the discovery of the harness to hitch the plow to an ox, rather than having it pulled by a person, and, second, the discovery of a harness that could hitch the plow to a horse, which was potentially swifter and more powerful than an ox, without choking the horse's long, vulnerable neck. These two discoveries were separated by about four thousand years. It took that much time for someone to think up the horse collar, which pressed against the shoulders of a horse rather than its neck. It was not until the twentieth century, after the development of tractors powered by internal combustion engines, that the modern gangplow (see image 7 in fig. 2.2) could be developed, replacing the single cutting blade of the traditional plow with as many as a dozen blades.[13]

The gangplow is but one of the numerous technological advances made during the Second Agricultural Revolution, which began about A.D.

1600 and involved changes not only in the hardware of agriculture but also in its biological practices, its sources of energy, and its organizational routines. The new technology of food production, including more prolific seeds, better rotation of crops, and improvements in planting and cultivation techniques, led to far more dramatic changes than were seen during the First Agricultural Revolution, eventually forcing the majority of the labor force out of agriculture, and also permitting the population to increase at a rate far higher than it had previously. The new technological breakthroughs after 1700 in manufacturing, transportation, trade, communications, and energy production were in many respects even more striking than those in agriculture. They gave rise to what economists call *modern economic growth*, which has provided many boons for society but is also responsible for many of the cultural and political crises of our time.

THE BENEFITS AND COSTS OF MODERN ECONOMIC GROWTH

In 1966, Simon Kuznets, winner of the third Nobel Memorial Prize in Economics in 1971, defined *modern economic growth* as a sustained increase in per capita income (gross national product, or GNP, divided by population) accompanied by an increase in population and by sweeping structural changes, some of which were socially disruptive. Among the structural changes he singled out were the change in the distribution of the labor force among economic activities (e.g., manufacturing, agriculture, service occupations), the movement of population from the countryside to the cities, and the change in the distribution of the annual output of goods and services (gross domestic product, or GDP) consumed by households, by business (also called *capital formation*), and by federal, state, and local governments (such as armaments, fire equipment, labor services, police protection, etc.). Although there had been sustained economic growth prior to the eighteenth century, premodern economic growth took the form of an increase in total income rather than in per capita income because of a tendency, first called to public attention in 1798 by Thomas Malthus, of population growth to press the limits of resources.[14]

At the beginning of the period of modern economic growth, the principal nations of the world, not only in Europe but also in Asia and the New World, had approximately equal per capita incomes, all of which were very low by current standards. Modern economic growth began first in Europe and initially proceeded at a relatively slow pace; only a handful of countries experienced the structural changes described by Kuznets prior to the twentieth century. Great Britain was among the first countries to experience such growth during the first half of the eighteenth century. The United States did not begin to experience such growth until the late eighteenth century, France during the Napoleonic era (the late eighteenth century through the mid-nineteenth). By the middle of the nineteenth century, the countries experiencing such growth included the Netherlands, Germany, Switzerland, Denmark, Norway, Sweden, Canada, and Australia.[15]

Japan and Argentina did not embark on the path of modern economic growth until the end of the nineteenth century. For Italy and a number of other European nations, modern economic growth was delayed until the beginning of the twentieth century. Except for Japan, modern economic growth did not extend to Southern or Eastern Asia until after World War II. The rates of growth in per capita income during the eighteenth century (about 1.2 percent per annum) were not as high as those achieved during the nineteenth century (about 1.4–1.7 percent per annum), and those of the nineteenth century were not as high as those achieved during the first six decades of the twentieth century (about 2.0–2.8 percent per annum). The latecomers, particularly the countries of Southeast Asia—Japan, South Korea, Taiwan, and China, among others—have experienced the most rapid rates of economic growth during the entire modern era, averaging over 6 percent per annum for several decades.[16]

As a result of the different dates at which countries experienced modern economic growth, large gaps developed between the average incomes of countries that once had been equally poor. By the 1850s, Britain, for example, enjoyed a real per capita income that was more than double the 1750 level. By 1960, British real per capita income stood at more than nine times the 1750 level. In contrast, in the 1960s, the real per capita income of nations such as India and China were still stuck at levels close to those that had prevailed two centuries earlier. Even Japan was still a relatively poor country in the mid-1950s.[17]

The first stage of economic growth in Britain, France, and most of the other early starters took place in agriculture. In Britain, the development of more intensive methods of land utilization (such as placing seeds in drilled holes and increased hoeing) and of new varieties of traditional crops, along with the introduction of new crops used for fodder (such as peas and clover, which added nitrogen to the soil), also raised the productivity of agricultural workers more rapidly than the rate of growth of the population. That is, the output of food increased more rapidly than did the population. Consequently, the average consumption of calories slowly increased, rising by 10 percent between 1700 and 1800 and by another 10 percent between 1800 and 1850.[18]

This blessing had a downside. Because agricultural workers' output of food increased more rapidly than the population, the supply of food came to exceed the demand for it. Many agricultural workers therefore became redundant and were pushed off the land, a process that began in the eighteenth century and continued through the twentieth. Some of these displaced workers remained in the countryside, where they joined the ranks of the rural unemployed. Others moved into the cities in search of jobs in trade or manufacturing. While some found urban jobs, others became part of a pool of homeless workers that hovered between 10 and 20 percent of the potential labor force during most of the eighteenth and nineteenth centuries.[19]

The Urban Explosion

Prior to the Industrial Revolution, only a small percentage of the population of the world lived in cities with populations of five thousand or more. As late as 1700, even in Britain, the most urbanized of the European nations, only 7 percent of the population lived in cities. The two largest cities of Europe were London, whose 550,000 people accounted for half of Britain's urban total, and Paris, whose 520,000 also accounted for nearly half the French urban population.[20]

It was only toward the end of the eighteenth century that the modern movement toward the rapid urbanization of society began to unfold. Britain led the way. By 1800, over a third of its population lived in cities, and London, with nearly 900,000 persons, was the largest city in Europe, leaping far ahead of Paris because of its extraordinary growth rate between 1750 and 1800.

However, the real urban explosion occurred during the nineteenth century. The urban transformation was again epitomized by London, whose population increased sevenfold, reaching 6.5 million in 1900. Paris, the third largest city in the world in 1900, with 3.3 million persons, had grown sixfold. The rate of urbanization was even more spectacular in the United States. New York, a port of modest size in 1800, grew over sixtyfold in a century, to become the world's second largest city. And Chicago, which did not even exist in 1800, had a population of 1.7 million in 1900, which ranked it fifth in the world. By the end of the nineteenth century, close to 40 percent of the people of Western Europe and the United States lived in cities.[21]

It is often said that the urban explosion was sparked by the expansion of the factory system, which absorbed the pool of unemployed urban labor. That proposition is misleading. During the first half of the nineteenth century, factories were powered primarily by water mills and hence had to be located at the fall lines of rivers, which were generally beyond the limits of the great cities. There were some cities, such as Manchester and Birmingham in Britain and Lawrence, Massachusetts, whose growth was closely related to the growth of factories. But, in cities such as London, New York, and Chicago, much more of the expansion of the labor force was related to trade, finance, professional services, government bureaucracies, construction, and artisanal crafts than to factory employment.

Migration played the central role in the growth of cities. The rapid growth of urban populations in the nineteenth century was much greater than the natural rate of increase (the difference between the birthrate and death rate) in both Europe and the United States. Indeed, death rates in London, Paris, New York, and other large cities were so high during most of the nineteenth century that, had it not been for massive immigration, these cities would have grown very slowly or even declined. For Britain and continental Europe, the migration was mainly internal, from the rural hinterlands to the cities, although at midcentury perhaps a third of London's population was either Irish or from continental Europe. In the case of the United States, the migration into the cities was mainly intercontinental. However, it too resulted from an excess of agricultural workers in Europe. Peasants pushed off the land by laborsaving changes in technology usually first sought employment in the cities of their own countries, before making the dangerous journey to the New World. These great migratory movements were highly destabilizing—socially, politically, and culturally—as is made apparent by the American experience.[22]

Technological changes that greatly reduced the cost of ocean transportation were a major factor in inducing millions of Europeans to cross the Atlantic. Prior to 1810, the voyage from Europe to North America was long (about thirty days), dangerous (about 5–10 percent of voyagers died on the high seas, and another 5–10 percent died within a year of landing because of diseases contracted during the journey), and expensive (passage charges were equal to the annual income of a European laborer). Between 1810 and 1860, the time of the journey was reduced by 75 percent (to about seven days), the average risk of death as a result of the journey was reduced by up to 90 percent, and passage charges were reduced by 90 percent.[23]

Technological change also transformed inland transportation. The introduction of the steamboat in 1803 and improvements in steam engines greatly lowered the cost of transportation on inland waterways and made it economically feasible to ship goods upstream on the Mississippi and Ohio river systems. Between 1817 and 1840, over three thousand miles of canals were constructed, improving passage on the Great Lakes and linking them to the navigable rivers. With the completion of the Erie Canal in 1825, linking the Great Lakes to the Hudson River and the Atlantic Ocean, vast amounts of land in Ohio, Indiana, and Illinois became commercially accessible. With agriculture and commerce no longer confined to the plains between the Allegheny Mountains and the sea, millions of workers, tradesmen, and their families, including many immigrants, migrated to the Midwest in search of economic opportunity. Major new cities such as St. Louis, Cincinnati, Chicago, Detroit, and Milwaukee sprang into being along these waterways.[24]

The conquest of land was reinforced by the development of the locomotive engine, which permitted railroads to compete for commercial traffic. The first commercial railroad in the United States, the Baltimore and Ohio, twenty-three miles long, was opened for traffic in 1828. By 1840, some three thousand miles of track were open to traffic in the United States. That figure increased to nine thousand miles in 1850 and thirty-one thousand miles in 1860. The transportation network was so dense on the eve of the Civil War that virtually every farm was within an easy journey of a railroad junction or a navigable waterway.[25]

The expansion of the transportation network shifted the locus of grain production from the seaboard states to the Midwest. The availability of rich prairie soils greatly reduced the price of grains throughout the country, which was a boon to urban consumers but undermined the livelihood of many farmers in the East. Unable to compete with cheaper Midwestern grain producers, farmers streamed out of the once-productive Connecticut River Valley during the 1840s and 1850s, seeking jobs in the often-glutted labor markets of Boston, New York, Philadelphia, and other Eastern cities.[26]

Of course, the expansion of the transportation network did not just destroy jobs; it also created them. Some Eastern farmers relocated to farmlands in the Midwest and were eventually better off economically. The construction of railroads and waterways created new nonagricultural jobs, as did the construction of residential and commercial buildings in the new and rapidly expanding Midwestern cities. Unfortunately, those who gained these new construction jobs were usually not those who had been driven off their farms. So, although total jobs may have increased as a result of technological change, new jobs often did not go to those who had lost their old jobs.[27]

The phasing of various new technologies also created great imbalances. This problem is illustrated by developments in English textiles. The first great technological advance in that industry was the mechanization at the end of the 1760s of the process by which cotton and wool were spun into yarn, which greatly reduced the cost of cloth and thereby increased its consumption. The increased consumption of cloth led to an increased demand for weavers, who still worked on hand looms. The initial effect of the mechanization of textiles, then, was quite salutary for hand-loom weavers, whose wages rose and whose numbers increased. By 1815, however, several decades after the revolution in spinning, weaving was mechanized, making hand-loom weavers uncompetitive and bringing ruin to the now-numerous practitioners of this craft.

The misphasing of new technologies showed up even more dramatically in the lag of those technologies needed to provide adequate housing, water supplies, sanitation, and public health in large cities. That gap and its grievous effect on American society and culture must be considered in more detail to understand the recurring religious-political cycles.

Cities and Cultural Destabilization

During the first quarter of the nineteenth century, there was little tension between cities and the countryside. The nation was in the midst of an evangelical revival during which both religious and political leaders celebrated the virtues of a society of farmers and merchants organized around villages and towns over those of a society based on commerce and industries organized around large cities. It was commonly argued that the countryside with its yeoman class "guaranteed the safety of property" and propagated "a due sense of independence, liberty, and justice."[28] Few anticipated the succession of urban problems that would soon engulf the North. The romantic attachment to agrarian life persisted through the whole of the nineteenth century and much of the first half of the twentieth.

As late as 1820, Americans thought that they could avoid the corruption and political chaos that massive cities had introduced to European society. Manufacturing in the United States was still more a rural than an urban pursuit because textile mills, grist mills, and ironworks were located next to the waterfalls that provided their power. Although they were numerous and substantial by 1820, the new factories were not yet viewed as a threat to the agrarian ideal. In 1820, it was still thought that, in a country like America, where, as Benjamin Franklin said, every man "can have a piece of land of his own," manufacturing was bound to occupy a small role in economic life. Experience had shown that few free men would willingly give up agriculture, where they were independent, and look to manufacturing for their livelihood, where they had to, as Franklin put it, "work for a master."[29]

Manufacturing, said Alexander Hamilton, secretary of the Treasury under George Washington, was useful mainly because it gave employment to women, children, and, as Hamilton labeled them, *redundant* males (i.e., men who could not perform agricultural work).[30] That judgment has been confirmed by the investigations of economic historians. Most of the hands in the great textile mills, the archetype of the factory system during much of the nineteenth century, were women and children. Such factories originally came into being in the United States only where, because of the heaviness of the labor involved, large numbers of women and children from the agricultural sector were underemployed (or lightly employed). In tobacco and cotton regions, where pay for women and children in agricultural labor was relatively high, large textiles mills were uncompetitive, and only small handicraft shops producing fine cloth, and staffed by male hand-loom weavers, thrived. Thus, the underemployment of female and child labor, combined with a general surplus of agricultural workers in the Northeast, gave a strong impetus to the growth of the factory system, an impetus that was abetted by the growing demand for manufactured goods.[31]

Even the two largest American cities in 1820, New York and Philadelphia, each with over 100,000 inhabitants, fitted comfortably into the vision of America as an agrarian nation. They were large because their excellent harbors and access to the rural hinterland made them the best centers through which to export America's agricultural surpluses and import the foreign merchandise craved by American farmers. Altogether, there were only sixty-one cities in the United States, and barely 7 percent of the population lived in them. Since the urban share of the population was slightly less in 1820 than in 1810, unchecked urban growth did not appear to be a menace. There were only six large cities in America at the time if one defines *large* as twenty-five thousand or more inhabitants. Thus, all but a few cities in 1820 were little more than overgrown villages, small enough to be managed without resorting to a professional police force, and light enough in population density to permit most families the space to own livestock and grow their own produce. All except the largest three or four cities were tightly knit communities that had not yet divided into class- and ethnicity-based neighborhoods, and they were walking towns, in the sense that all parts could easily be reached on foot.[32]

Economic growth after 1820 did not change the fundamental relation between the cities and the countryside in the South. As late as 1860, barely 10 percent of the Southern population lived in the cities. The change in the Northern cities was, by contrast, a veritable revolution in culture. Not only did the urban population of the Northeast expand at an unprece- dented rate during the last four decades of the antebellum era, but nearly half that population was concentrated in just two cities: Philadelphia and New York. By 1860, Philadelphia's population exceeded half a million, and New York's was close to a million. Although such large cities promoted certain elements of high culture and were showcases for new technology, it was not their achievements but the severe new problems that they posed that attracted the most attention.[33] Philadelphia, New York, and Boston were perceived as threats to social order (because they bred disease, crime, violence, and moral decay), to religious freedom (because they promoted godlessness and sin), and to popular democracy (because they promoted mob violence). This antipathy to big-city life reflected social and moral problems of unprecedented scope and severity. In New York, crime rates during the 1820s and 1830s rose more than four times as rapidly as the population, overwhelming the resources of the part-time police force.[34]

By the early 1840s, newspapers and government investigating commit- tees were decrying the uncontrolled, unpunished spate of murders and ri- ots, the commercialized vice, and the frequent robberies of both dwellings and businesses. Official estimates put the number of prostitutes in New York in 1844 at ten thousand, some of them "not even into the teens." Drunkenness was widespread, with one saloon "for every fifty persons in the city over the age of fifteen." There was also a mounting problem of "vagrant and criminal children" (estimated by police at over three thou- sand), some organized into rings of thieves by professional criminals, oth- ers individually engaged in acts "which for vileness and deep depravity, would absolutely stagger belief."[35]

The big cities of the 1840s and 1850s were not only incubators of crime and vice but also destroyers of the cultural vision of the founding fathers, who had warned that, like sores on a body, great cities would destroy the vigor of the Republic. By the late antebellum era, the prophetic metaphor had become a gruesome physical reality. Between 1790 and 1850, life expectancy in the North declined by 25 percent, and the decline in New York, Philadelphia, and other large cities was twice as great. Life expectancy at birth for persons born in New York and Philadelphia during the 1830s and 1840s averaged just twenty-four years, six years less than that of Southern slaves.[36]

This transformation of cities into death traps resulted from a population growth that outpaced the development of adequate housing stock and sanitation and water services. Thousands of lower-class families crowded into flimsy shacks and shanties. Many small, older houses originally intended for a single family were partitioned to hold three or more families. Thousands more people moved into windowless underground cellars, where they had to share space with their own livestock—pigs and fowl— as well as with omnivorous rats.[37]

THE POLITICAL CONSEQUENCES OF TECHNOLOGICAL CHANGE AND URBANIZATION

By the 1830s, the deep poverty and class conflicts of urban life seemed to threaten the stability of American society, much as they had threatened social stability in France and England. "I regard the size of some American cities," said the great French writer Alexis de Tocqueville, "and especially the nature of their inhabitants as a real danger threatening the future" of American democracy. Pointing to the "serious riots" that had recently occurred in Philadelphia and New York, he characterized the lower classes of "these vast cities" as "a rabble more dangerous even than that of European towns" and warned that the "passions that agitate" them would destroy America unless the "government succeeds in creating an armed force" that is "capable of suppressing their excesses." Such an armed force, the uniformed police, was of course created, first in New York, and soon after in Philadelphia, Jersey City, Baltimore, Chicago, Boston, and Cincinnati.[38]

Thus, the vast new cities of the nation were plunged into a new kind of urban politics, a politics that not only attracted professional politicians but also created large bureaucracies, required huge budgets, and provided new opportunities for personal enrichment. The struggle for control of these governments transformed local politics, bringing to the fore parties intent on keeping "the ignorant and the vicious" in check and other parties intent on becoming their champions.[39] The cities also became a focus of

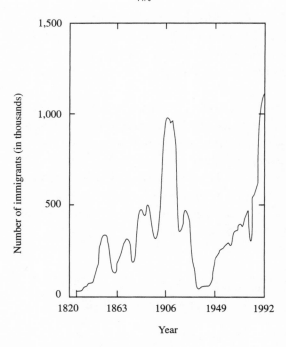

Figure 2.3 Cycles in annual immigration, 1824–1992.

SOURCES: HS (1975, 102–3) and SA (1996). See also Fogel, Galantine, and Manning (1992, entries 60–61, 67) and Fogel (1994c).

NOTE: This curve is a seven-year moving average of annual immigration data.

radical politics, both of the Left and of the Right. New ideas—for example, socialism—were introduced to America by foreign immigrants, especially those from Britain and Germany.

It was not socialism, however, but ethnicity and religion that became the principal base for urban politics in the late antebellum era. During the late 1830s and early 1840s, nativist parties became powerful enough to contend for political control in the major cities of the Northeast. From the mid-1840s on in Philadelphia, Boston, and New York, ethnic politics became the foremost basis for the formation of coalitions and the center of the struggle for power.

Politics and cultural conflict were exacerbated by economic conflicts caused by immigration. Pressure on labor markets varied over time because immigrants arrived in waves (see fig. 2.3), in response to economic and political developments in Europe.[40] The first of these waves, which began about 1830 and culminated in 1854, undermined the economic opportunities available to "Old Americans" (native-born children of native-born parents of the American branches of the dissenting Protestant churches of Northwest Europe, especially England). Between 1845 and 1854, immigration, mainly from Ireland and Germany, was so heavy that the total number of immigrants entering the country during these years exceeded the combined population of nine of the sixteen Northern states as reported in the 1850 census.[41] These "New Americans" (the foreign born and their native-born children, mainly Catholics and Lutherans from Ireland, Germany, and the Austro-Hungarian Empire) glutted nonagricultural labor markets and greatly depressed the wages of Old Americans, creating one of the most severe depressions in the economic status of a major segment of workers in American history.[42]

The Political Culture of the Antebellum Era

To understand why and how immigration destabilized American politics, it is necessary to understand the political culture of the antebellum era. Between 1832 and 1856, the era of the second American party system, the two main parties were the Democratic Party (established by Andrew Jackson in 1828 from the remnants of the party of Thomas Jefferson) and the Whig Party (established in the mid-1830's from the remnants of the Federalist Party of President John Adams and Treasury Secretary Alexander Hamilton). Both parties were national, with strong bases in both the North and the South. The Democrats tended to be more laissez-faire than the Whigs. They favored a universal franchise for white males and presented themselves as the party of the laboring classes and the ethnic poor. The Whigs wanted an activist government that promoted economic growth and, as the Republicans are today, were so closely associated with evangelical Protestantism that D. W. Howe, a leading historian of the party, called them "the evangelical united front at the polling place." Both parties had roughly equal strength in the North, South, and West.[43]

The national electoral campaigns during the years of the second party system played out mainly on economic issues, with Democrats presenting themselves as the friends of the laboring man and the Whigs as the instrument of the "money power." The Whigs denounced as demagogic the Democrats' attempts to set class against class, arguing that all those who worked for a living, whether employee or employer, whether factory worker or factory owner, belonged to the laboring classes. The Democrats were for low tariffs, blamed business cycles on the promiscuous issue of unsound paper money by banks, and wanted the public domain distributed to ordinary settlers in farm-sized parcels at modest prices, with the proceeds of such sales used to reduce the national debt. The Whigs, declaring that the federal government should promote rapid economic growth, wanted to subsidize the construction of railroads and canals with huge grants of public land and federal loans, establish high tariffs to protect American markets from competing foreign products, and institute federal programs to provide relief to those devastated by recession.

Politicians in both parties were initially unwilling to make the abolition of slavery a national political issue because they believed that the Constitution enjoined them from doing so. The Democrats, however, were expansionist and supported both the annexation of Texas and the war with Mexico, while the Whigs, Northerners and Southerners, opposed both. The Northern Whigs were more sympathetic to free blacks and fought to extend the franchise to them, while the Northern Democrats sought to exclude blacks from voting. There was, moreover, a small group of Northern Whigs in the House of Representatives who, in defiance of the party leadership, sought to use the House as a platform for constitutional arguments against slavery. These men, about eleven altogether at the beginning of the 1840s, were all from New England or the areas of the Yankee diaspora (such as upstate New York, Pennsylvania, or northern Ohio). All were proponents of enthusiastic religion, and several had been converted by Theodore Weld, one of the principal leaders of the abolitionist movement. As the antislavery and anti-Southern agitation continued in the North through the 1840s and into the 1850s, this ideology won increasing sympathy among Northern Whig legislators, enough so that it became a major embarrassment to Southern Whigs in the 1852 election, and many of them were defeated.[44]

Attitudes toward immigrants, especially toward Irish Catholics, German Catholics, and Lutherans, also undermined party unity, especially in the North, where 85 percent of these immigrants were located. Hostility toward immigrants (also known as *nativism*) peaked at the height of the first wave of immigration shown in figure 2.3. Nativism was especially acute from 1853 to 1855 because the high level of immigration coincided with a severe economic recession in the North. The severity of the recession and the inadequate response of Whigs and Democrats caused nativist evangelicals to bolt from both parties. The defections were so severe among the Whigs that the party splintered and was replaced by the Republican Party. Nativism reasserted itself during the post–Civil War wave of immigration, during the wave that peaked in the 1880s, and again with the huge wave that peaked during the first decade of the twentieth century.

The Political Realignment of the 1850s

The strong nativist movement during the late 1880s and the 1890s had a significant effect on political realignments in both the Democratic and the Republican Parties during the 1896 elections. Nativism also contributed to the urban and labor crises that gave rise to the Social Gospel movement. However, it is the political realignment of the 1850s that is most similar to the political realignment of the 1990s. It is instructive, therefore, to consider the circumstances that produced the Republican Party and embodied within it the coalition that dominated American politics during most of the federal elections between 1864 and 1928.

Prior to the election of 1852, the political domination of electoral contests by the Democratic and Whig Parties seemed secure. Both parties were strong at the state and local levels, sharing political offices at these levels roughly equally.[45] Between 1820 and 1860, internal trade became increasingly important, as technological change steadily undermined the self-sufficiency of farmers and promoted the rapid growth of nonagricultural employment. As a consequence, the main issues of national politics during the second party system were tariffs, regulation of the rapidly emerging banks, federal subsidies for transportation, and the free distribution of land in the public domain to settlers.

Only two small parties challenged the Democrats and the Whigs during these years. The abolitionists, the most radical of the evangelical reformers, working through the Liberty Party in 1840 and 1844, were unable to elect anyone to Congress, and their presidential candidate, James G. Birney, who was from a prominent slaveholding family in Kentucky, received a minuscule portion of the vote. Drawing their strength mainly from artisans and shopkeepers, who felt threatened by the huge influx of Catholic workers from Ireland and Germany, the nativists were successful in winning control of the New York City government in the 1844 elections and were able to elect a few congressmen in both New York and Philadelphia. Although they tried to organize themselves into a national party in 1845, their movement soon collapsed as the upturn in business conditions between 1844 and 1848 created an abundance of jobs.

The abolitionists became a significant factor in the election of 1848 by joining with a minority faction of the Democratic Party associated with former president Martin Van Buren and with a small antislavery faction of the Whigs, whose strength was mainly in Massachusetts. This coalition was drawn overwhelmingly from Old American immigrants and their descendants from England, Scotland, Protestant Ireland, and pietistic Germany. The central demand of the new party, which was called *the Free Soil Party*, was the provision of free land to free men in the territories, from which they meant to exclude slaveholders and slaves. With this coalition, the antislavery forces were able to win nine seats in the House and one in the Senate (held by Salmon Chase of Ohio, a dedicated abolitionist and one of the most brilliant political tacticians ever produced in the United States) as well as a smattering of seats in state legislatures and other local offices. However, most of these seats disappeared in the 1850 election, and the Northern vote for even a watered-down antislavery program slipped back to the levels of 1844. The Free Soilers did only slightly better in the 1852 elections.

Nativism, on the other hand, began to reawaken after the downturn of the economy in 1849 and again in 1853. These recessions, together with the huge increase of immigrants from both Ireland and Germany, had a negative effect on the wages of native-born workers. Operating through fraternal labor organizations, the nativists initially backed anti-immigrant candidates in both parties. By the beginning of the 1850s, the nativists were making themselves known in local elections, winning offices in Detroit and Pittsburgh on independent slates and threatening to win in other cities. By 1854, they had laid the foundation for a nationwide nativist campaign for the reform of local and state government. Sometimes using the name *American Party*, nativists entered into state and congressional elections, with devastating effects. In 1854, nativists won a third of the seats in the House of Representatives and swept all the state offices in Massachusetts. In 1855, nativists won victories in nine other states and made strong showings in another eight. So, a year before the election of 1856, the Know-Nothings (the name given the nativist American Party by Horace Greeley, Whig editor of the *New York Tribune*, owing to their refusal to divulge information about some of their organizations) confidently set their eyes on the White House, and the expectation that they would win was shared reluctantly by many of their opponents. In the deep South, most of the Whigs shifted into the Know-Nothing Party because the Whig Party was no longer viable in that region, scuttled by the outspoken antislavery sentiments of many Northern Whigs.[46]

Analysis of the election returns in the North for 1854 and 1855 reveals that support for the Know-Nothings came in roughly equal numbers from former Democrat and former Whig voters. The antislavery forces, particularly Senators Salmon Chase of Ohio and Henry Wilson of Massachusetts, recognized that this defection of Democratic and Whig voters in the

North provided an exceptional opportunity to create a new broad party based on an antislavery program, and they set about doing so. To this end, they organized slates at the state and local levels under the name *Republican*, hoping to win the nativist voters into their fold by combining abolitionism with a watered-down nativism. However, the Republicans did poorly in direct contests with the Know-Nothings in the 1854 and 1855 elections since voters were more responsive to the jobs issue than to an antislavery platform.

Despite this string of lopsided losses, the antislavery forces did gain predominance among the breakaway voters, and they did so with a suddenness that was dazzling. The turnabout came in fewer than six months. At the end of 1855, the Know-Nothings seemed to have the upper hand in the struggle for the control of the breakaway vote in all the key Northern states, with antislavery forces dominant only in Vermont, Iowa, Wisconsin, and Michigan. Six months later, the Republicans had jelled as a national political party under the influence of antislavery activists. The Know-Nothings, on the other hand, were split. The antislavery faction, which represented the bulk of the Northern Know-Nothings, was absorbed by the Republicans. Those Northern Know-Nothings, who were not primarily antislavery advocates, joined with Southern Know-Nothings to form the American Party, which nominated Millard Fillmore (conservative Whig and ex-president) to oppose the Republican candidate, John C. Frémont. Although Republican leaders had to maneuver adroitly to placate their Know-Nothing constituency, the control of the party (as is discussed in chap. 3 below) remained with the men who were committed to an antislavery policy as the overriding principle of the Republican coalition.

The preceding discussion gives an overview of the political realignment of the 1850s. The key development that relates the political realignment of the 1850s to that of the 1990s was the shift in the political allegiance of Northern Old Americans, who were mainly evangelicals. Their behavior was the decisive influence on the strength of the Republican coalition between 1856 and 1860. However, the Republican appeal also extended to some New Americans, especially among the German Lutherans and Catholics. Although the majority of these New Americans voted mainly for the Democrats, enough were brought into the Republican coalition to give Lincoln his margin of victory.[47]

About 76 percent of Lincoln's votes in 1860 came from ex-Whigs, and the balance was split nearly equally between ex–Free Soilers and ex–Democrats. Many ex-Whigs and ex-Democrats had voted for the Know-

Nothings before becoming Republicans. In other words, in 1860, the Republican Party was basically the Whig Party with the addition of enough votes from ex–Free Soilers and ex-Democrats to more than offset the loss of some former Whigs. The net effect of these shifts was to raise the Republican share of the Northern vote by 1.7 percent, just enough to give Lincoln his victory.[48]

Behind that slight increase in the overall Whig/Republican margin in the North was a flight of Old Americans (as was mentioned above, mainly evangelicals of New England ancestry) from the Democratic to the Republican Party. Between 1844 and 1852, the Northern evangelical vote was shared nearly equally by the two main parties. However, not only did the Northern Democrats appeal to the growing Catholic and Lutheran constituencies in the cities; they also abandoned their cheap-land policy (a key issue for the largely evangelical labor movement). These sins caused Northern evangelicals, the principal bearers of the antislavery ethic, to flee the Democratic Party in droves.[49]

The net effect of the consolidation of most Northern Old Americans in the Republican Party and most New Americans in the Democratic Party was to bring about the victory (by a razor-thin margin) of a Northern party on an antislavery, anti-Catholic program.[50] That realignment remained more or less intact until 1932. From the Civil War until the election of Franklin D. Roosevelt as thirty-second president, the Republican Party was purely Northern, based mainly on a Protestant constituency of Yankee ancestry, while the Democrats were largely a coalition of the new immigrants and their children (mainly Catholics and Lutherans) together with white Protestants from the "Solid South" (mainly conservative evangelical forerunners of today's fundamentalists and neoevangelicals).[51]

In the realignment of the 1850s, as in the realignment of the 1990s, it was the movement of evangelicals out of the Democratic Party and into the Republican Party that made the Republicans politically dominant. The Republicans maintained their hold on Northern evangelicals and their control of the federal government from 1864 to 1930, except when they were split (in 1885–89, 1893–97, and 1913–17). The Democrats began to recover from their loss of Northern evangelical support during the elections of 1896, 1900, and 1908, the three elections in which William Jennings Bryan, a politically liberal fundamentalist, was the Democratic nominee. However, it was not until 1932 that the momentum for change among liberal white evangelicals and black evangelicals became sufficient to make the Democratic Party the vehicle for the implementation of the

TECHNOLOGICAL CHANGE, CULTURAL TRANSFORMATIONS, AND POLITICAL CRISES

reform program of the Social Gospelers and their successors. That realignment is discussed more fully in chapter 3 below.

THE RISE OF THE PROFESSIONAL CLASS

Technological change brought about still another shift in American culture, one that is more subtle but in many ways more far-reaching in its political effect than either migration or urbanization: that is, the vast increase in professional occupations and the associated changes in higher education. Professionals are experts in fields that require high degrees of training, usually obtained in colleges and universities. Professions often have regulatory bodies that certify the competency of individuals to practice the occupation or attest to the fact that individuals have successfully completed a course of training for the occupation.

Throughout most of American history, the professional class constituted a small minority, generally less than 3 or 4 percent, of the labor force. Moreover, until the middle of the nineteenth century, professionals were overwhelmingly concentrated in three occupations: theology, law, and medicine. As late as 1840, these three fields accounted for two-thirds of the graduates of American colleges and universities, with theology alone accounting for nearly a third of the output. Those who entered the ministry outnumbered educators by more than three to one, authors and journalists by more than eighteen to one, and those in the government by more than twenty-five to one. It was not until the last quarter of the nineteenth century that the three original professions were overtaken. By 1900, engineering, the sciences, education, and a variety of commercial occupations were absorbing the great majority of college graduates.[52]

The preeminence of religious studies in American colleges and universities traces back to the origins of universities in medieval Europe as institutions authorized by the pope to teach theology, canon law, civil law, and medicine. Science as practiced in these medieval schools included not just medicine but also logic, mathematics, metaphysics, and natural philosophy (the equivalent of the natural sciences today). However, theology was considered preeminent.[53]

The main aim of colleges established during the colonial period, beginning with the founding of Harvard College in 1636, was to train learned men to be ministers in one or another of the Protestant denominations. The teaching programs of these schools, and of most institutions of higher learning founded between the Revolution and 1900, were patterned after the liberal arts courses of Oxford and Cambridge, emphasizing Latin, Greek, theology, biblical studies, moral philosophy and, somewhat less consistently, mathematics. As the nation grew, penetrating new areas of the continental wilderness, and as population grew from just 4 million at the time of the Revolution to 31 million in 1860, the desire for higher education intensified. By 1860, the institutions of higher education expanded from the nine established before the Revolution to over three hundred in 1860.[54]

Most of the new colleges were church affiliated, as were the nine established before the Revolution. Although they sometimes received financial support from state governments, the main initiative came from the denominations, which sought to maintain the intellectual standards of a growing ministry and to promote the dissemination of Christian knowledge. Control of these colleges was vested in private, self-perpetuating boards, and the colleges were financed primarily through private philanthropy, funds contributed through religious organizations, and tuition fees. At first, the new colleges offered a curriculum of traditional liberal arts, along the lines of the pre-Revolution colleges, but, as time wore on, they added courses in mathematics, moral philosophy, and natural philosophy. College presidents were almost always ordained ministers, and most faculty members were also ordained ministers or young men otherwise affiliated with their denominations. It was common practice for college presidents to teach a required course in moral philosophy, usually to fourth-year students.[55]

The quickening of technological change in the late eighteenth and early nineteenth centuries made applied science an increasingly important part of higher education. France set the standard with the establishment in 1795 of the École Polytechnique de France, which provided the engineers for Napoleon's armies. In the United States, technical education was stimulated by the Jefferson administration's ambitious program of canal and turnpike construction. In 1802, Congress voted to establish a corps of engineers with a training academy that was located at West Point. The academy was soon upgraded to a four-year program that offered excellent training in mathematics and the physical sciences, and it produced the original national corps of experts who constructed much of the nation's canal, railroad, common road, bridge, reservoir, and sewage systems. Many graduates of West Point became professors of mathematics or natural philosophy in colleges and universities throughout the nation. Additional engineering schools were opened in Troy, New York (Rensselaer Polytechnic

Institute, 1824), Brooklyn (Polytechnic Institute of Brooklyn, 1854), and New York City (Cooper Union, 1859).[56]

The growth of scientific teaching within the denominational colleges was typified by Yale University, which, partly in response to the striking advances made in chemical technology during the preceding half century, established a chair in chemistry, mineralogy, and geology in 1802. A medical department was established in 1810 and a school of engineering in 1852. In 1854, the courses in chemistry and engineering were combined into the Sheffield scientific school, which a decade later expanded to include the agricultural sciences and applied mechanical arts. Similar developments took place at Harvard, where the medical school was founded in 1782, the Lawrence scientific school in 1847 (offering courses in physics, chemistry, and engineering), and the Museum of Comparative Zoology in 1859 (to promote biological studies).

The establishment of state universities in the Midwest further promoted the secularization of the curriculum. The University of Michigan, for example, was founded in 1837 under a state charter that required it to be nonsectarian. That provision was originally interpreted to apply only to Protestant denominations. Although biblical studies and daily worship were required of all students, the teaching program had a strong utilitarian component, reflected in courses in mathematics, chemistry, astronomy, zoology, and medicine. Michigan was also the first state to provide funds for the establishment of a college of agriculture (1857), setting off a movement that culminated in congressional passage of the Morrill Land Grant Act of 1862. Under this act, each state received large quantities of public land to establish colleges teaching those branches of learning related to the agricultural and mechanical arts.[57]

The movement to reform the curriculum of institutions of higher learning accelerated during the last three decades of the nineteenth century, led by Harvard and Johns Hopkins in the East and by Michigan and Wisconsin in the Midwest. These reforms included modernizing the undergraduate curriculum by adding numerous courses in the humanities (modern languages, English literature and literary criticism, systematic ethics [independent of theology], history), the social sciences (political science, economics, psychology, and anthropology), and the natural sciences (chemistry, physics, zoology, botany, mineralogy, and geology). In addition, curricula became less rigid, and, by the end of the century, most universities permitted students, usually beginning with their third year, to choose which courses they wished to take (the elective system) and also to choose their concentration (their major). Another innovation was the introduction of graduate schools and research that were separate from and beyond undergraduate training. This accelerated the trend toward separate professional schools of law, theology, and medicine within universities. Professional schools were also established in such new disciplines as commerce, education, journalism, agriculture, architecture, mining, and social work. Paralleling the change in curriculum was a change in teaching methods. Daily recitations in which students translated Latin and Greek under the watchful eye of the teacher were replaced by lectures by professors and by seminars in which teachers and students jointly discussed problems of research.[58]

The modernization of colleges and universities before 1900 involved substantial secularization. Biblical studies remained, but the Bible increasingly was studied primarily as a literary or historical work, according to developing canons of literary and historical scholarship. Worship was reduced from twice daily to once daily and later to weekly. Compulsory chapel often became interdenominational, with services often focusing on ethical rather than theological issues. The taking of attendance at chapel lapsed. The prevalence of ordained ministers as university presidents dwindled. Even Princeton, the leading Presbyterian university and theologically conservative, elected a lay member of the church as president in 1902: Woodrow Wilson, the future governor of New Jersey and president of the United States.[59]

By 1900, colleges and universities were poised for a vast increase in the demand for their product. In a sense, the reforms of the preceding half century had returned higher education to its original purpose, vocational training. However, in place of the one professional occupation—the ministry—that the founders of Harvard, Yale, and the other pre-Revolution colleges had in mind, the post–Civil War leaders of higher education sought to produce persons trained in all the professions demanded by the new technologies of the nineteenth century.[60]

Interestingly, technological change increased the demand not only for scientists and engineers but also for graduates trained in the humanities, social sciences, and business management. The explosive growth of high school education was a response to the high-technology industries of the late nineteenth century and the early twentieth (industries based in electricity, chemistry, and the first wave of office automation, printing and publishing), which demanded manual workers with a higher level of education than had previously been expected. The fifteenfold increase in high school students created a huge market for college-trained high school teachers.[61]

The demand for graduates in the humanities was also related to the burgeoning growth of the mass media. During the last three decades of the nineteenth century, daily newspapers fell in price, increased the number of pages and the number of editions printed, ran drawings and photographs, and added literary material, gossip columns, cartoons, display advertising, and separate editorials. Circulation boomed, expanding from under 1 million to over 15 million daily copies between 1870 and 1900 and then to 42 million daily copies between 1900 and 1929. Behind these developments were such crucial technological advances as high-speed rotary presses, the linotype machine, color printing, photoengraving, and the array of technologies that promoted urban growth, including rapid transit systems, electricity, central heating, and pasteurized milk.[62]

Advertising was a critical factor in reducing the cost of newspapers and new popular magazines. In the 1890s, mass-circulation magazines selling at ten cents per copy came into being, including *McClure's* and *Cosmopolitan*. A decade later, these and such other magazines as *Ladies Home Journal, Collier's,* and the *Saturday Evening Post* each had circulations that ran into the hundreds of thousands. College graduates were in demand to work on those magazines as well as to write copy and produce the artwork for the new advertising agencies. The talents and skills of humanities graduates were also in demand in the new industry of popular entertainment (movies, vaudeville, the popular songs of Tin Pan Alley, radio, and eventually television), although in entertainment, college graduates had to compete with the products of informal apprenticeship systems.[63]

Part of the growth in the demand for social scientists also came from the media. Newspapers and magazines that featured stories about social reform (muckraking) found that they could make use of historians, economists, and sociologists. Ida Tarbell began her career at *McClure's* with biographies of Lincoln and Napoleon but then turned her talents to an exposé of the operations of Standard Oil. In eighteen installments running from November 1902 to May 1904, she provided a scholarly indictment of the practices used by John D. Rockefeller to create the oil trust.[64]

However, the movement for social reform, which sought government intervention to cure the social ills of the era, created an even bigger market for college graduates: the government. Labor bureaus, set up in numerous states and in the federal government, needed economists and sociologists with the skill to design and execute surveys of working conditions and standards of living. Similar skills were required by the Bureau of the Census, the U.S. Industrial Commission, and the Interstate Commerce Commission. Various congressional investigations, such as the Senate Select

Committee on Transportation and the Senate Committee on Finance, also needed social scientists. Economists too were drawn into state investigations such as those of public utilities in Wisconsin and of the New York Stock Exchange in New York.[65]

Businesses needed students trained in engineering and the sciences. Chemists were in high demand not only by firms manufacturing dyes and other industrial chemicals but by the oil industry, the steel industry, and the food-processing industries. Such new and rapidly growing industries as public utilities, telephonic communications, railroads, and the manufacture of electrical equipment and internal combustion engines demanded large numbers of electrical, mechanical, chemical, and civil engineers.[66]

As businesses grew larger, more integrated, and more complex, the professionally trained managers began to replace the owner-manager (often an artisan) who ran the smaller firms of the first half of the nineteenth century. Some professionally trained managers came out of engineering, some out of law, and some out of the schools of business management founded first at Pennsylvania in 1881 (the Wharton School of Finance and Economy), at Chicago (1898), at Dartmouth, California, NYU, and Wisconsin (all in 1900), and at Harvard (1908). By 1915, some forty business schools had been established.[67]

The growing demand for college-trained personnel by business and government led to extraordinary rates of growth in higher education. Undergraduate enrollment at colleges and universities increased more than fourfold between 1870 and 1900, when it stood at 232,000. It increased again by over fourfold during the next thirty years, reaching 1.1 million in 1930. The huge growth in enrollment resumed after World War II, going from 2.8 million in 1960 to 13.7 million in 1990.[68]

As a result of this vast expansion in higher education, professional occupations in 1997 accounted for about 33 percent of the labor force, and the composition of these occupations had changed from a century before. The clergy, which dominated intellectual life in the 1890s, in 1997 represented less than 1 percent of the professional class. In 1997, journalists and authors, social and natural scientists, college and university teachers, and mathematicians each outnumbered members of the clergy. As if in answer to the appeals of the modernists, a secular class of experts on the natural and social worlds has usurped the monopoly that theologians once had on these domains.[69]

The new professionals have played three important roles in the establishment and perpetuation of the egalitarian state. They provide most of the personnel who manage the egalitarian state, both as designers and as implementers of policy. The government today employs one-fifth of all physical scientists, one-third of all life scientists, three-eighths of all mathematicians, and more than a quarter of all social scientists. Even cabinet posts, once filled almost exclusively by politicians and businessmen, are now increasingly claimed by professionals. There were, for example, four Ph.D. economists in President Jimmy Carter's cabinet.[70]

In addition to having a strong vested interest in the egalitarian state, professionals have an ideological predisposition toward it. The orientation is related partly to their professional training, which, in keeping with the egalitarian creed, emphasizes their obligation to serve society. Moreover, for many professionals, higher education has been a principal channel for upward economic and social mobility. They have therefore gladly accepted the role assigned to them by the principles of the Third Great Awakening: to guide society to a solution of the problems of poverty and social strife. Hence, they have taken the lead among those designing new policies and institutions that will permit the egalitarian state to fulfill its historic, if not divine, mission. In the circumstances that prevailed in the late nineteenth century, some of them argued that equality of condition should supersede equality of opportunity as the principal touchstone of progress, although they remained committed to meritocracy as a professional standard.[71]

The professional class has become the principal possessor of an increasingly important form of capital: human capital, the value of which is today more than twice as great as the value of land and reproducible material assets. Today, the leading owners of capital are not landlords or capitalists in the traditional sense but professionals and other possessors of labor skills.[72] Although the professional class has a strong interest in preserving the value of its human capital, it would be a mistake, I believe, to view its dedication to egalitarian principles as primarily economic. For reasons more fully spelled out in the next chapter, its commitment to egalitarianism is probably more ethical than economic. Whatever the reason, the professional class is the principal political foundation for modern egalitarianism, not only because of its central role in designing and implementing egalitarian policy, but because it represents a huge portion of the political support for candidates who commit themselves to such policies.[73]

Although the large share of capital assets owned by professionals may be a minor factor in the predominant ethical values of this class, it is a major factor in the search for a viable way of completing the unfinished egalitarian agenda and of successfully developing a new agenda, which is the topic of chapter 5 below.

The development of such a large core of highly trained professionals was a concomitant of the acceleration in technological change and the resulting increase in human control over the environment, which in turn produced major improvements in human physiology. The synergism between technological change and improvements in human physiology was first noted by investigators studying the causes of the long-term reduction in mortality.

THE EMERGENCE OF TECHNOPHYSIO EVOLUTION

The synergism between technological and physiological improvements has produced a form of human evolution that is biological but not genetic, rapid, culturally transmitted, and not necessarily stable. Dora Costa (an economist and biodemographer at MIT) and I call this process, which is still ongoing in both developed and developing countries, *technophysio evolution*.[74]

Unlike the genetic theory of evolution through natural selection, which applies to the whole history of life on earth, technophysio evolution applies only to the past three hundred years of *human* history and particularly to the past century. Despite its limited scope, technophysio evolution appears to be relevant to forecasting likely trends over the next century or so in longevity, the age of onset of chronic diseases, body size, and the efficiency and durability of vital organ systems. It also has a bearing on such pressing public policy issues as the growth in population, pension costs, and health-care costs.

The theory of technophysio evolution rests on the proposition that, during the past three hundred years, particularly during the last century, human beings have gained an unprecedented degree of control over their environment—a degree of control so great that it sets them apart not only from all other species but also from all previous generations of Homo sapiens. This has enabled Homo sapiens to increase its average body size by over 50 percent, to increase its average longevity by more than 100 percent, and to improve greatly the robustness and capacity of vital organ systems.

Figure 2.4 helps show how dramatic the change in our control of the environment after 1700 has been. Figure 2.4 also highlights the astounding acceleration of technological change over the past two centuries, including the advances in the technology of food production after the Second Agricultural Revolution (which began about A.D. 1700), advances that were far more dramatic than those constituting the earlier breakthrough since they permitted population to increase at so high a rate that the line indi-

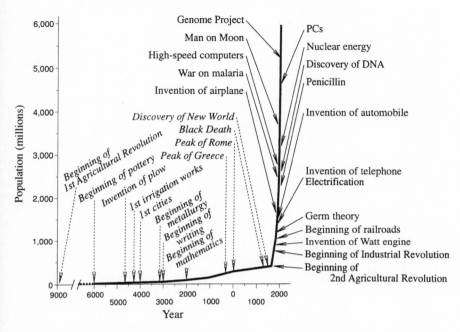

Figure 2.4 The growth of world population and some major events in the history of technology.

SOURCES: Cipolla (1974); Clark (1971); Fagan (1977); McNeill (1971); Piggott (1965); Bronowski (1973); Derry and Williams (1960); Trewartha (1969); and Bishop (1936). See also Allen (1992, 1994); Slicher von Bath (1963); and Wrigley (1987).

NOTE: There is usually a lag between the invention of a process or a machine and its general application to production. *Beginning* means the earliest stage of this diffusion process.

cating population growth rises almost vertically. The new technological breakthroughs in manufacturing, transportation, trade, communication, energy production, leisure-time services, and medical services were in many respects even more striking than those in agriculture. Figure 2.4 shows the huge acceleration in both population growth and technological change during the twentieth century. The increase in world population between 1800 and 1999 was seven times as great as it had been during the whole previous history of humankind.

The most important aspect of technophysio evolution is the continuing conquest of chronic malnutrition, which was virtually universal three centuries ago. Even the English peerage, with all its wealth, had a diet during the sixteenth and seventeenth centuries that was deleterious to health. Although abundant in calories and proteins, aristocratic diets were deficient in vitamins and included large quantities of potentially harmful

Table 2.1 Daily Energy Available for Work after Body Maintenance Needs Were Met, France, England and Wales, and the United States, 1700–1994 (in Calories)

Year	France	England and Wales	United States
1700[a]		720	2,313
1705	439		
1750		812	
1785	600		
1800		858	
1803–12			
1840			1,810
1845–54			
1850		1,014	
1870	1,671		
1880			2,709
1944			2,282
1975	2,136		
1980		1,793	1,956
1994			2,620

SOURCE: Fogel and Floud (1999).

NOTE: The entries are expressed in consumption per equivalent adult male aged twenty to thirty-nine, to adjust for differences in age and sex ratios.

[a] Prerevolutionary Virginia only.

substances, especially alcoholic beverages and salt. A diet heavy in salt and alcohol probably increased the incidence of liver, renal, gastrointestinal, and cardiovascular disease among peers who survived to middle age and may have contributed to their high mortality rates at age forty and over. But the bad dietary habits of the peerage were probably most harmful to unborn children because ladies of the realm were apparently consuming well over three ounces (eighty-five grams) of absolute alcohol per day on average—more than enough to produce a high incidence of birth defects.[75]

Most people in 1700 were chronically malnourished, not because their diets abounded in toxic substances or were qualitatively deficient, but because of severe deficiencies in dietary energy (the amount of energy made available to the body by the ingestion of food). Table 2.1 shows that, in rich countries today, some eighteen to twenty-six hundred calories of energy are available to fuel the work activities of a typical adult male, age twenty to thirty-nine.[76] During the eighteenth century, however, France produced less than one-third the current U.S. amount of energy for work, and Britain was not much better off. Only the United States provided potential energy for work equal to or greater than late twentieth-century levels during the eighteenth century and the early nineteenth, although some of that energy was wasted owing to the prevalence of diarrhea and other conditions that undermined the body's capacity to utilize nutrients.

One implication of these estimates of calorie availability is that, during the eighteenth century and much of the nineteenth, mature adults must have been very small by current standards and less physically active. Today, the average American male in his early thirties is about 177 centimeters (70 inches) tall and weighs about 78 kilograms (162 pounds). Such an individual requires about eighteen hundred calories daily for basal metabolism (the amount of energy needed to maintain body temperature and the functioning of vital organs when the body is fully at rest, measured at least fourteen hours after the last meal) and a total of twenty-three hundred calories for baseline maintenance (the energy for basal metabolism plus vital hygiene, including the digestion of food). If either the British or the French had been that large during the eighteenth century, virtually all the energy produced by their food supplies would have been required for basic body maintenance, with little available to sustain work. To have the energy necessary to produce the national products of these two countries around 1700, the typical adult male must have been quite short and very light.[77]

The Connection between Malnutrition, Body Size, and the Onset of Chronic Disease

Recent studies have established the predictive power of height and weight at early ages with respect to the onset of chronic disease and premature mortality at middle and late ages. Variations in height and weight appear to be associated with variations in the chemical composition of the tissues that make up the vital organs, in the quality of the electrical transmission across membranes, and in the functioning of the endocrine system and other vital systems. Nutritional status thus appears to be a crucial link connecting improvements in technology to improvements in human physiology.

Research on this topic is developing rapidly, and some of the new findings are yet to be confirmed. The exact mechanisms by which malnutrition and trauma in utero or early childhood are transformed into organ dysfunctions are still unclear. What is agreed on is that the basic structure of most organs is laid down early, and it is reasonable to infer that poorly developed organs may break down earlier than well-developed ones. The principal evidence so far is epidemiological, although there are some suggestions as to possible mechanisms.[78]

With these caveats in mind, recent research bearing on the connection between malnutrition, body size, and the onset of chronic disease can con-veniently be divided into three categories. The first category involves forms of malnutrition (including the ingestion of toxic substances) that cause permanent, promptly visible physiological damage, as is seen in the impairment of the nervous systems of fetuses resulting from excessive smoking or alcohol consumption by pregnant women. It appears that pro-tein calorie malnutrition (PCM) in infancy and early childhood can lead to a permanent impairment of central nervous system functioning. Folate and iodine deficiency in utero and moderate-to-severe iron deficiency dur-ing infancy also appear to cause permanent neurological damage.[79]

Not all damage caused by retarded development in utero or infancy as a result of malnutrition shows up immediately. In a recent series of studies, D. J. P. Barker (of Southampton University, England) and his colleagues have reported that such conditions as coronary heart disease, hypertension, stroke, non-insulin-dependent diabetes, and autoimmune thyroiditis be-gin in utero or in infancy but do not become apparent until midlife or later. In these cases, individuals appear to be in good health and function well in the interim. However, early onset of the degenerative diseases of old age appears to be linked to inadequate cellular development early in life.[80]

Certain physiological dysfunctions incurred by persons suffering from malnutrition can, in principle, be reversed by improved dietary intake, but they often persist because the cause of the malnutrition persists. If the malnutrition persists long enough, these dysfunctions can become irre-versible or fatal. This category of consequences includes the degradation of tissue structure, especially in such vital organs as the lungs, the heart, and the gastrointestinal tract. Malnutrition also has been related to im-pairment of immune functions, increased susceptibility to infections, poor wound healing, electrolyte imbalances, endocrine imbalances, and, in adults, dangerous cardiac arrhythmias and increased chronic rheumatoid disorders.[81]

Thermodynamic and Physiological Factors in Economic Growth

So far, I have focused on the contribution of technological change to phys-iological improvements. The process has been synergistic. Elsewhere, I describe in more detail how improvements in nutrition and physiology have contributed significantly to the process of economic growth and tech-nological progress.[82] Here, I merely point out the main conclusion. Tech-nophysio evolution appears to account for about half of British economic growth over the past two centuries. Much of this gain was due to the improvement in human thermodynamic efficiency. The rate of converting human energy input into work output appears to have increased by about 50 percent since 1790.

THE ACCELERATION OF TECHNOLOGICAL CHANGE AND ETHICAL TURBULENCE

Today, parents want assurance that their children will lead better lives than they themselves have led. That is a peculiarly modern expectation. For thousands of generations, the normal expectation was that things would *not* change.[83] Even when long-term changes were under way, they were so gradual that they were hardly noticeable from one generation to the next. The changes that were apparent were in the rhythm of the seasons or in the stages of life. But these patterns were repeated generation after generation. There was also awareness of the periodic disasters that made life so uncertain—natural disasters such as floods, droughts, and plagues and such primal man-made disasters as wars and enslavement. In these circumstances, codes of behavior were embodied in religious injunctions and were enforced by priests, kings, and gods.

Some dreamed of change, such as those who wanted to fly. Testimony to the antiquity and the ubiquity of that idea is found in the Greek, Roman, Norse, and Arabian myths that pictured gods riding chariots, boats, or flying horses across the sky. Half a millennium ago, Leonardo Da Vinci, the great Florentine artist, engineer, and scientist, thought that human flight was a practical possibility. He designed a heavier-than-air flying machine, but it remained only a drawing in his notebooks.

The realization of this ancient dream symbolizes the incredible speed with which scientific knowledge and technological capacity have changed during the twentieth century. The first successful motor-driven flight took place in 1903, but the fragile aircraft of Wilbur and Orville Wright traveled only a few hundred feet. Just sixty-six years later, a man was standing on the moon, talking to another man on earth, as hundreds of millions of people around the world listened in on that conversation and watched the images broadcast across the void of space.

The cascade of new scientific knowledge and new technologies that underlie the great improvements in the American standard of living, in health, and in longevity during the twentieth century has also produced a series of ethical crises. Some crises, such as the heated debate over the right to life, do not depend on recent technological advances. Other disputes, however, are directly linked to new technological capacities far beyond anything previously contemplated. The debates over the way to resolve these unique ethical issues are ongoing.

It is now possible, for example, for infertile couples to conceive a child through in vitro fertilization, a procedure in which a number of eggs are removed from a woman's ovaries and fertilized with sperm in a petri dish. The procedure involves the simultaneous fertilization of all the eggs, which are then frozen for a period. Later, one of the fertilized eggs is implanted in the woman's uterus. If the implantation does not take, a second egg is implanted, and so on, until an implanted egg yields a viable fetus. Is it ethical to interfere with the natural process of conception in this way? If there are fertilized eggs left over, is the destruction of the leftover fertilized eggs, each of which had split into four to eight cells before being frozen, tantamount to abortion? Leaders of the Roman Catholic Church and of some Protestant churches believe that it is. There is also an ethical dispute over whether the excess fertilized eggs of one couple should be made available to other infertile couples.[84]

Numerous other ethical disputes have emerged from progress made in the biomedical sciences. Ultrasound—a nonintrusive method of visualizing a fetus in utero—was developed to aid in prenatal care. However, it can also be used to aid women seeking selective abortion—that is, women who have conceived multiple fetuses but want to give birth to only one child. Moreover, if the ultrasound examination reveals the sex of the fetuses, the parents can elect to retain the fetus of the preferred sex. Ultrasound, amniocentesis, and other prenatal tests can reveal fetal abnormalities, raising the controversial issue of the termination of a pregnancy when such abnormalities are discovered. A related set of disputes turns on the use that may be made of placental tissue (the afterbirth) and of aborted fetuses. Is it ethical to use them for medical research or to supply cellular material to treat illness?[85]

The replacement of failed vital organs with organs obtained from other individuals immediately after death has also given rise to a series of contentious issues. The disputes here have ranged over such matters as how to define death, the regulations governing precedence in the receipt of donated organs, and who is eligible to obtain such operations. The rationing of organs for transplantation is part of the broader issue of how to ration medical care, particularly access to expensive, high-tech procedures that cannot be made available to everyone.[86]

Issues of medical ethics have reached beyond the borders of medicine and have become matters of public controversy and political strife. Some people have lost confidence in the integrity of physicians, viewing them as self-aggrandizing individuals more interested in their own fame and fortune than in the welfare of their patients. The complexity and intensity of the debates has given rise to a new subdiscipline—medical ethics—replete with its own textbooks, journals, and meetings. Review boards have been established at all medical research institutions to examine and approve the protocols of all research projects involving human or animal subjects before these projects can be undertaken.

Medicine is not the only area in which new technologies have provoked public alarm. E. O. Wilson, the noted Harvard sociobiologist, has warned that humanity may be committing suicide by disregarding environmental concerns.[87] In recent years, many advances in science and technology seem to induce foreboding that extends beyond the available evidence. Although it is now established that the use of fossil fuel for heating and to generate electricity is resulting in the warming of the earth's atmosphere, the extent of this effect is still uncertain. Some fear that coastal cities will be flooded and commerce disrupted, but it is also possible that a warmer climate worldwide may have beneficial effects. Many worry that the use of genetic engineering to create wonder drugs and to increase agricultural productivity will inadvertently introduce deadly new organisms and produce new scourges.[88]

Even electricity, so long a symbol of a modern economy, the principal energy source in American homes, offices, and factories, and the driver of all those appliances that reduce household drudgery and make the home an entertainment center, has been declared a menace to health. Some investigators have found that electromagnetic fields generated by power lines can affect the natural flow of hormones and other bodily chemicals across the cells of the body. Although it is theoretically possible that electromagnetic fields could cause a variety of diseases, including learning disorders, miscarriages, and cancer, the evidence to sustain such speculation is wanting. Nevertheless, some social critics were quick to accuse utilities and public health officials with conspiring to conceal the threat to health caused by power lines, cellular telephones, personal computers, television sets, and even electric clocks.[89]

Such claims leave most scientists and engineers aghast. An editorial in *Science*, the leading journal of the American scientific community, deplored the "scare-of-the-week" tactics of some public interest groups. These tactics, said the editorial, cause the public to believe that "complete safety is a feasible goal" and that the persistence of danger is the result of "chicanery, negligence, or incompetence." The public, the editorial continues, must recognize that a risk-free society is impossible and that attempts to attain one are prohibitively expensive. There are numerous deaths from falls on stairs every year, but no one advocates the replacement of all staircases by elevators. In the same way, the editorial concludes, the danger of pesticides must be balanced against the value to the poor of cheaper fruit and vegetables.[90]

The incredible rate at which the economy and society are changing causes people to lose their bearings. They fear not only for their safety but also for their livelihoods. Some Americans believe that technological change will rob *them* of their jobs, even if it allows others to prosper. Others fear that technological change will help international competitors more than it helps the U.S. economy. In the 1950s, it was said that the Soviet economy would soon outstrip the American. In the 1970s and 1980s, the specter was Japan, which threatened to dominate lagging American industries in everything from basic steel to consumer electronics and automobiles. In the 1990s, it is not just Japan but the rest of Asia as well as the Latin American countries that, many believe, are robbing America of jobs and forcing American wages down to their levels.

The persistence of gloom, despite a credible record of achievements, suggests that the malaise about the economy is more moral and psychological than economic. Everything seems inadequate when measured against perfection. So even technology has become a symbol of failure because it is incapable of delivering perfection. Moreover, the notion of balancing the benefits against the costs or of balancing one set of risks against another, so common to the thinking of physicists, chemists, engineers, and economists, does little to quell the foreboding of those who seek assurance.[91]

This chapter has described the disruptive effect of technological change on the prevailing culture and the ensuing social and political strife. During the Second Great Awakening, the most disruptive new technologies were those that lowered transportation costs (steamboats, canals, and railways), spread the population beyond the Allegheny Mountains, and introduced new means of production (the factory system in textiles, iron making, and milling). Lower transportation costs encouraged huge waves of Catholics from Ireland and of Catholics and Lutherans from Germany and the Austro-Hungarian Empire to migrate to the United States. The synergism between the factory system and intercontinental migration promoted the rise of large cities, which became the focal point of ethnic riots and reshaped politics along ethnocultural lines.

The principal technological changes after the Civil War were associated with increasing economies of scale, especially in railroads, utilities, petroleum refining, steel production, food processing and distribution, chemical manufacture, and consumer appliances relying on electricity. These new large-scale industries required highly trained personnel, not only in the basic sciences, but also in business and engineering, to provide the managers needed to oversee complex production operations and to supervise the development of far-flung national and international markets. As a consequence of these new demands, professionals, who made up only a small fraction of the labor force at the beginning of the twentieth century, now represent close to one of three workers at the end of it. The enormous advances in health and life expectancy during the twentieth century also revealed the existence of a synergism between the changes in technology and improvements in human physiology that ushered in the era of technophysio evolution. Whatever the advantages of technological progress to standards of living, there also arose severe dislocations in culture as a result of the lag in the adjustment of human institutions to the dramatic technological changes. The necessary adjustments were eventually brought about by political processes similar to those that have characterized the opening phase of the Fourth Great Awakening. It is to those political processes that I now turn.

THREE

The Triumph of the Modern Egalitarian Ethic

The Fourth Great Awakening did not spring full-blown, like Athena from the head of Zeus. The Fourth Great Awakening evolved gradually out of the technological changes that disrupted the prevailing culture and out of the repeated efforts to adjust institutions to radically new modes of production and consumption. The process of adjusting human institutions to the accelerating technological changes of the past two centuries has been protracted and increasingly difficult. It is characteristic of those creating new reform agendas to portray those holding to the old one as enemies— and vice versa. The current conflict between the leaders of the Fourth and the Third Great Awakenings turns on the nature of inequalities in American society and the role that government should play in resolving them. To understand the nature of that conflict, we must first consider how the doctrines of the Third Great Awakening gained ascendancy.

The fundamental egalitarian doctrine championed by the leaders of the Third Great Awakening, and the doctrine that came to dominate the twentieth century, raised equality of condition over equality of opportunity. That doctrine, which for convenience I shall call *modern egalitarianism,* has three components: first, a conviction that society as a whole would be better off if income is transferred from the rich to the poor; second, a belief that the state is the proper instrument to effect such redistribution; and, third, the development and implementation of public policies and a variety of institutions to effect such redistribution. Modern egalitarianism assumes that these income transfers will raise the general level of well-being.

It is wrong to presume that modern egalitarianism began with the rise to dominance of popular democracy. Quite the contrary, its roots can be traced back to two of the most successful and ruthless autocrats in the history of the Western world, Henry VIII of England and Louis XIV of France, who intervened aggressively in grain markets to ensure an ample supply to such favored constituencies as London, Paris, royal retainers, and the army.[1] Autocracy is not the only perverse force that contributed to its development. The international wars of the past five centuries were also instrumental in producing modern egalitarianism, as was the use of military force to suppress internal dissent.[2] Famines were another factor in the rise of modern egalitarianism, but famines of the sixteenth, seventeenth, and eighteenth centuries were not, as Thomas Malthus and so many others have thought, primarily the result of natural misfortune. They were more often man-made disasters, the product of nationalistic politics and of the failure of government policy. These misguided policies endured for so many generations partly because dominant religious creeds countenanced and rationalized such events as calamities of supernatural origin brought on by the misbehavior of the afflicted.

Important as it is, political exigency is only one of the factors that has shaped the institutions and ideology of modern egalitarianism. New technologies that drastically altered the material conditions of life and the way in which individuals related to one other represent another critical factor. The efforts of the clergy and other ideological innovators to realign fundamental beliefs with perceptions of modern realities were also critical to the emergence of modern egalitarianism.

Much of this chapter is concerned with unraveling the complex interrelations between the experience of and beliefs about poverty and how they affected its definition, the explanation of its existence, and the obligations of the redeemed toward the poor. Much of the ideological foundation for modern egalitarianism was laid during the Second Great Awakening, when holiness and virtue were equated with disinterested benevolence. That doctrine gave a powerful impetus to the social reform movements of the nineteenth and twentieth centuries. The Third Great Awakening completed the ideological foundation for modern egalitarianism by making social rather than personal corruption the chief source of sin and by making individuals the innocent victims of poverty and social corruption.

FAMINE POLICY AS THE SEEDBED OF THE EGALITARIAN STATE

Raising taxes to finance wars of national unification was one of the two main economic problems that confronted the new nation-states during the sixteenth, seventeenth, and eighteenth centuries. The other was famine: the periodic shortage of grain that prompted widespread food riots. These riots undermined public order and threatened the stability of monarchical governments. It was also widely believed that famines were responsible for the periodic mortality crises that afflicted the laboring populations of the new nations. That theory was formalized at the end of the eighteenth century by Thomas Malthus, an English parson and one of the founders of modern economics, who maintained that periodic famines and the ensuing mortality crises (increases in mortality rates substantially above the average rate) were the main mechanisms by which a balance was kept between a population that grew too rapidly and a food supply that grew too slowly.

The institutions that were put in place some four hundred years ago to cope with famines provided the model for the egalitarian state of the twentieth century. The debate over these institutions also established the intellectual battle lines, which endure to the present day, between defenders and critics of modern egalitarianism. Of the many famous participants in the debates over redistribution, Malthus looms largest. He roundly condemned the poor laws of his country that prevailed in the 1790s as utter failures since the transferred income promoted a higher birthrate among the poor. Periodic famines and the associated mortality crises were his main proof that the failure of the poor to control their "passions" had caused the rate of population growth to outstrip the rate of increase in the food supply, although he acknowledged that improved agricultural practices might make it possible for the food supply to increase more rapidly than the population.[3]

Malthus was right in his assertion that there had been periodic famines but wrong in his belief that the mortality crises were caused by famine or even that mortality crises were responsible for the high mortality rates of the preceding three centuries. As a result of recently developed time series that extend back to 1541 for England and to 1676 for France, we now know that these two countries' mortality crises, which were relatively rare, accounted only for a small fraction of total deaths. Even in France, where crisis mortality was relatively severe, there is no half century in which mortality crises accounted for more than an eighth of total deaths. In both England and France, more than 97 percent of the reduction in the crude death rates (deaths per thousand persons in the population) of preindustrial times resulted from the decline in "normal" mortality.[4]

Famines, Hardship, and Relief Measures in England

Although famines were not the mechanism that brought population and the food supply into equilibrium, they did create great hardship, including death, for poor workers. Famines also provoked food riots, which British monarchs saw as a serious threat to the stability of their regimes. In England during the late Tudor (from Henry VIII [r. 1509–47] to Elizabeth I [r. 1558–1603]) and early Stuart (from James I [r. 1603–25] to Charles I [r. 1625–49]) eras, containing the damage caused by grain shortages was a primary objective of the state. The basic strategy of the Crown between 1520 and 1640 was to leave the grain market to its own devices during times of plenty, except to guard against abuses of weights and measures and to foil plots to corner markets. Even these measures provoked hostility from provincial justices and traders, who resented the attempts of the central government to usurp local rights. As a result of their pressure, the Long Parliament (1640–53) passed legislation that made it impossible for a uniform system of weights and measures to be established until the nineteenth century.[5]

In years of grain shortage, however, the Crown overrode the complaints of traders, merchants, brewers, bakers, and other processors. In 1587, and in subsequent years of dearth, the Privy Council (Queen Elizabeth's cabinet) issued a Book of Orders instructing local magistrates to determine the grain inventories of all farmers, factors, maltsters, and bakers; to force holders of inventories to supply their grain to artificers (artisans) and laborers at relatively low prices; to suppress wasteful consumption of grain by taverns and unnecessary expenditures of grain in manufacturing; and to prevent all export abroad and limit transportation at home.

It was, of course, easier to issue such orders than to enforce them. Despite the incentives—the specter of popular upheaval—that spurred the authorities, they found it difficult to gain control of inventories or to curb the rise of prices. Grain continued to be exported abroad or sold to brewers. Innkeepers who had contracted for their supplies before the harvest insisted that their contracts be enforced. When maltsters complied with suppression orders, they often found themselves prosecuted by customers who had sent barley to them to be malted. Caught in the middle, many tradesmen and processors were driven to poverty by regulations intended to prevent it. The procedure enraged farmers and tradesmen, who were subject to the arbitrary searches of bailiffs and constables, often on no better grounds than the testimony of a common informer.

Because of the resistance of landlords, farmers, merchants, maltsters, and other owners of grain stock, it has been argued that government efforts to gain control of grain surpluses and to reduce the volatility of prices were a failure. Some hold that the paternalistic restrictions of the government were actually counterproductive since the efforts to uncover hidden stocks of grain caused alarm and pushed prices up. Instead of promoting greater efficiency in the market, these restrictions thwarted the activities of middlemen, whose function was balancing demand and supply by moving grain from places in which it was abundant to those in which it was scarce.[6] Others believe that Tudor-Stuart paternalism actually worked by the time of the Stuarts. Although the scheme to ration grain on behalf of the poor might not have been immediately effective, numerous instances can be cited during the reigns of James I and Charles I in which concealed grain was brought to market and sold to the poor at reduced prices.[7]

The paternalistic system began to unravel with the Civil War in England (1642–46). The heavy-handed intervention of the Privy Council with local authorities in order to relieve poverty was, indeed, one of the grievances of the opposition to Charles I. Although the victory of Parliament over the king enabled those who sought free markets and the protection of property to have their way, the paternalistic system did not collapse at once. The same inertia at the local level that had made it so difficult for Elizabeth and the early Stuarts to effect their reforms now operated in the opposite direction. Although the landholders and merchants who dominated Parliament developed a legislative program aimed at unshackling farmers, producers, and merchants from the restraints that had been imposed on them, local authorities continued to prosecute those who sought to profit from dearth at the expense of the poor. However, as Parliament implemented its new program, local authorities veered eventually in the new direction, and the paternalistic apparatus atrophied.

It was the abandonment of the Tudor-Stuart program of food relief, not natural disasters or the technological backwardness of agriculture, that subjected England to periodic famines for two additional centuries. That conclusion is implied by a statistical analysis, which shows that, during the period from 1600 to 1640, when government relief efforts were at their apogee, the variability of wheat prices declined to less than a third of the level prevailing during the preceding era. The analysis indicates that there is less than one chance in ten thousand that such a large drop could have been caused by chance variations in the weather. Nor is it likely that the sharp rise in the variance of wheat prices during the last six decades of the seventeenth century was the result of chance variations in the weather.

In the absence of government action to reduce prices during grain shortages, workers took to the streets, and price-fixing riots became a standard feature of the eighteenth century. During the early decades of the eighteenth century, the government sought to cope with such outbreaks by enforcing vagrancy and settlement laws and by repression.[8] During the late 1750s, however, after food riots of unprecedented scope and intensity, renewed proposals emerged for vigorous government intervention in the grain market (a return to Tudor-Stuart policies), including the reestablishment of public granaries. As the battle over these questions ebbed and flowed during the next half century, the government at the local and national levels gradually shifted toward more vigorous intervention in the grain market.

English efforts to provide a safety net for the ultrapoor (the bottom 20 percent of the income distribution) were far more vigorous than those in France. Despite efforts down to the end of the ancien régime (1789) to extend the system, relief in France was organized primarily on a voluntary basis, and mainly by the church. Estimates made for the 1770s put the annual subsidy to the ultrapoor in the neighborhood of about 3.5 livres per head, which could buy about an ounce and a half of bread per day.[9] In England, by contrast, the relief of the poor became a responsibility of the state. Although administered at the parish level before 1834, when Parliament outlawed outdoor relief for the able-bodied poor, the extent of such relief had grown rapidly between 1750 and 1801, increasing at a real rate of 2.3 percent per year, or nearly three times as fast as the rate of growth of either national income or the pauper class.[10] Consequently, by the early 1790s, relief to the ultrapoor had become substantial, more than doubling the income of households in the lowest decile of the income distribution.

The climax of the English system of poor relief came with the development of the Speenhamland system in the 1790s, which provided "allowances in aid of wages" sufficient to maintain an adequate supply of food for a worker and his dependents. Although that principle came under heavy attack by Malthus and others in subsequent generations, the principle prevailed and is embodied in the way in which the poverty line is drawn in the United States today and in various welfare programs aimed at aiding families with dependent children.

Many European visitors to America during the late colonial period and the early years of the new Republic commented on how much better off the ordinary laborer was in the United States than in England or France. Such observations have led some historians to draw the erroneous conclusion that income must have been much more equally distributed in the United States than in England about 1800. Recent statistical studies have revealed that, although the distribution of income and wealth was fairly egalitarian at the settlement of the Massachusetts and Virginia colonies, by the time George Washington became president inequality was a hallmark of society.[11] Despite the absence of a hereditary nobility, ownership of land and buildings (the principal sources of nonlabor income during that age) had become as highly concentrated in the United States as in England.[12]

How is this apparent conflict in evidence to be resolved? How can highly unequal distributions of income and wealth in both nations be reconciled with much better standards of living for ordinary workers in America than in England? The answer is that the average *level* of American income was so high that the poor of America had a higher standard of living than many English shopkeepers, professionals, craftsmen, and small farmers.[13] This advantage is particularly obvious in the consumption of food. Households at the threshold of poverty by American standards (i.e., at the twentieth centile of consumption) had better diets than 70 percent of English households. Or, to put it another way, only one American household in a thousand had a diet as poor as the typical English household on the relief rolls.[14]

Early Relief Measures in the United States

Despite the absence of a large pauper class, the Americans, even in colonial times, established programs for poor relief along English lines. Each of the towns, as well as the handful of cities that dotted the Eastern Seaboard before 1800, had adopted poor laws and established an apparatus to administer them. These laws required close kin (parents, grandparents, children, and grandchildren) to take financial responsibility for their impoverished relatives. If there were no such relatives and the impoverished people had not established legal residence in the locality (which often required having lived there for a year), they would be "warned out" of the community, escorted across the border of a town or county. If legal residence had been established, relief was provided from public funds for those unable to work: orphaned children, the aged, the crippled, the blind, and the insane. As in England, the funds for such relief were obtained from local taxes, and the relief programs were locally administered.[15]

Indigent people were provided for in three main ways. First, girls were placed with families that would educate them in the household arts, and boys were trained in a trade. Since the cost of apprenticeship came from public funds, children were often put out to the families that charged the lowest fees. Second, almshouses were established that took in not only able-bodied children and aged adults but also the lame, the blind, the insane, the sick, and indigent pregnant women. In this respect, almshouses were the forerunners of insane asylums and hospitals; such important public hospitals as Bellevue in New York City, Baltimore City Hospital, and General Hospital in Philadelphia began as almshouses. Almshouses also took in able-bodied indigent adults. Such adults usually constituted only a small proportion of the inmates, and they were required to work, often on a farm connected to the almshouse, while they received moral instruction aimed at making them fit to return to the labor force. Care provided in almshouses was referred to as *indoor relief*. The third form of care for the needy, called *outdoor relief*, involved grants in cash or in commodities to persons living in their own homes whose incomes were inadequate to provide basic necessities.[16]

Private charities supplemented public assistance. Some charities were organized through churches. Each Quaker meetinghouse, for example, maintained a poor fund to be used by its members in times of disaster. "Beneficial societies," fraternal organizations of workers that also provided insurance in the case of ill health and death benefits to widows, were numerous. Some societies were organized along craft lines, others along ethnic lines. These societies gave rise to trade unions and organized many of the strikes that occurred during the 1830s, 1840s, and 1850s. The strengthening of the ethic of benevolence during the First Great Awakening, and the central role assigned to it by the new theologies of the Second Great Awakening, led to the formation of an array of interdenominational charitable organizations headed by ministers and by lay leaders of the evangelical churches, many of which focused on the relief or rescue of the urban poor. Among these organizations were the Society for Employing the Poor (Boston), the Society for the Relief of Half Orphan and Destitute Children (New York), the Ladies Orphan Society (Philadelphia), and the Association for the Relief of Respectable, Aged, Indigent Females (New York).[17]

These charitable organizations were products of the wave of reli-

giousness of the Second Great Awakening, which began toward the end
of the 1790s in New England but rapidly spread to the rest of the nation
and gained momentum after the close of the War of 1812. The benevolent
movement surged in the 1820s and 1830s and then continued with some
fluctuations to the end of the 1850s. The religious intensity of the movement derived partly from the older Calvinist doctrines of Congregational-
ist and Presbyterian theologians. The Second Great Awakening, however, was also spurred by significant modifications in these Calvinist doctrines. While retaining and even intensifying mysticism and piety, New
England theologians developed a modified Calvinism called the *New Divinity* that emphasized that sinners had the capacity to realize salvation
through personal struggle against inner and outer corruption. As the New
Divinity unfolded, "revivals came to be understood less as the 'mighty acts
of God' than as the achievement of preachers who won the consent of
sinners."[18]

The Second Great Awakening was also shaped by the rise of the
Methodist Church in America. Organized for the first time in Baltimore
in December 1784, with a creed derived from the Church of England and
using Wesley's modification of the Anglican Book of Common Prayer, the
Methodist Episcopal Church grew at a phenomenal rate in every region
of the country. By 1850, with over 1.25 million members, it was the largest
Protestant denomination in the republic.[19]

The theology of Wesleyan Methodism accepted man's sinful state but,
unlike Calvinism, emphasized the possibility of everyone achieving grace
by faith, not just the elect. Rejecting the doctrines of predestination to
damnation of all but a relatively small elect and the irresistibility of grace
to those on whom it was bestowed, Wesleyans declared both "that men
could resist the Spirit and fall from grace"[20] and that sincere Christians
could, by appropriately ordering their lives, achieve not just salvation but
perfection; that is, they could become "perfected in the love of God and
man and wholly delivered from sin."[21] Although Northern and Southern
Methodists disagreed on how far the purging of sin could go, the life of
every committed Methodist became a search for sanctification or sinlessness. That ultimate objective was available to everyone and could be
achieved through the dynamic interaction between divine grace and human will. The quest for perfection required piety, austerity, and benevolence—not just self-examination, but the promotion of an enthusiasm for
holiness among others.[22]

Another significant development was the emergence of the Baptists
as a popular denomination. One of the three original Puritan denomina-

tions, the Baptists grew slowly after the establishment of their first church in Rhode Island in 1639. A century later, there were still just ninety-six Baptist churches with about 100,000 members—less than a quarter of the Congregational membership. Then Baptist missionaries fired up by the First Great Awakening (the New England revivalist movement of 1730–60) successfully undertook the immense task of evangelizing the stream of migrants at the Southern frontier.

With the pushing of the frontier beyond the Allegheny, Baptist influence accelerated. The denomination's membership increased more than tenfold in sixty years, reaching over 750,000 at midcentury. The Baptists' success was due in large measure to the vigor with which they organized revival meetings, their appeal to emotions rather than intricate theological arguments, and their widespread use of ministers who traveled west with their flocks. Although often unlearned, these Baptist preachers exuded zeal and warmth, moving people to such "overpowering emotions" that they often experienced "seizures, convulsions, and uncontrollable weeping."[23]

The revivalist movement among the Congregationalists and Presbyterians of New England differed significantly from that led by Methodists and Baptists. Although both denominations reflected a modified Calvinism that offered sinners the possibility of salvation through struggle against worldly corruption, the New England movement was more sedate and intellectual, less personal, less emotional, and less inwardly oriented. To be sure, the New Divinity stressed the need for an inner conversion, but it also absorbed rationalistic Scottish philosophy and recognized the human capacity to act virtuously. The aim of this New England theology was not to demystify religion but to make mystical experience relevant to the needs of the time. One of the central tenets of the New Divinity was that self-love was sinful and that "true virtue consists in 'disinterested benevolence,' even unto complete willingness to be damned if it be for the greater glory of God." This emphasis went in two directions. It helped promote "a benign, optimistic, and utterly respectable Christian rationalism," which eventually emerged as the Unitarian schism. But it also served to turn reformed Calvinism in the direction of fighting inner corruption by engaging in movements for "moral reform and social benevolence." In so doing, an army of "missionaries and humanitarians" was inspired to create an array of new organizations to facilitate such work, thus bringing into being "the benevolent empire."[24]

As elaborated by Charles Grandison Finney, the most charismatic figure of the Second Great Awakening, the movement for social reform was not just an appendage but an indispensable feature of the struggle for purification. Salvation, he said, required "that the reborn became totally unselfish or totally altruistic." Sin, in his view, consisted of selfishness, and "all holiness or virtue" resided in "disinterested benevolence." Reformed sinners should strive to be "useful in the highest degree possible," to "make the world a fit place for the imminent return of Christ." Their spirit had to be that of the reformer; they were "committed" to "the universal reformation of the world," to the "complete and final overthrow" of "war, slavery, licentiousness, and all such evils and abominations."[25] Although criticized by some orthodox ministers, Finney was far from a radical in either religion or politics. One of the consequences of his campaigns, however, was the emergence of increasingly radical religious beliefs that became known as *religious ultraism* and that spread throughout the Western regions that Finney and his holy band evangelized.[26]

Rooted in a passionate devotion to American democracy and a belief in the possibility of the ultimate perfection of society, ultraism was also nourished by a fear derived from Calvinism that, unless these goals were continually promoted, the natural tendency was toward degeneracy. Religious ultraism was propagated not only by radicals but by some of the most conservative men in religious life. To nearly all the evangelical leaders, conservatives and liberals alike, revivalism was a fight not only for the spiritual regeneration of a naturally sinful people but against powerful satanic forces that promoted corruption and vice in American life.[27]

A struggle against Satan on so many fronts required not only a vast expansion of the clergy but also a means of drawing all reformed sinners into the campaign. The solution to this problem was found in a new form of voluntary society, administratively independent of the churches, but manned by both clergy and devout lay members of churches. Shortly after the turn of the nineteenth century, a variety of organizations "for the promotion of Christian knowledge and education" came into being under the inspiration or prodding of English evangelicals. For example, Bible societies were established in Philadelphia in 1808 and in Connecticut, Massachusetts, Maine, and New York in 1809. By 1815, the number of these societies had grown to 108, with at least one in every state in the Union, and amalgamation into an interdenominational national organization (the American Bible Society) followed a year later. While the Bible societies spread the word of God, a related group of societies, beginning with the New England Tract Society of 1814, began to publish and distribute pamphlets that defined a code for the daily behavior of devout Christians. Still other types of organizations, the Sunday schools, were created to teach Christian values to children. The Sunday school movement was initiated in England by the Wesleyans during the late eighteenth century and was later taken up by the Clapham sect (an influential group of English evangelicals and reformers), whose members pressed the idea on their American friends.[28]

The enormous success of the "united front" of missionary and educational organizations in reviving religious zeal led evangelicals to return to their broader goal of shaping the moral and political character of the American nation. Beginning in 1817, they began to expand the societies of the benevolent empire beyond the original bounds of missionary work and religious education by forming a series of single-issue organizations that increasingly made social rather than personal corruption the principal source of sin. Initially concentrating on issues and methods relatively remote from politics (such as persuading individuals to abstain from intoxicating liquors or persuading prostitutes to reform themselves), the evangelicals gradually reasserted their influence in the political arena.

THE REFORM AGENDA OF THE SECOND GREAT AWAKENING

The reform agenda of the disciples of the Second Great Awakening was extraordinarily ambitious and daring. There was no evil in the social order that was not targeted by some group of evangelical reformers. Many of these reform movements were quite radical, challenging long-standing practices and beliefs, and it is the most influential of these that now must be considered.

Justice to Indigenous Americans

A case in point is the rise of the movement to protect "American Indians" from white exploitation and to assimilate them into Christian society.[29] The leader of this movement was the Reverend Jedidiah Morse, pastor of the First Congregational Church of Charlestown, Massachusetts, one of the most orthodox Calvinists of his day, a powerful figure in both the church and politics and a vigorous defender of the faith. When in 1808 Harvard University appointed a Unitarian to its chair in divinity, Morse resigned from its board of overseers and led in the establishment of Andover Seminary, which was dedicated to producing ministers who would uphold Calvinist orthodoxy.[30]

It was Morse who energized the campaign for justice for American Indians, bringing to public attention the immorality of white traders who plied Indians with ardent spirits while using chicanery to steal their lands. Morse also condemned plans developed by the federal government to force Indians off their traditional lands and resettle them west of the Mississippi. He argued that the policy of the government should be the assimilation of Indians into white society through education in the Bible and the teaching of farming and artisanal crafts. He worked closely with the American Board of Commissioners for Foreign Missions, which established a school for the Cherokees and sent missionaries to other tribes. To further promote favorable government and voluntary activities on behalf of Indians, and to oppose forced deportation, he established the American Society for Promoting the Civilization and General Improvement of the Indian Tribes. Morse also called on the government to prohibit private trade with Indians, making trade with all Indians a monopoly of the federal government since that was the best way to end the persistent fraud. His most radical proposal, however, was for government policies aimed at promoting intermarriage between Indians and whites. "They would then be literally of one blood with us," he wrote, "be merged into the nation, and saved from extinction."[31]

Women's Rights and Temperance

Women's rights was another radical reform movement that emerged from the religious ultraism of the Second Great Awakening. Ignoring the Pauline injunction that women be silent, Finney involved women in his religious crusades, allowing them to pray in public, allowing women to join men on the "anxious benches" during the all-night vigils that he made a critical part of the effort to see a sinner through a conversion, and making women as much as men the target of his crusades. Many of the leaders of the early feminist movement were converts of Finney's crusade, including Elizabeth Cady Stanton, who in 1848 wrote a "Declaration of Sentiments" that spelled out the program that guided the feminist movement for the next seventy years and still inspires feminists today. Other early feminist leaders, such as Lucretia Mott and Susan B. Anthony, who as Quakers were part of a tradition that encouraged women to be outspoken and to serve as preachers, were educated in the political tactics of radical reform through their experiences in the temperance and abolitionist movements.[32]

Feminism was too radical a concept to gain much support before the Civil War. It was a divisive issue even among abolitionists. Only the followers of William Lloyd Garrison pointed to the similarities between discrimination against blacks and discrimination against women, which extended even into abolitionist societies. Gathering into his organization such outstanding women as Mott, Anthony, Stanton, and Lydia Maria Child (novelist and editor of an abolitionist newspaper), Garrison opened the pages of his newspaper, the *Liberator*, to a wide-ranging discussion of women's rights, including the right of women to vote and to hold office. Garrison split the American Anti-Slavery Society (AASS) when he nominated a woman to become an officer at the annual meeting in 1840. That act led many of the initial organizers of the AASS to resign and to organize a new antislavery society that excluded women.[33] Garrison and his feminist allies continued to link women's rights and black rights as twin crusades, down through the end of the Civil War. Throughout the war, Anthony fought vigorously for constitutional amendments that would guarantee the civil rights of both blacks and women. However, the Fifteenth Amendment limited the extension of the franchise to black males.[34]

The temperance movement also contributed significantly to the development of women's rights. The Puritans were not teetotalers. "Drink," said Increase Mather, the president of Harvard University between 1685 and 1701, "is in itself a creature of God, and to be received with thankfulness."[35] Of course, Puritans expected that, like all other food, alcoholic beverages would be consumed in moderation, and they denounced drunkenness. Alcohol consumption increased sharply during the eighteenth century, dropping slightly during the Revolution and for a few years afterward owing first to an interruption in the West Indian supply of molasses from which New England rum was made, then to the high tax that was placed on domestic whiskey. However, with tax evasion, improved distilling technology, and rising income, the consumption of distilled spirits climbed to five gallons per capita annually, which is close to twice the current rate of consumption. In addition, Americans drank large quantities of fermented liquor, especially hard cider (which is 10 percent alcohol). Alcohol consumption reached a peak during the 1820s, when, according to the best available estimates, a quarter of all males were occasional or perpetual drunkards. It was also believed that there were about 100,000 female drunkards, about 3 percent of the population of adult females.[36]

In 1826, the American Temperance Society was established to coordinate the activities of numerous local temperance organizations seeking to persuade individuals to renounce the consumption of distilled spirits. Initially, the campaign focused on obtaining, whenever possible, personal pledges of total abstinence, although hard cider and wine were initially excluded from the pledge, as was the use of distilled spirits for medical purposes. As religious zeal intensified, the consumption of intoxicants became a sin rather than merely an unhealthy departure from decency, a sin that could be eradicated only by immediate and total abstinence. This campaign was so successful that, between 1830 and 1840, average consumption rates fell by over 50 percent. However, only a minority of the population abstained totally.[37]

Lyman Beecher, one of the principal revivalists of the Second Great Awakening, and other temperance leaders argued that it was hopeless to expect those addicted to alcohol to abstain voluntarily. From the mid-1830s, the main focus of the temperance movement was the use of state power to prohibit the production and distribution of alcoholic beverages. After some successes in prohibition at the local level, the movement focused on the passage of state prohibition laws. Such laws were passed in thirteen states between 1846 and 1855, but most were soon abandoned. At the end of the Civil War, only two states, Maine and Massachusetts, still had prohibition laws in effect.[38]

The postwar drive came from the Woman's Christian Temperance Union (WCTU), which was founded at a national convention held in Cleveland in November 1874. Many of the delegates were active in church missionary societies, some had been active in voluntary organizations supporting the Union army, and some had participated in grassroots "pray-ins" at saloons in several Eastern and Midwestern states throughout 1873 aimed at forcing proprietors out of business. Under the leadership of Frances Willard, who was first elected corresponding secretary and then served as president from 1879 until her death in 1898, the WCTU became not only a powerful force promoting the prohibition of alcoholic drinks but also a major factor in the women's rights movement. Among the other reform movements promoted by the WCTU were the teaching of temperance in public schools, the criminalization of sexual intercourse with women under the age of eighteen, and women's suffrage.[39]

The campaign for prohibition reached a new level with the formation of the Anti-Saloon League, established in Ohio in 1893 and nationally in 1895. Although its roots were in the evangelical churches, the Anti-Saloon League was less ideological than the WCTU, functioning like a modern single-issue lobby to line up support for prohibition in state legislatures and Congress regardless of a legislator's moral behavior or stance on other issues. As a result of its work, the number of dry states increased from three in 1903 to thirty-two in 1916. The campaign for a constitutional amendment began in 1913 and aimed at electing congressmen from either party who pledged to vote for prohibition. With overwhelming dry majorities in both the House and the Senate, the Eighteenth Amendment cleared Congress in December 1917 and was adopted in January 1919, when it was ratified by the thirty-sixth state, Nebraska.[40]

Just seventeen months later, the Nineteenth Amendment to the Constitution, which gave women the right to vote, was passed. Most of that long struggle was led by Stanton and Anthony, through the National Woman Suffrage Association, which later became the National Suffrage Association. Although little headway was made in gaining the vote during the nineteenth century (only five states had voted for women's suffrage— New Jersey, Wyoming, Utah, Colorado, and Idaho), women had won a wider place for themselves in education and the professions, in the trade union movement, and in various aspects of church life.[41] The Progressive movement remained cool to female suffrage until 1912, when Theodore Roosevelt enthusiastically endorsed it. An additional impetus came from the successes of the English suffrage movement led by Emmeline Pankhurst. The large number of women working in war industries and services during World War I provided the increased public support needed for winning the issue. The Nineteenth Amendment passed Congress in June 1919 and was proclaimed as law in August 1920, when Tennessee became the thirty-sixth state to ratify it.[42] After this victory, the women's movement became quiescent for several decades and did not revive until the 1960s.

Public Education

In 1840, the population of the Northern states had the highest literacy rates (over 90 percent) in the world.[43] That achievement resulted in large measure from Puritan traditions that made the instruction of all members of the family in the reading of the Bible a central facet of life. The schooling of children was pushed further during the Second Great Awakening with the Sunday school movement, which was highly successful both in its educational and in its evangelical objectives. The tradition of publicly funded schools goes back to two laws passed by the Massachusetts General Court (the legislature of the Massachusetts Bay Colony) in the 1640s. The first law made all parents and ministers responsible for ensuring that children could read the Bible and could understand the principles of religion and the laws of the colony. Under the second law, towns of fifty or more families were required to create elementary schools, towns of one hundred or more families were also required to create Latin grammar schools, and both types of schools were to be supported by local taxes. The much larger population of the mid-eighteenth century made it necessary to divide the towns into school districts governed by a school committee whose task was to disperse funds in a manner that ensured the quality of education. This model of education was replicated in all parts of New England except Rhode Island, which maintained that the responsibility for educating children rested with the family.[44]

The principal educational issues of the era of the Second Great Awakening were the maintenance of the quality of education, the secularization of the schools, and the provision of free, universal elementary education to all children. Under the provisions of the Tenth Amendment of the Constitution, the control of education has been left primarily to the states. However, the "general welfare" principle of the Preamble and the doctrine of implied powers have been used to permit the federal government to promote education. That policy began even before the ratification of the Constitution when, in the Land Ordinance of 1785, Congress required the proceeds from the sale of the sixteenth lot (a square mile) of every township (thirty-six square miles) in the public domain to be reserved for the support of education in that township. This provision was confirmed in the Northwest Ordinance of 1787, which declared: "Religion, morality, and knowledge, being necessary to good government and happiness of mankind, schools and the means of education, shall forever be encouraged."[45]

During the early decades of the Republic, several states struggled to establish high-quality public school systems, aided and prodded by the voluntary organizations of the Second Great Awakening. Massachusetts led in this endeavor. In 1837, it established a state board of education, which, under the leadership of its first secretary, Horace Mann, embarked on a program of educational reform that became a model for the rest of the nation during much of the nineteenth century.

Down through the beginning of the nineteenth century, Massachusetts and Connecticut remained "Bible commonwealths" with "established churches," which meant, among other things, that these states levied taxes that were used to support the churches. "Establishment also meant that the Congregational Church continued to ensure that the curriculum of the elementary schools prepared students to understand the Bible and taught them proper religious and moral principals. Thus, in Connecticut, under state law, new schoolmasters had to be certified by the nearest minister of a Congregational church.[46]

The rising strength of other denominations, however, particularly of the Presbyterian, Baptist, and Methodist Churches, and the Unitarian schism within the Congregational Church in Massachusetts brought Congregational control over education to an end. By 1826, these other denominations were strong enough to insert a clause into a state education statute that admonished school boards not to select books "which were calculated to favor any particular religious sect or tenet."[47] This development led Congregational leaders strongly to endorse nonsectarian religious instruction.

Nonsectarian meant Protestant. The term did not include Roman Catholics, with whom all the Protestant denominations were at war, an ideological war that was the basis for the nativist anti-Catholic campaign that eventually produced the Know-Nothing Party of the 1850s and gave the Republican Party its strong anti-Catholic tinge during the nineteenth century.[48] Even Horace Mann, a Unitarian firmly committed to nonsectarian instruction, assured Protestant leaders that "all the practical and perceptive parts of the Gospel" would "be sacredly included" and all "dogmatical theology and sectarianism sacredly excluded." Although he insisted on allowing the Bible "to speak for itself," only the King James Version was given speaking privileges. Roman Catholics insisted that their Bible should also have such privileges in public schools or else that public funds should be given to support Catholic schools on a proportionate basis. But the Catholic position was defeated in pitched political battles at the state and local levels throughout the nineteenth century.[49]

Even the primers were deeply steeped in evangelical Protestant theology. *The New England Primer, or Milk for Babes,* the most widely used primer prior to the publication of the McGuffey readers, taught the alphabet with such sentences as, "Except a Man be born again, he cannot see the Kingdom of God." The McGuffey readers, which were dominant during the last half of the nineteenth century, also promoted evangelical Protestant beliefs.[50]

Horace Mann was in the forefront of the movement to make elementary education free, universal, and compulsory. Calling the public schools "the greatest discovery ever made by man," and holding education up as the instrument that would keep opportunity open to the poor and prevent revolutions of the European type, he pressed for the adoption of a compulsory education law in Massachusetts. The state legislature responded in 1852, making it the pioneer on this issue. Gradually, free and compulsory education was introduced, first throughout the North, then in the South.[51] The drive for universal public education emanated not only from various voluntary organizations of the evangelical united front but also from beneficial and fraternal organizations of labor, which were very active on this question in the Middle Atlantic and Midwestern states. In many cases, it was the clash between Protestant workers and the Catholic Church, which championed the rights of immigrant workers, that made state aid to education politically explosive and promoted the powerful nativist movements of the 1850s, the 1880s, and the 1890s.[52] Religious issues still swirl around public schools; leaders of the Fourth Great Awakening are seeking to reintroduce religious values and activities into school life; and, in many cities, pitched battles are under way as reformers seek to rescue failing schools from the grip of incompetent bureaucrats. Nevertheless, public support for expanding educational opportunity is strong at the dawn of the new millennium.

Urban Reform

The explosive growth of the cities after the 1820s, which was for most of the nineteenth century concentrated mainly in the North, created large, new bureaucracies that offered ample opportunity for graft and other forms of corruption. To control the politics of the cities, the contending parties created political machines that cemented supporters' loyalties by dispensing licenses, patronage, and charity to them. In return, the parties received supporters' votes and bribes. Between 1840 and 1860, foreign-born Catholics and Lutherans and their adult children emerged as the majority of voters in the large Northeastern and Midwestern cities. Hence, political control of these cities turned largely on the capacity of each party to marshal these foreign-born voters.

The Democrats generally proved far more adept at this contest than the Republicans. In such cities as New York, Boston, and Philadelphia, the Democratic Party became deeply entrenched among foreign-born Catholics and Lutherans even before the Civil War. New York was the first city to give rise to an urban political machine, one that dominated the Democratic Party and chose the politicians who held office. By the beginning of the last quarter of the nineteenth century, machine politics was established in many of the major cities of the North, and immigrants and their children began to replace the Old Americans as political bosses and officeholders.[53]

The movement for urban reform was closely associated with nativism. Much of the impetus came from artisans and shopkeepers, who complained that foreign workers were undercutting established wages, threatening to undermine the public school system, and buying licenses and petty public offices from corrupt city officials who hankered after their vote. The failure of either the Whigs or the Democrats to respond to their complaints moved these disaffected artisans and shopkeepers, most of whom were Protestants, to launch their own tickets. Running on reform platforms, they achieved notable victories in New York and Philadelphia in 1844 and in Pittsburgh, Detroit, Boston, and other Northern cities between 1851 and 1855, before being absorbed into the Republican Party.[54]

After the Civil War, upper- and middle-class Protestants joined with nativist workers in calling for urban reform and the restriction of immigration. Among the elite were charity leaders who were overwhelmed by the task of caring for the huge number of indigent immigrants who arrived during the early 1880s. There were also university-trained reformers who thought that only professionals could provide both the ethical leadership and the scientific talent needed to run modern cities. The urban reformers took aim at the political bosses, who, after 1870, were increasingly foreign-born Catholics or their children, many of them Irish. By the 1890s, Irish political bosses controlled the Democratic Party machinery, the mayor's office, the city councils, and police and fire departments in most of the large municipalities.[55]

The urban reform movement was one of the areas in which the divergence between the ethics of the Second and those of the Third Great Awakening became apparent, and it is useful to consider this distinction briefly before continuing to recount the reforms of the Second Great Awakening, whose final phase extended to the early 1920s. Reformers of the Second Great Awakening focused on making city government more efficient, on providing vital services, and on making these services less costly. They sought to replace appointees of the political machines with professional managers and to put an end to the sale of licenses and to kickbacks to government officials. The reformers saw that the strength of the machines lay in the immigrant voters who supported them. In this connection, the reformers sought to build nonpartisan coalitions to institute the desired reforms, and they introduced new forms of city management, replacing the mayor (a politician) with a city manager (a technician) and the city council with a commission of experts in the provision of city services. They also lowered taxes, enforced blue laws, and closed down saloons. At the state level, they introduced such democratic reforms as the referendum, the recall of elected officials, and direct primaries.[56]

When the reformers of the Third Great Awakening became involved, they identified big business as the principal source of urban corruption. The immigrants, they maintained, were the victims of both the political bosses and the giant corporations. Social Gospelers emphasized social welfare programs such as settlement houses (which aided disadvantaged children) and vocational schools (which educated immigrants and their children so that they could obtain better jobs) and the municipal ownership of utilities. They also established commissions of social scientists and other experts to study the problems of cities by collecting and analyzing data.[57] Such studies by experts have become essential in the promotion of new reforms and today form the platforms for numerous campaigns for legislative change.

The Abolition of Slavery

The abolition of slavery was the most radical and far-reaching of the reforms sought by the evangelicals of the Second Great Awakening, especially with respect to the emergence of an egalitarian ethic. Believing that personal freedom was a necessary condition both for heavenly salvation and for the earthly perpetuation of popular democracy, the abolitionists mounted an unprecedented attack on slavery because it permitted one group of people to exercise unrestrained personal domination over another. The proposition that such power was by itself profoundly evil and corrupting was the original basis for the condemnation of slavery by the religious radicals who initiated the campaign (no matter how overlaid with political expediency it became), and that proposition continued to impel the antislavery crusade throughout its history. The proposition was the logical outcome of the theologies of both Quakers and evangelicals. Believing that "all men were equal before God," associating "moral evil with institutions of the external world," and holding that it was within the capacity of men to achieve salvation by unselfish acts and unremitting struggle against inward and outward evil, slavery loomed both as a barrier to the exercise of the free will through which slaves could obtain salvation and as a corrupter of the masters. Personal domination was condemned as a sin, and those who sought it were denounced as usurpers of power that belonged only to God.[58]

Several factors made the abolition of slavery an exceptionally difficult undertaking. First, the United States was constructed on a compromise that legitimated slavery, most notably in the clause that permitted Southern states to include three-fifths of the slave population in the totals that determined representation. The Constitution not only recognized slavery and made it lawful but also guaranteed that the power of the federal government would be employed to protect the master's right to his human property. Nowhere in the Constitution was there a word regarding the rights of slaves or the obligations of masters to treat them humanely. Such matters would continue to be regulated by state governments and courts, as they had been in the colonial era, and hence were beyond federal juris-diction.[59]

Ideology was another barrier to the success of the abolitionist move-ment. For the better part of a century, slavery posed a severe moral di-lemma to the leaders of the American Revolution and to other enlightened men of goodwill throughout the Western world. The root of the dilemma was the rationalistic doctrine of natural rights, which linked freedom and justice with the inviolability of property and which was the philosophical platform of the American Revolution. Men who had rebelled because the confiscatory taxes of the British Parliament and the arbitrary regulations of the Crown had diminished their wealth were bound to be confounded by the demand for the compulsory abolition of slavery. Despite anguish and desire, most of the founding fathers and their intellectual heirs were unable to find an apt solution to the conflict between the natural right of the enslaved to their freedom and the natural right of the masters to the security of their property.

The escape from the dilemma was led by militant evangelical reform-ers, who were also deeply involved in the temperance and women's rights movements. Convinced that they were divinely inspired, they rejected out of hand the proposition that material gain or any other worldly consider-ation could justify the degree of domination that slavery gave one group over another. American abolitionism began as a theological rather than as a political movement. Proclaiming that, no matter how well slaves were treated, slaveholding in and of itself was sinful, the abolitionists called on the churches to expel all slaveholders who would not repent. Despite very substantial successes within the principal Northern evangelical churches, enough to cause the Southern branches of the Presbyterian, Methodist, and Baptist churches to split from the Northern branches and form their own denominations, abolitionists could not win full acceptance for their doctrine. When the leadership of the Northern evangelical churches maintained that the mistreatment of slaves was a sin but that mere owner-ship was not, the main body of abolitionist leaders decided to go over the heads of the church hierarchies by injecting the issue into the political arena.

The first problem in configuring the issue politically was that the Whig and the Democratic leaders vehemently refused to include the abo-lition of slavery in their parties' platforms. Consequently, the abolitionists developed a multipronged approach. As was noted in chapter 2 above, they launched a third party, the Liberty Party, which interjected the moral issue of slavery into the 1840 elections. They also worked closely with sympathetic Northern Whigs and Democrats in Congress and in state and local governments to find ways of promoting limited antislavery issues that could win wider support than the 3 percent who voted for outright abolition in 1840. One of these demands, as was mentioned in chapter 2, was the reservation of public land in the territories for free white men, excluding Southern slaveholders and their slaves.

By the 1840s, convinced by the ferocity of the resistance to their appeals, abolitionists concluded that slaveholders were hopelessly corrupt, gave up the effort to use moral suasion in the South, and focused all their energy on rallying the North to a minimalist antislavery program even though the approach entailed a dilution of their moral position. At the core of the new approach was an indictment of Southern morality and culture, an indictment set forth in a book written by Theodore Weld (who had been a member of Finney's Holy Band), his wife, Angelina Grimké, and his sister-in-law, Sarah Grimké (the Grimké sisters were also early leaders of the feminist movement). That book, *American Slavery as It Is: Testimony of a Thousand Witnesses* (1839), became one of the most powerful social indictments ever written and, among other things, provided the basis for Harriet Beecher Stowe's immensely popular book and play, *Uncle Tom's Cabin* (1852). Slavery, Weld argued, was like alcohol; it was intoxicating. Anyone who was ensnared by the desire to exercise absolute power over another human being was bound to be brutal. Weld's elaboration of that theme went a long way toward transforming Northern perceptions of the South. Southerners, in Weld's view, were brutal not only to slaves but to each other; Southerners were an unstable and lazy people who combined their lust for power with a passion for violence and pagan pleasures.

The abolitionists extended their indictment of the South by propagating the theory of the slave-power conspiracy. That theory implied not just the unconstitutional use of the federal government to protect and promote the interest of slave owners but a more far-reaching plot against American freedom, a plot aimed ultimately at the complete subjugation of free people. The plot was unfolding in a series of steps that began with the seizure of the federal government by slave owners immediately after the ratification of the Constitution. It then progressed toward the suppression of the democratic rights of Northerners to free speech, free assembly, free press, and free elections. The foundation of the political conspiracy, the abolitionists asserted, was the three-fifths clause of the Constitution, which gave slaveholders political power far beyond their number. As a result, the North had been reduced to the position of a "conquered province."

The attractiveness of the slave-power conspiracy as a political rallying cry became apparent almost as soon as it was aired. It meshed well with long-held fears that the democratic liberties of ordinary people were threatened by invisible but malevolent minorities who secretly wielded catastrophic political influence. From the slave-power conspiracy, the abolitionists finally passed over to the charge that Northerners were victims of an economic conspiracy by the slave power, a conspiracy aimed at using the federal government to enhance the wealth of slave owners at the expense of the farmers and workers of the North. The slave owners were intent on seizing land in Missouri, Kansas, and other Northern territories and flooding Northern markets with slave labor and slave-produced products.[60]

However secular the arguments became, the abolitionists believed that the destruction of slavery was the moral imperative of the age. "Slavery must fall," said the Reverend William E. Channing, a founder of the Unitarian Church, in the 1840s, "because it stands in direct hostility to all the grand movements, principles, and reforms of our age, because it stands in the way of an advancing world."[61] The end of slavery gave an enormous boost to egalitarianism not only because it freed the slaves but also because it created conditions favorable to a continued struggle for the democratic rights of the lower classes, black and white alike, and for the improvement of their economic conditions, not only in America, but everywhere else in the world. The fall of slavery neither ushered in the millennium nor produced a heaven on earth, but it vitalized all the grand movements, principles, and reforms of Channing's age and of the Third Great Awakening. Moreover, the success of the techniques for coalition building developed during the 1840s and 1850s demonstrated that, in a democratic society, legislative action could become an instrument of radical reform. That lesson shaped the tactics of the leaders of both the Third and the Fourth Great Awakenings.

THE THIRD GREAT AWAKENING AND THE EMERGENCE OF A NEW EGALITARIAN ETHIC

There is no sharp line separating the end of the era of the Second Great Awakening and the beginning of the era ushered in by the Third Great Awakening. Quite the contrary, the last fifty years of the religious-political cycle of the Second Great Awakening overlap with the first forty years of the Third Great Awakening. Moreover, many of the novel theological and ethical innovations of the Third Great Awakening emerged gradually and then evolved considerably. Many of the individuals who shaped the theology, ethics, and reforms of the Third Great Awakening originally accepted those of the Second, only gradually moving in a new direction.[62]

Consider the movements for compulsory elementary education, the abolition of child labor, and the protection of women from exploitation by factory owners, which later became closely identified with the Third Great Awakening. These movements were actually initiated before the Civil War by reformers of the Second Great Awakening and continued to be promoted by them throughout the last phase of the second religious-political cycle. During the 1870s and 1880s, before the Social Gospel movement had emerged, more than half the states had adopted compulsory education laws. Similarly, about a quarter of the states had adopted laws prohibiting child labor before 1880, and an additional fifteen states adopted such laws during the 1880s. When the Social Gospel movement came into being by the 1890s, it embraced these issues and sought to extend them by campaigning for laws to increase the number of weeks of required attendance in school, raise the minimum age of employment, and reduce the hours of work permitted in manufacturing, mining, and retailing.[63]

Transformations in Economic Thought

The gradual shift in thought can be seen in the realm of economic theory. The principal economic theorist of the Second Great Awakening was the Reverend Francis Wayland, president of Brown University and one of the most influential figures in the Northern Baptist Church before the Civil War. His treatise *The Elements of Political Economy* was the most widely used economics textbook from the time it first appeared in 1837 until the outbreak of the Civil War.

Viewing economics as a subfield of moral philosophy, Wayland defined the subject as "the science of wealth." The word *science* meant a systematic arrangement of God's laws so far discovered. It is obvious, he wrote, "that the Creator has subjected the accumulation of the blessings of life to some determinate laws." It followed that "no man can grow rich without industry and frugality." Personal liberty and private property, he believed, were two of the fundamental principles of moral science, but liberty was dependent on the protection of private property. Property, he said, was founded on the "will of God," and it was acquired directly as his immediate gift (as with land) or by labor. Property could also be acquired indirectly by exchange. But exchange required well-defined property rights.[64]

Turning to labor, Wayland drew on the theories of David Ricardo and Thomas Malthus, arguing that laborers' excessive fertility tended to increase their numbers and therefore reduce the wages of labor to the point of starvation and death. On the other hand, when capital increased more rapidly than labor, wages tended to rise so high that a flow of foreign labor into the country was induced, which, in turn, brought wages back toward the level of subsistence. Because capital generally increased faster than the population in the United States, "distressing poverty" was rare except when precipitated by intemperance, indolence, and similar vices. The favorable demand for labor and the lagging supply made it possible for industrious workers to accumulate capital in a relatively short period of time.[65]

Combinations of laborers (such as unions) were useless, wrote Wayland, because they thwarted the laws of competition, which determined the proper level of wages. Combinations were also counterproductive and unjust because they deprived laborers of the right to dispose of their labor (work for wages) and, as with legislative interference, they were destructive of industry. He opposed charity to able-bodied workers because it would promote indolence if they did not experience the penalties of idleness. However, he favored the support of the "superannuated, the sick, and infants in public workhouses."[66]

Very similar views were held by the Reverend John Bascom during the early decades of his career. During the Civil War, he argued that the tactics of trade unions, especially strikes, were vicious attempts by incompetent workers to prevent workers with "superior intelligence, economy, and integrity" from achieving the benefits of free competition.[67] By the mid-1880s, however, when Bascom was serving as the fifth president of the University of Wisconsin, he deplored the prevailing lack of sympathy for trade unions. Capital, he charged, was combining in ways that made the contest between capital and labor highly unequal. Consequently, government should curb the tyranny of big business and favor labor more. The state, he believed, had to become a vehicle for social improvement, including a mild redistribution of income from the rich to the poor.[68]

Bascom's change of economic heart was typical of many of the leaders in the emerging Social Gospel movement. It would be a mistake to presume that this evolution reflected a change in underlying spirit, from complacency to compassion. The reformers of the Second Great Awakening could hardly be called complacent. They were imbued with the ethic of benevolence. Their ambition was to make the world "a fit place for the imminent return of Christ." They were committed to the "universal reformation of the world" and to the "complete and final overthrow" of "war, slavery, licentiousness, and all such evils and abominations."[69] They were prepared to expend their fortunes and to risk their reputations, and sometimes their lives, in such originally unpopular causes as the rights of American Indians, women's rights, and the abolition of slavery. They willingly taxed themselves in order to bring public education and higher education to those who were too poor to pay for it themselves.

The divergence in economic policy between reformers of the Second and those of the Third Great Awakenings stemmed from three factors: structural changes in the economy; the inadequacy of older theories of poverty in an industrial age; and a shift in the theories of man's relationship to God.

Structural Changes in the Economy

During the first two decades of the nineteenth century, the U.S. population clung to the coast of the Atlantic Ocean and the Gulf of Mexico and to the rivers that emptied into them. The movement west had begun, but vast stretches of land between the Appalachians and the Mississippi were still largely uninhabited. Prior to the building of the Erie Canal (1817–25), even the western part of New York State was still a frontier. The economy was structured relatively simply, with 80 percent of the population in agriculture and the balance split between manufacturing and services. Cities, which still held a mere 5 percent of the population, had plenty of open space, and most households maintained some livestock and gardens, which provided a significant proportion of their food supply.

In such a world, there was very little unemployment or distressing poverty among able-bodied males. Paupers were mainly the elderly, widows (with or without children), orphans, the sick, and the disabled. In New York State, persons falling into these categories accounted for hardly 1 percent of the population. Able-bodied males unable to sustain themselves were primarily drunkards and those who needed aid only for short periods of time.[70]

In such a world, the evidence seemed to sustain the theory that, at least for the able-bodied, poverty was the wages of sin. There were few impediments to work, none that appeared to be endemic in the economy, and there was an empire of virgin land beckoning to those who were dissatisfied with their current condition. America truly seemed to be a nation in which every adult male who wished to could become a prosperous yeoman.

New technology, embodied in steamboats, canals, turnpikes, and railroads, stimulated the growth of great cities and attracted millions of immigrants. With the rise of the cities, however, came an increase in pauperism, which presented many dilemmas, especially with respect to how to finance and care for those so afflicted.[71]

The development of credit markets and the emergence of a banking system brought on a series of recessions, the first of which occurred from 1819 to 1820. However, this recession affected mainly the propertied classes, whose loans were suddenly recalled, and only a small proportion of ordinary workers (some textile mills were forced to shut their doors). At the height of the recession, the unemployment rate was probably about 4 percent. In any case, the recession was short-lived.[72]

No one at the time, of course, knew that recessions were going to become endemic. To the extent that there was anything wrong with the economic system per se, the fault seemed to lie with bankers, who willfully and selfishly manipulated financial markets for their own benefit, or so Andrew Jackson charged. That accusation created one of the main programmatic divisions between the Democratic and the Whig Parties. However, the effect of bank policy was more obvious to independent proprietors (farmers, merchants, manufacturers), who depended on bank loans, than to ordinary laborers.[73]

More serious in creating distress among the laboring classes were the huge waves of immigrants streaming into Northern cities and transforming the urban landscape. The resulting glut of the labor markets was viewed by economic theorists as transitory because there were still vast stretches of virgin land begging for workers. Moreover, the huge construction enterprises, especially those connected with the building of canals and railroads, created an enormous demand for manual laborers and craftsmen. So great was this demand for labor that construction chiefs willingly bore the expense of moving laborers to construction sites, first in New England and the Middle Atlantic states, then in the Midwest. The labor shortage induced many railroads to advertise for labor in Europe.[74]

Rates of pauperism started to rise sharply in the late 1820s, reaching a peak around 1830. However, the new pauperism was concentrated mainly in the major Northeastern ports of entry for immigrants. The situation was most acute in New York State, where paupers constituted 10 percent of the population in 1830. Most of these paupers were foreign-born able-bodied males and their families who had just arrived and needed only temporary help before moving west or finding jobs in urban areas, especially Manhattan or Brooklyn. Immigration, combined with bank panics in 1837, 1843, and 1854, pushed the pauper rates as high as 15 percent. Although the problems of financing these emergencies were severe, somehow the money was found, through charity and taxes.[75]

Although nativist workers clamored for a tariff on immigrants that would protect them from the competition presented by foreign workers, most evangelical leaders viewed the problems of labor and poverty as transitory and pointed to the shortage of workers elsewhere in the country. To Horace Greeley, editor of the *New York Tribune,* there was a simple solution: provide free homesteads in government territory to landless laborers in New York and other port cities. Not only would land thereby be made accessible to wage earners, but the bargaining position of those workers who remained in the cities would also be strengthened, reversing the polarization of urban dwellers and creating new markets in the West for the products of Eastern merchants and manufacturers. "Every smoke that rises in the Great West," wrote Greeley, "marks a new customer to the counting rooms and warehouses of New York."[76]

The pace of structural change in the economy intensified after the Civil War. The rate of investment reached an all-time high during the 1870s and 1880s, symbolized by the vast expansion of the railroad network, which exceeded the total value of railroad construction prior to the Civil War. In addition to new lines, many of the old roadbeds were reconstructed, with heavy steel rails taking the place of lightweight iron. Passenger and freight cars became larger and heavier and engines more powerful. The total new investment in railroad equipment and track during the peak year of the 1880s exceeded the entire national investment of the United States in 1850.[77]

Such huge expenditures in capital formation—not only in transportation, but also in manufacturing—were associated with companies of unprecedented size. In the case of the steel industry, for example, there was an enormous expansion in the optimal size of blast furnaces. In 1850, there were hundreds of enterprises with blast furnaces, no single one of which produced more than 1 or 2 percent of the national output of pig iron. The Bessemer process, however, by which steel is manufactured from molten pig iron, required blast furnaces of unprecedented size. As a consequence, by 1880, the entire country's output of Bessemer steel was produced by just thirteen plants. Other industries in which new technologies required a much larger plant size in order to function economically were petroleum, food production, transportation equipment (including automobiles), machinery, and chemicals. Such large units produced, not for local markets, but for national, and sometimes international, markets.[78]

The optimal size of a company turned not only on the technology of a particular operation, such as blast furnaces or, in the petroleum industry, refineries, but also on such issues as the size and location of markets and transportation and other distribution costs. These considerations reflected both the enormous expansion of urban markets and the new technologies that drastically reduced the cost of transportation and communication. As a result, efficient firms could compete in distant markets in which inefficient producers had previously been protected by the natural barriers of high transportation and distribution costs. Between 1870 and World War II, in one industry after another, small firms were pushed out of many lines of business or confined to smaller and smaller sections of their industries.[79]

The losers in this competitive struggle did not accept their fate stoically but appealed to the government for legislation that would offset their technological disadvantages. Small millers in upstate New York demanded reductions in their freight rates to make them more competitive with large-scale millers in Milwaukee. Small banks that charged higher interest rates in their local markets demanded protection from the Eastern banks that began offering comparable services at lower rates. Small refineries called on legislators to prevent Standard Oil from undercutting their markets with what they described as "predatory pricing." Farmers in Iowa condemned the railroads for charging them more to ship a ton of wheat two hundred miles to Chicago than it cost to ship that same ton nine hundred miles from Chicago to New York City.[80]

Farmers, Workers, and Small Businesses Confront Robber Barons

Thus, the last quarter of the nineteenth century and the first quarter of the twentieth witnessed a fierce confrontation between the new big businesses and traditional businesses. On the one side were multimillionaires, the robber barons. On the other were small rural and urban businesses, farmers, and those who labored for the robber barons.

Railroads were the earliest and the most persistent target. During the railroad-building boom that followed the Civil War, state and local governments outdid each other in offering tax exemptions and other inducements for companies to lay track through their areas. Once the railroads were completed, however, discontent arose with the structure of rates, the quality of service, and the failure of railroads to pay their fair share of taxes.

Led by the principal farmers' organization in the Midwest, the Grange, lobbies were successful in passing state laws regulating the railroads and raising taxes on railroad properties and in bringing suits in the courts.

This regulatory movement was temporarily thwarted at the state level when, in 1886, the Supreme Court ruled that it was up to the courts rather than state legislatures to determine the reasonableness of railroad rates. Just one year later, however, the federal government joined the assault on the railroads with the Interstate Commerce Act of 1887, which established the Interstate Commerce Commission. Three years later, in 1890, Congress approved the Sherman Antitrust Act, which struck out against every contract "in the form of trust or otherwise, or conspiracy in restraint of trade or commerce among the several states."[81]

The widespread financial distress of farmers during the 1880s and 1890s, due partly to the increasing burden of debt in an era of declining prices, led them to demand that the federal government free them from the clutches of bankers by intervening in a wide variety of issues. Dissatisfied with the supply of mortgages and the rates that were charged by local banks, farm organizations and, later, the Populist Party called for the establishment of an agency of the federal government to supply such loans and to accept stored grain as prime collateral. To ease the burden of interest rates, farmers and, later, populists called on the federal government to issue paper money and to mint silver. Other demands included the nationalization of railroad and telegraph lines and the withdrawal of government lands from the market.[82]

Labor also protested, often using its most powerful weapon, the strike. During the Civil War, the first of the great Railroad brotherhoods was organized among locomotive engineers, and that example was followed by other groups of workers on and off the railroad. By 1870, there were thirty-two national trade unions, and most of the larger cities had also established trade assemblies and publications. The most violent strike of the postwar era began during July 1877 in response to wage cuts on many of the railroads east of the Mississippi. Trains were halted by workers, and troops were brought out to deal with angry mobs. Buildings were burned and blood spilled in Baltimore, Pittsburgh, and other major railroad centers. Before it was over, about one hundred people were killed, and property damage ran into the millions. The conflict was so bloody it revived fears that America could be visited by a revolution such as that which occurred in France in 1789. Those fears were reawakened in 1892 and again in 1893 when strikes at the giant Carnegie Steel Company and the Pullman Palace Car Company touched off pitched battles and mob violence requiring state

militias and federal troops to reestablish order.[83] Labor strife led some reformers to doubt the prevailing theories of poverty and to question
whether the frontier was still an adequate safety valve for urban labor. It is
these doubts that gave rise to the modern egalitarian ethic.

Reconsideration of the Theory of Poverty

By the early 1890s, the old theories of poverty no longer seemed adequate.
During the depression of the 1890s, urban unemployment rates rose to
over 18 percent. America was experiencing the worst economic disaster of
the century. Moreover, what had once seemed like a limitless empire of
potential farmland was now fully occupied, a point that became clear when
the 1890 census announced that the frontier was closed. Horace Greeley's
call for unemployed young men in Eastern cities to go west no longer
made sense when Western farmers were also protesting their economic
distress and seeking to limit the increase in the agrarian labor force. Of
course, the country was also still attempting to deal with the massive numbers of immigrants who continued to arrive from Europe—immigration
levels reached all-time highs in the 1880s and again shortly after the turn
of the century.[84]

Such a world left little room for the belief that there was still excess
demand for labor and that every adult male who wished to could become
a prosperous yeoman. Business-cycle recessions, no longer new, appeared
to be returning more frequently and becoming increasingly severe. Most
of those who were unemployed in the depression of the 1890s were neither
immigrants nor idlers but industrious workers thrown out of jobs that they
did not want to leave. Many were also burdened with debt, which, together with steadily declining price levels, made economic survival difficult
even for cautious farmers and small proprietors. Urban poverty was clearly
endemic, and the dysfunctions in the economy were clearly systemic.[85]

These systemic problems had grown beyond the voluntary organizations that had been created to deal with poverty during the first phase of
the Second Great Awakening. What needed to be reformed were institutions, not just indolent workers. Who needed to be rescued were exploited
women and children, not just drunkards. What needed to be resisted was
not the conspiracies of the trade unions. The true conspiracies against
competitive markets were organized by the mammoth corporations, the
trusts, and the railroad pools. It was the failures of the economic system
that were at issue.

In actuality, the average real wages and annual incomes of workers increased by 50 percent between 1860 and 1890. Despite the huge waves of immigration in the 1870s and 1880s, despite the strikes and numerous other expressions of discontent, the economy was able to absorb an unprecedented increase of labor in its nonagricultural sector. Why, then, were there such bitter labor protests, and why were reformers so deeply concerned about the course of the economy?

The answer turns to a large extent on the frenetic pace of technological change. While the Bessemer furnace increased the demand for workers at steel mills, it led to the loss of jobs in iron mills and foundries that could not compete effectively with the new steel products. The same kind of turmoil was created in petroleum, meatpacking, textiles, transportation vehicles, and wholesale and retail distribution. Moreover, numerous handicraft skills were made obsolete by the development of machines that could perform the same functions more quickly and more cheaply. Although far more new jobs were created than old jobs were lost, those who obtained the new jobs were often new immigrants, and those who lost the old jobs were often either native-born workers or longtime residents.

The insecurity arising out of technological change was increased by job loss owing to plant relocation and the intensification of business cycles. Job security was also undermined by the response of the corporations to the unions, with strikers losing more often than they won and frequently being replaced with new immigrants.[86]

Job insecurity does not tell the whole tale of the plight of workers. Nor do indexes of real wages by themselves portray the difficult conditions of life in the burgeoning cities. One of the worst features of the age was the extraordinarily bad housing in which many workers lived. In cities such as Boston, New York, and Philadelphia, housing densities in the tenement districts were shockingly high, and so were death rates. During decades that reformers called a *gilded age* and *a great barbecue* for the upper classes, infant death rates in the working-class slums continued to exceed 20 percent. The tenement districts acted as a reservoir for infectious diseases that escalated into epidemics, ravaging not only the rest of the city but eddying out into the suburbs and the rural areas as well. Periodic epidemics of cholera, typhoid, and typhus stunned the nation. Urban death rates were raised to frightening peaks as millions of immigrants crowded into the already-overstrained tenement districts. The inequality that appalled the Social Gospelers existed not only in income but also in health and life expectancy.[87]

Social Gospel economists saw both the good and the bad in the American economy of the late nineteenth century. The great scientific and tech-

nological advances made them optimistic about the possibility of achieving the kingdom of heaven on earth in the immediate future. However,
businesses had grown so large, and robber barons were so rich and arro-
gant, that they constituted an impediment to reaching that goal. Believing
that prices of products were inflated through monopoly control and that
collusion among employers frequently pushed wages below subsistence
levels, Social Gospelers argued that labor unions needed to be favored in
order to compensate for the unfair power exercised by the giant industrial
corporations.[88]

The state would have to intervene in those places where unions were
too weak to control corporate power. Richard T. Ely, an economist at the
University of Wisconsin and a leading exponent of the proposition that
capital had become too powerful, sought to redress the balance by getting
the state to intervene on the side of labor. In papers and books published
during the last two decades of the nineteenth century, he argued that the
state should be an "ethical agency whose positive aid is an indispensable
condition of human progress." He called for the taxing of the monopoly
profits of the corporations in order to finance the poverty programs of the
state. He and John R. Commons, a fellow economist at Wisconsin and
later doyen of labor economics, also called on the government to limit the
hours of labor, to ensure a minimum wage adequate for subsistence, and to
provide greater job security. They also advocated the restriction of foreign
immigration. That restriction would allow the worker to obtain "the highest possible share of the social product in return for his personal abilities."[89]
Unions also helped achieve this goal, said Commons, by restricting the
supply of labor.

Modernism and Inherent Goodness

Important as it was, the development of a new economic theory that took
account of systemic deficiencies in the economy could not by itself produce
a modern egalitarian ethic that emphasized equality of condition rather
than equality of opportunity. Such a shift required the destruction of the
doctrine of innate depravity, which, in turn, rested on the doctrine of original sin. Catholics and Protestants have somewhat different interpretations
of original sin, but they both involve the belief that God's punishment of
Adam extended to all his descendants. Catholic theologians believed that
the punishment "left the human mind and will intact, but deprived men
and women of the grace that would enable them to attain their original
destiny." Protestant theologians went further, describing "sin as a perver-

sity encompassing human nature in its entirety, including the mind and will."[90] During much of the nineteenth century, Calvinist theologians debated whether Adam alone sinned, with his punishment extended to all his descendants, or whether all Adam's descendants directly participated in Adam's sin because they were all in Adam.[91]

Methodist theologians of the early nineteenth century were more optimistic, arguing that Christ's death provided atonement for the entire human race and thus removed the "obstacle of not being able to please God." While no one is born guilty, "all are born without the vital influence of God."[92] In other words, individuals were not born with grace but had the capacity to obtain it through the free exercise of will. The failure to seek God's grace would inevitably result in human pollution, corruption, and depravity. Even this more optimistic view held individuals, rather than society, responsible for sin.

The theological arguments just described presumed the historical accuracy of the Book of Genesis. That assumption received a powerful blow with the appearance of Sir Charles Lyell's *Principles of Geology*. Published in three volumes between 1830 and 1833, it called the biblical account of Creation into question, providing evidence that the earth evolved over hundreds of millions of years. The effect of that discovery on belief in biblical inerrancy is illustrated by the recollections of Ida M. Tarbell, one of the most famous of the muckraking journalists. Born in 1857, raised in a devout, warm, and intellectually engaged Methodist household in western Pennsylvania, she was fifteen when she read with "horror and amazement" Hugh Miller's *Testimony of the Rocks*, which attempted to reconcile geology and Genesis. She could not accept Miller's contention that the "biblical day" was really "an eon." "If this was true," she asked, "why did the Bible describe so particularly the work of each day" and end with " 'and he rested on the seventh day' "? She found it difficult to accept an explanation that required her to believe that "words could have other meaning than I had always given them." A Bible that "did not mean what it said, was not the rock I had supposed my feet were on."[93]

Tarbell was not the only one disturbed by the "biblical day"; it became a chief issue in a major part of the Christian world. The crisis was greatly intensified by the publication of Charles Darwin's *The Origin of Species* in 1859 and *The Descent of Man* in 1871. During these difficult confrontations between science and religion, Tarbell thought of leaving her church but decided against it because of the ethical guidance of the Bible. "Scientists," she wrote at age eighty-two, "offered nothing to guide me in human relations, and they did not satisfy a craving from which I could not escape;

that was the need of direction, the need of that which I called God and which I still call God."[94]

Belief in the inerrancy of the Bible may have received its sharpest blow from German "scientific history," with its strict rules for evaluating historic languages (philology), writing (paleography), documents (diplomatics), seals (sphragistics), and coins (numismatics) and for the identification of medieval and ancient weights and measures.[95] These new disciplines were carried over into Bible studies, which had long been the center of Christian theology. Imported with scientific history was a skepticism regarding the belief that Scripture recorded the infallible words of God. It was assumed, especially on the Continent, but also in Britain, that the principles of "textual criticism" (the collection, ordering, and assessment of myriad word-by-word variations in thousands of different manuscript copies of the Bible) and "higher criticism" (the systematic evaluation of the sources of the Bible, making use of philology, paleography, diplomatics, and the other new historical sciences) were appropriate methods of biblical interpretation. Traditional interpretations based on revealed knowledge or doctrine were denigrated and dismissed.

The traditional imputation of the authorship of the first five books of the Old Testament to Moses was replaced by the theory that these books were written by many individuals long after the events they described. Similar evidence was presented to support the proposition that the prophetic books were written after the events they foretold and that the gospel writers reported not facts but the idealized beliefs of early Christians. The general thrust of contextual criticism and source criticism was to dispute the miraculous nature of the Bible, treating it as an inspirational book, but not the word of God.

These propositions undermined centuries of intricate theology based on the doctrines of original sin and innate depravity. The modernists tended to emphasize the natural goodness of man, and sin was reinterpreted "chiefly as error and limitation which education in morals and the example of Jesus could mitigate, or else as the product of underprivilege which social reform could correct."[96] Ethics replaced theological doctrine as the foundation of the Christian Witness, and to many modernists the Sermon on the Mount became the core of the Bible. Social Gospelers insisted that the ethics of the Sermon on the Mount applied to economic and political institutions as much as to individuals.

Modernists, especially the Social Gospelers, were optimistic about the human capacity for doing good and about the potential for creating a kingdom of heaven on earth. Walter Rauschenbusch, the most eminent expositor of the Social Gospel, believed that "the immense latent perfectibility in human nature" was revealed by the extraordinarily rapid scientific and technological progress of the United States. He expected the control of social forces to do for the twentieth century what the control of natural forces by science had done during the nineteenth century. Writing in 1907, he predicted that his grandchildren would see the realization of God's kingdom and viewed the previous nineteen centuries of Christian influence as a long preliminary stage of growth. This optimism and millennial enthusiasm gave the Social Gospelers a powerful burst of energy in promoting reforms that they were sure would bring about the "great day of the Lord for which the ages waited, and count us blessed for sharing in the apostolate that proclaimed it."[97]

The rejection of the doctrine of innate depravity paved the way for the central doctrine of the Social Gospel, which held that social reform was a precondition for the personal salvation of those in the grip of poverty. In the case of alcohol, for example, the new doctrine implied that few impoverished individuals could be freed from its corrupting influence merely through evangelical appeals. Not only did the power of the state have to be used to place alcoholic beverages beyond the reach of those corrupted by them, but the state also had to intervene to end the conditions that were thought to make alcohol so attractive: the grinding hours of labor, the low wages that kept workers trapped in corrupting poverty, the growing threat of unemployment that undermined self-respect, and the concentration of wealth and power in the hands of a few whose exercise of privilege and personal corruption undermined faith in America's millennial potential.[98]

As it evolved, this so-called New Theology gradually abandoned the emphasis on the inherent sinfulness of humankind and veered toward an emphasis on the innocence of the newborn. If adults were corrupt, they were corrupted by a sinful social order. Adherents of the New Theology veered away from the tenet of free will, not by returning to the Calvinist view of predestination, but by emphasizing the social corruption of the innocent young. Those who grew up in a corrupt society could not be blamed if they failed to rise above their environment. They were not sinners in the original meaning of that term: individuals who purposely violated the known will of God. They were victims of a corrupt society that denied them the education and opportunities needed to choose virtuous behavior or to be viable amid the crushing competition of contemporary urban society.

CAPTURING IDEOLOGICAL CITADELS AND INSTALLING NEW EGALITARIAN POLICIES

The third religious-political cycle began with a phase of religious revival that intensified religious beliefs and ushered in reinvigorated ethics and theological principles. As with the two previous Great Awakenings, there were both orthodox and more liberal aspects connected with the religious excitement. In the two previous Awakenings, the liberal wing represented a retreat from strict Calvinism, but this time the retreat went so far among some of the liberals as to reject the supernatural elements of religion altogether.

The Two Sides of the Third Great Awakening

In the two previous Awakenings, there was a single unifying experience, the conversion, that transcended whatever differences there might have been on theological issues. The conversion experience was an intense, highly concentrated, life-transforming, physical and emotional experience. It was a moment of crisis in which one turned away from a life of sin and committed oneself to a new life in Christ, partaking of the saving power of God.[99]

As modernist theory grew stronger, the supernatural aspects of religion diminished among those creating the New Theology, and conversions ceased to be central to their missionary work. Social reform increasingly replaced personal reform as the center of the struggle to perfect American society. In the place of a transcendent God, "modernists argued that God was present in and revealed through the progress of history and the evolution of culture. God worked through natural laws, not by miraculous intervention in the natural order."[100] Such a theory led to unity between the sacred and the secular, and, for some, the secular component increasingly overwhelmed the sacred. To many of those who embraced the Social Gospel message, the value and truth of religion were shown by the capacity to create God's kingdom on earth rather than in the hereafter. The essence of religion became the elimination of poverty and inequality.

These two sides of the Third Great Awakening were not initially distinct. When Dwight L. Moody, the great revivalist of the end of the nineteenth century, brought his orthodox message to university campuses during the 1880s, he found a receptive audience among students already exposed to Darwinism and the higher criticism. The enthusiasm that he aroused among students led to the establishment of the Student Volunteer Movement, a missionary organization. However, that enthusiasm also promoted support for social crusades that continued during the first three decades of the twentieth century. Embracing social concerns did not necessarily mean that one had to abandon either belief in the supernatural or concern for personal purification. Some of the most ardent reformers, including Josiah Strong, a Social Gospeler who was instrumental in promoting interdenominational organizations to rally the churches for reform, retained their belief in the supernatural and in the importance of conversions. Yet Strong and others like him insisted that the "ethics of Jesus applied not just to the individual but to economic and political structures as well."[101]

The differences between these two components of religious intensification did not threaten to become an outright split until more than two decades into the revival phase of the Third Great Awakening.[102] Even those who had sought a conversion experience but were unable to achieve it, such as Washington Gladden, who is often described as the originator of the Social Gospel, did not campaign against those who believed in conversion; instead, they sought to rally all Protestants to the social side of the Christian Witness. The conversion campaigns led by Moody and, later, by revivalist Billy Sunday reached millions of people and led many to their rebirth, despite the growth of modernist sympathies.

The revival gave rise to a zeal for reform that matched that touched off by the Second Great Awakening. The coalitions developed after the turn of the twentieth century (around such issues as temperance, the protection of children and women in manufacturing and mining, women's suffrage, and political corruption) and included individuals whose ethics were derived from both the Second and the Third Great Awakenings. The campaigns were so effective that they resulted in the passage of four new amendments to the Constitution (the Sixteenth through the Nineteenth) in the span of just a half dozen years. Although for some the zeal was ignited by the conversion experience, for others it was ignited by a modernist enthusiasm for the imminent realization of God's kingdom on earth as powerful as that which impelled Calvinists.

The revival phase of the Third Great Awakening also gave rise to an even more earnest and mystical movement with increased emphasis on conversions. The first Pentecostal churches emerged during the opening decade of the twentieth century, and, since then, the movement has become the most rapidly growing section of evangelical Protestantism, not only in the United States, but throughout the world. Pentecostals believe that the original conversion experience should be followed by another intense experience of "spirit baptism," which is evinced by such gifts of the Holy Spirit as healing and "speaking in tongues," a state during which an individual speaks in human languages of which he has no knowledge or in a "heavenly language" that has no known meaning. This movement spread rapidly among impoverished blacks and whites, giving rise to over three hundred distinct denominations.[103]

The latent split between the conservatives and the modernists did not break into the open until the close of World War I. The prelude to the battle was the publication between 1910 and 1915 of a series of twelve volumes called *The Fundamentals*. The distinguished group of conservative theologians who contributed to these volumes sought systematically to set forth their objections to the New Theology in a scholarly manner. During the 1920s, differences turned into theological warfare aimed at purging liberals from positions of authority in the principal evangelical denominations. At the same time, a public campaign was mounted to eliminate the teaching of evolution in public schools.[104]

The fiercest intramural battles took place in the Northern Baptist and Presbyterian denominations. The conservative effort to remove modernists from positions of authority climaxed with the case of the Reverend Harry Emerson Fosdick. Although ordained a Baptist minister, Fosdick was serving as the pulpit minister at the First Presbyterian Church in New York City when he delivered a sermon that questioned the belief in the virgin birth, denied the inerrancy of the Bible (which he said was incredible to the modern mind), and called for reconsideration of belief in the Second Coming of Jesus Christ. Efforts to expel Fosdick outright without trial were made at the 1924 General Assembly of the Presbyterian Church. Those efforts were thwarted by less militant fundamentalists, who permitted Fosdick to resign. Then, at the invitation of John D. Rockefeller Jr., Fosdick became pastor of the Park Avenue Baptist Church (later renamed the Riverside Church when the congregation moved into its new building next to Columbia University), a stunning rebuff to the conservatives.[105]

The campaign to rid the public schools of Darwinian theory came to a head one year later with the famous Scopes "monkey" trial. In 1925, the Tennessee legislature banned the teaching of any theory that denied the story of divine creation as taught in the Bible or that argued that man had descended from lower orders of animals. Backed by the American Civil Liberties Union, John T. Scopes, a science teacher in Dayton, Tennessee, confessed to having taught Darwinian theory. William Jennings Bryan, the former presidential candidate of the Democratic Party and the secretary of state under Woodrow Wilson, was the prosecutor. Scopes was defended by Clarence Darrow of Chicago, a religious skeptic and famous trial lawyer. This trial became the first great media event, with a troop of reporters wiring stories throughout the nation and around the world ridiculing the "rural yokels" and Bryan's defense of the literal truth of the Book of Genesis. Although Scopes was found guilty, his conviction was reversed on a technicality by a higher Tennessee court. Bryan died shortly after the trial, and the secular press declared the Scopes trial a victory of science over superstition.[106]

Under siege by the powerful liberal press, the fundamentalist campaign to purify the churches of the modernist heresy ground to a halt. The more militant fundamentalists withdrew from the mainline Northern churches, founding new fundamentalist denominations. Founding their own schools, publishing houses, and missionary agencies, they created an all-encompassing subculture of their own within which they pursued their educational, religious, and personal goals. It was not until the 1950s that they again sought to engage the public at large.[107]

Laying the Foundation for a Modernist Egalitarian Coalition, 1890–1920

It was one thing to proclaim the new doctrine that poverty was the source of sin; it was quite another to work out a practical program for redistributing income from the rich to the poor. A substantial barrier had to be overcome. Americans were far more addicted to private property than they were to alcohol. Political viability required programs that served the goal of redistributing income and wealth from the rich to the poor without appearing to undermine the rights of propertyholders. Not only did such programs have to be invented, but the public had to be persuaded that they were superior to the reforms advocated by disciples of the Second Great Awakening, who initially had the upper hand within both religious circles and the two main political parties.

The Social Gospelers worked diligently within their denominations to create sympathy for the plight of wage earners and to point up the avarice of the leaders of big business. One of the principal breakthroughs came in 1908, when the Social Creed of the Methodist Church was adopted. Declaring its fraternal interests in the aspirations of workers, the Methodists characterized the goals of unions as fundamentally ethical. Other points in their Social Creed included "equal rights and complete justice for all men in all stations of life"; "protection of the worker from dangerous machinery, occupational diseases, injuries and mortality"; the abolition of child labor; the regulation of the working conditions of women to safe-guard their physical and moral health; the gradual reduction of hours of labor "to the lowest practical point, with work for all"; the provision of "a living wage in every industry"; and the "most equitable division" of the output of industry "that can ultimately be devised." That creed was also adopted by the Federal Council of Churches, which represented thirty-three denominations and, from its inception in 1908, displayed a keen con-cern with social issues.[108]

Social Gospel leaders also moved vigorously to mobilize universities to support egalitarian legislative programs. Richard T. Ely's effort to found a national organization that would rescue the discipline of economics from the clutches of classical theorists is a case in point. Of the fifty people who gathered at the first organizational meeting of the American Economic Association (AEA) in 1885, more than twenty were, or had been, practic-ing clergy. The nonbinding platform that was adopted called for the united efforts of churches, the state, and science to promote social reform. Toward that end, the AEA awarded a series of prizes for essays proposing programs on such matters as the protection of women wage earners, the institution of state and local taxation, the evils of unrestricted immigra-tion, the housing of the urban poor, and the curbing of industrial acci-dents.[109]

Winning coalitions on such issues were more often established at the state than at the federal level. In the case of women, statutes were widely enacted limiting the workday to nine hours and the workweek to fifty-four hours. Twelve states also passed laws providing for the establishment of minimum wage rates for women, and five prohibited night work for women. Another issue that gained widespread support was that of safety and health, especially in factories and mines. Laws were enacted in thirty states making employers liable for accidents caused by defective machinery and requiring the establishment of insurance programs to cover industrial accidents.[110]

The effort to promote outright egalitarian legislation at the federal level met with mixed success. Most of the issues singled out in the Social Creed of the Methodist Church were easier to pursue in state legislatures and city councils, although, in 1916, Congress prohibited the interstate transportation of manufactured goods produced by factories employing children under age fourteen or children under sixteen who worked more than eight hours in any day or six days in any week. Labor was also success-ful in adding a clause to the Clayton Antitrust Act of 1914 that exempted trade unions from the conspiracy provisions of the Sherman Antitrust Act and prohibited courts from issuing restraining orders or injunctions against strikes. This was only a temporary victory for labor, however. Although Samuel Gompers, the head of the American Federation of Labor (AFL), hailed the Clayton Act as the Magna Carta of working people, the courts effectively nullified these clauses during the 1920s.

The most effective boost to organized labor took place during the years 1917–18 and was a by-product of World War I. The diversion of a sixth of the labor force into the army created a seller's market in labor that pushed up wages. To ensure uninterrupted production, President Woodrow Wilson created the National War Labor Board (NWLB), which was responsible for settling labor disputes. The board prohibited strikes but recognized the rights of unions to organize and bargain collectively. It also supported an eight-hour workday. The combination of strong markets for labor and the favorable policies of the NWLB enabled unions to negotiate favorable labor contracts and promoted the growth of union membership, which more than doubled between 1910 and 1920, reaching 12 percent of the nonagricultural labor force. However, the gains of labor were drastically eroded during the 1920s as courts freely issued injunctions against trade unions and the unions lost most of the gains of the war years.[111]

World War I also created a favorable climate for the passage of legislation putting an end to unrestricted immigration. The labor movement and the Social Gospelers had been pushing for various types of restrictive legislation from the 1880s on. The central demand was the imposition of a literacy requirement, which would have reduced immigration to a fraction of prevailing levels. Such legislation passed Congress in 1897 but was vetoed by President Grover Cleveland. Subsequent legislation was vetoed by President William Howard Taft in 1913 and President Woodrow Wilson in 1915. It was vetoed again by Wilson in 1917, but this time Congress overrode the veto. In 1921, Congress shifted to a quota system that made it possible to place more severe restrictions on immigration from Southern and Eastern Europe.[112]

Although the antitrust policies of Presidents Theodore Roosevelt, William Howard Taft, and Woodrow Wilson have often been described as important contributions to egalitarianism during the Progressive era, there is less to that claim than meets the eye. The principal achievements in this area were ideological. The muckraking literature attacking the Standard Oil Company, Wall Street, the health and employment practices of the meatpacking industry, and the corruption of the railroad corporations aroused the public against big business and created a climate favorable for government action against them. When Roosevelt ran for reelection in 1904, he made trust-busting a campaign issue and initiated legal action against the Standard Oil Company, the Consolidated Tobacco Company, and the Northern Securities Company (a railroad trust). Altogether, thirty-seven antitrust cases were brought by the Roosevelt administration, forty-three by the Taft administration, and fifty-three by Wilson's first administration. However, the net effect of these prosecutions was not very great. Court rulings established the principle that individual companies could not conspire to control prices or restrain trade, but they upheld the general right of smaller companies to merge into larger ones, thus permitting a single firm to control a substantial portion of an industry, provided that they were not conspiring with remaining rivals or otherwise acting to prevent new companies from entering the market.[113]

Moreover, regulatory agencies such as the Interstate Commerce Commission may have done more to cartelize some industries than would private pools and trusts, which, lacking the sanction of law, frequently failed in their attempt to maintain a monopolistic level of prices. Recent economic analyses have revealed that the net effect of such regulatory agencies has frequently been to enforce collusions between management and unions to raise wages and profits at the expense of consumers.[114]

Of the various reforms of the Progressive era, taxing the income of corporations and individuals was probably the most important institutional step toward the realization of the egalitarian state envisioned by the Social Gospelers. In 1900, customs receipts from tariffs and excise taxes on such products as alcoholic beverages, tobacco, and sugar constituted 93 percent of the revenues of the federal government.[115] Federal expenditures began rising rapidly in the 1880s, largely as a result of a substantial expansion in pensions for veterans of the Union army. Promoted by a very effective veterans organization, the Grand Army of the Republic, and by competition between the Republicans and the Democrats for the votes of Northern veterans, the total cost of pensions doubled between 1880 and 1890 and rose by another third between 1890 and 1896, by which time veterans' pensions accounted for about 45 percent of federal outlays. To meet the increasing expenditures, Congress raised tariffs and excise taxes a number of times during the 1880s and early 1890s, touching off a mass protest movement among farmers and small business owners in the South and Midwest.

The demands of farmers and small business owners found political expression in the formation of a third party, the Populist Party, and also through the Democratic Party. The Populists demanded cuts in the tariff and excise taxes, which they wanted replaced by a federal income tax on the top 5 percent of individual incomes and on the profits of corporations. The campaign for the income tax was led in the House by William Jennings Bryan, then a Democratic representative from Nebraska, who had been elected with Populist support. Although Bryan and his allies were not able to prevent an increase in tariffs, they were able to add an income tax amendment to the tariff bill by nearly a straight party vote. The federal income tax became law in August of 1894 but was struck down by the Supreme Court the following year on constitutional grounds. Further action on a federal income tax was delayed until 1909, when Democrats introduced a constitutional amendment that won overwhelmingly in both houses and was ratified by the states, becoming the Sixteenth Amendment to the Constitution in February 1913.[116]

In 1913, the combined yield on individual and corporate income taxes was relatively low, accounting for under 4 percent of total federal revenue. The exigencies of the war, however, justified sharply raising taxes on individuals and even more so on corporations. Although these taxes seemed exceptionally high by the standards of the time, once established, they were difficult to cut. Some reductions in tax rates were made during the 1920s, but the level of rates remained far above those that were in force before the war.[117]

In 1907, Walter Rauschenbusch, the Social Gospeler, believed that the forces of egalitarianism were on the march and that the promised day would be achieved before long. When he died in 1918, he was more disillusioned by the outbreak of World War I than by the failure of egalitarian gains to transform human nature. Although there had been ideological gains in the condemnation of greedy corporations, the movement toward economic concentration continued at a brisk pace during the 1920s. The gains that trade unions had made during World War I were sharply reversed during the 1920s, and, by the eve of the Great Depression, the membership of the AFL had returned to its 1910 level. Nor had the liberals defeated the conservatives within the ministerial ranks of the Northern evangelical churches. Despite liberal domination of religious and philosophical thought in the universities, the fundamentalists remained in control of the governing organizations of the mainline churches. It was not until the more militant fundamentalists withdrew from the mainline churches, disheartened by their inability to expel the modernists, that this valuable resource came under the control of the modern egalitarians.

Installing the Welfare State, 1930–70

By the mid-1930s, the Social Gospel was superseded as a theological movement, but its social philosophy was more vigorous than ever. It was carried forward between 1930 and 1970 by scholars and reformers who had been educated in that philosophy. Some of these experts had also been involved in the mobilization of the economy during World War I and had observed the successes and the shortcomings of that effort. Favorable conditions for the transformation of Social Gospel philosophy into social and economic policies were provided by the Great Depression. Unemployment rose to unprecedented heights during the 1930s, far exceeding the levels that had prevailed during the depression of the 1890s. At the high point of the Great Depression in 1933, over 30 percent of the labor force was unemployed. During the rest of the 1930s, average annual unemployment ranged between 14 and 24 percent.[118] This unprecedented unemployment provided the context for the avalanche of legislation between 1933 and 1968 that established the welfare state.

Since the 1890s, politicians had been turning to academics with increasing frequency to provide expert knowledge and to design social policies. The early pattern is illustrated by the career of John R. Commons, who was trained in economics at Johns Hopkins University during the late 1880s and taught at Wesleyan (in Connecticut), Oberlin, Indiana University, and Syracuse University before coming to the University of Wisconsin in 1904, where he taught until his retirement in 1932. During his academic career, he prepared a report on immigration for the U.S. Industrial Commission, drafted Wisconsin's civil service law (1905), its public utility law (1907), and its workmen's compensation act (1911), and organized and directed Milwaukee's Bureau of the Economy and Efficiency (1911–13). He also served on Woodrow Wilson's U.S. Commission on Industrial Relations (1913–15), represented four Western states before the Federal Trade Commission on the discriminatory price policies of the United States Steel Company in 1923, and was an economic adviser to the House Committee on Banking and Currency. The legislation that he and his students drafted for Wisconsin served as models for measures enacted by the New Deal administration of President Franklin D. Roosevelt, including the Social Security Act of 1935.[119]

What was remarkable in Commons's time became ordinary during the 1930s. Roosevelt established a "brain trust" of academic specialists to advise him on economic and social policies. Congress demanded an increasing output of economic intelligence from the Commerce Department and other agencies of the executive branch. Congress also established such independent agencies as the Temporary National Economic Committee (TNEC) to investigate problems of industrial concentration and other issues bearing on the long-term prospects of the economy. This utilization of highly trained specialists was made possible by the enormous—sixfold—increase in advanced degrees—master's and doctorate—between 1920 and 1940. Most of the new corps of specialists accepted the precepts of modernism and embraced its egalitarian ideals. They looked for guidance, not to the Bible, but to the foundational texts and journals of their disciplines.[120]

There was little demand for these specialists in Washington until the onset of the Great Depression. According to Walter Salant, one of the first economists hired in Washington, there were hardly a hundred economists employed by the federal government in 1931, even if one counted statistical clerks. By 1938, the middle of Roosevelt's second administration, the number of economists employed by the government had risen to five thousand. Today that number stands at over twenty thousand.[121]

The turning point in the government's demand for economists came in 1932, when the Senate passed a resolution calling on the Bureau of Foreign and Domestic Commerce to prepare estimates of the national income of the United States for the preceding three years. Since the bureau lacked a specialist capable of directing the study, it asked the National Bureau of Economic Research (NBER), a private, nonpartisan research organization, to permit Simon Kuznets, one of its economists, to take charge of the project. The report he produced, using a combination of government and NBER personnel, represented the beginning of a revolution in government responsibility for economic intelligence. The national income statistics developed by Kuznets provided such striking insights into the operation of the economy that the government soon established a National Income Division in the Department of Commerce to prepare annual estimates, with one of Kuznets's former students, Robert Nathan, as its head. Other important new programs brought large numbers of economists into the Department of Commerce—for example, thanks to new sampling procedures, the Bureau of the Census was able to obtain regular monthly reports on the size of the labor force, the level of unemployment, retail sales, and retail and wholesale prices. Large numbers of economists were also employed during the 1930s by the Department of Treasury, the Department of Agriculture, the Department of the Interior, the Federal Reserve Board, the TNEC, and the National Resources Committee.[122]

World War II pushed the employment of economists in government to unprecedented levels. As MIT Professor Paul A. Samuelson, winner of the Second Nobel Memorial Prize in Economics, put it in 1943, that war was "an economist's war." Economists working in the Planning Division of the War Production Board, led by Robert Nathan, were responsible for ensuring an adequate output of war materials without crippling the civilian economy. They demonstrated that targets developed by the procurement office of the United States Army were unrealistic and convinced Roosevelt to adopt their projections, which turned out to be on the mark. Economists also ran the civilian side of the economy through the Office of Price Control. And economists, working in the Treasury, designed the program for financing the war, including the development of the withholding system, which made it possible to extend the income tax from a tax on the rich to a tax on the entire population. Economists, along with historians and political scientists, provided the personnel for the research division of the Office of Strategic Services (the predecessor to the Central Intelligence Agency), where, among other tasks, they chose targets for the nightly bombing runs over Germany.[123]

Economists were so effective during the war and made so positive an impression on business and political leaders that, in 1946, Congress established the Council of Economic Advisers to provide the president with guidance on economic issues. The Full Employment Act of 1946 obligated the federal government to develop programs aimed at full employment and steady prices, focusing attention on economic issues. That was but one of the postwar measures indicating that the federal government had taken responsibility for managing the economy and correcting systemic deficiencies in the modern industrial system.

Economic planning during and after World War II provided a salutary environment for the trade union movement. Despite wage controls, the real income of workers rose by 70 percent during the war. Protections provided to trade unions, including the right to strike, which was won early on in the New Deal years, were extended during the war years, when the market for labor was unusually favorable. By 1945, there were nearly 15 million union members, representing over 35 percent of the nonagricultural labor force. Even though the share of workers in the trade unions started to decline after 1945, the power of the union movement over the economy continued to expand well into the 1960s, as demonstrated by the number of workers involved in strikes and by the salutary effects of trade unions on the wages of their members.[124]

During the postwar period, fiscal policy was also used to promote the redistribution of income. The boldest initiatives occurred during President Lyndon B. Johnson's War on Poverty. Payments to retirees, families with dependent children, injured workers, and the unemployed were substantially increased. Medicare, which provided medical coverage for the elderly, and Medicaid, which provided it for the indigent, were created as new entitlements.[125]

The expansion of higher education following World War II may have been the greatest contribution to the redistribution of income. Although the proportion of the population aged eighteen to twenty-four attending college had risen steadily during the first four decades of the twentieth century, developments after World War II represented a significant expansion of opportunity. Enrollments in institutions of higher education increased more that fivefold between 1940 and 1970, and the share of persons aged eighteen to twenty-four in colleges and universities rose to over 30 percent. The turning point was the GI Bill of Rights, which provided full tuition and a large proportion of living expenses to virtually all veterans of the Second World War. The success of that program led to a widespread policy among universities of providing scholarships to qualified applicants who could not pay for their education. Financial support to students from middle- and lower-class families was also provided by the federal government through a program of low-cost loans to college students and through increased appropriations by legislatures to state universities.[126]

Not only was much of the economic egalitarianism preached by the Social Gospelers realized during the postwar era; these years also gave rise to a concept of cultural egalitarianism that was hardly contemplated by liberals at the beginning of the century. The movement based on this concept was a by-product of World War II. The Axis powers based their ideological campaign on nineteenth-century anthropological theories that presumed a hierarchy of ability by race and ethnicity. The United States responded by championing the new anthropological theories of Franz Boaz, the founder of social anthropology in the United States, who argued for the equality of races. After the close of the war, the continuing practice of racial, religious, and ethnic discrimination in employment, educational opportunities, and numerous other aspects of life became intolerable to many in a generation educated in the belief that all people were innately equal. The earliest gains were made by the campaigns against religious discrimination, climaxed by the election of John F. Kennedy, a Roman Catholic, to the presidency in 1960.

Racial barriers to equal opportunity were more difficult to overcome. It was not until nearly two decades after Germany's surrender that government-sanctioned discrimination in employment because of race, color, religion, sex, or national origin was outlawed, along with segregated facilities in public accommodations and in public schools. Although the struggle to enforce the Civil Rights Act of 1964 was exceedingly difficult, the effort was enhanced by the Voting Rights Act of 1965 and the Twenty-Fourth Amendment (ratified in 1964), which eliminated poll taxes, literacy tests, and other long-existing barriers to black equality in political life. Still another new weapon was delivered by the Civil Rights Act of 1966, which prohibited discrimination in the rental or sale of housing and provided sanctions against interference with the equal rights of all Americans in education, employment, travel, and jury service. Behind this legislation and its implementation was a movement for civil rights that had become a major political factor in American life.[127]

The 1960s also saw the revival of the women's movement, which had been relatively quiescent for nearly four decades. Women active in the campaigns for minority rights became conscious of the failure of these movements to articulate an adequate program of equal opportunity for women. The feminist movement that emerged in the 1960s was, in many ways, more radical than the other reform movements of that decade because it challenged a wide array of cultural norms. It not only demanded an end to discrimination against women in occupational opportunity and compensation but also attacked the prevailing view that the primary role of women was in nurturing the family.

The battle flag was hoisted in 1963 by Betty Friedan, whose book *The Feminine Mystique* led to widespread questioning of prevailing views on the psychology of women, the value of marriage, and the role of women in society. The National Organization for Women (NOW), founded in 1966 with Friedan as its first president, challenged all aspects of the gendering of behavior and quickly became the largest and most powerful women's group. Among the campaigns launched by NOW was one in support of passage of an Equal Rights Amendment (ERA), which aimed to end gender discrimination in employment, including, ironically, much of the protective legislation for women won by reformers before 1920, on the grounds that it impeded women's occupational opportunities. Although the ERA was never passed, the campaign for it promoted the growth of the women's movement. NOW also championed the right of women to legal abortion, a right upheld by the Supreme Court in its 1973 decision in

Roe v. Wade. NOW gave a powerful impetus to the gay rights movement with a 1973 resolution calling for "civil rights legislation designed to end discrimination based on sexual orientation."[128]

The Changing of the Guard

By the late 1960s, the third religious-political cycle was about eight decades old, and its disciples were at the peak of their influence, commanding ideological institutions and key social and economic agencies of government. Of course, those who occupied positions of intellectual leadership and led the new reform campaigns were not the initiators of the Third Great Awakening. The initiators were born just before, during, or just after the Civil War. They were educated during the ideological crisis ushered in by modernist theology. Even when divided on critical issues of theology, they found common ground on a wide range of social reforms. Although some issues, such as the expansion of education, the protection of children and women employed in manufacturing, the extension of suffrage to women, and the prohibition of alcohol in beverages, were left over from the Second Great Awakening, they were embraced by those steeped in modernism and the Social Gospel. Those who promoted reform movements distinctive to the Social Gospel—the assault on big business, the defense of trade unions, and the use of fiscal policy to redistribute income—received their university education toward the end of the nineteenth century and exercised their influence over thought and policy primarily during the first three decades of the twentieth century.

The generation that designed the economic and social reforms of the New Deal, that ran the economy during World War II, and that ushered in the early postwar phases of the welfare state was born mainly during the three decades surrounding the turn of the twentieth century and received its university training between World War I and the Great Depression. By the eve of World War II, the social sciences had grown far beyond the religious issues that marked their emergence as professions. The standards of these disciplines had become akin to those developed in the natural sciences. Strict procedures for the collection and analysis of data, including the new methods of statistical inference, were increasingly common aspects of social scientists' training. Social scientists also fully accepted the role that modernists and Social Gospel theologians had assigned them: the development of government policies that could solve the social and economic problems of an urban industrial society. The idea that the government should accept responsibility for managing the economy after peace was achieved seemed natural to them, and their training and experience prepared them to undertake the tasks assigned them by the New Deal and post–World War II governments.

Those who helped design and implement the Great Society and the War on Poverty were born mainly during the 1920s, 1930s, or early 1940s, and they received their university training during the tail end of the Great Depression, World War II, and the two decades following the close of the war. Their education was even more secular than that of their predecessors. Unless they were specialists in the history of their disciplines, little in their academic training connected the mathematical models of economic and social behavior to which they were exposed, and to which they contributed, to the theological issues that had given rise to their disciplines. To many in that generation, especially among economists, although contributing to public policy was a part of the mission of the discipline, it was no longer at its center. This is not to say that large numbers of economists and other social scientists did not continue to concern themselves with policy issues, but, for many of those "doing economics," especially those who received their degrees in the 1960s and 1970s, the "pure science" of the discipline was an end in itself. That ethos did little to prepare the practitioners for the intellectual bombshell that exploded when the Fourth Great Awakening intruded on their consciousness.

This chapter has traced the rise of the modern egalitarian ethic from its beginnings in the sixteenth-century efforts of the new nationalist governments of England and France to provide famine relief. It was, however, the reform program of the Second Great Awakening that established the immediate context for the emergence of modern egalitarianism. The reforms of the Second Great Awakening stemmed from the assumption that egalitarianism would be promoted by increasing equality of opportunity. The application of that principle gave rise to some of the most radical demands in American history, including equal rights for indigenous Americans, women's rights, prohibition, and the most radical of all the demands, the abolition of slavery.

After the Civil War, the disciples of the Second Great Awakening promoted such reforms as universal primary education, protection for children and women in the workplace, and the restriction of unlimited immigration. However, they failed to recognize that the closing of the frontier and the concentration of production in a relatively small number of very large industrial firms had undermined the principle of equality of opportunity. Ordinary workers in such industries as public utilities, transportation, iron and steel manufacturing, petroleum refining, food distribution, and chemical and electric appliance manufacturing could no longer expect to become the masters of their own modest enterprises or to rebuff the attempts of their employers to lower wages, nor could they expect to find new, more expansive opportunities in the West.

Modernist reformers focused on this glaring shortcoming by substituting the principle of equality of condition for that of equality of opportunity. Although they continued to pursue such unrealized reforms of the Second Great Awakening as the expansion of educational opportunity, Prohibition, protective legislation for women and children, and women's suffrage, they developed a new program of fiscal reforms aimed at redistributing income from the rich to the poor. They also supported the right of trade unions to strike and encouraged other institutions that would raise wages. Their most notable accomplishment was the transformation of the federal government into a welfare state committed not only to economic equality, but also to cultural equality. It is now necessary to consider the effectiveness of their legislative program in promoting the goal of equality of condition. Without such an assessment, it is not possible to properly evaluate the efficacy of the reform program of the Fourth Great Awakening, which focuses on spiritual (immaterial) equality and seeks a return to the principle of equality of opportunity.

FOUR

The Egalitarian Revolution
of the Twentieth Century

The techniques that leaders of the Fourth Great Awakening are using to mobilize winning coalitions for their reforms are not new. They are copied from the techniques fashioned by modernists during the Third Great Awakening, techniques that were extraordinarily effective in promoting the modernist agenda. These techniques made it possible for the modernists to shift much of the responsibility for poverty and crime from the individual to society. Other achievements of the modernists include the legalization of the right to strike and the establishment of a vast network of regulatory agencies to monitor and control the behavior of businesses. Income taxes were levied on both corporations and individuals, and the proceeds were used to finance entitlement programs that redistributed income to the poor. Job security was enhanced partly by increasing the share of the labor force that is directly employed by the federal, state, and local governments and partly by instituting unemployment insurance.[1] Laws were enacted that prohibit discrimination in employment for reasons of race, ethnicity, or gender. These accomplishments reveal the political potency of the modernist movement.

The capacity to turn the government into an agency that promotes greater equality in the distribution of material resources does not mean that the redistribution actually achieved improved welfare in the manner envisioned by the reformers. This chapter assesses the extent of income redistribution that has actually taken place during the past century as well as the share of this income redistribution that can be attributed to the policies and laws promoted by disciples of the Third Great Awakening. The chapter also provides several measures of the overall welfare gains that can be attributed to the egalitarian reforms.

Measuring the costs and benefits of various policies leads unavoidably to a discussion of technical issues: determining the properties of alternative measures, identifying the complex interactions between various policies, sorting the negative and positive components of these interactions, and assessing retrospectively which issues were beyond the reach of policy or better handled by letting the natural course of economic and social processes work themselves out. I have sought to summarize the findings of these inquiries in a manner that is informative to the general reader, highlighting the conundrums and puzzles that remain to be resolved and the information gaps that still need to be closed.

Issues that require the skills of such specialists as econometricians and biostatisticians have been relegated to technical reports published elsewhere. Many issues that seem purely technical are actually complex amalgams of technical and ethical judgments, as Amartya Sen, the 1998 Nobel Laureate in economics, has demonstrated.[2] A number of these subtle ethical considerations are pointed up in this and the next chapter. Some of the most important of the measurement issues are still under analysis. I have summarized findings to date, indicating points that are still unresolved.

In assessing the contribution of particular policies to a more equal distribution of resources, I pay attention not only to indexes of real wages and to measures of the inequality of income distributions but also to biomedical measures of health and welfare, especially measures of chronic malnutrition. Nutritional status needs to be singled out not only because it was the original focus of egalitarian concerns but also because we now know that malnutrition severely reduced the level of labor productivity and accounted for a surprisingly large, even preponderant, amount of the homelessness and pauperism of the past. The biomedical measures include improved approaches to the estimation of survival levels of calorie consumption and the calorie requirements of various types of labor, epidemiological studies of the connection between stature and the risk of both mortality and chronic disease, and epidemiological studies of the connection between the body mass index (BMI), the standard measure of weight adjusted for height, and the risk of mortality.

All in all, I review eight different measures, four economic (per capita income, real wages, the Gini ratio, and homelessness) and four biomedical (stature, BMI, life expectancy, and the prevalence rates of chronic illnesses [morbidity]). The different measures capture different aspects of the increases or declines in welfare, and they do not always agree. There is as much insight to be found in the disagreements among these indices as in the agreements among them. One of the principal findings of this chapter is that the economic measures tend to overestimate the welfare gains of ordinary people during the nineteenth century and underestimate such gains during the twentieth century. It is my judgment that, on the whole, the biomedical measures are more illuminating indices of the gains in material egalitarianism than are conventional economic measures.

The first two parts of this chapter contrast the modest egalitarian gains that took place during the nineteenth century with the remarkable gains realized during the twentieth. The third part describes new techniques that make it possible to probe more deeply than ever before into the nature of the escape from hunger and premature death. The discussion is followed by an evaluation of the contribution of government policies to the egalitarian achievements of the twentieth century, including an examination of the proposition that economic growth and egalitarianism are conflicting goals.

I then assess the effectiveness of several of the major egalitarian programs instituted by the leaders of the Third Great Awakening. This assessment deals with five major achievements and one glaring failure. The chapter closes with a discussion of the difficulties facing anyone attempting to use the government as an agency of egalitarian reform. The difficulties stem partly from the speed with which technology is changing, partly from long lags between the time certain policies are put in place and the time payoffs are apparent, partly from rigidities in political processes.

Although the United States is the principal focus of this chapter, some attention is paid to developments in Europe, particularly in Great Britain, in order to put American achievements, or the lack thereof, into a broader perspective.

THE MODEST PROGRESS IN WORKING-CLASS CONDITIONS DURING THE NINETEENTH CENTURY

At the beginning of the twentieth century, there was no compelling evidence that could refute the Marxist proposition that the absolute, or at least the relative, standard of living of the working class in Europe and America had deteriorated as a consequence of the rise of capitalism.[3] Indeed, during the early decades of the twentieth century, many outside Marxist circles raised alarms about the deterioration in the living conditions of the working class. In England, for example, the large proportion of men rejected by recruiters for the Boer War provoked concern among authorities, a concern that was heightened by data that seemed to show that men who reached maturity about 1900 were shorter than those who had reached maturity at the time of the Crimean War, in the mid-1850s. These results seemed to be confirmed by the studies of British living standards published in 1901, which found that 27 percent of the population were living in such deep poverty that their consumption of food, clothing, and shelter fell below the level needed to maintain physical efficiency. A study of the standard of living more than a decade later found little improvement.[4]

Similar findings were reported in the United States, where about one-third of the men examined for induction into the army during World War I were deemed unfit for service because of chronic impairment of health. As late as the 1920s, Paul H. Douglas, an influential labor economist at the University of Chicago and later a U.S. senator from Illinois, found that the real wages of American workers over the two and a half decades preceding World War I had been constant. More recent studies have provided somewhat more optimistic assessments of the progress in living standards before World War I.[5] However, the older studies were not very far off the mark. Although the period from the middle of the eighteenth century to the end of the nineteenth has been hailed justly as the Industrial Revolution, as a great transformation in social organization, and as a revolution in science, these great advances brought only modest and uneven improvements in the health, nutritional status, and longevity of the lower classes before 1890. It was not until well into the twentieth century that ordinary people in Europe and America began to enjoy the levels of nutrition and longevity that characterize our age. Whatever contribution the technological and scientific advances of the eighteenth and nineteenth centuries may ultimately have made to this breakthrough, escape from hunger and high mortality did not become a reality for most ordinary people until the twentieth century.

Figure 4.1 summarizes the available data on U.S. trends in average stature (which is a sensitive indicator of the nutritional status and health of a population) and in life expectancy since 1720. Both series contain striking cycles. They both rise during most of the eighteenth century, attaining substantially greater heights and life expectancies than prevailed in England during the same period.[6] At the time of George Washington's administration, Americans had a four-inch advantage in height and a

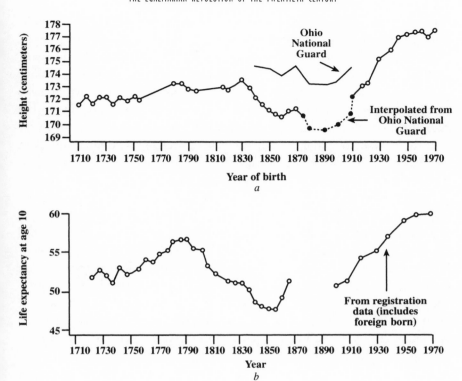

Figure 4.1 Panel *a*, Trend in the mean final height of native-born, white American males. Panel *b*, Trend in the life expectancy of native-born, white American males at age ten.

SOURCES: Fogel (1986a); Costa and Steckel (1997).

NOTE: Height is by birth cohort, and life expectancy at age ten is by period.

twenty-year advantage in life expectancy at birth over the English. Life expectancy began to decline during the 1790s and continued to do so for about half a century. A new rise in heights, the one with which we have long been familiar, probably began with cohorts born during the last decade of the nineteenth century and continues to the present.

Figure 4.1 reveals, not only that Americans achieved World War II heights by the middle of the eighteenth century, but also that they reached levels of life expectancy that the general population of England and even the British peerage did not attain until the first quarter of the twentieth century.[7] The early attainment of relatively modern stature and relatively long life expectancy is surprising. Yet, in the light of the evidence that has accumulated in recent years, it is by no means unreasonable. By the second quarter of the eighteenth century, Americans had diets that were remarkably nutritious by European standards and particularly rich in protein. Moreover, the American population was low in density, probably below the threshold needed to sustain major epidemics of such diseases as smallpox. The low density probably also reduced exposure to the crowd diseases of the nineteenth century (such as tuberculosis and rheumatic fever) that took a heavy toll of life in both England and America. This is not to say that there were no epidemics in America between 1725 and 1800, but, with the exception of a few port cities, outbreaks of epidemic diseases appear to have been much milder in America than in England.

Similar cycles in height appear to have occurred in Europe. For example, Swedish heights declined by 1.4 centimeters between the third and the fourth quarters of the eighteenth century. Hungarian heights declined sharply (5.2 centimeters) between the third quarter of the eighteenth century and the first quarter of the nineteenth. There also appears to have been regular cycling in English heights at maturity throughout the nineteenth century, although the amplitude of these cycles was more moderate than those of the American or Hungarian cycles. A second height decline, accompanied by a rise in the infant mortality rate, occurred in Sweden during the 1840s and 1850s.[8]

This evidence of cycling in stature and mortality rates during the eighteenth and nineteenth centuries in both Europe and America is puzzling. The overall improvement in health and longevity during this period is less than might be expected from the rapid increases in per capita income indicated by national income accounts for most of the countries in question.[9] More puzzling are the decades of sharp decline in height and life expectancy, some of which occurred during eras of undeniably vigorous economic growth. This contradiction of vigorous economic growth and very limited improvement, or even reversal, in the nutritional status and health of the majority of the population suggests that the modernization of the nineteenth century was a mixed blessing for those who lived through it. The problem at hand, then, is the identification and measurement of the negative aspects of modernization that temporarily offset such benefits as the leap forward in scientific knowledge, the remarkable technological innovations in agriculture, transportation, industry, and commerce, and the marked gains in labor productivity. Before attempting to resolve this puzzle, it is necessary to examine the trend in conditions during the twentieth century.

THE REMARKABLE REDUCTION IN INEQUALITY
DURING THE TWENTIETH CENTURY

The record of the twentieth century contrasts sharply with that of the two preceding centuries. In every measure that we have bearing on the standard of living, such as real income, homelessness, life expectancy, and height, the gains of the lower classes have been far greater than those experienced by the population as a whole, whose overall standard of living has also improved.

The *Gini ratio* (also called the *concentration ratio*) is the measure of the inequality of the income distribution most widely used by economists.[10] This measure varies between zero (perfect equality) and one (maximum inequality). In the case of England, for example, for which the longest series of income distributions is available, the Gini ratio stood at about 0.65 near the beginning of the eighteenth century, at about 0.55 near the beginning of the twentieth century, and at 0.32 in 1973, when it bottomed out, not only in Britain, but also in the United States and other rich nations.[11] This measure indicates that over two-thirds of the reduction in the inequality of income distributions between 1700 and 1973 took place during the current century. The large decrease in such inequality, coupled with the rapid increase in the average real income of the English population, means that the per capita income of the lower classes was rising much more rapidly than was that of the middle or upper classes during this long period.[12]

A similar conclusion can be drawn from the data on life expectancy. In 1875, there was a gap of seventeen years between the average length of life of the British elite and that of the population as a whole. There is still a social gap in life expectancy among the British, but, today, the advantage of the richest classes over the poorest is only about two years. Thus, about seven-eighths of the social gap in longevity has disappeared. As a consequence, the life expectancy of the lower classes increased from forty-one years at birth in 1875 to about seventy-five years today. That is a remarkable improvement. Indeed, there was a larger increase in life expectancy during the past century than there was during the previous 200,000 years. If anything sets our century apart from the past, it is this huge increase in the longevity of the lower classes.

Data on stature also indicate the high degree of inequality during the nineteenth century. At the close of the Napoleonic Wars, a typical British male worker at maturity was about five inches shorter than a mature male of upper-class birth. There is still a gap in stature between the workers and the elite of Britain, but now the gap is only on the order of an inch. Height differentials by social class have disappeared in Sweden and virtually disappeared in Norway, but they have not yet done so in the United States. Statistical analysis across a wide array of rich and poor countries today shows a strong correlation between stature and the Gini ratio.[13]

Weight is another important measure of inequality. Despite the great emphasis in recent years on weight reduction, the world still suffers more from problems of undernutrition and underweight than from overweight, as the World Health Organization has repeatedly pointed out. Although one should not minimize the afflictions caused by overnutrition, it is important to recognize that, even in rich countries such as the United States, undernutrition remains a significant problem, especially among impoverished pregnant women, children, and the aged.

That the secular (long-term) increase in body build is due primarily to the great improvement in socioeconomic conditions over the past several centuries, rather than genetic factors, can be seen by considering Holland. The average final height of adult males was only sixty-four inches in that country during the middle of the nineteenth century. The corresponding figure today is nearly seventy-two inches. An increase of eight inches in just four generations cannot be due to natural selection or genetic drift because such processes require much longer time spans. Nor can it be attributed to heterosis (hybrid vigor) because Holland has remained relatively homogeneous and because the effects of heterosis in human populations have been shown both empirically and theoretically to have been quite small. It is hard to come up with credible explanations for the rapid increase in heights that do not turn on environmental factors, especially on improvements in nutrition and health. These environmental factors appear to be still at work. Stature is still increasing, although at a somewhat slower rate, and nations have not as yet reached a mean height that represents the biological limit of humankind given current biomedical technology.[14]

Homelessness is another indicator of the dramatic reduction in inequality during the twentieth century. Until the middle of the nineteenth century, between 10 and 20 percent of the population in Britain and on the Continent were homeless persons whom officials classified as vagrants and paupers. Estimates of vagrancy and pauper rates in the United States during the nineteenth century are less certain, but these rates appear to have reached European levels in the major cities during the 1830s, 1840s, and 1850s. When we speak of homelessness in the United States today, we are talking about rates under 0.4 percent of the population.[15] Many of the homeless today are mentally ill individuals prematurely released from psychiatric institutions that are inadequately funded. Many others are chronically poor, young, and inadequately trained for the current job market.

RECENT TECHNIQUES FOR STUDYING THE EFFECTS OF CHRONIC MALNUTRITION ON HEALTH AND MORTALITY

Of the five measures that have been used so far to characterize and compare the extent of inequality in the nineteenth and twentieth centuries, two are strictly economic. The Gini ratio of income distributions is a financial measure that tracks changes in the concentration of income. Homelessness is also an economic measure that, although it focuses on one particular asset, is indicative of command over other basic necessities of life. The other three measures are of a biomedical nature. The relevance of one of them, life expectancy, to the assessment of economic well-being is obvious. This section is concerned with the relevance of height and of the body mass index (BMI) to the assessment of chronic malnutrition and to other aspects of well-being, including their capacity to predict mortality and morbidity rates.

In common parlance, *diet* and *nutritional status* are often treated as synonyms. However, to nutritionists and epidemiologists, these are distinct terms. The distinction needs to be kept in mind when discussing the relation between improvements in nutritional status and the secular decline in mortality. *Nutritional status* denotes the balance between the intake of nutrients and the claims against it. It follows that an adequate level of nutrition is not determined solely by *diet*, which is the level of nutrient intake, but varies with individual circumstances. Whether one's diet is nutritionally adequate depends on such matters as one's level of physical activity, the climate of the region in which one lives, and the extent of one's exposure to various diseases. As Nevin S. Scrimshaw, University Professor Emeritus at MIT and winner of the World Food Prize in 1991, once pointed out, the adequacy of a given level of iron consumption depends critically on whether an individual has hookworm or malaria.

Thus, a population's nutritional status may decline at the same time that its consumption of nutrients is rising if the extent of its exposure to infection or the degree of its physical activity is rising even more rapidly. It follows that the assessment of the contribution of nutrition to the decline in mortality requires measures, not only of food consumption, but also of the claims on that consumption. To avoid confusion, I will use the terms *diet* and *gross nutrition* to designate nutrient intake only. All other references to nutrition, such as *nutritional status, net nutrition, nutrition, malnutrition,* and *undernutrition* will designate the balance between nutrient intake and the claims on that intake.

Height and the BMI are now the two most widely used measures of malnutrition. They are part of a broader class of *anthropometric* measures (measures of the human body) used by public health authorities to assess the general health and nutritional status of populations. The BMI is calculated by dividing weight (measured in kilograms) by height (measured in meters squared). The index is designed to indicate whether individuals are heavy or light for their stature.

Final height (height at maturity) and the BMI measure different aspects of net nutrition. Although changes in height during the growing years are sensitive to current levels of nutrition, mean final height reflects the accumulated past nutritional experience of individuals over all their growing years, including the fetal period. Thus, it follows that, when final heights are used to explain differences in adult mortality rates, they reveal the effect, not of adult levels of nutrition on adult mortality rates, but of nutritional levels during infancy, childhood, and adolescence on adult mortality rates. A weight-for-height index, by contrast, reflects primarily the current nutritional status. It is also a net measure in the sense that the BMI reflects the balance between intakes and the claims on those intakes. Although final height is determined by the cumulative nutritional status during an entire developmental age span, the BMI fluctuates with the current balance between nutrient intake and energy demand. A person who is short relative to the modern U.S. or West European standard is referred to as *stunted.* Those with low BMIs are referred to as *wasted.*

The Predictive Capacity of Height and BMI

Extensive clinical and epidemiological studies over the past two decades have shown that height and BMI at early ages predict the risk of morbidity and mortality at later ages. The predictive power of the BMI and height with respect to mortality and morbidity is indicated by figures 4.2 and 4.3. Figure 4.2 reproduces a diagram by Hans Waaler, a Norwegian epidemiologist, that shows the relation between BMI and the relative risk of death in a study of 1.8 million Norwegians. Although the observed values of the BMI ranged between 17 and 39, over 90 percent of males had BMIs within the range 20–29. Within this range, the curve is fairly flat, with the relative

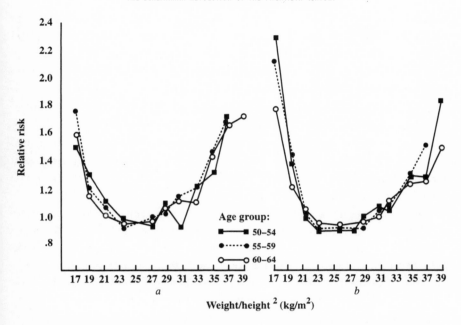

Figure 4.2 The relation between the BMI and prospective risk of death among Norwegian adults aged fifty to sixty-four at risk between 1963 and 1979. Panel *a*, Males. Panel *b*, Females.

SOURCE: Waaler (1984).

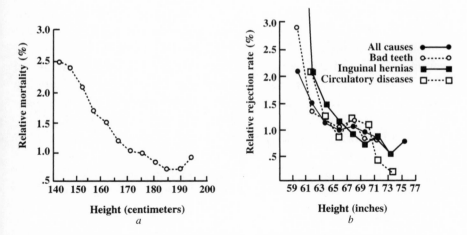

Figure 4.3 A comparison of the connection between height and relative risk in the third quarter of the nineteenth and twentieth centuries. Panel *a*, Relative mortality rates among Norwegian men aged forty to fifty-nine between 1963 and 1979. Panel *b*, Relative rejection rates for chronic conditions in a sample of 4,245 men aged twenty-three to forty-nine examined for the Union army.

SOURCES: For fig. 4.3*a*, Waaler (1984). For fig. 4.3*b*, Fogel et al. (1986).

risk of mortality hovering close to 1.0 (which indicates average mortality). At BMIs under 20 and over 29, however, the risk of death rises quite sharply as the BMI moves away from its mean value. The BMI curves are relatively symmetrical, which indicates that high BMIs are as risky as low ones. Notice that women are more likely than men to die at low BMIs and that men are more likely than women to die at high ones. Although figure 4.2 does not show this, different diseases are associated with each of the sides of the BMI curve. Underweight persons are more likely to die from infectious diseases such as tuberculosis and measles and from lung and stomach cancer. Persons with high BMIs are more likely to die from coronary heart disease and colon cancer.[16]

Panel *a* of figure 4.3 shows the relation between stature and the relative risk of dying at mature ages. It reproduces another diagram by Waaler, which shows that short Norwegian men aged forty to fifty-nine at risk between 1963 and 1979 were much more likely to die than tall men. Indeed, the risk of mortality for men with heights of 165 centimeters (65.0 inches) was on average 71 percent greater than that of men who measured 182.5 centimeters (71.9 inches). In the Norwegian case, the optimum height was about 190 centimeters (between 74 and 75 inches). For that height, the risk of dying was about 30 percent less than the average Norwegian death rate among middle-aged men.[17]

Although height and BMI are effective predictors of mortality at young ages (younger than five) and at middle and late ages, they do not consistently predict mortality rates between ages fifteen and thirty.[18] These measures do, however, predict the likelihood that late adolescents and young adults will have particular chronic diseases. Panel *b* of figure 4.3 shows several curves that relate height to the odds that men of military age would be rejected because of specific chronic illness during the American Civil War. Notice that the "all causes" rejection curve is nearly identical to the Norwegian mortality curve in panel *a*. It thus appears that malnutrition early in life creates a predisposition to develop chronic diseases in adolescence and early adulthood that can kill at later ages.[19]

Explaining the Cycles in Height, BMI, and Mortality

Why did height, BMI, and life expectancy move in cycles from the last quarter of the eighteenth century to the last quarter of the nineteenth? What were the negative aspects of modernization that, for the great majority of the population of that period, offset such benefits as the growth of productivity in agriculture, industry, and transportation? These cycles seem paradoxical to investigators who believe that the rapid economic growth achieved during that century should have raised the standard of living of the lower classes in the United States, England, and several Continental nations by more than it appears to have done. Research into this puzzle so far has focused on four principal possibilities. These are overrapid urbanization, increased geographic mobility, increases in population that were more rapid than the increase in the food supply, and increases in the inequality of the distribution of income.[20]

Although the mix of factors tending to retard improvements in nutritional status and health varied from one country to another, one factor stands out more than any other: overrapid urbanization. In both Europe and the United States, the population of cities grew far more rapidly during the nineteenth century than at any other time in history.[21] The mortality rate appears to have been correlated both with the size of the city and with the rapidity of its rate of growth. In the United States during the 1830s, cities with populations of over fifty thousand had death rates more than twice as high as those of rural areas, and similar patterns have been observed for Europe.[22] The exact threshold at which city size began to affect mortality rate varied with time, place, and circumstance, but, in the United States during the mid-nineteenth century, cities of about twenty-five thousand persons appear to have marked the threshold of significant elevation in mortality rates.[23]

Increased geographic mobility significantly affected mortality rates and also exacerbated urban mortality rates. A classic example is the spread of the cholera epidemic of 1849–50 in the United States. This epidemic was brought to American shores in December 1848 by two ships carrying German immigrants, one bound for New York, the other for New Orleans. Although New York–bound passengers who had contracted cholera were kept in quarantine when the ship arrived, others were allowed to enter the city. Within a few days, the disease broke out in the immigrant districts of the city, then spread first to the predominantly native-born, lower-class districts nearby and eventually to upper-class districts. In the case of the second ship, public health officials were able not only to tie the spread of the disease to New Orleans to the disembarkation of the immigrants there but to follow the movement of cholera up the Mississippi and its tributaries. As immigrants from the infected ship boarded river steamers, cholera broke out aboard these ships and then in the cities at which the steamers called, including Memphis, Nashville, Louisville, Cincinnati, Wheeling, Pittsburgh, and St. Louis. Soon after it reached these cities, cholera broke out in the surrounding countryside.[24]

Despite the drama of the cholera epidemic, internal migration was probably more important than foreign migration in spreading disease in the United States during the nineteenth century. The migration of many Easterners to the Midwest via New Orleans appears to have been a major factor in making malaria endemic in the Midwest as far north as Madison, Wisconsin, during the 1820s, 1830s, and 1840s.[25] The upsurge of malaria in the North following the Civil War appears to have been the consequence of the return of large numbers of Union army men who became infected while serving in the South.[26]

There was an important interactive effect between urbanization and migration in addition to their independent effects. Overcrowded housing, the crisis in public sanitation brought on by decades of exceptionally rapid population growth, and poor personal sanitation among tenement dwellers made the large cities of Europe and United States reservoirs of disease, not only undermining the health of urban residents, but also infecting the surrounding rural areas. The mechanisms through which urban diseases were transmitted to the countryside were trade and the rotation of labor between the cities and the surrounding countryside.[27]

The pressure that population placed on the food supply may have played some role in the cycling of heights.[28] One recent study has found that this was the case in Hungary between the second quarter of the eighteenth century and the first quarter of the nineteenth.[29] However, such general pressure on the food supply does not seem to be a likely explanation for the decline in heights and in life expectancy in the United States shown in figure 4.1 above. Calories available for human consumption appear to have increased between 1840 and 1860. In any case, both average calorie and average protein consumption were high throughout the period of decreasing stature and life expectancy, exceeding 3,600 calories and 120 grams of protein daily per *equivalent adult male* (a system of rating the calorie consumption of individuals as a fraction of the average calorie consumption of males aged twenty to thirty-nine).[30]

The fact that average food consumption of Americans (gross nutrition) remained high from 1830 to 1860 does not imply that the average amount of nutrients available to sustain physical development (net nutrition) remained high. Indeed, the fact that average stature declined by several centimeters implies either that more of the food ingested failed to be metabolized or that claims on the intake of food were increasing. The spread of malaria in the North associated with the increased migration of persons bound for the Midwest through New Orleans, the apparent rise in diarrheal diseases (including cholera and typhoid) in both the cities and the countryside, and the higher prevalence of typhus, tuberculosis, respiratory infections, measles, and other diseases associated with rapid urbanization after 1820 provide the mechanism necessary to reconcile an apparently satisfactory level of food consumption with the observed decline in stature.[31]

Since permanent stunting occurs largely at ages under three, declines in final heights during the nineteenth century raise questions about the synergism between nutritional status and disease in utero and in early childhood.[32] Physical development before age three could have been retarded because of increased infections suffered by pregnant mothers, increased contamination of the foods fed to young children, or increased use of opiates (in elixirs) to pacify infants or because weaning and early childhood diets were low in protein.[33] Early childhood diets that contained barely adequate amounts of protein when exposure to disease was low could have become inadequate as the incidence of disease increased.[34] Since disease interrupts growth, the amount of protein required to bring about full catch-up growth following an episode of infection may be double the normal requirement.[35] In the American case, an increase in the proportion of time in which children under age three were sick or in the process of recovery could explain the sharp decline in final heights despite the large and relatively constant quantities of meat consumed by older persons from 1840 to 1860.[36]

THE ROLE OF GOVERNMENT POLICY IN REDUCING INEQUALITY

Such leaders of the Social Gospel movement as Richard Ely and Washington Gladden were convinced that state intervention was an indispensable condition for significant egalitarian advance. Now, a century later, most of the Social Gospel agenda has been implemented, and it is possible to evaluate the role played by the government. The Social Gospelers sought to decrease inequality, not by increasing BMIs or reducing Gini ratios per se, but by improving infant and maternal nutrition, eradicating impurities in food and drugs, improving housing and sanitation, and raising wages relative to property income. Nevertheless, the BMI, Gini ratios, and life expectancy can be used to measure the success of such programs in improving the quality of life among the poor and other groups.

What is at issue in this section is not whether the government could be made an agent for the reforms demanded by the Social Gospelers (in fact, it became such an agent), but whether the reformers read previous experience properly, and whether the legislation and regulations that were implemented as a result of their campaigns accounted for most of the egalitarian gains outlined in this chapter. Since the government's role varied from issue to issue, evaluation of the effectiveness of the state in promoting egalitarianism must be issue specific.

Famine

The elimination of famine is the most obvious area in which government policy was effective because the periodic famines of the early modern era were not natural events but political events. In England, for example, there never was a time from 1500 on in which national inventories of grain fell so far below their usual levels that famines (acute starvation brought on by sharply elevated prices) are properly characterized as unavoidable natural disasters. This surprising discovery does not imply that nonfamine levels of consumption were adequate by modern standards. Quite the contrary, even during years with normal harvests, the English population of the sixteenth, seventeenth, and eighteenth centuries was so poorly fed that the majority suffered from chronic malnutrition, which, we now know, seriously undermined health and elevated mortality rates. However, such substandard nutritional levels were considered normal given the prevailing agricultural technology.

Recent estimates indicate that, even during the most severe combination of famine years, the decline in the production of grains and other foods did not exhaust the inventories carried over from one year to another. For example, during the year with the worst harvest in three centuries, the grain supply was sufficient to feed the population and the livestock without encroaching on the seed reserve and still leave a carryover inventory that was about 40 percent of normal to serve as a buffer against misfortune in the next year. In most of the years that have been designated as famine years in Britain after 1500, the decline in grain output was in the neighborhood of 5 percent, a shortfall that could easily have been covered by carryover inventories, which normally equaled a third or more of average annual production.[37]

Famines were brought about primarily by the governments of new nation-states during periods of anticipated shortages. Fearful that they might not be able to feed their troops, the capital city, and other favored constituencies, government agents entered the major grain-producing areas, demanding large quotas of grain at prearranged prices. In France, the prior claims of the government were sanctioned by law, and no one else was permitted to purchase grain until governmental quotas were satisfied. The effect of this policy was to make the demand for inventories by those who owned them exceedingly inelastic (quantity demanded remains nearly constant when price increases) because the owners of inventories also had obligations to their own troops, to their own retainers, and to clients of various sorts. As a consequence, shortfalls in grain production as small as 5 percent were capable of raising grain prices by nearly 50 percent, forcing the poor to reduce their already meager consumption of grain by a quarter, and forcing the ultrapoor onto starvation diets.[38]

Does the last point contradict the analysis in chapter 3, which held that the paternalistic policies put into practice by James I and Charles I broke the cycle of famines by forcing owners of inventories to sell grain to the poor at affordable prices? No. The state first created the problem and then found a solution. In both instances, the leaders of the new nation-states were driven by nationalistic goals, which required the elimination of all internal threats to the stability of their governments and the military defeat of external enemies. These nationalistic leaders probably were not aware that they were creating the problem. They railed against "engrossers," by which they meant landlords, grain merchants, and brewers, without apparently realizing that the state was the biggest engrosser of all, the principal force that drove the elasticity of the demand for inventories to exceedingly low levels and that sent the price of grain skyrocketing.

Chronic Malnutrition and Mortality

To what extent was the cycling in height, BMI, and mortality during the nineteenth century caused by a failure in government policy? Since upsurges in disease (closely associated with migration and overrapid urbanization) appear to have been the principal source of the cycling, at least in the United States, the answer to this question turns on whether government policy contributed significantly to the rate of urbanization and migration.

Even posing this question might seem ridiculous since the regulation of urban growth today appears to require administrative mechanisms that are beyond the capacity of even the current large federal and local bureaucracies. However, paradoxical as it may seem, reducing the rate of urban growth was well within the capacity of the modest federal government of the antebellum era. The failure of the government to act left in place policies that promoted excessive growth in the large cities (those with populations over twenty-five thousand), which were the main reservoirs of disease during most of the nineteenth century.[39]

One feasible way of regulating urban growth was through the regulation of immigration.[40] About 80 percent of the growth of Northern cities between 1820 and 1860 was the result of immigration, and the balance resulted from the natural increase of the urban population. Hence, reducing immigration rates by two-thirds would have reduced the rate of urban growth by half, which would have made housing less crowded and public sanitation more manageable. Urban labor had long demanded a reduction in the rate of immigration and had proposed a mechanism to regulate it: a tariff (an entry tax) on immigrants. However, despite heavy public pressure to regulate immigration, first Congress and then a succession of presidents blocked action until well into the twentieth century.[41]

The reluctance to act is understandable since limiting immigration posed profound ethical, political, and economic issues.[42] Not only was there a national ethic that made America a refuge for those fleeing political oppression in Europe and for the victims of famine, but immigration policy was at the center of the political struggle for power. Since 85 percent of all immigrants settled in the North, the huge waves of immigration during the 1830s, 1840s, and 1850s shifted the electoral balance between the sections and made it possible for a party based exclusively in the North to gain control of the federal government. Many Southern politicians recognized the danger and joined with nativists in supporting legislation that would have curtailed immigration, but they could not prevail. Strong economic interests were aligned against demands for limitations on immigration. Farmers benefited from the growing urban markets for their products. Land owners, urban and rural, benefited as the increasing density of population sent property values skyrocketing. Employers benefited because the rapid growth of the labor force kept wages relatively low. Native, propertyless laborers were the primary group that suffered from the competition for jobs brought on by unrestricted immigration. However, as a minority of the population during most of the nineteenth century, they lacked the strength to prevail in the political arena.

Although the federal government was unable to regulate urban growth, state and local officials introduced public health programs that significantly reduced the exposure to disease. These included the development of safe water supplies, the inspection of milk, meat, and other foods, the control of housing density, and the improvement of sewers and garbage collection, combined with bans on the dumping of garbage in residential areas. Local governments also established effective systems of quarantining persons with potentially lethal diseases that reduced the transmission of cholera, typhoid, and other dreaded urban killers.

The combined effects of improvement in diet and the reduction in claims on diet through public health programs had a significant effect on mortality rates, not only in the United States, but also in the leading nations of Western Europe. In the case of France, for example, 90 percent of the decline in mortality between 1705 and 1870 appears to have been due to a reduction in chronic malnutrition, which was reflected in substantial increases in height and body mass. Since 1870, however, especially after the mid-1930s, factors other than those that act through height and BMI (such as advances in surgery and chemotherapy) have become increasingly important.[43]

To complete an assessment of the government's contribution to the escape from chronic malnutrition, we need to know how much of the gain was due to improvements in the diet and how much was due to the reduction in exposure to infectious diseases. Work on this question is still at an early stage, and the eventual outcomes of many issues are hard to predict, but several of the preliminary findings are worth noting.

It appears that, during the last quarter of the eighteenth century in both England and France, the average level of calorie intake and protein consumption was so low that large proportions of the population were bound to have been vulnerable to high morbidity and mortality rates. Moreover, while both the per capita supply of food and its distribution improved, the gains were modest by comparison with the advances of the twentieth century. In France, for example, it was not until the second quarter of the nineteenth century that the average daily calorie consumption reached levels currently prevailing in India. Although in France calorie intake increased by about 50 percent between about 1830 and about 1880, meat consumption remained relatively low, averaging just 1.7 ounces (48 grams) daily per capita during the third quarter of the nineteenth century. Moreover, because the distribution of meat was highly unequal, the poorest third of the population consumed hardly 0.3 ounces (8.5 grams) per day, or about 2 ounces (57 grams) per week.[44] So, until the twentieth century, the backwardness of agriculture, combined with an exceedingly unequal distribution of meat and with the inadequate vegetable protein that was then available, left large sections of the French population severely deprived of protein.

Such low levels of meat consumption were not confined to France. Available evidence indicates that average daily meat consumption at the turn of the twentieth century was below 2.0 ounces (57 grams) per capita in Sweden, Norway, and Austria-Hungary. British consumption, the highest in Europe, probably averaged about 2.6 ounces (74 grams) per capita daily.[45] It was not until after World War II that these nations reached the levels of meat consumption achieved in the United States more than a century earlier.[46]

The fact that, in the mid-nineteenth century, the American diet provided enough high-grade protein to permit considerable catch-up from the interruption in growth caused by disease goes a long way toward explaining why the final heights of native Northern white farmers born about 1830 averaged 68.7 inches (174 centimeters). Yet, without any apparent deterioration in their diets, the final heights of farmers born about 1860 averaged only 67.2 inches (171 centimeters), 1.5 inches (4 centimeters) below their earlier level, and almost 3 inches (8 centimeters) below levels of white American males born about 1955.[47] For reasons indicated in the notes to this chapter and elaborated elsewhere, these differentials suggest that improved diet and reduced exposure to disease were factors of roughly equal importance in eliminating chronic malnutrition.[48]

It thus appears that, as with famines, government policy had a significant but mixed effect on the incidence of chronic malnutrition, health, and mortality. By encouraging, or at least failing to restrain, urban growth, which overtaxed the public health system during the early and middle nineteenth century, governments contributed to the upsurge in epidemics that produced the cycling in stature and mortality. Later in the nineteenth century, and in the early decades of the twentieth, vigorous public programs were launched to supply pure water, improve sewage systems, quarantine those stricken with infectious diseases, and promote early inoculation against those diseases for which vaccines existed. On the other hand, the government had relatively little to do with the improvement in diet, which appears to have resulted primarily from factors beyond the direct influence of government policy, such as advances in agricultural productivity.[49] Improvements in diet after 1800 played a larger role in the alleviation of hunger and high mortality in Europe than in the United States.

The Gini Ratio

As already noted, in both Britain and the United States, the income distribution has become much more equal. The Gini ratios of both countries dropped by about a third between the 1870s and the 1970s.[50] Only a small part of this large decline in inequality was due to government fiscal programs that directly transferred income from the rich to the poor.

The factor accounting for most of the reduction that has so far been achieved in the inequality of the income distribution is the decline in the relative importance of land and physical capital, and the increasing importance of human capital (labor skills), in the process of production. The share of national income going to owners of land and capital has declined to less than half of what it was in the mid- or late nineteenth century, while the labor share has nearly doubled. Since labor income is much more equally distributed than the income from land and physical capital, these shifting shares explain about three-quarters of the equalization in pretax incomes that occurred during the twentieth century.[51]

The substitution of human for physical capital in the production process resulted from changes in technology and in the composition of consumer purchases. Agriculture was and is the sector of the economy that makes the greatest use of land and physical capital. Great advances in productivity combined with limited increases in demand have reduced agriculture from the largest sector of the economy to one that accounts for barely 2 percent of the gross national product. On the other hand, the service sector, which depends far more on labor than on land or physical capital, has increased its share in the national product from 10 percent to over 60 percent. So changes in technology and in demand rather than an egalitarian government policy explain why human capital has become more important than physical capital in the production process.

One should not leap from this last point to the conclusion that the egalitarian state played a minor role in the equalization of pretax incomes. Quite the contrary, the state did much to equalize incomes through the subsidization of education. By making primary and secondary education compulsory and free, the state endowed poor and middle-class children with large amounts of highly valuable human capital. This endowment of the relatively poor was further extended by the establishment of free state and city universities and by the GI Bill (1944), which enabled more than 8 million veterans of World War II to obtain vocational and college educations. After World War II, private universities also enhanced the endowment of lower- and middle-class children by greatly expanding scholarship programs. Although some of the expansion of higher education was supported by private philanthropy rather than by federal, state, or local taxes, private philanthropy was encouraged by the tax laws. Tax exemptions for contributions to educational institutions were another way of transforming the income produced by the land and physical capital of the rich into the human capital accumulated by children from the middle and lower classes. Because of school segregation and similar barriers to entry into apprenticeship programs, blacks, Hispanics, and other minorities were largely barred from these opportunities, creating a gap, described more fully below, that has been only partially closed in recent years.

Homelessness

The relatively generous poverty program developed in Britain during the last half of the eighteenth century, which nearly doubled the income of the ultrapoor, and the bitter attacks on that program by Malthus and others have given the impression that government transfers played a major role in the secular decline in beggary and homelessness.[52] Nothing could be further from the truth. Despite the relative generosity of English poor relief between 1750 and 1834, beggary and homelessness fluctuated in the range of 10–20 percent. Despite the substantial reduction in the proportion of national income transferred to the poor as a result of the harsh poor law reform of 1834, homelessness declined sharply during the late nineteenth century and the early twentieth.

The fact is that government transfers were incapable of solving the problem of beggary and homelessness during the eighteenth century and much of the nineteenth because the root cause of the problem was chronic malnutrition. Even during the most generous phases of the relief program, the bottom fifth of the English population was so severely malnourished that it lacked the energy to perform adequate levels of work. The typical adult male in the bottom 3 percent of the British income distribution lacked the energy for regular work altogether. The next 10 percent had the energy for a little strolling each day, enough for a career in beggary, but not much more. Such people were severely stunted and had low BMIs, making them highly susceptible to disease.

At the end of the eighteenth century, British agriculture was simply not productive enough to provide more than 80 percent of the potential labor force with enough calories to sustain regular manual labor. On average, England produced only about 2,060 calories per capita, which is about 8 percent less than consumption in India today. It was the huge increases in English productivity during the later part of the nineteenth century and the early twentieth that made it possible to feed even the poor at relatively high calorie levels. Begging and homelessness were reduced to exceedingly low levels only when the calorie consumption of the bottom fifth of the population was sufficient to permit regular work. The principal way in which government policy contributed to that achievement was through its public health programs. By reducing exposure to disease, more of the calories that the poor ingested were made available for work.

It thus appears that government action aimed at improving living conditions produced mixed results. Famines were precipitated by bad policies and later eradicated by more felicitous policies. Homelessness was reduced to low levels by the growth of agricultural productivity, which was outside the domain of government policy. The decline in inequality during the Third Great Awakening was due mainly to technological change beyond the scope of government, but the subsidization of secondary and higher education contributed to the more equal distribution of labor skills. Public health programs, which successfully counteracted some of the worst aspects of overcrowding in large cities, were generally quite successful.

MAKING ECONOMIC SENSE OF THE DISCREPANCIES BETWEEN ECONOMIC AND BIOMEDICAL MEASURES OF INEQUALITY

As already noted, traditional economic measures of the standard of living, such as per capita income and indices of real wages, sometimes conflict with biomedical measures such as stature, BMI, and life expectancy. What are we to make of a situation in which real wages were rising, as apparently occurred in England during the last three quarters of the nineteenth century, while heights and BMIs of the working class remained at relatively low levels, showing little increase over half a century?[53] How should we characterize conditions of workers in the United States between 1820 and 1860 if real wages were generally constant or rising, sometimes quite rapidly, but heights and life expectancy were decreasing?[54] During an era in which from 50 to 75 percent of workers' income was spent on food, is it plausible that workers' overall standard of living was improving even as their nutritional status and life expectancies were declining? Although these questions are not yet resolved, they are now being vigorously investigated.[55] It may be fruitful to consider some of the new issues about the course of the standard of living and their implications for the measurement of inequality that are suggested by the anthropometric and demographic data.

If cholera and other diseases that afflicted the United States during the nineteenth century were acts of God, unrelated to the functioning of the economic system, they would pose no special problem for the resolution of the controversy over whether the standard of living (the consumption level of food, clothing, and shelter) for urban workers increased or decreased during the Industrial Revolution. However, economic growth, the spread of disease, and the concomitant increase in morbidity and mortality rates were intricately intertwined. Not only was internal migration responsible for as much as 50 percent of the increase in measured per capita income during the antebellum era, but it was also a principal factor in the spread of cholera, typhoid, typhus, malaria, dysentery, and other major killer diseases of the era.[56] Increasing population density, another concomitant of economic growth, also increased the prevalence of various diseases, raising the level of malaria, enteric diseases, and diseases of the respiratory system.

The increase in mortality between 1790 and 1860, therefore, indicates that, even if wage rates in localities characterized by a high incidence of disease fully reflected the "bribe" (the extra wage compensation) that workers demanded for the increased risks involved in living in these areas, a downward adjustment in real wages is necessary since national income accounting procedures treat the bribe as an increase in national income when it is merely a cost of production. Different ways of correcting estimates of the unmeasured cost of mortality, and of adjusting the national income accounts accordingly, have been developed by economic theorists. Their research indicates that much of what appears to have been a rise in real wages between 1790 and 1860 is spurious and that the apparent growth in average real wages over these years should be reduced by at least 40 percent.[57]

So far, I have stressed that measures of per capita income exaggerate economic growth because they fail to remove costs of production from the measure of real income. This point is akin to Kuznets's correction of national income for wages paid to police because crime is not a benefit but a cost of urban production.[58] (In national income accounting, wages paid to government employees are counted as a benefit to society when in fact they are a cost of living in urban areas, where crime rates are higher.) However, even when average real wages are appropriately adjusted, the bearing of this line of argument on the measurement of trends in inequality during the nineteenth century is obscure because we lack the detail needed to correct the variations of income among wage earners as well as between wage income and other types of income. The veil is lifted somewhat, however, if we switch from the conventional economic measures of inequality to the biomedical measures. Data on life expectancy in Great Britain reveal that, although the life expectancy of the lower classes remained constant or actually declined in some localities, during much of the nineteenth century the life expectancy of the upper classes rose quite sharply. From the beginning of the Industrial Revolution to the end of the nineteenth century, the gap in life expectancy between the upper and the lower classes increased by about ten years. Similarly, the gap in stature (height) between members of the upper and members of the lower classes appears to have increased between the end of the Napoleonic Wars and the beginning of the twentieth century.[59]

In other words, the biomedical data suggest that the disparity between the upper and the lower classes increased during much, if not most, of the nineteenth century. This is a different finding than that obtained from calculations based on income distributions, which suggest that, during most of the nineteenth century, the inequality of the English income distribution remained constant.[60] Such discrepancies between traditional economic measures and biomedical measures suggest that, for the nineteenth century, the biomedical measures are more laden with economic information than are the traditional economic measures, at least insofar as assessing secular trends in inequality is concerned.[61]

A preference for biomedical measures over conventional economic measures of inequality seems even more warranted when dealing with the issues of the twentieth century. In both the British and the American cases, life expectancy increased dramatically between 1890 and 1930—by about fourteen years in Britain (a 31 percent increase) and by about sixteen years in the United States (a 36 percent increase).[62] Over the same period, as figure 4.1 shows, stature increased in the United States by about 6 centimeters. However, in both the British and the American cases, measures such as the share of income held by the top 5 or 10 percent of the income distribution show that inequality was relatively constant over this period or that it might have increased slightly.[63] The experience of the depression years is even more paradoxical. In the United States, the annual unemployment rate between 1931 and 1939 varied but was never less than 16 percent; for half that period, unemployment ranged between 20 and 25 percent. Yet, between 1929 and 1939, life expectancy increased by four years, and the heights of men reaching maturity increased by 1.6 centimeters.[64]

The resolution of the paradox turns on the huge social investments made between 1870 and the end of World War I, the payoffs of which were not counted as part of national income during the 1920s and 1930s even though they produced a large stream of benefits during these decades. I refer, of course, to the huge social investment in biomedical technology, whose largest payoffs came well after the investment was made. Included in this category are not only direct federal investment in biomedical research, which remained modest before 1950, but also the expansion of clinical medicine practiced in a vastly expanded network of hospitals established on scientific principles and the quadrupling of higher education in medicine. These developments not only contributed to public health but also laid the basis for the cumulative increase in the quality of that education and the international expansion of the stock of knowledge about the biology, chemistry, and epidemiology of disease. Perhaps the social investments that contributed most to unmeasured income were the construction of facilities to improve the supply of water, the cleaning up of the milk supply, the development of effective systems of quarantine, and the cleaning up of the slums.

The point is not merely that these benefits are often excluded entirely from national income accounts, and from the measures of real wages, or are greatly undervalued when some aspects are included, but that these benefits accrued disproportionately to those with modest incomes. That those who occupy the lower rungs of society have gained more from certain forms of unmeasured income is revealed by the biomedical measures because they show by how much the gap in life expectancy, in stature, and in BMI that once existed between the upper and the lower classes has been reduced.

The discussion of omitted variables (unmeasured additions or subtractions from measured income) so far indicates that much less progress was made by the lower classes during the nineteenth century than is shown by conventional measures and that, as some have argued, the relative condition of the working class may have deteriorated during major parts of the century. The implication for the twentieth century is the reverse: omitted variables lead to an underestimate of the absolute and relative gains of the lower classes. Would these conclusions still hold if another omitted variable, leisure, were brought into consideration?

Although there were some gains in leisure for the lower class in the United States and Britain during the nineteenth century, they do not appear to have occurred until well past the middle of the century. Of the roughly twenty-five-hour reduction in the workweek between 1860 and 1990, not more than five or six hours were eliminated before 1890, as will be shown in chapter 5 below. Moreover, the scope of leisure-time activities was narrow, limited primarily to carousing in bars and attending church. Although there were antecedents during the nineteenth century, spectator and participatory sports were limited by the long workday, and public libraries, movies, radio, television, and the like are mainly products of the twentieth century.[65]

Kuznets, the leading designer of the U.S. national income accounts, which estimate the annual value of the national product, recognized the large underestimate of economic growth occasioned by the omission of leisure (which took such forms as home improvement, sports, and home-produced entertainment) from these accounts. Valuing the increased daily hours of leisure of workers at the average wage, he pointed out, would raise per capita income in the late 1940s by about 40 percent. Today, the figure is closer to 120 percent. If such a computation were undertaken for each of the deciles of the income distribution, it would be apparent that those in the top decile experienced less of a gain in leisure since the highly paid professionals and businesspeople who populate the top decile work closer to the nineteenth-century standard of thirty-one hundred hours per year than to the current middle-income standard of about eighteen hundred hours. The variety and quality of leisure-time activities have also improved less for the upper than for the lower classes. The upper classes still have a proclivity for those expensive amusements that are most fully measured—opera, concerts, drama, literature. That proclivity, combined with their longer workweek, means that they spend less of their time engaged in those forms of leisure activity, such as watching television, videotapes, and spectator sports and listening to recorded music, for which the unmeasured gains have been greatest.[66]

IS CONFLICT BETWEEN ECONOMIC GROWTH AND FAIRNESS UNAVOIDABLE?

If government action aimed at reducing inequality inevitably led to a reduction in the total output of a nation or to a decline in the rate of increase in total output, the desirability of such action would be open to question. It is often argued that income transfers from households at the top of the income distribution to those at the bottom are self-defeating because they undermine the drive and initiative of the most skillful workers, adversely affect the structure of labor skills, and reduce the rate of technological advancement. Suppose, for example, that income transfers via fiscal policy legislated by Congress that were sufficient to reduce the Gini ratio from 0.40 to 0.35 also caused the economy to stagnate. (Recall that the Gini ratio measures inequality of income distribution and varies between zero [perfect equality] and one [perfect inequality].) It is possible to show mathematically that more than a third of all households would be worse off one year after the legislation took effect and that more than two-thirds would be worse off after five years. After ten years, even those households that had benefited the most from the initial redistribution, the bottom tenth of the income distribution, would be worse off under the egalitarian fiscal policy than under the progrowth policy.[67]

There are three difficulties with this argument. First, its central assumption, that even modest reductions in income concentration are bound to have a large negative effect on economic growth, is not supported by the available evidence. An examination of the relation between the Gini ratios and the growth rates of eighteen prosperous countries between 1965 and 1987 shows that countries that have the nine lowest Gini ratios grew slightly more rapidly on average than those that have the nine highest Gini ratios. Moreover, as I have previously emphasized, growth rates of the currently rich nations have been higher during the twentieth century than during the nineteenth, yet it is the twentieth century that has witnessed the greater reduction in inequality.[68]

Arguments that assert the existence of a conflict between egalitarianism and economic growth are generally theoretical, but they do not rest on a well-worked-out theory of the optimal income distribution. The basis for the speculations is much more primitive: it is merely the proposition that income differentials are necessary to encourage individuals to engage in risky or undesirable occupations or in occupations that require long and arduous training. For example, it takes an average of twelve years of training beyond high school to become a board-certified surgeon. Not only is the out-of-pocket cost of such training quite high, but the income that is forgone during this long training period is large.[69] Obviously, few individuals would undertake such arduous and expensive training if, on certification, they could earn no more on average than an ordinary laborer.

Reasonable as that argument might appear, it does not tell us just how much larger the income of surgeons should be than that of ordinary laborers. Recently, the average pretax income of surgeons from professional activities has been about ten times larger than that of ordinary laborers. However, surgeons typically work about 1.5 times as many hours as ordinary laborers.[70] On an hourly basis, surgeons on average receive about 6.4 times the compensation of ordinary laborers.[71] Is that differential too large? Could we reduce the average hourly differential from 6.4 to 5 without impairing the quality of the service that surgeons provide? Would the quality of surgeons' work increase significantly if their hourly compensa-

tion were raised to eight times that of ordinary laborers? There is no generally accepted theory of optimal compensation differentials for surgeons (as
compared with ordinary labor) or for any other highly skilled professionals
that can be used to answer such questions.

In the light of the empirical evidence, and in the absence of a sound
theoretical case to the contrary, a further reduction in the Gini ratio from
the neighborhood of 0.4 to the neighborhood of 0.3 seems possible without seriously impairing growth rates. However, how best to pursue such a
reduction is a complicated issue. Misguided policies may actually exacer-
bate inequality, as happened during the late 1970s and 1980s, when, under-
estimating the increase in the demand for college-trained personnel, policy
makers cut back on programs supporting entry into college and graduate
programs. As a result, the rate of growth of the salaries of highly trained
persons has considerably exceeded the rate of growth of per capita income,
a development that contributed to the increase in the Gini ratio (i.e., income inequality) in recent years.[72] Nor should egalitarian policies punish
diligence or excellence by unduly taxing those whose income is high because they work harder or are more skilled. Even in occupations such as
surgery, which attracts some of the most diligent and talented persons in
the nation, there are significant variations in hours worked and in skill. As
a result, those in the top tenth of the distribution of surgeons' income earn
six times as much as those in the bottom tenth.[73]

THE SUCCESSES, AND A FAILURE, OF SOCIAL REFORM

The Social Gospelers were convinced that the imminent achievement of
God's kingdom on earth was possible, and they designed a program of
economic and social reform to bring about that end. Now, a century later, few would claim that God's kingdom has arrived, but much has been
accomplished. How does the balance sheet on the main egalitarian accomplishments and failures during the era of the Third Great Awakening
add up?

Gains in Life Expectancy

Of the numerous egalitarian successes during the twentieth century, the
most impressive by far is the gain in life expectancy, which has increased
twenty-nine years since 1900 for the American population as a whole. In
1900, only half a birth cohort was still alive at age forty. Today, 95 percent

of a birth cohort is alive at age forty, and it is not until age seventy-nine that only half are left.

When the figures are broken down by racial category, it turns out that, since 1900, life expectancy has increased by thirty-eight years for blacks and by thirty-three years for whites. Although there is still a six-year gap in life expectancy between blacks and whites, half the gap that existed in 1900 has been eliminated. The greatest reduction in mortality has been among infants and children under five years of age. Mortality rates at these ages have declined by about 95 percent since 1900.[74]

Great gains have also occurred in the cities, especially in the urban slums. Indeed, many working-class districts, once reservoirs of diseases, are now healthier than rural areas, although both have gained immensely in overall health. Comparing the sexes, the gain in life expectancy has been about five years more for women than for men. In recent years, however, the gap in longevity between men and women has begun to narrow. The increase in life expectancy of women has slowed as the cohort of women that smokes heavily moves into the older ages.

As pointed out earlier in this chapter, much of the increase in life expectancy has to do with improvements in technology. However, the reform movements had a significant effect on the speed with which opportunities created by technological change were realized and on the breadth of the distribution of the benefits. Cases in point are the pure-water movement, the improvement in sewage systems, and the provision of vaccines to all children regardless of income. The massive public investment in medical education and hospitals had slower but, in some ways, more far-reaching effects.

Improvements in Health

The gains in health are as impressive as the reduction in mortality rates. Consider the case of tuberculosis, which, during the nineteenth century, accounted for between one-quarter and one-sixth of all deaths in the United States, Britain, and other countries. Today, tuberculosis has been nearly wiped out everywhere in the developed world. Despite a recent upsurge in AIDS-related and other types of tuberculosis, the disease remains at very low levels compared to health conditions in the United States a century ago or conditions prevailing in the Third World today. Rheumatic heart disease, which killed nearly as many people as tuberculosis a century ago, has also been nearly wiped out. As with tuberculosis, rheumatic heart disease was more prevalent among working-class families in the crowded tenement districts of cities than among the well-to-do. Still other one-time infectious scourges now have either been completely vanquished, as in the case of smallpox globally or poliomyelitis in the Western Hemisphere, or become in the developed nations relatively innocuous childhood diseases, as in the case of scarlet fever, measles, whooping cough, and chicken pox. Social reform contributed to the speed of technological change in health sciences and delivery systems by subsidizing medical and pharmacological research and by subsidizing medical education.

The Gains of Labor

Virtually all the labor reforms sought by the Social Gospel movement have been achieved. Child labor in manufacturing has been eliminated. The real annual earnings of industrial workers have risen by nine times between 1890 and 1996 (when fringe benefits but not earnings accumulating in pension funds are included), while hours worked per year have declined dramatically.[75] The dream of a ten-hour day and a sixty-hour week was superseded by the dream of an eight-hour day and a five-day week. That dream—and more—has also been achieved.

Women's wages have, on average, risen 50 percent more rapidly than those of men over the past nine decades. Much of this gain was because women moved from low-paying service and manufacturing jobs into the white-collar ranks. Also significant was the increase in the job experience of the average female worker. The gains have been most rapid among highly educated workers (those with four or more years of college). However, there is still a 15–20 percent gap in compensation between the sexes. Moreover, in order to achieve parity, many professional women have had to choose between marriage and career.[76]

From 1940 through 1980, the wages of black males relative to white males nearly doubled, rising from a ratio of 43 percent to a ratio of 73 percent. Part of the reduction in black/white earnings differentials resulted from the migration of blacks from the South to the North; part resulted from a compression in the wage structure that lifted persons at the low end of the wage distribution (where many blacks were concentrated) relative to those at the high end. However, the main factor in the convergence between black and white earnings over the past five decades has been the rise in the length and quality of education available to blacks, although, after 1964, affirmative action also appears to have played a role. Once again, the greatest gains were at the highest levels of education. By the end of the 1970s, young college-educated black males were earning over 90 percent of the wages of their white counterparts. During the 1980s, however, the progress toward equalization in wage rates came to a halt and in some cases actually reversed as a result of unfavorable labor market conditions in such regions as the "Rust Belt," related to the relative decline in the demand for consumer durables.[77]

The goals of the Social Gospelers with respect to the rights of trade unions have also been realized. As indicated in chapter 3 above, the legislation and practices of the New Deal established the right of labor to bargain collectively and to strike in order to enforce its demands. Unions were also effective in raising compensation by an estimated 15 percent for unionized workers as compared with nonunionized workers. Despite these legal victories, unions in the private sector of the economy have declined sharply since the early 1970s, partly because of the relative decline of businesses in which unions were once concentrated. For a time, the overall size of the trade union movement remained relatively constant owing to the growth of unions in the public sector. By 1990, however, overall unionization had dropped to about 13 percent of nonagricultural employment, just about the level that existed on the eve of World War I.[78]

Gains in Education

All the gains so far discussed are closely related to the spread and intensification of education. It is ironic that the campaigns of the evangelical churches to inculcate children in their religious doctrines should have been far more successful in promoting economic growth and technological change (as the content of education became secular) than they were in ensuring the predominance of one set of religious ideals over all others. Not all the original objectives were self-defeating. In many ways, the secularization of education represented victories for the reformers of both the Second and the Third Great Awakenings because many ideas that stemmed from religious doctrine were converted into the democratic foundations of the secular American state. The campaign to make elementary education universal was nearly won before the beginning of the Third Great Awakening. By 1890, about 86 percent of children between the ages of five and fourteen were already enrolled in elementary schools. The principal contribution of the Third Great Awakening was to spread elementary education in the South, where participation rates in the 1890s were only about two-thirds of the national level for whites and about 40 percent of the national level for blacks. By 1950, despite segregation, Southern blacks drew abreast of Southern whites, and the South as a whole was at virtual parity in numbers, if not quality, with national figures for participation in elementary schools. Currently, about 98 percent of the school-age children nationwide are enrolled in elementary schools.[79]

The greatest advances in education during the third religious-political cycle were at the high school and college levels. Between 1890 and 1950, high school graduates as a proportion of seventeen-year-olds rose from under 4 percent to nearly 50 percent. The change in high school education during these years was in more than numbers. There was a major shift in the content of education. Prior to 1900, schools were almost exclusively preparatory academies for colleges, and their curricula focused on Latin, Greek, and the classics. Between 1900 and 1940, the curricula of high schools shifted, not only to an emphasis on English and mathematics, but also to accounting, typing, mechanical drawing, and other skills increasingly demanded by businesses. This was particularly true with respect to white-collar jobs, which, shortly after the turn of the twentieth century, began to require a high school diploma, or at least several years of high school.

Such requirements were introduced more slowly in blue-collar jobs. But, between 1909 and 1940, many industries, especially those in what would have been considered the more high-tech categories, began relying primarily on high school graduates even for blue-collar jobs.[80]

The growth of high school education had a significant effect on the changing role of women in the labor force. Prior to the twentieth century, women found employment primarily in domestic work and manufacturing. During the first four decades of the twentieth century, however, women found more and more jobs in offices and in retail sales as secretaries and clerks. This shift was closely correlated with the sharp increase in female attendance in high school, beginning with women born between 1900 and 1920. As the century wore on, married women became an increasing proportion of the female labor force and, as with single women, were primarily employed in white-collar occupations.[81]

The effect of social reforms and technological change on egalitarian opportunities was also striking at the college level. Among persons born during the first decade of the twentieth century, only about 9 percent graduated from college; about 30 percent of those born in the 1950s graduated from college. Nearly all this increase took place after World War II and was closely related to the vast expansion of higher education made possible by the GI Bill of Rights, the bundle of educational benefits provided to veterans of World War II and later extended to veterans of the Korean War. Because it was predominately males who were eligible for these sub-

sidies, the proportion of males graduating from colleges increased more
rapidly than that of females. By the 1970s, however, this gender gap was
virtually eliminated. Although gender parity in higher education made it
possible for women to gain parity in many professions, they paid a much
heavier price than men for their careers. Nearly 50 percent of women
graduating from college in the late 1960s and early 1970s were childless
in their forties. Those women who chose to have children paid a substantial price in career attainment in professional and executive occupations.
Among college-educated women in their mid- to late forties today, only
about one-sixth have been able to achieve "the elusive goal of 'family' and
career."[82]

Changes in the Condition of the Poor

The improvement of the condition of the poorest 20 percent of households
is one of the most notable accomplishments of the third religious-political
cycle. The real income (money income adjusted for inflation) of these
households increased nineteenfold between 1890 and 1990, several times
more than the gain in the balance of the households, the upper four-fifths.
The poor of the 1990s are relatively rich by 1890 standards because, a century ago, only households in the top 10 percent of the income distribution
had real incomes that exceeded our current poverty line.

Not only has the poverty line been regularly redefined upward, rising
at a remarkable rate, but the share of family households falling below each
new poverty line has decreased steadily. In 1890, about 30 percent of such
households fell below the poverty line as it was then defined. By 1954, only
20 percent fell below the poverty line of that year. Today, hardly 15 percent
of households fall below the poverty line.

The stabilization of the economy with respect to seasonal and cyclic
fluctuations contributed to the alleviation of poverty. During the nineteenth century and the early twentieth, incomes fluctuated sharply with
the seasons, especially in the North, because many workers were laid off
between mid-November and the beginning of April. Among the hard-hit
industries were construction, inland and coastal navigation, milling, grain
and produce distribution, and manufacturing industries that employed
waterpower. Some manufacturing industries that were sheltered from the
elements also operated at relatively low rates because the seasonally low
incomes reduced the demand for their products. Much of the subsequent
reduction in seasonal unemployment resulted from changes in technology.

The provision of unemployment insurance may also have improved the income positions of seasonal workers during slack months.

Reduction in the volatility of business cycles also alleviated poverty. Recent statistical analyses of unemployment data indicate that, during the late nineteenth century, the odds that a manufacturing worker would become unemployed over a four-year period (about the length of a typical business cycle) were seven times greater than in recent decades. Business cycles have moderated significantly since World War II. Recessions have become shorter and milder, while the period of recovery has become longer and more vigorous. Whether these gains are due to greater success in the government's management of monetary and fiscal policy is still a matter of debate. There is more agreement that the shift from fiscal to monetary policy (from expenditures by Congress to control of the money supply by the Federal Reserve Bank) as the principal means of managing the business cycle has been salutatory and that the Federal Reserve Bank has become more adept in making use of the tools at its disposal. The changing structure of the economy has also served to moderate business cycles. Since output and employment are more volatile in manufacturing than in services, the sharp reduction in the manufacturing share of the labor force and the large increase in the share of the labor force employed by the government have contributed to stability.[83]

Whatever merit there may be to criticisms of government poverty programs, those programs have made a difference to households at the low end of the income distribution. In 1990, about $22,000 was taken through taxation, on average, from each of the households in the top fifth of the income distribution, and about 40 percent of that amount ($8,800) was paid, on average, to each of the households in the bottom fifth of the income distribution, raising low incomes almost fourfold. Most of the transfer took the form of social security, Medicaid, and Medicare, but unemployment insurance, food stamps, and other state and federal welfare payments accounted for about 15 percent of transfers.[84]

The Failure to Promote Moral Behavior

Despite the enormous gains in life expectancy, health, education, and real income and the nineteenfold increase in the real income of the poor, the Social Gospelers' effort to reform human nature, to crush evil, and to create God's kingdom on earth through income redistribution has failed. The failure was already obvious in the late 1920s and early 1930s when one of the leaders of neo-orthodox theology, H. Richard Niebuhr, harshly criticized liberal theory: "A God without wrath," he said, "brought men without sin into a kingdom without judgment through the ministrations of Christ without a Cross."[85]

The theory projected by the Social Gospelers, and embraced by modernism generally, held that cultural crises could be resolved by raising incomes. That theory has been given a long trial and has turned out to be incorrect. Despite the sharp rise in incomes, especially at the low end of the income distribution, the moral crisis of the cities remains unresolved. Although income transfers have gone far beyond the mild redistributions advocated by Bascom, Ely, and Commons, such problems as drug addiction, alcoholism, births to unmarried teenage girls, rape, the battery of women and children, broken families, violent teenage death, and crime are generally more severe today than they were a century ago.[86]

Oddly, the sharpest increases in indicators of moral decay came after, not before, the "war against poverty" of the 1960s and 1970s. The rate of what the Census Bureau called *illegitimate births* until the mid-1970s but now calls *births to single women* (never married) had been below 5 percent for most of American history. However, this rate rose to nearly 30 percent between the election of President John F. Kennedy and today. There was a similar jump in overall crime rates and in alcohol consumption between 1960 and 1980, after which there was a slight downturn. Over the same period, the proportion of children living in one-parent households more than doubled. According to recent polls, the increasingly determined search of the young, and not so young, for sexual gratification and sensual titillation generally has led many adolescents to shun the restraints counseled by the Social Gospelers. Entertainment and the media, supported by the huge advertising budgets of beer and liquor, tobacco, gambling, and other industries (including state and local governments) that thrive on promoting casual sex, heavy drinking, smoking, and lotteries, not only drowned out the message of restraint and fidelity preached by the ministry, but caused some religious leaders to embrace the counterculture as the inevitable trend of modern society. As a result, the coalitions of the first half of the twentieth century that had succeeded in promoting antivice legislation at local, state, and federal levels divided, and laws prohibiting alcoholic drinks, pornography, gambling (now called *gaming*), adultery, and other vicious habits were either repealed or attenuated. To many liberals, moral vices became illnesses (addictions) better treated by secular therapists than by legal prohibition or moral suasion.

The theory that society is the source of sin has undermined personal responsibility for bad behavior, and such words as *vicious habits, vices,* and *moral deviance* have dropped out of favor. Although Gladden, Ely, Raushenbusch, and other Social Gospelers called on the poor to embrace such virtues as sobriety, modesty, thrift, and industry and to shun preoccupation with pagan pleasures, many of their successors reject such puritanical ethics and defend the counterculture.[87] Liberal equivocation on the older virtues has created the vacuum into which the leaders of the Fourth Great Awakening have rushed. Cultural reform, they argue, must be pursued primarily at the individual level, with an empathy and warmth better achieved by churches and organizations such as Alcoholics Anonymous than by government bureaucracies.

THREE LESSONS ON GOVERNMENT AS AN AGENCY OF EGALITARIAN REFORM

What lessons are there to be learned from the successes of the Social Gospel movement in turning the government into an agency for implementing its program of egalitarian reform? I would single out three.

First, evangelical congregations have been very effective instruments for detecting the negative effects of new technologies and changes in economic structure on the lives of their parishioners and for advancing programs of reform. These congregations might be called America's original focus groups, in that they not only provided a forum in which the discontented could speak out but also promoted the early detection of emerging economic and social crises that required the attention of church leaders. Such interactions also made it possible for church leaders, both lay and clerical, to review the adequacy of the prevailing social policies, public appeals, and aspects of the prevailing theology, especially ethics. Such interactions also made it possible for leaders to formulate programmatic demands and develop strategies that could mobilize home and far-flung congregations. It was this process of early program formulation and the preexisting network of organizations with passionate members and earnest leaders that made the evangelical churches the leading edge of populist reform movements. Movements started anywhere, such as the campaign against segregated buses in Montgomery, Alabama, could be turned into united fronts by creating single-issue organizations and by making use of denominational and interdenominational publications, standing and ad hoc committees, and the resources of college and university campuses to rally support for their demands. Sympathetic souls in the emerging mass media could also be rallied to support the causes.

The second lesson arising from the Social Gospel movement is that it is difficult to change the existing policies of local, state, and federal legislatures, which are often torn by the demands of diverse constituencies. Moreover, when new policies are installed at the federal level, they are often poor reflections of the reforms demanded by populists, inadequately funded, halfheartedly enforced, and frequently resisted by other agencies and levels of government. As a consequence, it may take decades for an effective program to be implemented. But, because of the extraordinary rate of technological change, the structure of the economy may have changed so much in the interval that the targeted reforms may no longer be relevant.

Consider the case of campaigns for the control of railroads. Three decades elapsed between the consolidation of railroads into trunk lines with rate structures that outraged farmers and merchants and the passage of the Interstate Commerce Commission (ICC) Act in 1887. Yet, like the flurry of state legislation a decade earlier, this effort to regulate railroad rates proved to be ineffective. Resistance by railroads and adverse court decisions limited ICC jurisdiction and permitted the railroads to capture the regulatory process and use it to curtail competition among railroads serving the same territories. In the interim, technological change gave rise to the automotive industry and later to commercial aviation. Competition from motor vehicles and airlines put heavy downward pressure on the passenger and freight rates of railroads. After 1916, railroad transportation began a long era of decline. From 1920 on, federal legislation and regulation were focused, not on how to curtail railroad profits, but on how to shore them up with subsidies and on other ways to sustain railroad services.

Finally, there is a tendency for new and old waves of egalitarian reformers to misunderstand each other's concerns. Disciples of the Second Great Awakening were slow in recognizing that, by itself, their reform program was no longer adequate in a world of confrontations between powerful big businesses and alienated workers who could no longer count on the demand for labor outstripping the supply. They were also slow in recognizing the far-ranging changes in the structure of the economy that were exacerbating the insecurities of labor. As a consequence, the split between the disciples of the Second and Third Awakenings became a major obstacle to the implementation of reforms required by these structural changes. At the same time, disciples of the Third Great Awakening dismissed the relevance of personal responsibility as a key element in the struggle against corruption. Even as they denounced the corruption of the rich, they embraced a theory that corruption among the poor could be solved primarily, if not exclusively, by improving their material conditions. By remaining at loggerheads, these two camps of egalitarians missed opportunities to collaborate on a set of reforms that could have addressed both sides of the problem. A very similar tension exists today. Leaders of the Third and Fourth Great Awakenings often denounce each other and shun collaboration on measures that could advance egalitarian goals.

FIVE

The Emergence of a Postmodern Egalitarian Agenda

At the dawn of the new millennium, two mighty camps of egalitarians are arrayed against each other. Disciples of the Third Great Awakening are determined to uphold the principle of equality of condition and to extend their progressive program of reforms. Disciples of the Fourth Great Awakening are equally determined to reinstate equality of opportunity as the reigning principle. Each camp champions an extensive list of moral and legislative reforms, one a response to modern industrial society, the other addressing new, postmodern concerns.

As important and as relevant as they are, the unrealized economic reforms of the Third Great Awakening cannot be the main elements of an egalitarian program for the era that is now unfolding. To assume that intensification of the struggle for the completion of the old agenda is enough to advance egalitarianism in a world that is changing rapidly and radically is to repeat the error committed by the later reformers of Second Great Awakening. They failed to understand that technological and structural changes in the economy and society had created many new issues that emerged with considerable urgency during the late nineteenth century and became even more urgent as the twentieth century unfolded.

Now, at the dawn of the new millennium, it is necessary to address such postmodern concerns as the struggle for self-realization, the desire to find a deeper meaning in life than the endless accumulation of consumer durables and the pursuit of pleasure, access to the miracles of modern medicine, education not only for careers but for spiritual values, methods of financing an early, fruitful, and long-lasting retirement, and increasing the amount of quality time available for family activities. Unlike the reform agenda of the Third Great Awakening, that of the Fourth emphasizes the spiritual needs of life in a country where even the poor are materially rich by the standards prevailing a century ago and where many of those who are materially rich are spiritually deprived.

Nor can current legislative success be the principal measure of what is needed to continue the advance of egalitarianism in the decades ahead. Three of the principal programmatic demands of the Second Great Awakening (female franchise, prohibition, and universal primary education) were embodied in constitutional amendments or state laws during the period in which the theories and programs of the Third Great Awakening surged to the forefront. Indeed, the reformist zeal promoted by the Social Gospelers reinforced the zeal of the reformers of the Second Great Awakening in bringing about many of the legislative victories of the late nineteenth century and the early twentieth.

The principal shortcoming of the later disciples of the Second Great Awakening was not a lack of compassion or good intent but a failure to understand the limitations of a program shaped to deal with inequality in a largely rural society of farms and small businesses that was relatively homogeneous in terms of religion and ethnicity. Such a program was inadequate to deal with the problems of big businesses, industrial concentration, and extended unemployment in a society that was highly urbanized and increasingly diverse in terms of religion and ethnicity.

The new equity issues in the United States do not arise from the shock of rapid urbanization, the destruction of small businesses by competition from industrial giants, the massive destitution created by the prolonged unemployment of up to one-quarter of prime-aged workers, the disappearance of the frontier as a safety valve for urban unemployment and poverty, or the undernutrition and premature death of the great majority of urban workers and their family members. Quite the contrary, the new issues are to a large extent the product of the *solutions* to these problems, achieved by a combination of economic growth and the successes of the reforms advocated by the Social Gospelers, their allies, and their successors.

The emerging egalitarian crisis arises partly from the fact that people are living much longer than they did in 1900 and that life spans will likely continue to increase for the foreseeable future. The emerging crisis is also related to the changing nature and distribution of work and leisure, changes so drastic that our current vocabulary is inadequate to describe them. The new crisis also has to do with enormous changes in the structure of consumer demand, which are creating overabundance in some areas (such as the excessive consumption of calories and fat) and severe shortages in others (such as health services at all ages). It also has to do with those adolescents and young adults whose education and vision leave them increasingly unable to cope with this new world or to share in its abundance, effectively estranging them from the mainstream of society.

Although the low levels and unequal distribution of food, clothing, shelter, and health care are still the most burning equity issues in the low- and moderate-income countries that constitute the majority of the world's population, a new and urgent set of distributional issues has arisen in the United States and the other very rich nations, where the share of lifetime hours spent in working for a living has become exceptionally small by either historical or Third World standards. In these rich countries, overeating is a more common problem than undereating, and opportunities for self-realization (opportunities to fulfill one's potential) are more unequally distributed than food, consumer durables, or health care.

The problem of self-realization has distinct aspects, and different solutions, for the young and the aged, for ethnic and racial minorities, and for women, yet all fuel the moral crisis that is the hallmark of our age and the greatest threat to the survival of our society. To achieve self-realization, each individual must have an understanding of life's opportunities, a sense of which of these opportunities are most attractive to him or her at each stage of life, and the requisite educational, material, and spiritual resources to pursue these opportunities. In the era that is unfolding, fair access to spiritual resources will be as much a touchstone of egalitarianism as access to material resources was in the past.

Spiritual resources are not limited to those found in the sacred realm but include the whole range of immaterial commodities that are needed to cope with emotional trauma and that, more often than not, are transferred between individuals privately, rather than through the market. Such resources include a sense of purpose, a sense of opportunity, a sense of community, a strong family ethic, a strong work ethic, and high self-esteem. Although the majority of Americans, especially those over forty, find many of these resources in the ethics and creeds of their religion, there are numerous other codes of behavior and theories of life that inspire virtue and lead to success in coping with the challenges and pitfalls of modern life. Various quasi-religious organizations and movements have developed—secular humanism, civil religion, and various secular philosophies—and their nature and content are widely debated by scholars.

Severe inequality in the distribution of spiritual resources results in part from changes in the structure of the economy and of social institutions through which immaterial resources are transferred. Spiritual deprivation is due in part to the glorification of hedonistic impulses and instant gratification by the media and advertising; this has diverted many children and adolescents from the quest for self-realization. Also involved are the improvements in human physiology that have contributed to the rapid growth of the elderly population, without an adequate corresponding growth in social institutions to minister to their spiritual and physiological needs.

The growth of the elderly population has given rise to the problem of intergenerational equity, which now looms as a barrier to the self-realization of both older and younger cohorts and which threatens to become the most divisive issue of the era that is unfolding. Intergenerational equity involves not only the assurance of appropriate standards of living at different stages in the life cycle but also the assurance that one generation will not be made to suffer a disproportionate share of the burden of financing a lifetime of self-realization. Among the most pressing problems are methods of financing more expensive systems of education, higher costs of health maintenance, and much longer periods of retirement than hitherto anticipated. Also pressing is the need to develop arrangements that permit prime-aged workers shorter work weeks and greater flexibility in hours worked during the day, the week, and the year so that they can attend to their own and their family's spiritual needs.

Lifelong learning is another new equity issue. It involves, first of all, greater access to college and technical education, through the bachelor's degree or its equivalent, for adolescents and young adults. Also needed is a higher level of training in technical skills for high school and junior college graduates unable to undertake the bachelor's degree. Lifelong education for adults in midlife should offer opportunities not only to upgrade skills required to earn a living but also to extend knowledge in the arts and humanities, an important part of self-realization and an essential aspect of accumulating spiritual resources. By far the most severe educational inequities, and the most difficult and expensive to solve, are those that afflict the elderly.

In the era that is unfolding, international equity, that is, equity among nations with respect to both condition and opportunity, will become an increasingly critical issue. The most obvious aspect is the contrast between overnutrition in the rich nations and malnutrition among hundreds of millions of children in the poor nations, malnutrition so severe that their lives are as mean and brief as the lives of poor children in Europe during the age of Charles Dickens. Potentially more explosive, however, is the rapid economic growth of countries with a combined population of over 2 billion people, particularly in South and East Asia, whose products are streaming into our markets and causing dislocations among American workers. This process, which will continue for several decades, poses the highly charged issue of how to accommodate such growth in relatively poor countries while protecting the living standards of those American workers who feel under siege.

The emphasis on spiritual matters promoted by the Fourth Great Awakening will influence international relations. The aggressive pursuit of American values may clash with what other peoples see as their individual and national interests, and such clashes could intensify as a result of the unusually high rates of economic growth in the emerging market countries. Of particular concern is the role that China will play in the near future. Its authoritarian tradition, its sense of having suffered under the heel of Western imperialism, and its enormous pride in its own culture and traditions could pit it against American ambitions to extend our democratic and egalitarian values to all corners of the world. Moreover, given China's rate of economic growth, it could become an exceedingly powerful foe within a decade and a half and, in twenty-five to thirty years, the most powerful foe the United States has ever had to confront. If international equity as defined by both the United States and China is not assiduously pursued by both nations, the long-feared Armageddon might be precipitated.

To many disciples of the Third Great Awakening, *spiritual equity* is a red flag that conjures thoughts of reactionary assaults by the religious Right. Like it or not, the reform agenda spelled out by the religious Right, with its focus on the restoration of the traditional family and its emphasis on equality of opportunity, more fully addresses the new issues of egalitarianism than does the agenda of the Third Great Awakening. The upsurge of religiosity associated with the Fourth Great Awakening is inspiring millions who have experienced religious revival to minister to the alienated young and the depressed elderly, to counter the drug, tobacco, and alcohol cultures, and to reinforce the traditional family. Those who are suspicious of the Promise Keepers (an organization of enthusiastic Christian men that focuses on, as their literature put it, "uniting men through vital relationships to become Godly influences in their world") or dislike some planks of the Contract with the Family (the reform agenda of the Christian Coalition) should not throw the baby out with the bathwater but should organize their own movements to reinforce traditional families (families dedicated to procreating and rearing children to maturity), to provide mentors to alienated young people, to provide moral support for single mothers, and to enrich the lives of preschool children.

If properly integrated, the unrealized aspects of the egalitarian agenda of the Third Great Awakening and the new agenda of spiritual reforms will become mutually reinforcing. For women, self-realization requires an end to glass ceilings and the creation of conditions that make careers and families fully compatible. For African Americans, self-realization requires not only an end to overt and covert forms of discrimination but training and the spiritual resources that will enable those who are alienated to compete successfully for mainstream economic opportunities. For all those in poverty, particularly the young, education that provides the technical and spiritual (immaterial) endowments needed for successful competition in the rapidly changing economy is a necessary condition for self-realization.

The divisive disputes over the urgency of supplying material and immaterial needs between the disciples of the Third and those of the Fourth Great Awakenings could become a major obstacle to progress, as occurred a century ago when the two main egalitarian camps of that era, the traditionalists and the modernists, assaulted each other. The problem is not merely one of recognizing the salience of the new spiritual issues (including international equity) and, in some cases, their political precedence. It is also necessary to reformulate some of the older analyses and solutions to take account of changes in the structure of the economy and in the desires of consumers at all levels of the income distribution. Some of these structural changes have been obscured by their complexity. Other changes have been obscured because their effects cross disciplinary lines, and an interdisciplinary perspective is needed to appreciate their magnitude and implications.

THE CHANGE IN THE STRUCTURE OF INDUSTRIAL ORGANIZATION

The new egalitarian agenda has been shaped by changes in the structure of industrial organization that have reversed the trend toward economic concentration, which had as one of its consequences the separation of the workplace and the home. Early in the nineteenth century, practically all those in the labor force worked where they lived. This was certainly true of farmers, who then constituted 80 percent of the labor force. It was also true of most manufacturing workers, weavers, spinners, tailors, cabinetmakers, shoemakers, and most metalworkers, who worked in one room of their house while they and their families lived in the rest.

Technological changes between 1800 and the Civil War led to the building of enterprises employing increasingly large numbers of workers. However, even in 1860, large-scale enterprises were still quite exceptional. Despite the attention given to them in such stories as Margaret Mitchell's *Gone with the Wind,* plantations such as Tara, which employed hundreds of slaves, were few and far between. Hardly 2 percent of all slaves lived on such large plantations. The typical plantation consisted of just three or four slave families.[1] The same was true of the cotton textile industry. The majority of the factory hands in this industry worked in firms employing fewer than a hundred workers.[2]

The rush toward economic concentration began during the last third of the nineteenth century and was promoted by new technologies, which, as we have seen, gave striking competitive advantages to large-scale firms. That process continued for more than half a century and even spread to some parts of the service sector. The opening of the new building of the New York Insurance Company in downtown Manhattan in 1907 was a culture shock. Every morning, five thousand workers left their homes all over New York City and the nearby suburbs and spent their day in a single building that held enough people to be a small-sized city.[3] By the early 1930s, in one industry after another, a handful of firms dominated production. Just four firms produced 80 percent of all steel ingots; two firms produced over 90 percent of all aluminum output; four firms produced 90 percent of all automobiles; one firm, the DuPont Company of Delaware, produced 60 percent of all industrial chemicals; three firms accounted for 70 percent of rubber production; and, even after the breakup of the Standard Oil Company, just six firms produced nearly all refined petroleum.[4]

By the eve of World War II, the problem of industrial concentration had become so severe that the government hired hundreds of economists to study the problem and set up the Temporary National Economic Committee (TNEC) to oversee these investigations and produce recommendations for action. But, before the business of the committee was over, World War II had broken out, and the government relied on the efficiency of big business to make America the "arsenal of democracy." The war effort enhanced the tendency toward economic concentration. Continued domination of the economy by a relatively small number of giant firms seemed to be inevitable for the indefinite future. Despite such laws as the Sherman Antitrust Act and the Clayton Act, despite the unfair practices exposed by the TNEC, economic concentration was deemed likely to increase in peacetime.[5]

Joseph Schumpeter, the leading theorist of technological change and economic growth during the first half of the twentieth century and legendary figure in the Economics Department at Harvard University, dealt with this problem in a highly influential book published during World War II. Carefully analyzing the economies of scale that promoted economic concentration, he found that the benefits of concentration exceeded whatever evils were associated with it. Despite their collusive and monopolistic practices, Schumpeter concluded, economies of scale allowed large firms to produce more cheaply than small, competitive firms. America would have to learn to live with industrial concentration, with the government doing whatever it could to restrain the worst practices of big business.[6]

Such forecasts were off the mark. Economic concentration did not continue to increase after the close of World War II. Quite the contrary, the most rapidly growing sector of the economy in recent decades has been establishments employing fewer than one hundred workers. Part of the explanation for the surge in small businesses is the change in the structure of the economy. There has been a dramatic shift from industry (manufacturing, transportation, utilities, construction, and mining), where economies of scale are marked, to services (trade, finance, insurance, health care, entertainment, and government), where small firms are often the most dynamic. This shift toward services was already under way prior to World War II but received little attention at that time. However, the share of the labor force working in industry declined from 44 percent in 1920, to 28 percent in 1983, to 24 percent in 1994. The Bureau of Labor Statistics forecasts that the industrial share of the labor force will continue to decline during the next decade, reaching 20 percent by 2005—less than its share in 1850. Meanwhile, the share of the labor force in services has increased from 38 percent in 1920 to 66 percent in 1994, and it is expected that the services share will reach over 70 percent during the current decade. Only about a third of the increase in the service sector of the economy is due to the growth of the government.[7] The increase in the services share is due mainly to changes in the structure of consumption and in the use of time.

CHANGES IN THE USE OF TIME AND THE STRUCTURE OF CONSUMPTION

Since technophysio evolution is still ongoing, it is likely that improvements in health, life expectancy, and average income will also continue.

Table 5.1 Secular Trends in Time Use: The Average Hourly Division of the Day
of the Average Male Household Head, Based on a 365-Day Year

	Ca. 1880	Ca. 1995	Ca. 2040
Sleep	8	8	8
Meals and essential hygiene	2	2	2
Chores	2	2	2
Travel to and from work	1	1	.5
Work	8.5	4.7	3.8
Illness	.7	.5	.5
Subtotal	22.2	18.2	16.8
Residual for leisure activities	1.8	5.8	7.2

One concomitant of these changes has been a change in the structure of
consumption. A century ago, the typical household in OECD nations
spent 80 percent of its income on food, clothing, and shelter. Today, these
commodities account for less than a third of consumption. Many people
are alarmed at this and other recent changes in the structure of consumption, particularly the reduced role of manufactured products, which they
fear may presage economic and social decadence and portend a reversal in
national fortunes. A similar state of mind was widespread at the end of
the nineteenth century. But, then, it was the decline of agriculture and the
rise of industry that was the focus of concern. Those who identified the
good life with agriculture feared life in an urban and industrial age. Now
it is life in a service society that promotes anxiety.[8]

Changes in Hours of Work and Uses of Time

Changes in hours of work and in the average division of the day have par-
alleled the changes in the structure of industry. For persons in the labor
force before the Civil War, whether agriculture or industry, the workyear
typically ran fifty-one weeks, the workweek was typically six or six and a
half days, and the workday averaged ten to twelve hours. All in all,
allowing for illness, holidays, and inclement weather, the typical worker in
1880 averaged about thirty-one hundred hours of labor per year. That
amounts to about eleven hours of work per day over a workyear of 290
days or nearly nine hours per day over the 365 days of the calendar year.[9]

Table 5.1 shows the remarkable reduction in the workyear that has occurred for males in the American labor force over the past century.[10] *Sleep*

and *meals and essential hygiene,* which are biologically determined, required about ten hours of the day in 1880, as they do today. The remaining fourteen hours represent "discretionary" time. *Chores* and *work* both involve tasks necessary for earning and maintaining a standard of living. Much of what was once called *chores* is today often called *do-it-yourself* or *sweat equity.* Disagreeableness is not the criterion for including an activity in the category *chores* since then, as now, some chores, such as gardening and cooking, could be pleasurable, as was true of other categories of work. *Chores,* like *work,* denotes economic compulsion, whether that compulsion is administered by a "boss," the invisible hand of the market, or is self-administered in order to ensure the maintenance of standards of living. *Work* denotes the principal activities involved in earning a living (farming, smithing, carpentry, clerking, teaching, etc.), while *chores* denotes work routines of lesser magnitude often uncompensated but necessary for well-being. *Illness* is based on surveys indicating days restricted to home, and *travel to and from work* takes account of such items as a farmer's walk from his house to the fields.

The most notable feature of table 5.1 is the large increase in leisure time available to the typical male worker.[11] His leisure time has tripled over the past century as his workyear declined from about 3,109 hours to about 1,730 hours today.[12] The residual shown for leisure does not allow for changes in the quality of leisure over time. One aspect of the change in quality is the reduction in travel time to and from public events, which could well have consumed as much time as the public events themselves in 1880. In 1995, when time available for leisure activities by the typical household head exceeded the time spent at work, only about a quarter of leisure time is devoted to public events; most leisure time was spent at home in front of the television set. Going to the saloons in 1880 probably involved only a short walk in cities, but the distance was usually substantial in rural areas. For the typical household head in the late nineteenth century, there was little beyond churches and saloons that qualified as regular leisure-time activities. The image of higher forms of leisure that linger in sentimental depictions pertains mainly to the leisure class, the top 10 percent of the income distribution.[13]

Table 5.1 also forecasts the division of the average day in 2040. It shows that, by that date, more than half the discretionary day will be devoted to leisure activities. The forecast is for a reduction of the workyear from the current average of about 1,730 hours to just 1,400 hours, with the average workweek down to 30 hours, paid holidays up to 30, and sick days at 12.

This forecast may underestimate the rate of the continuing decline in work hours since the workyear is already at 1,650 hours in France, 1,600 hours in Germany, and 1,400 in Sweden.[14]

The reduction in the average workday between 1880 and 1995 did not come about as an accident. Shorter hours were one of the most insistent demands of the labor movement since the mid-nineteenth century. As the workday and the workweek grew shorter, economic and social theorists debated the significance of this development. Karl Marx described it as a means of increasing worker exploitation. The reduction in the workday, he argued, was offset by an increase in the intensity of work per hour so large that the total amount of labor extracted from workers was actually increased. Progressive economists such as Richard T. Ely and John R. Commons saw the reduction in the workweek as a means of raising wages since the effect was to reduce the supply of labor. Beyond that, they and other Progressives, and now also the disciples of the Fourth Great Awakening, promoted the reduction in the workweek as a step toward the democratization of leisure and as a necessary measure to permit the intellectual and spiritual elevation of workers.[15]

As it turns out, American workers conformed more to the Progressive view than to the Marxist one. They have often indicated their willingness, through collective-bargaining agreements, to work more intensely in order to raise their wages and shorten their hours of work. As their incomes rose, they used some of the extra money to buy more and better food, clothing, and shelter and other, more luxurious commodities, but the lion's share of the increase in income has been spent on purchasing leisure.[16] Most such purchases are made indirectly by forgoing opportunities to earn additional income needed to buy more food, clothing, shelter, consumer durables, and services.

The pattern among women was similar to that of men. The workday of women in 1880 was somewhat longer, and in some respects may have been more arduous, than that of men. Although we do not have survey data on women before the 1930s, there is considerable evidence that, in households of working farmers, artisans, and manual laborers, wives rose before their husbands and continued working until bedtime. That routine suggests a workday that may have run about 15 minutes longer than that of males, amounting to perhaps 8.75 hours per day, on the basis of a 365-day year, or 3,200 hours annually.[17]

As a result of the mechanization of the household, smaller families per household, and the marketing of prepared foods, the typical nonemployed married woman today spends about 3.4 hours per day engaged in housework; if she is employed, the figure for housework drops to 2.1 hours. However, women in the labor force average about 4.6 hours per day engaged in paid labor. Hence, combining "work" with "chores," men and women work roughly equal amounts per day, and both enjoy much more leisure than they used to. The principal difference is that the gains of women have come exclusively from the reduction in hours of housework while the gains of men have come from the reduction in the hours of paid labor.[18]

I have so far retained the common distinction between work and leisure, although these terms are already inaccurate and may soon be obsolete. The distinction was invented when most people were engaged in manual labor for sixty or seventy hours per week and was intended to contrast with the highly regarded activities of the gentry or their American equivalent, Thorstein Veblen's leisure class. However, it should not be assumed that members of the leisure class were indolent. In their youth, they were students and athletes. In their young adult years, they were warriors. In middle age and beyond, they were judges, ministers of state, parliamentarians, bishops, other high officeholders, landlords, planters, merchant princes, and patrons of the arts. Whatever they did was for the pleasure it gave them since they were so rich that earning money was not their concern.

Hence, *leisure* is not a synonym for *indolence* but a reference to desirable forms of effort or work (*work* is to be understood here in the physiological rather than the economic sense). As George Bernard Shaw put it, "Labor is doing what we must; leisure is doing what we like; rest is doing nothing whilst our bodies and our minds are recovering from their fatigue."[19] To some extent currently, and more so in the future, as the average workweek declines toward twenty-eight hours and retirement routinely begins at age fifty-five, these terms will lose their pejorative connotations. *Work* will increasingly mean activity under the compulsion of earning income regardless of whether the effort is manual or mental. And *leisure* will mean purely voluntary activity, as was characteristic of the English gentry or Veblen's American leisure class, although it may incidentally produce income. In order to avoid confusion, in the balance of this chapter I reserve the word *work* for use in its physiological sense, an activity that requires energy over and above basal metabolic rate (BMR). Activity aimed primarily at earning a living I will call *earnwork*. Purely voluntary activity, even if it incidentally carries some payment with it, I will call *volwork*.

FIVE

Changes in the Structure of Consumption

Why have hours of earnwork declined so much in recent years? Many have argued that it is because of technologically induced unemployment, citing the high unemployment rates (up to 20 percent) in such rich countries as France, Germany, Spain, Sweden, and Switzerland. In some of these countries, employed workers are reported to have reluctantly reduced their hours of employment, their earnwork week, in order to increase the number of jobs available for the unemployed.[20] However, the same decline in earnwork hours has taken place in countries with low levels of unemployment, such as the United States (5 percent unemployment) and Japan (3 percent unemployment). Moreover, hours of earnwork have been declining throughout the rich countries for more than a century. This long-term decline reflects developments much more profound than the public spirit of the employed who selflessly share their jobs with the unemployed or even of much-criticized errors in recent public policy. Although erroneous policies help explain why some current unemployment rates are so high, why some rates of economic growth are relatively low, and why take-home pay is relatively low in some of the rich countries, they do not explain the persistent secular decline in the earnwork day or week.

It is not only daily and weekly hours of earnwork that have declined. The share of lifetime discretionary hours spent in earnwork has declined even more rapidly. Table 5.1 dealt only with the hours of earnwork of persons in the labor force. It did not reflect the fact that the average age at which people enter the labor force is about five years older today than it was in 1880 or that the average period of retirement for those who live to age sixty-five is about fifteen years longer today than it was in 1880. A century ago, 92 percent of American males aged sixty to sixty-four were in the labor force. Now, only about 50 percent of this age group is still in the labor force; the other 50 percent are retired. A century ago, only one of five males aged sixty-five and older was retired. Today, six of seven are retired. Male retirement rates have recently increased in the age group fifty-five to fifty-nine. Once hardly 3 percent, these rates are now up to 15 percent and still increasing rapidly.[21]

All in all, the lifetime discretionary hours spent earning a living have declined by about one-third over the past century (see table 5.2) despite the large increase in the total of lifetime discretionary time.[22] In 1880, four-fifths of discretionary time was spent earning a living. Today, the lion's share (59 percent) is spent doing what we like (volwork). Moreover, it appears probable that, by 2040, over three-quarters of discretionary time will

Table 5.2 Estimated Trend in the Lifetime Distribution of Discretionary Time

	1880	1995	2040
Lifetime discretionary hours	225,900	298,500	321,900
Lifetime earnwork hours	182,100	122,400	75,900
Lifetime volwork hours	43,800	176,100	246,000

be spent doing what we like, despite a further substantial increase in discretionary time owing to the continuing extension of the life span. It is the abundance of leisure time that promotes the search for a deeper understanding of the meaning of life and fuels engagement with the issues of the Fourth Great Awakening.

Why this deep desire for volwork? Why do so many people want to forgo earnwork, which would allow them to buy more food, clothing, housing, and other goods? The answer turns partly on the extraordinary technological changes of the past hundred years or so. Not only have the number of hours of labor that the average individual needs to obtain his or her food supply been greatly reduced, but housing, clothing, and a vast array of consumer durables have become so inexpensive in real terms that the totality of material consumption requires far fewer hours of labor today than was required over a lifetime for food alone in 1880.

Indeed, we have become so rich that we are approaching saturation in the consumption not only of necessities but also of goods that were in the very recent past thought to be luxuries and that were only dreams during the first third of the twentieth century. Today, there is an average of nearly two cars per household in the United States. Even among the impoverished, 70 percent of households have at least one car. In the case of television, there are 0.8 sets per person (2.2 per household). On some items, such as radios, we seem to have reached supersaturation—there is now more than one radio per ear (5.6 per household). Our society is so well saturated with consumer durables, in fact, that even the poorest fifth of households are well endowed with them.[23]

Consequently, the era of the household accumulation of consumer durables, which sparked the growth of many manufacturing industries during the decades following World War II, is largely over in the United States. Most future purchases of consumer durables in the United States will be by those replacing items or establishing new households. In the case of automobiles, for example, over 90 percent of all new sales over the past five years represent the replacement of older vehicles, less than 10 percent additions to the existing stock. In some recent years, the number of

Table 5.3 The Long-Term Trend in the Structure of Expanded Consumption
and the Implied Income Elasticities of Several Consumption Categories

Consumption Class	Distribution of Expanded Consumption (%)		Long-Term Income Elasticities
	1875	1995	
Food	49	5	.2
Clothing	12	2	.3
Shelter	13	6	.7
Health care	1	9	1.6
Education	1	5	1.6
Other	6	7	1.1
Leisure	18	68	1.5

NOTE: Expanded consumption is the sum of conventional expenditures plus the imputed value of leisure time. Health care and education include government and employer expenditures plus out-of-pocket expenditures. Columns may not add to 100 because of rounding.

old cars retired has actually exceeded the number of new cars sold. Although the production of computers and related devices used as consumer durables is growing more rapidly than the population, it is unlikely that the durables sector of the economy will reclaim its former share of the labor force in the foreseeable future on the basis of domestic sales.[24]

The point is not merely that we are reaching saturation in commodities that once defined a high standard of living and quality of life but also that the hours of labor required to obtain those commodities have drastically declined. In 1880, the typical household required 1,405 hours of labor in the marketplace to acquire its annual food supply, not counting the household labor necessary to prepare meals. Today, less than 20 percent of that amount of labor (about 260 hours) in the marketplace will pay for the food consumed by the typical household. Moreover, far fewer hours of household labor are required to prepare the food, not only because of the automation of the kitchen, but because most food is now purchased partially or fully prepared, often in restaurants. Similarly, clothing—more abundant, more colorful, more durable, and easier to care for than in 1880—is obtained with about three-eighths of the labor required a century ago. All in all, the commodities that used to account for over 80 percent of household consumption can now be obtained in greater abundance than previously, with less than a third of either the market or the household labor once required.[25]

Table 5.3 shows how sharply the U.S. distribution of consumption has changed over the past 120 years. Food, clothing, and shelter, which accounted for about 74 percent of consumption (expanded to include the value of leisure time) in 1875, accounted for just 13 percent of expanded consumption in 1995.[26] Leisure, on the other hand, has risen from 18 percent of consumption to 68 percent. The expenditure category *other*, which consists mainly of utilities and services, has risen only slightly as a percentage of consumption, partly because of the great reduction in the cost of these services. As table 5.3 shows, the long-term income elasticities (the percentage of change in consumption caused by a 1 percent change in income) of the demand for food and clothing are below 0.5, and the elasticity of the demand for shelter is closer to but still below 1.0. The implication of elasticities below 1.0 is that the share of these commodities will decline as income rises. On the other hand, the elasticities of demand for leisure (volwork), education, and medical services (both preventative and curative) are over 1.0, which means that their share in national income will rise as income rises. Even if these elasticities decline somewhat during the next forty-five years, it is still likely that the burden of health care and retirement will require a substantially larger share of gross domestic product than has been allowed in most recent forecasts.[27]

More conventional forecasts have been compromised, not only by the failure to take adequate account of the growth in the consumption of leisure, but also by a failure to recognize differences in the time preference for leisure. Leisure can be taken while still in the labor force by varying daily, weekly, and annual hours of work. Or leisure can be taken in a block later in life by varying the age of retirement. Different households have different time preferences for leisure, which depend partly on the uses of leisure and partly on their lifetime targets for levels of various categories of material consumption. On average, the consumption of leisure time after retirement has grown more rapidly than the consumption of leisure time before retirement. In 1880, only a quarter of lifetime volwork was taken after retirement. Today, nearly half is taken after retirement.

Today, ordinary people wish to use their liberated time to buy those amenities of life that only the rich could afford in abundance a century ago. These amenities broaden the mind, enrich the soul, and relieve the monotony of much of earnwork. They include travel, athletics, the performing arts, education, and shared time with family. The principal cost of these activities is often measured, not by cash outlays, but by outlays of time.

Today, people are increasingly concerned with what life is all about. That was not an issue for the ordinary individual in 1880, when nearly the whole day was devoted to earning the food, clothing, and shelter needed to sustain life. A half century from now, perhaps even sooner, when increases in productivity make it possible to provide goods in abundance with half today's labor, the issue of life's meaning, and other matters of self-realization, will take up the bulk of discretionary time.

Dismantling Standard Working Hours

In the mid-nineteenth century, most earnwork occurred outdoors, which meant that hours worked per day and days worked per year were controlled by the rhythms of nature. During the summer, hours of earnwork were longer in the North than in the South, but that disparity was offset during the winter, when the North had fewer hours of daylight than the South. Year-round, in both regions, the rule was that earnwork extended from sunup to sundown. Over the seasons, daylight hours in both regions averaged twelve per day. Allowing for meals, travel to and from work, and other constraints, the earnwork day typically lasted about 10.5 hours. The number of days worked per week and per year also varied with natural conditions. Rain, snow, floods, and dry spells affected working conditions, including those of factories, where water- or wind power was the primary source of nonhuman energy, although factories could extend the working day past sundown by using oil lamps or candles to provide artificial illumination.

During the late nineteenth and early twentieth centuries, average hours of earnwork gradually diminished as more and more earnwork moved indoors. Despite the diffusion of steam engines, internal combustion engines, and electricity, which freed the earnwork day and year from limitations imposed by nature, employees preferred fewer rather than more hours of earnwork. Legislative efforts to force employers to limit the workday to ten hours and the workweek to six days were generally unsuccessful prior to World War I, except in the cases of women and children. By 1929, however, only 30 percent of manufacturing employees worked more than fifty-four hours per week, and the average workweek had declined to forty-four hours. With the passage of the Federal Fair Labor Standards Act just before the outbreak of World War II, and to a greater extent thereafter, unions were able to negotiate contracts requiring payment of overtime rates for more than forty hours worked per week.[28] During the 1950s and 1960s, even heavier premiums were imposed for weekend work or weekly hours in excess of forty-eight. This compensation structure had two effects. For those who earnworked over forty hours, overtime represented a further increase in average pay rates, contributing to the rise in the average real annual income of workers. As their incomes rose, workers generally preferred to take their greater income in the form of volwork. So the average lifetime hours of earnwork continued to diminish, although most of the reduction took the form of earlier retirement rather than shorter workweeks.

The entry of married women into the labor force on a large scale after World War II was a major step toward dismantling standard hours. Women with children often sought earnwork that could be performed at home. They also preferred part-time over full-time jobs. And many married women, with or without children, preferred jobs that would permit them to work in blocks of time lasting several months, after which they could take several months off without losing the opportunity to return. By the late 1970s, perhaps 20 percent of married women and single women with children had developed such work arrangements.[29]

The proportion of households in which both spouses were employed rose to 30 percent in 1960 and increased steadily during the early decades of the Fourth Great Awakening. A number of complex factors slowed down the rate of growth of households in which the husband and wife both earnworked, particularly the marked increase in the divorce rate. In those households where marriages have remained intact, the share of earned income contributed by wives has risen dramatically, from 17 to 36 percent. Moreover, it is in households that tend to be stable and in which wives bring in a sizable income that experiments in the development of nonstandard hours of earnwork have been pursued most vigorously by both spouses. Highly trained married men and women with skills that are in high demand have led the participation in such new work modes (defined below) as regular part-time work, blocks of work punctuated by blocks of released time, job sharing, flextime, telecommuting, hoteling, compressed work, early retirement, and postretirement earnwork arrangements.[30]

Job sharing is an arrangement permitting two or more individuals to share the duties of a job, with compensation, including fringe benefits, prorated. *Flextime* permits workers to vary their hours or days of work. *Telecommuting* permits a worker to perform all or part of a job at home or at a site other than the company premises, usually making use of a computer, fax machine, and other electronic devices to transmit the product of work. Under *hoteling,* a worker has no permanent office at the company premises but reserves an office (and sometimes a secretary) by the hour or day as needed. *Compressed work* permits an employee to put in a full week of work in three or four days. Other departures from standard work arrangements include pregnancy and health leaves, midcareer breaks (often for educational purposes), and sabbaticals.

These new flexible arrangements are desired by an increasing number of workers, both men and women, who want a life that is not overwhelmed by earnwork. They do not measure success simply by how much their income increases or how rapidly they are climbing the corporate ladder. Although money and social status matter, they are content with a simpler lifestyle that places greater emphasis on such values as family life, shared relationships, spiritual growth, religious faith, and good health. A poll conducted by *U.S. News and World Report* in late 1995 reported that 48 percent of American adult earnworkers had either cut back on hours of work, declined a promotion, reduced their commitments, lowered material expectations, or moved some place offering a quieter lifestyle during the preceding five years. Those who preferred more free time even if it meant less income outnumbered by about three to two those who preferred to earn more money even if it required more time. A journal of labor management recently described the growing disillusionment with the corporate rat race of employees who "don't need, or want, 80-plus-hours-a-week jobs. They may not even want 40-hour jobs. And they don't mind giving up big chunks of their paychecks." What is at issue to such employees is time—time to enjoy the things they have, time to spend with their families, time to figure out what life is all about, and time to discover the spiritual side of life.[31]

In the mid-1980s, most corporations looked on nontraditional work arrangements with a jaundiced eye. Flextime and telecommuting were generally considered disruptive arrangements that might be granted occasionally to star workers. Today, a wide array of corporations views these alternative working arrangements as part of an inventory of personnel policies that increase corporate productivity and reduce absenteeism, labor turnover, and the cost of office space. In a recent survey, more than 86 percent of large establishments reported that they had to address family and diversity issues to remain competitive in the current marketplace. Most of these employers, especially establishments employing more than a thousand workers, believed that flexibility in employment improved worker morale. Some 94 percent of firms offer some form of flexible work arrangements. The most common was regular part-time work (79 percent), which usually included prorated fringe benefits, but flextime was in use among 38 percent of firms and was under consideration in another 11 percent.[32] Telecommuting was the most rapidly expanding form of alternative work arrangement, with two-thirds of the Fortune 1000 companies reporting such programs in place. About 11 percent of the labor force (nearly 16 million workers) telecommutes, and the number of telecommuters is growing by over 2 million per year. Many companies also reported offering a variety of convenience services, including automatic teller machines, postal services, laundry and dry-cleaning services, work-site centers for child care and fitness, and preretirement planning services.[33]

Although the average annual hours of earnwork undertaken by family *heads* has continued to decline over the past quarter century, the combined hours of earnwork undertaken by *families* has increased, especially at upper income levels. In households with both husbands and wives present, hours of total earnwork provided by both spouses increased by 24 percent since 1969.[34] These extra hours are concentrated in prime working ages, and they are one of the main ways that couples are financing early retirement. The drive to acquire or to retire early sometimes exacerbates the rat race, but not always. In today's world of flexible earnwork, the involvement of both parents in the marketplace need not undermine family life and may even enhance it. In some cases, families in which both spouses jointly provide fifty to sixty hours of weekly earnwork, the family's earnwork week has been reduced to just three or four days. In other cases, either the mother or the father performs earnwork largely at home, while both make use of flexible hours.

NEW ISSUES OF DOMESTIC EQUITY: GUARANTEEING PENSIONS AND HEALTH CARE

Changes in the structure of industry, the use of time, the organization of work, and the structure of consumption have given rise to a new set of egalitarian issues, some material and some spiritual, that constitute the reform agenda of the Fourth Great Awakening. The most urgent of the new material issues is guaranteeing workers the pensions and health-care services to which they are entitled. The threat to entitlements, however, is not so much an issue between socioeconomic classes as it is a conflict between generations. Unlike the situation a century ago, the crisis in entitlements today is due, not to predatory business policies, but to well-intended government policies that were reasonable at the beginning of the twentieth century but are inappropriate for the beginning of the twenty-first.

Nor is this problem peculiar to the United States. OECD nations generally are faced with crises in their pension and health-care systems, not because they are poor, but because they are, by historical or Third World standards, exceedingly rich. It is the enormous increase in their per capita incomes over the past century that permitted the average length of retirement to increase fivefold, the proportion of a cohort that lives to retire to increase sevenfold, and the amount of leisure time available to those still in the labor force to increase over threefold.[35] Policy makers are now haunted by the fear that it is not possible to maintain and extend these achievements without bankrupting governments.

Funding Abundant Leisure and Health Care

The forecasts embodied in tables 5.1 and 5.2 imply that, by 2040, those still in the labor force, as conventionally defined, will have over fifty hours per week of leisure (volwork), the average age of retirement (the beginning of the full-time volwork or the end of regular earnwork) will begin about age fifty-five, and the average duration of full-time volwork will approach thirty years. Will OECD nations have the resources to afford amounts of leisure that once would have been considered luxurious and also provide high-quality health care for an additional seven or eight years of life?

Assuming that the per capita income of OECD nations will continue to grow at a rate of 1.5 percent per annum, the resources to finance such expanded demands will be abundant. This is a reasonable growth rate, below the long-term experience of the twentieth century.[36] Consider a typical new American household established in 1995 with the head aged twenty and with the spouse earning 36 percent of the income of the head (i.e., the spouse works part-time). Such a household could accumulate the savings necessary to retire at age fifty-five, with a pension paying 60 percent of its peak life-cycle earnings, by putting aside 14.7 percent of annual earning from the year that the head and spouse enter the labor force.[37] That pension would permit retirees at age fifty-five to maintain their preretirement standard of living, with a real income that would rank them among the richest fifth of householders today.

By putting aside an additional 9.8 percent of income, the household can buy high-quality medical insurance that will cover the entire family until the children (the analysis assumes that there are two) enter the labor force and also cover the parents' medical needs between the time they retire and age eighty-three (assumed to be the average age of death in their cohort). Saving an additional 7.8 percent of income will permit parents to finance the education of their children for sixteen years, through the bachelor's degree at a good university.

What I have described is a *provident fund* (a fund that makes provision for the future) of the type recently introduced or under consideration in some of the high-performing Asian and South American economies.[38] I have assumed that the savings would be invested in conservatively run funds, such as the Teachers' Insurance and Annuity Association/College Retirement Equities Fund (TIAA/CREF), to which most American universities subscribe on behalf of their faculties. These pension funds could be managed by the government, by private firms, or as joint ventures. The only requirement is that the funds invest in a balanced portfolio of government and private securities that yield a respectable rate of return and are kept insulated from irrelevant political pressure. As in TIAA/CREF, individuals may be permitted modest latitude in choosing among investment opportunities.

The point of the example is that prospective real resources are adequate to finance early retirement, expanded high-quality education, and an increasing level of high-quality preventative and curative medical services (I estimate that medical expenditures will increase to between 18 and 20 percent of gross domestic product by 2040). The typical working household will still have 68 percent of a substantially larger income than is typical today to spend on other forms of consumption. Since current levels of food, clothing, and shelter will require a decreasing number of hours of work during the family's life cycle, dropping to about 20 percent of earnwork hours just before retirement, families will be able to increase their rate of accumulation in consumer durables and housing, or increase expenditure on such consumables as travel, entertainment, and education, or further reduce hours of earnwork, or retire before age fifty-five.

Embedded in my simulation is a suggestion for modernizing current government systems of taxation and expenditure. Close to half of what are called *taxes* actually represent deferred income or forced savings. In these cases, the government does not collect money for its own benefit but merely acts as an intermediary in order to ensure that money needed for later use (such as retirement by individuals) is set aside for the stated purpose and then delivered to households when needed. The particular form of intermediation exercised by the U.S. government, however, is quite peculiar. Instead of setting up an account in the name of the individual doing the savings, the government transfers the funds to a person who had earlier deferred consumption. At the same time, it promises the current taxpayer that, when he or she is ready to retire, the government will find new tax-payers to provide the promised funds. Under normal circumstances, OECD governments provide this form of intermediation quite efficiently. The costs of administering the U.S. social security system, for example, is just four-fifths of 1 percent of expenditures.[39]

The problem with the current system, aside from the fact that it gives the impression that personal savings are actually taxes, is that its operation is subject to heavy political buffeting. As a consequence, rates of return on the savings for deferred income are highly variable and often far lower than they would have been had they been invested in a fund similar to TIAA/CREF. Moreover, the current system is affected by variations in the fertil-ity and mortality rates that have created financial crises and thrown into doubt the government's promises that it will be able to provide the money supposedly set aside for later retirement income, health care, or education.

The crisis, then, is not in a nation's resources for providing extended retirement, improved health care, and extended education but in the ex-ceedingly clumsy system for financing these services. The crisis is to a large extent due to accidents of history. When the original social security sys-tems were established in various nations prior to World War I, they were intended to be class transfers, a transfer of income from the rich to the poor. The level of transfer was modest, supplying the elderly with barely enough food to keep them from starving. Such payments were not gener-ally expected to cover the cost of housing or other necessities of life. More-over, only a small percentage of a cohort was expected to live long enough to become eligible for the benefits, and the average duration of support was expected to last only a few years. Under these circumstances, a tax of 1 or 2 percent on the income of the richest 5 percent of the population was adequate to fund the program. The rich of Prussia and Great Britain were prepared to bear this cost for the sake of political stability.[40]

Over the course of the twentieth century, however, the enormous in-crease in life expectancy and the rising standard of living led to much longer periods of retirement and much higher levels of support after retire-ment. Such programs could no longer be financed through a highly con-centrated class tax. To support more expensive pension systems, taxes had to be extended to the entire working population. In so doing, social secu-rity programs were transformed from redistribution schemes into systems of forced savings, although the transformation in the basic nature of these systems was obscure to most participants.

Modernization of the essentially self-financed programs for retire-ment, health care, and education from their current unsustainable systems of financing to a more transparent system of forced savings in provident funds will not be easy. If provident funds were being established anew, as they are in, say, Malaysia, no special problem would confront the OECD nations. All individuals currently in the labor force would be required to set aside a quarter to a third of their income in a TIAA/CREF type of account to use later for the specified purposes. Although that can also be done in rich countries that currently have social insurance systems, those countries are confronted with the burden of meeting trillions of dollars of debt to savers under the old system. It is immoral and politically impossible to default on this obligation. Nevertheless, because of demographic factors and the unstoppable movement toward early retirement, some adjustment in the old system will have to be made.[41]

The stumbling block in shifting to a more transparent system is political, not economic. Although the United States and other OECD nations are rich enough to afford early retirement and high-quality health care, these appear to be provided by taxing relatively young working people for the benefit of retired older people. Moreover, the increased demand for health care and longer periods of retirement will require increasing that tax from current levels, about 15 percent of payrolls, to the neighborhood of 25 percent of payrolls because, by 2030, only two people will be paying into social security and Medicare for every one person receiving benefits (currently about 3.25 persons are paying in per beneficiary).

Such a tax is economically feasible. Even if the economy grows at only 1.5 percent per capita annually, the average incomes of workers in 2030 will be about 56 percent higher in real terms before payroll taxes and about 38 percent higher after payroll taxes. In other words, providing undiminished benefits through the current government plan will not reduce future taxpayers to penurious standards of living but actually leave them with posttax real incomes substantially higher than they are today.

Is such a plan politically feasible? Could politicians persuade workers *today* to accept an additional tax burden equal to between 10 and 15 percent of their after-tax earnings by arguing that the income of individuals after the new tax will still leave them with a third more income than people had a generation ago? Such appeals to "how much better off you are than in olden days" does little to assuage anger at being overtaxed. The search for a more transparent system of funding retirement and health care is therefore a search for a plan that will not cause a catastrophic political explosion either today or in 2030.

Despite the public rhetoric against privatizing social security, the United States is actually in the process of doing so if by *privatizing* one means increasing the share of total lifetime savings for retirement not intermediated by the government. The principal form of privatizing is the delay in the age at which full social security income will be made available to retirees. In 1983, Congress mandated that the normal age for the payment of social security would be delayed from sixty-five to sixty-seven by the year 2025. Currently, there is growing support in Congress to delay the normal starting age to seventy. The public argument for delay is that the huge improvement in life expectancy and health since the social security system was instituted makes it feasible for individuals to stay in the labor force longer.

But the proposal to delay the onset of social security by five years is the equivalent of a cut in the value of social security payments by 37 percent. In other words, to replace the income taken from them by the delay, individuals who want to retire at age sixty-five and live at the level that social security would have made possible will have to save privately an amount equal to about 37 percent of payments to Social Security. Moreover, as income increases, the demand for retirement will increase. The average age of retirement, currently sixty-three, will probably drop to about sixty or younger. Since the social security system will not pay for extra years of retirement, individuals will have to save privately a sum that is even greater than their payments to social security. In other words, the delay of the onset of social security to age seventy, combined with the failure to provide additional government-mediated savings to cover the cost of the early years of retirement, means that, in effect, half the system will have been privatized by 2025.[42]

The difficulty with this road to privatization is that it puts the entire burden of the shift toward a transparent, readily understandable system on a single generation, the baby boomers.[43] It would be fairer, and more expedient politically, to spread the burden of the transition over several generations. A number of proposals that address the issue of intergenerational equity in this manner have emerged in both the United States and other OECD nations.[44]

Concerns over the transition to a transparent system of life-cycle savings relate also to the problem of equity for the poor. I have focused my analysis on the typical (median or average-income) household in order to demonstrate that the economies of OECD nations have the prospective resources to permit early retirement, expanded educational opportunities, and expanded medical care. Unfortunately, the income of some households is so low that saving 32 percent of earnings would not provide them with a provident fund large enough to support adequate retirement, health

care, and education. This is a problem, not of inadequate national resources, but of inequity. Such inequities can continue to be addressed by
redistributing income from high-income to poor households by means of
taxes and subsidies. Correcting these inequities does not require restricting
retirement or health care.

Some investigators worry that the interclass transfers already built into
social security may be lost during a switch to provident funds. However,
now that the system has matured, the interclass transfers are relatively
modest. They can be recouped with subsidies to the provident funds of
those whose earnings are too low to provide a decent minimum standard
of living. A tax of 2 or 3 percent applied progressively on the top half of
the income distribution would be sufficient to raise the pensions of those
with inadequate incomes above the poverty line. Such a tax has been accepted by the well-to-do in the past and should be acceptable in the
future.[45]

The Virtue of Increased Spending on Health Care and Retirement

What, then, is the virtue of increasing spending on retirement and health
rather than on goods? It is the virtue of providing consumers in rich countries with what they want most. It is the virtue of not insisting that individuals must increase earnwork an extra ten hours a week or an extra twenty
thousand hours per lifetime in order to produce more food or durables
than they want, just because such consumption will keep factories hum-
ming. The point is that leisure-time activities (including lifelong learning)—volwork—and health care are the growth industries of the late
twentieth century and the early twenty-first. *They* will spark economic
expansion during our age, just as agriculture did in the eighteenth century
and the early nineteenth and as manufacturing, transportation, and utilities did in the late nineteenth century and much of the twentieth.

The growing demand for health-care services is due primarily, not to
a distortion of the price system, but to the increasing effectiveness of medical intervention. That increase since 1910 is strikingly demonstrated by ex-
amining the data on hernias in table 5.4.[46] Prior to World War II, hernias
were generally permanent, and often exceedingly painful, conditions.
However, by the 1980s, about three-quarters of all veterans who had ever
had hernias were cured of them. Similar progress over the seven decades
between 1910 and the 1980s is indicated by the line on genitourinary conditions, which shows that three-quarters of those who had ever had such
conditions were cured of them. Other areas where medical intervention

Table 5.4 Comparison of the Prevalence of Chronic Conditions among Union Army Veterans in 1910, Veterans in 1983,[a] and Veterans in 1985–88,[b] Aged 65 and Above (%)

Disorder	1910 Veterans	1983 Veterans	1985–88 Veterans
Musculoskeletal	67.7	47.9	42.5
Digestive	84.0	49.0	18.0
Hernia	34.5	27.3	6.6
Diarrhea	31.9	3.7	1.4
Genitourinary	27.3	36.3	8.9
Central nervous, endocrine, metabolic, or blood	24.2	29.9	12.6
Circulatory[c]	90.1	42.9	40.0
Heart	76.0	38.5	26.6
Varicose veins	38.5	8.7	5.3
Hemorrhoids[d]	44.4		7.2
Respiratory	42.2	29.8	26.5

SOURCES: See Fogel, Costa, and Kim (1993).

[a]Reporting whether they had specific chronic conditions.

[b]Reporting whether they had specific chronic conditions during the preceding twelve months. The veterans were responding to the U.S. National Health Interview Survey (NHIS).

[c]Among veterans in 1983, the prevalence of all types of circulatory diseases will be underestimated because of underreporting of hemorrhoids.

[d]The variable indicating whether the 1983 veteran ever had hemorrhoids is unreliable.

has been highly effective include the control of hypertension and the reduction in the incidence of stroke, the surgical removal of osteoarthritis, the replacement of knee and hip joints, the curing of cataracts, and chemotherapies that reduce the incidence of osteoporosis and heart disease.[47] It is the success in medical intervention, combined with rising incomes, that has led to a huge increase in the demand for medical services.

THE STRUGGLE FOR SPIRITUAL EQUITY

Although modern economic growth is about three centuries old, it is only in the past half century, mainly during the era of the Fourth Great Awakening, that the process pushed the rich nations of the world onto a plane previously contemplated only by dreamers: saturation in the consumption of the main categories of consumer products. Some proponents of egalitarianism insist on characterizing the *material* level of the lives of the poor today as being as harsh as it was a century ago. Failure to recognize the enormous *material* gains made over the last century, even for the poor, impedes rather than advances the struggle against chronic poverty. In rich nations, the principal characteristic of those afflicted by chronic poverty is their *spiritual estrangement* from mainstream society. Although material assistance is an important element in the struggle to overcome spiritual estrangement, such assistance will not be properly targeted if one assumes that improvement in material conditions naturally leads to spiritual improvement.

That proposition, so widely embraced by the more secular of the Social Gospelers, did more to promote the consumerism of the 1920s and 1930s than to produce spiritual regeneration. The middle and working classes became preoccupied with the acquisition of automobiles and those household appliances made possible by electricity: irons, lamps, telephones, toasters, refrigerators, radios, and washing machines. It was this consumerism that led such Progressive critics of the era as Vernon Parrington, pioneer in the development of intellectual history, to decry the "cash-register" mentality of modern urban life.[48] Electricity, combined with the new leisure made possible by declining hours of work, promoted forms of entertainment more enticing than church; those new entertainments promoted such sins as smoking, drinking, drug use, and forbidden sex. The media's promotion of these bad habits was excoriated by Washington Gladden, Josiah Strong, and numerous other clergy on both sides of the old lights/new lights split. Those clergy saw such habits as a direct assault on religious values and on the church. Yet they were unable to stem the tide.[49]

As pointed out in chapter 4 above, the economist's traditional measures of income inequality are inadequate measures of both egalitarian gains and egalitarian failures. They focus on a variable—money income—that currently accounts for less than half of real consumption and that, in a generation, may slip to just a quarter of real consumption. The most serious threats to egalitarian progress—certainly, the most intractable forms of poverty—are related to the unequal distribution of spiritual (immaterial) resources. The aim of this section is to identify those spiritual resources that are most critical to egalitarian progress and to discuss ways of distributing these resources to those most deprived of them, a group that includes but is not limited to the chronically poor, the alienated young, the defeated midlifers, and the estranged elderly.

The Democratization of Self-Realization

Self-realization requires good health and extensive leisure. The process of technophysio evolution is satisfying these conditions. Self-realization also requires, however, an answer to the question that persons with leisure have contemplated for more than two thousand years. How do individuals realize their fullest potential? Technophysio evolution is making it possible to extend this quest from a minute fraction of the population to almost the whole of it. Although those who are retired will have more time to pursue this issue, even those still in the labor force will have sufficient leisure to seek self-realization either within their professional occupations or outside them.[50]

One implication of this analysis is that decision makers both in government and in the private sector now need to review existing policies for their bearing on the timely growth of institutions that will satisfy an expanding demand for volwork. Some may consider it premature to speculate on the new forms of human activity that will come into being in order to provide solutions to the quest for self-realization. Nevertheless, I believe that one of the solutions will be lifelong education—education, not to train for an occupation, but to provide a better understanding of ourselves and our world. What is required is more than an expansion of existing universities and other forms of adult education. Entirely new educational forms are needed that aim at satisfying, not only curiosity, but also a longing for spiritual insights that enhance the meaning of life, that combine entertainment with edification and sociality. These include reading circles and informal seminars for the elderly, usually voluntarily led by one of their number more expert than the others in some field of intellectual endeavor. Such seminars may move from one topic to another, depending on the interests of the participants and the variety of expertise among them. I believe that the desire to understand ourselves and our environment is one of the fundamental driving forces of humanity, on a par with the most basic material needs. We are lucky to be living in an age that offers vast amounts of time, much longer lives, and better health to satisfy this urge. But we are also faced with a new set of equity issues that could become more divisive than those that threatened stability a century ago.

The Maldistribution of Vital Spiritual Resources

Self-realization does not mean merely fulfilling one's desires, no matter how debased they may be. To those philosophers who have developed the concept, self-realization means the fullest development of the *virtuous* aspects of one's nature. Among them was John Dewey, the leading pragmatic philosopher between the two world wars and an early architect of secular religion, who argued that self-realization required immersion in the political struggle to create a better world.[51]

The realization of an individual's potential is not something that can be legislated by the state, nor can it be provided to the weak by the strong. It is something that must develop within each individual. Moreover, which aspect of his or her potential an individual chooses to develop most fully, such as choosing an occupation, can be purely an aesthetic consideration. Dewey and one of his chief disciples, Richard Rorty of the University of Virginia, contend that, in a democracy, self-realization is "a particularized creative project of individual growth."[52] The emphasis on individual choice does not mean that other individuals and institutions play no role in shaping choice. Quite the contrary, the quality of the choices made and the range of opportunity taken up depend critically on how well endowed an individual is with spiritual resources. These spiritual resources are unequally distributed among young and old, among men and women, among various ethnic groups, and among rich and poor. The rich who are continuously preoccupied with sensual gratification are as likely to fail in self-realization as are the poor who share that preoccupation. Although the rich who suffer from addictions may have the wealth to buy treatment from physicians, character and religious counseling may serve as well, if not better, both for them and for the addicted poor.

Before considering how best to equalize the distribution of spiritual resources, it is first necessary to consider what these resources are and which ones are most vital in the quest for self-realization by particular individuals or groups of individuals.

Of all the maldistributed spiritual resources, *sense of purpose* may be the most important. Deprivation of this sense is widespread among the alienated young and the depressed elderly. This absence also afflicts the frustrated and bewildered of all ages, rich and poor alike. William Julius Wilson, professor of sociology at Harvard, has described the role of persistent poverty in depriving those locked into the underclass of a *vision of opportunity*. Without a vision of opportunity, there cannot be a purposeful struggle for self-realization. Even with such a vision, opportunity cannot be realized if individuals do not have a sense of a virtuous purpose in life. For opportunity to be realistic, an individual must also have *a sense of the mainstream of work and life,* a sense of where opportunities are and how to pursue them. The young need this sense if they are to develop their ideas of how they want to exercise their opportunities, the old if they are to see how they can fit into the world of retirement.[53]

Another cluster of poorly distributed immaterial resources relates to solidarity and diversity. Of these, perhaps the most important is *a strong family ethic.* I have in mind more than just a belief in the value of the traditional family. There must be a palpable commitment on the part of parents to love their children above all others, a commitment that their children can count on unequivocally. There must also be an intergenerational commitment from mature children to do for their own children what their parents did for them. The mature children must also be prepared to provide aid and comfort when their parents are no longer able to care for themselves. Complementing the family ethic is *a sense of community* with others outside the family, a solidarity with neighbors, ethnic compatriots, coreligionists, professional colleagues, classmates, and members of one's race and gender. Such a sense not only reinforces the family ethic and provides solace in a competitive world but also facilitates the transition from kin solidarity to *a capacity to engage with diverse groups.* The world outside the family and the community is diverse. To achieve success in it, one must appreciate, learn from, and have the capacity to lead or follow foreigners and other strangers. This engagement with outsiders must be based on *an ethic of benevolence,* a resolve to be of service to others, not because of the esteem attached to givers of charity, but because of a considered duty to humanity and a commitment to make the world a better place.

To many individuals, self-realization is achieved, to a considerable degree, through an occupation. Success in occupations requires *a work ethic.* That ethic embraces the idea that work is a duty, that, if a task is worth doing at all, it is worth doing well, and that diligence is both moral and pleasurable. The execution of a work ethic requires *a sense of discipline.* Discipline is not a gift but a learned pattern of behavior. It pertains not only to an occupation but to all aspects of life. It is a necessary ingredient in all purposeful activities. One important aspect of discipline is *the capacity to focus and concentrate one's efforts.* Discipline requires more than purposefulness and dedication. It also requires *a capacity to resist the lure of hedonism,* to control self-indulgence, to remain faithful to a commitment despite strong impulses and other distractions.

Few quests for self-realization are undertaken with adequate knowledge of what is entailed. No matter the field, textbooks invariably leave out essential information. Typically, the successful realization of a goal requires *a capacity for self-education* along the way. Self-education is facilitated by *a thirst for knowledge* that helps overcome the cost of learning, which is often measured in confusion and tedium. The more ambitious quests for self-realization require *an appreciation for quality.* Very often, the difference between an average performance and an outstanding one rests in the discernment of details. Quality involves pushing beyond the obvious and taking intellectual risks. Assimilation of all the preceding immaterial resources requires *self-esteem*, a belief in one's capacity to succeed in an undertaking. The more ambitious the undertaking, the higher the level of self-esteem required. One aspect of high levels of self-esteem is the capacity to overcome the repeated failures that usually accompany ambitious goals.

Each of the fifteen spiritual resources just outlined must be possessed in moderation. There is an optimal amount of each spiritual resource, which will vary from one individual to another. Too much of a sense of purpose turns dedication into ruthlessness. Too little purpose may cause one to be uncompetitive in a given pursuit. Similarly, too high a level of self-esteem may lead individuals to compete for opportunities for which they are ill equipped, and such failures can easily lead to despair. Excess self-esteem also produces vanity and undermines the capacity to learn from others. Too much engagement with diverse groups may undermine family and community ties. Inadequate engagement with diverse groups may deprive one of adequate breadth of knowledge and predispose one to ignorant superstitions and prejudices.

Approaches to the Redistribution of Spiritual Resources

A common characteristic of the fifteen spiritual resources just described is that they are transferred from one individual to another mainly very early in the life of the recipient. Self-esteem and a sense of family solidarity are transferred to babies along with milk and pabulum. Other spiritual resources begin to be transferred during the toddler years, including a sense of discipline, a capacity to resist or control impulse, and a sense of community. Passing on stories and nursery rhymes such as "This little piggy" and recounting the autobiographies of the mother and father and family histories going back two or three generations convey such spiritual resources as a work ethic (the piggy that goes to market not only gets the goods but is hugged and caressed), a sense of the mainstream of work and life, an ethic of benevolence, a vision of opportunity, and a thirst for knowledge.

In my own case, my love for mathematics began on my father's knee, when he told me stories about his childhood life and education in Odessa, including the barriers that Jews in czarist Russia had to overcome to obtain an education. I was not too young to notice the awe with which my father spoke of his *Gymnasium* (high school) mathematics teacher. These early reminiscences also taught me the importance of ethnic solidarity and the capacity of a young immigrant father to engage with diverse groups.

Although these early transfers of spiritual resources are enriched and expanded by primary, secondary, and college education and by occupational and other later life experiences, the salience of these later transfers depends in no small measure on what happens at home before formal education begins. It is, therefore, necessary to remedy the maldistribution of spiritual resources early in life because the most spiritually deprived infants will often be borne by single, teenage mothers, who are themselves spiritually deprived.

One remedy is a major expansion of prenatal care, not only to provide health care to more unwed pregnant teenagers, but also to provide instruction to all mothers on the newly discovered aspects of the nurturing of their fetuses and infants. Expectant teenage mothers need to be counseled, not just about diet and avoiding smoking and drinking alcohol, but also about the virtues of talking and singing to their unborn babies and about beginning the process of transmitting immaterial resources along with milk and pabulum.

Some young mothers and fathers are too deprived, or too young, to call on their own life experiences to transmit a sense of discipline and of opportunity, a work ethic, a family ethic, a sense of self-esteem, and a knowledge of the mainstream of work and life. The deprivation can be addressed by promoting a system of mentoring, taking advantage of the increasingly large number of retired men and women who have abundant spiritual resources. Such mentoring programs would be useful, not only for the toddlers and their mothers and fathers, but also for the elderly who are looking for ways to enrich their retirement years.

Another program targeting very young children involves the expansion and spiritual enrichment of nursery and day-care programs. One aspect of this expansion should be the encouragement of houses of worship to convert basements and other unused facilities into space suitable for nursery programs. Such remodeling could be encouraged by competitive grants from private foundations and public programs. One advantage of facilities based in houses of worship is that they can draw on large pools of volunteers, many of them retired professionals, and thus lower the cost of quality day-care facilities for working and would-be working parents. Once again, the possibility of engaging in such uplifting volwork is helpful to the elderly.

The potential role of parochial schools at the primary and secondary levels in addressing the maldistribution of spiritual resources ought to be reconsidered. Wilson reported that, in Chicago, blacks from Catholic high schools scored as well on tests as whites but that blacks from inner-city public schools performed more poorly.[54] Not enough information is available to allow us to determine how much of the better performance of blacks in Catholic schools is due to a higher quality of education and how much is due to the fact that blacks in the Catholic schools come from families with higher incomes and more immaterial resources than those at inner-city public schools. In New York City, however, inner-city Catholic primary schools outscored the inner-city primary public schools by 10–17 percent in reading and math.[55]

In utilizing the resources of houses of worship for the redistribution of immaterial resources, great care is needed both to safeguard freedom of religion and to ensure the separation of church and state. One way to do that is to make such grants competitive so that denominations that wish to join the effort to extend the network of values-oriented nursery schools must undergo professional peer review. Peer review for grants from public sources for converting facilities should be secular, the composition of the review committee encompassing a wide range of beliefs. The boards certifying that these programs meet professional standards should be similar to other educational certifying organizations.[56] The cost of tuition should be met, not by subsidies to schools, but by grants directly to students (or their parents)—the way in which the GI Bill of Rights operated—so that the money received can be used at any approved nursery school, regardless of whether the sponsoring organization is the church, government, or private business.

Still another approach is the encouragement of mentoring organizations directed at older children, preteens, teens, and those in their early twenties, a notion widely supported by adherents of the Fourth Great Awakening. A number of highly successful organizations, such as the Girl Scouts, the Boys and Girls Clubs of America, and the Promise Keepers, are already in existence. The focus of government agencies' and private foundations' policy in this area should be on ways of extending the outreach efforts of these programs, including efforts to involve retirees who are seeking outlets for their creative capacities.

Redistributing Spiritual Resources to the Elderly

It has been widely noted that the income of the elderly has increased considerably over the past three decades.[57] Today, the median income of households in which the head is over age sixty-five is comparable to the median income of households with heads under age sixty-five.[58] In the late 1950s and early 1960s, however, the bulk of elderly households were concentrated in the lower deciles of the income distribution and were deprived of those consumer durables that younger families were busily accumulating. Indeed, the elderly represented the main core of those with incomes below the poverty line.[59]

Despite the improvement in their material conditions of life, including comfortable stocks of consumer durables, the elderly today suffer from a maldistribution of immaterial resources that traces back to the conditions of their youth. Persons age eighty today were born in 1919 or 1920. Only 43 percent of that cohort graduated from high school, and less than 15 percent entered college. Even among the youngest cohort of the elderly, those born in 1934 and 1935, only half graduated from high school, and about 20 percent entered college.[60] These cohorts also suffered from high infant death rates, high levels of infectious diseases, and early onset of chronic diseases, as compared with cohorts born since World War II.

Hence, despite their relatively high levels of income and stocks of consumer durables, the elderly today command markedly low levels of spiritual resources. Depression, alienation, and substance abuse are common.[61] Those who are most afflicted are lonely, have few communal contacts, are living in retirement homes rather than in their own homes, and sense a loss of control over their personal lives.[62] Recent studies also indicate that those who lacked immaterial resources early in life have difficulty in attaining self-realization after retirement.[63]

I have emphasized level of education because recent studies indicate that the capacity of the elderly to engage effectively in physical activity is strongly correlated with education early in life. Education also affects cognitive ability and the rate of illness.[64] Consequently, individuals who were not adequately educated in youth are, for that reason, among others, relatively undersupplied with both physiological and spiritual resources in late life.

Despite the long reach of youthful deprivation, there are enough other factors affecting the quality of life for the elderly to permit redistribution that compensates for previous deficits. On the physiological side, for example, there are effective medical interventions that can increase the quality of life and longevity. Although the elderly are eligible for Medicare to pay for treatment, the quality of treatment is variable, and many individuals may be shunted to low-quality care. Moreover, some procedures, such as hernia operations, are denied, or are more reluctantly ordered, for the elderly than for the middle-aged.

Because spiritual resources are so unequally distributed among the elderly, different programs are needed for different strata. The minority of those currently elderly who are well educated, the 14 percent with at least a bachelor's degree, most of whom had professional careers, have developed some innovative programs.[65] In Great Britain, one of these is called the University of the Third Age. This educational program is aimed, not at providing credentials for those about to embark on new careers, but at satisfying the thirst for knowledge. It is based on the proposition that education, and the acquired knowledge and skills, is a source of self-satisfaction, even if it does not enhance an individual's employability. As Peter Laslett, Cambridge University don and one of the founders of the University of the Third Age, put it: "Reading in a literature, mastering a language, unraveling a point in logic or philosophy, understanding the objectives set for themselves by poets, painters, novelists or architects, these things extend your appreciation and your mastery of your world, your objective and your subjective world as well. They are fulfilling, and adding to other people's knowledge is the most fulfilling of all."[66]

Programs such as the University of the Third Age will become increasingly important as the baby boomers and other of the more highly educated cohorts of the post–World War II era begin to retire. However, today, and for the next decade, the bulk of the elderly lack the skills to create and participate in such high-level programs as the University of the Third Age. A recent survey of adult literacy revealed that more than half the elderly population suffers from functional illiteracy. These individuals may be able to sign their names or read very simple material, but they cannot follow instructions for taking medicine or cope with a variety of documents encountered in daily living.[67]

Those who suffer from low levels of literacy can be educated but require programs geared to their level. Peer tutoring by the more highly educated elderly on an individual basis or in small groups appears to be effective. Such programs may be aimed at raising reading levels, at coping with transportation schedules and similar documents, or at improving quantitative skills. Engaging the elderly in intellectual activity has a significant influence on their physiological performance. Recent studies reveal more physiological plasticity than was previously suspected. The capacity for self-improvement continues into old age, and appropriately designed programs can return diminished individuals to earlier levels of functioning. Simple activities at home, for example, can raise the level of hormones that stimulate the central nervous system.[68]

Peer tutoring has a two-way effect since it benefits both the tutored and the tutor. Both gain from involvement in social networks that enhance mood, combat depression, and reduce the risk of suicide. For widowed men, the benefits are physiological as well as psychological. Men in situations that provide greater social support experience significantly lower loss of cortisol, epinephrine, and norepinephrine (hormones that reduce pain, stimulate the functioning of the heart, and improve electrical transmission across cells). Statistical analysis indicates a positive relation for both men and women between social support and physical performance.[69] For the tutors, being active in such productive and emotionally rewarding activities serves to retain a sense of relative youthfulness. Thus, because it is effective, because it is emotionally rewarding, and because it is what the tutors want to do, volwork adds significantly to the national product.

The productive nature of this type of volwork points up the misleading character of current practice in the construction of national income accounts. Were tutors paid by government or private agencies, their work would be counted as income. Nor is this a trivial oversight. Volunteer work by retired individuals averages over 218 hours per volunteer annually.[70] If valued at the average hourly compensation of a counselor in the public schools, the average peer tutor adds about $5,000 (in 1996 dollars) annually to the gross domestic product.[71] Of course, tutoring by the elderly is not limited to assisting their peers. Many tutoring or mentoring programs, such as those of the Promise Keepers and the National Retired Teachers Association, are directed at youngsters.[72]

Arguments that downplay the importance of voluntary efforts and insist that only government agencies or private organizations that pay care givers can do the job miss several important considerations. Volworkers themselves gain emotionally and physiologically from their service. Deprived of the opportunity to be useful in this way, their loss in self-esteem might turn some of them from care givers into patients. If such services are added to the workload of an HMO, the average cost of health care would be significantly elevated and the willingness of employers and taxpayers to fund overall health-maintenance programs reduced. The attempt to keep costs in check would significantly reduce the quality of the service delivered to the emotionally needy. Even the most conscientious government social worker with a heavy caseload can hardly be expected to provide adequate emotional support in the brief period available per client per month. The available time might be adequate for monitoring the use of welfare payments but hardly constitutes involvement in a social network for those at high risk of depression. Finally, since the taxes to fund government programs for the elderly come out of the paychecks of younger workers, the substitution of professional for volunteer programs increases the political tension between generations.[73]

With the elderly, as with the young, it is necessary to reconsider the role of religious organizations, by far the largest potential pool of peer tutors for the deprived elderly in the country. The elderly, especially women and ethnic minorities, are far more active in organized religion than are young adults. Sociological studies indicate that religiousness is an important determinant of a sense of well-being among the elderly. This is due partly to the wide array of services provided for old persons by religious groups, ranging from housing developments and nursing homes to the organization of social and educational activities, personal counseling, and the provision of such aids to the disabled as home visitation, meal preparation, minor home repair, and transportation. The doctrines of most religious groups in the United States promote intergenerational obligations and emphasize the possibilities for spiritual growth and fulfillment in late life. Central to many religions is the belief that self-realization is a function, not of age or of past vicissitudes, but of obedience to the ethical commands of a transcendent being, no matter how old one may be.[74] Fear that the mobilization of religious groups for the redistribution of immaterial resources will inadvertently promote organized religion in America is probably misplaced. The Princeton-Gallup survey of religious attitudes for 1994 revealed that 76 percent of the elderly, but only about a third of persons under age thirty, believe that religion is very important in their lives. This pattern of increasing religiousness with age appears to be a constant feature of American life as far back as the evidence permits us to go.[75] Moreover, the extent of religiousness among successive cohorts does not appear to have increased significantly over time. Stability in religious identification is also consistent with the notion of religious-political cycles in American history. In the Fourth Great Awakening, as in the past, these cycles turn, not on the extent of belief in the existence of a transcendent being, but on the emergence of new ethical priorities, of a new political agenda consistent with the new ethical priorities, and of a realignment within the party system that makes the advocates of the new agenda politically dominant.

It follows that governmental agencies handling applications from church-sponsored organizations on behalf of the elderly must act evenhandedly in order to correct the maldistribution of immaterial resources. The standard has already been established by the peer-review bodies that grant research support to scientists working at church-sponsored hospitals and universities. The appropriate issue is whether a program will make a significant contribution to the immaterial needs of the elderly. The nature of the sponsoring organization should enter into consideration only insofar as it bears on the capacity of the organization to implement the program.

Some Differences between Redistributing Material and Immaterial Resources

Use of fiscal policy to correct the maldistribution of income (a material resource) is based, explicitly or implicitly, on the ethical proposition that those households at the top of the income distribution have more income than they ought to have. This concentration of income at the top is the fundamental source of the maldistribution that fiscal policy aims to correct by taxing the rich and subsidizing the poor. Although the top 10 percent or so are left somewhat worse off materially, the transfer is justified by the belief that the gain to the poor so outweighs the loss to the rich that the procedure is virtuous. Indeed, it might even be argued that, by being charitable in this way, those at the top are actually gaining spiritually.

What about the case of spiritual redistribution? Are spiritual resources maldistributed because virtue is too heavily concentrated? The government cannot legislate the transfer of virtue as it does that of money income. Even if it desired to do so, those rich in virtue or in the family ethic or in benevolence could not transfer spiritual resources by writing out checks denominated in virtue, benevolence, or family solidarity. Those poor in these spiritual resources acquire more of them only through the process of self-realization, through a concerted effort to develop as fully as possible the virtuous aspects of their nature.

Those rich in spiritual resources can help those who are spiritually deprived by counseling them, providing spiritual companionship and moral support, informing and teaching those who are deprived about existing opportunities and procedures, and helping raise their self-esteem. Not only does this process of redistributing spiritual resources leave those who have been deprived better off; it also increases the spiritual resources of those who have them in abundance. Good works add to their pleasure, sharpen their sense of benevolence, improve their ability to engage with diverse groups, deepen their sense of community, and improve their discipline. Thus, in working to correct spiritual inequity, everyone is made better off. To use the language of economists, spiritual redistribution is not a fixed-sum game in which some people can become better off only if other people are made worse off. It is a game in which total resources increase and the share of the deprived in this larger total may also increase without in any way diminishing those who have a superabundance of spiritual resources.

THE UNREALIZED ASPECTS OF THE THIRD GREAT AWAKENING'S EGALITARIAN AGENDA

Completing the revolution in education is perhaps the most important of the unrealized aspects of the egalitarian agenda of the Third Great Awakening, and it is an issue that can win support among adherents of the Fourth Great Awakening. The educational achievements of the nineteenth and twentieth centuries far exceed the original expectations of past generations of reformers. Now, not only is there virtually universal primary and secondary education, but half of all high school graduates enter college—a feat that was declared impossible in the 1940s, when the GI Bill of Rights was under consideration. Nevertheless, the current state of educational opportunity is unsatisfactory.

The demand for college graduates with bachelor's and professional degrees is expanding more rapidly than the supply. On the other hand, the supply of workers with just high school degrees is growing more rapidly than the demand. As a result of both these developments, the hourly earnings of those with bachelor's and professional degrees are rising relative to the hourly earnings of more poorly educated workers. The consequent increase in the inequality of the hourly earnings distribution has alarmed many, not only disciples of the Third Great Awakening, but also those of the Fourth Great Awakening, neither of whom wish the egalitarian gains of the first three-quarters of the twentieth century to be undone.

Efforts to correct the situation by raising taxes and increasing entitlements have not worked, partly because of the tax revolt, and partly because most households in the lower fifth of the income distribution are not dependent on welfare payments. Efforts to limit the hourly earnings of the well-to-do by artificial means, whether practiced by the government or by corporations, have also failed, as is demonstrated by the effort to reduce the fees paid to physicians. After a brief interlude of apparent success, both Medicare and HMO payments to doctors have resumed rising more rapidly than the consumer price index.[76] Efforts to suppress the demand for physicians' services by rationing them have largely collapsed in the face of consumers who insist on high-quality, high-tech, and high-cost treatment. Meanwhile, little has been done to increase the flow of new physicians out of medical school since policy makers thought that rationing demand, rather than increasing the supply of physicians and other health specialists, was the policy of choice.

Government policies aimed at raising the relative earnings of lower-level manual and service workers have failed because they have been fashioned to meet the modernist egalitarian agenda rather than the needs and conditions prevailing during the era of the Fourth Great Awakening. Account must be taken of the reasons for the current stagnation in the demand for low-level manual workers, of which there are three: First, continuing advances in computer technology have made it possible to have machines replace people in an expanding range of manual and service tasks. Second, globalization in the production of many industrial products has substituted foreign for domestic labor, leaving workers in import-competing industries worse off, a condition that is not directly assuaged by the rise of jobs in the export sector. Third, the approaching saturation in consumer durables has also reduced the growth in the demand for workers in these industries, which in the past were the main reservoir for well-paid jobs for high school graduates. It is sometimes argued that new technological discoveries will boost the demand for workers in the consumer durables sector. But that forecast has not held up so far, nor is it likely to work since technological change has reduced the production cost for these products so rapidly that the net effect on the demand for labor is negative. There are, for example, fewer domestic production workers in computer manufacturing today than there were a decade ago.[77]

The main solution to the relative stagnation in the wages of high school–trained workers is to reduce their supply by educating more of them for higher-level technical and professional jobs. Given the rate of decline in the supply of good jobs for those with only high school training, an appropriate target is a doubling in three decades of the share of those receiving bachelor's degrees and a similar increase in high-level technical training. This target is consistent with the rate of expansion in higher education after World War II, which was financed by the GI Bill of Rights when per capita income was less than half of what it is today.

The efficacy of education in reducing wage inequality is based on the best current forecasts of the likely direction of technological change, the demand for conventionally defined output, and the demand for leisure. Improved education is also vital to improved health throughout the life cycle. Recent studies have shown that education at all ages has a significant effect on the efficiency of physiological systems well into late ages. Moreover, legislation supporting expanded educational opportunity is politically feasible since such legislation has wide support among adherents of the Fourth Great Awakening.

The completion of the educational revolution of the Third Great Awakening will not be cheap. The expansion of prenatal counseling; mentoring programs for deprived mothers, alienated youngsters, and the aged; the expansion of higher education (for careers); and the development of lifelong educational programs, including such new programs as the University of the Third Age—all this will likely raise the share of national resources expended on education from about 7 to about 11 or 12 percent of national income.[78] Such an expansion is appropriate because increased education conforms with both individual and national goals and because it is demand driven. It is affordable because basic needs—food, clothing, and shelter (including consumer durables)—will require a diminishing share of national income, and the resources needed to expand education will therefore be released.

Many of the resources needed to implement the expanded educational program will come from volwork rather than earnwork. It is important that those who want to advance egalitarian objectives let go of the belief that only paid workers are effective. Volunteers have been the backbone of past reform movements, and that of the Fourth Great Awakening will be no exception. Even many current government programs, especially at the local level, are staffed by volunteers and, because of limits on taxation, could not otherwise be implemented.[79]

The Debate over Measuring Changing Inequality

As pointed out in chapter 4 above, between the mid-nineteenth century and the late 1960s or early 1970s, various measures of conditions of life, including both financial measures (such as the Gini index of the concentration of income) and biomedical measures (such as life expectancy), have shown a pattern of declining inequality. Since the early 1970s, however, the Gini ratio and other comparable financial measures have shown increasing inequality in the income distribution of households, although biomedical measures continue to show declining inequality. The rise in the Gini ratio has attracted a great deal of attention from both the media and social scientists.[80] It has been widely interpreted as an indication that the economic gains made by the poor during the first two-thirds of the twentieth century are under assault and that living conditions for the chronically poor have deteriorated over the past quarter century.

Income can become more unequally distributed among families for a variety of reasons, not all of which have the same social implications. Consider, for example, the case of two forty-five-year-old toolmakers, each of whom is paid $20.00 per hour. One toolmaker, John, prefers a short workweek, many long weekends, and a month-long summer vacation, and plans to keep working until age sixty-five. The other toolmaker, Harry, plans to retire at age fifty-five and, to finance such early retirement, works thirty-two hundred hours a year.

John's eighteen-hundred-hour workyear gives him an annual income of $36,000, which puts him in the middle of the fifth decile (somewhat below the median) of the income distribution.[81] Although he drives a six-year-old car and lives far out in the suburbs, he is satisfied with his family's level of consumption, and he has plenty of time to spend with his family, is a vestryman in his church, and is the coach of his son's Little League team. Harry has had to forgo many of these leisure-time activities. He rarely attends church, partly because he often works on Sundays, and partly because he loves watching professional football and basketball on his thirty-six-inch, surround-sound television, which gives him the feeling of actually being at the game. Although Harry drives a newer, larger car than John, most of his extra earnings go into saving for retirement.

Although the cumulative life-cycle earnings and the total life-cycle hours of leisure of the two men are similar, between ages forty-five and fifty-five Harry will report an annual income of $74,205, which is 106 percent more than John's income, enough to put him in the top fifth of the income distribution. Consequently, differences in Harry's and John's choices in lifestyle and in how to distribute similar cumulative lifetime hours of leisure between early to mid-adulthood and later life appear as much different conditions of welfare during their prime working ages.[82]

The Increase in Income Inequality since the 1970s

These lifestyle issues and choices between current and later leisure explain most of the increase in the inequality of the income distribution since the early 1970s. Differences in hours worked by the household head explain about 45 percent of the increase in the Gini ratio between 1969 and the end of the 1980s. Differences in hours worked by spouses explain nearly another 10 percent. Consequently, the total hours worked by the richest 10 percent of families rose, while the total hours worked by the poorest 10 percent declined, which explains most of the rise in inequality.[83] It is the failure to appreciate this institutional change that has misled disciples of the Third Great Awakening into believing that America is drifting back to the conditions that made the income distribution of the 1890s so deplorable.

The fact is that, in the 1890s, the richest 10 percent worked fewer hours than the poorest 10 percent. Today, the reverse situation prevails.[84] This is only one of many factors that makes the analysis of the inequality of the income distribution during the era of the Fourth Great Awakening far more complex than it was during the early decades of the twentieth century. Another important change is in the nature of the households that are now represented at the top of the income distribution. About 54 percent of the families in the top 10 percent today are there only because both the head and the spouse are in the labor force. Another 12 percent of families are in the top decile because they are at the peak age for their occupation. They did not earn enough to be in the top income decile a few years earlier, and they will not be there a few years later.[85]

Between the late 1960s and the late 1980s, the hours worked by the industrious professionals and highly skilled technicians who dominate the highest income decile increased by 12 percent. By contrast, the hours worked by those in the poorest decile declined by 20 percent. Some observers have jumped to the conclusion that the drop in hours worked is due, not mainly to the voluntary consumption of leisure, but to an inability to find work. However, an examination of the expenditures of the bottom decile contradicts that assumption. Despite the decline in hours worked, and despite a 28 percent decline in real income, the real expenditures of families in the bottom decile rose by over 11 percent between the early 1970s and 1994.

How can people whose real income is declining spend more? It is not because their expenditures are supported by public assistance since such payments were taken into account in calculating their income. It is because the majority of these poor households in 1994 were not chronically poor.

The majority of the families found in the lowest income decile during any given year normally earn enough to place them in the middle or upper deciles of the income distribution. Some of these transient low-income families are business owners who had a bad year. Some are professionals on sabbatical. Others are heads or spouses (or both) who have taken time off from work for educational or family purposes. Some were downsized. Whatever the reasons, these households were able to sustain their normal level of consumption by supporting themselves out of accumulated wealth. Only about a quarter of the families in the bottom 10 percent of the income distribution in 1994 were chronically poor. The other three-quarters had both transient low incomes and enough accumulated wealth to sustain their normal consumption levels.[86]

Consequently, most of the recent rise in the Gini ratio is not due to structural changes that threaten to reproduce the deplorable distributional conditions of the 1890s. The consumption standards at the low end of the income distribution today are far above those of the middle classes in the 1890s. Hence, to reassert the Social Gospel analysis of the inequality of the income distribution of the 1890s in the 1990s is to befuddle rather than to advance egalitarian reforms. A new drive to promote consumerism will solve neither the problem of spiritual deprivation nor the profound alienation of neglected youths. It will not eliminate glass ceilings, nor will it reduce the widespread depression among the aged.

Study of the rise in the Gini ratio has helped identify the chronically poor, those whose incomes fell below the poverty line for two years in a row and who lacked the accumulated wealth needed to maintain consumption levels above income levels. In 1992 and 1993, slightly under 4 percent of all families were chronically poor. About two-thirds of these families, 2.5 percent of all families, had incomes that placed them in the bottom decile of the income distribution. The balance had incomes that placed them in the bottom half of the second lowest income decile. However, their consumption levels were well below the median consumption level of the second decile. Thus, chronically poor households, the bulk of them headed by unmarried mothers (with the father absent), contain many of the spiritually deprived individuals that William J. Wilson has brought to public attention.[87] Government and private programs to aid such families are essential, but, to be effective, such programs must be focused on providing those families with those immaterial resources essential to an escape from the underclass.

Two other factors, more injurious than those so far discussed, have contributed to the rise in the Gini ratio. One is the relatively rapid rise in professional incomes during the 1980s. The other is the stagnation of the income of individuals with only high school degrees. One of the ironies of the reduced share of income held by landowners and owners of physical capital, the principal source of the long-term decline in the Gini ratio, is that the overall shape of the income distribution has become quite sensitive to changes in the structure of demand for different categories of highly skilled labor.[88] Moreover, since it takes a relatively long time to train highly skilled personnel, adjustments in supply tend to lag behind increases in demand. Consequently, any errors made by policy makers in projecting the rate of increase in demand for highly skilled labor may result in shortages that drive up the income of those possessing the desired skills.

This appears to be precisely what happened during the 1980s, although the policy errors began in the mid-1970s, when education and government officials reached the conclusion that the demand for highly skilled personnel was declining and that, unless the supply were cut back, the market would soon be glutted.[89] As a result, admissions to various Ph.D. programs were reduced, and fellowship and loan programs were cut back. In contrast to the 1960s, when the number of Ph.D.'s conferred annually nearly tripled, between 1975 and 1982 the number of Ph.D.'s conferred declined by about 10 percent and then remained relatively constant throughout the balance of the decade.[90]

In such fields as medicine, dentistry, and law, cutbacks after 1975 were more modest, generally lagging those for Ph.D.'s by about a decade. Degrees conferred in law declined after 1980, in dentistry after 1983, and in medicine after 1984. In the case of master of business administration (MBA) degrees, growth remained brisk until 1985, then stagnated for most of the balance of the decade. In no case did the increase in output keep up with the growth of the demand in these fields. As a consequence, the rate of increase in compensation in these fields exceeded the rate of growth in per capita income during 1980s. In the case of surgeons, for example, real income increased by about 39 percent between 1981 and 1988, while real gross national product per capita increased by only 16 percent.[91]

The rise in the average compensation of highly trained personnel is only part of the explanation for why the rich got richer during the 1980s. About 3.3 percent of households in 1980 earned $50,000 or more. Because of inflation, it took about $71,800 to have the same purchasing power in 1988 as $50,000 had in 1980. If we designate persons with incomes of $71,800 or more in 1988 and $50,000 or more in 1980 as *rich*, then the real income of the rich grew by 134 percent during the eight years in question, which was more than ten times the income growth in the balance of households. Indeed, the rich, who represented hardly 3 percent of all households in 1980, accounted for 42 percent of the total increase in income.[92]

The principal reason for the growth in the income of rich households was not that the average compensation of highly trained persons increased but that their numbers increased. The number of rich households nearly doubled between 1980 and 1988. Only about a third of the growth in the real income of the rich was due to an increase in the average level of compensation. About two-thirds of the growth was due to the rise in the number of rich households.[93] The ranks of the rich increased during the 1980s despite the slowdown in the production of highly trained persons because the shortage of personnel led employers to bid more for new entrants in given professions and to promote these new entrants more rapidly than usual. To some extent, the training requirements for entry were lowered. But all these measures were not enough to meet the rapidly growing demand for professionals, so real salaries in some new professions grew more than twice as rapidly as real per capita income.[94]

The Importance of Education

The experience of the 1980s suggests a way not only of reversing the undesirable part of the recent increase in inequality but of further increasing egalitarianism: return to the pre-1975 policy of vigorously promoting higher education. Although it might be economically feasible to promote egalitarianism through a renewal of the drive to extend education, is it politically feasible? I believe that it is: broadening educational opportunity is as central to the reform program of the Fourth Great Awakening as it was to that of the Third Great Awakening. Education is an issue that is of as much concern to evangelicals as to secular egalitarians. As previously noted, the American enthusiasm for universal education traces back to the Puritans, who promoted literacy in order to permit each individual to study the Bible. Since they believed that the capacity to understand the Bible depended on a reader's breadth of knowledge and learning, the Puritans also promoted a deep study of all past writings, not just Christian writing, but also those produced in Greece, Rome, and the Arab world during their golden ages.

The most direct inheritors of Puritan traditions, New England evangelicals, were in the forefront of the nineteenth-century movement for the establishment of free schools for the education of children from the lower classes. As Yankees poured out of New England after 1750, streaming across the northern tier of New York State, across Ohio's Western Reserve, and into the counties above the forty-first parallel in Indiana, Illinois, Wisconsin, and Iowa, they took their passion for education and their penchant for the establishment of free schools with them. The mark of their accomplishment can be seen in the census records for 1850 and 1860, which reveal much higher literacy rates in the counties of the Midwest above the forty-first parallel than in those below it. It was evangelicals who also led the way in the establishment of institutions of higher learning and in the later broadening of the curriculum of these institutions, thus laying the basis for America's leading role in the development of the sciences, engineering, and other fields on which so much of twentieth-century economic growth has depended.[95]

Using education to promote egalitarianism allows a concentration on the most disadvantaged sections of the population: blacks, Hispanics, the poor generally, and women, who outnumber men as undergraduates. There is now a well-established tradition in education that financial aid should be awarded, not equally, but on the basis of need. This principle became deeply embedded in higher education after World War II, when the leading universities agreed that all those admitted would receive as much financial aid as was needed to make up the difference between their ability to pay and the cost of tuition, fees, supplies, room, and board. For some severely disadvantaged students, there were also allowances for clothing and miscellaneous living expenses. Where university funds were insufficient, students could obtain federal loans at very low interest rates.

These precedents allow plenty of scope for programs that target particularly disadvantaged children. For example, families dependent on the earnings of teenagers could receive subsidies sufficient to compensate them for the lost income during the years of a child's education, provided that the child is enrolled in school and remains in good standing. The same principle could be extended to unwed teenage mothers, whose subsidies could include child care, which is needed if they are to be competitive. Persons on welfare rolls could be retrained for the labor market by tying welfare payments to participation in appropriate educational programs.

It should not be overlooked that some of the staunchest opponents of socialism have also been the most ardent supporters of free education for all. If these individuals had been asked to join in confiscating the land and industrial capital of the rich and redistributing it to the poor, they would have fiercely opposed such blatant socialist schemes. Yet they participated in what may have been the largest socialist enterprise in history: the transfer from the rich to the poor and the middle classes of a form of capital that exceeds the value of all privately held land and industrial capital, human capital.[96] Very often, it is the form of a reform, rather than its content or ultimate effect, that is the barrier to its adoption.

THE INEQUALITY OF THE INTERNATIONAL DISTRIBUTION OF INCOME

There is one glaring exception to the list of egalitarian achievements during the past century or so. The international distribution of income is far more unequal than it used to be. Today, the Gini ratio for the international distribution of income is about 0.64, which means that, among countries for which such information exists, differences in the average income across nations exceed the differences within any single nation.[97] One would have to go back a century or more to find countries in which income was so unequally distributed within national boundaries as it is among nations today.

The current effort to promote greater equality in the international distribution of income is the quintessence of the postmodern egalitarian agenda and the clearest indication that the reform program of the Fourth Great Awakening is superseding that of the Third. The Social Gospelers paid little attention to the plight of the poor in the less-developed regions of the world. Nor did they counsel their followers on the need to share American abundance with the starving poor of Europe and Asia. Quite the contrary, they led the campaign to restrict foreign immigration into the United States, as a measure to raise the living standards of American workers. There was little embarrassment in Social Gospel circles that, in doing so, they were reducing living standards in foreign countries. Charity begins at home was the watchword of the modernists, many of whom supported American imperial aspirations.

The recent surge of concern about international egalitarianism is more than a new phase in the unfolding of the ethics of benevolence. And it is more than a by-product of the new drive to evangelize the world. It is also a response to the realities of economic change, especially in Asia, where a number of once poor countries today are among the most dynamic, rapidly growing nations in the world. Because these countries are converging on the income levels and military capacity of the OECD nations, the United States and Europe have had to reassess their economic, diplomatic, and social policies toward Asia, especially toward the so-called high-performing Asian economies (HPAEs), which are described below in more detail.

Ironically, in the eighteenth century, when inequality *within* European countries was high, inequality *across* countries was exceptionally low.[98] The Gini ratio for the distribution of income across countries was about 0.07, which implies a distribution that is close to perfect equality. The anomaly existed because the countries that we now consider highly developed were actually a bit poorer per capita than were the countries that constitute the Third World today, the underdeveloped or developing countries. In the middle of the eighteenth century, most countries were very poor by current standards, with some a little less poor than others. Indeed, at that time,

China had a higher per capita income than Western Europe. However, one should not confuse the opulence of the emperor's court, especially as depicted in the movies and on television, with the condition of the population as a whole. Per capita income in China in 1750 was little less than a quarter of what it is in China today.

The divergence in income since 1750 between today's rich nations and the Third World may have been due partly to the exploitation of the latter by external powers, especially before World War I. That issue is still unresolved, although the latest research suggests that internal feuding rather than imperial exploitation was the principal factor in the economic regression experienced by Third World nations until the early years of the twentieth century.[99] However, the main reason for the divergence was the remarkably high, and relatively steady, rates of growth made possible by the Industrial Revolution in the handful of nations that we now call *rich*. It has been estimated that, between 1830 and 1950, the per capita income of these nations quadrupled. It quadrupled again between 1950 and 1990, and today they are sixteen times as rich as they were in 1830. Third World countries have grown richer also, but their growth did not begin until the start of the twentieth century, and, even then, they grew slowly until after World War II. Today, their real per capita income is only about three times as large, on average, as it was in 1830.[100]

Over the past forty years, income has been growing more rapidly in a subset of Third World countries than in OECD countries. Hence, there has been some reduction recently in the inequality of the international distribution of income. Nonetheless, international inequality remains extremely high. The per capita income of people in Bangladesh is hardly a twentieth of that in the United States. Their life expectancy is twenty-four years less than ours. Their average educational attainment is barely a sixth of ours. Their average daily consumption of calories is 45 percent less than ours, and a quarter of their population is on the verge of starvation. Bangladesh is not the poorest of nations. About 1.5 billion people are either worse off, or not much better off, than the people of Bangladesh. It has been estimated that over a third of the children under five in developing countries (180,000,000) are as severely malnourished as the ultrapoor of England and France were before the French Revolution.[101]

What can the United States do to promote greater equality on a global scale? Some say that the provision of serious aid would bankrupt the United States because the impoverished in the Third World are so numerous and their needs so great. Others argue that charity begins at home and resist any proposals that might divert funds from our own needy. Still others maintain that only a small fraction of the aid that we supplied abroad would reach the needy because corrupt officials will divert most of the aid to their own consumption.

However, these objections do not apply to the single most effective policy that we can pursue with respect to the needy abroad, which is to keep our markets open to products of Third World countries. Exports are a powerful engine for promoting the economic growth of developing nations. This proposition is supported by the nineteenth-century experiences of the United States and Canada, which used exports of raw materials to finance the growth of their manufacturing industries and transportation networks and to attract direct foreign investment from abroad. There was a strong correlation worldwide during the nineteenth century and the early twentieth between the rate of economic growth in developing nations and the level of foreign investment in them.[102]

Exports have also been a powerful engine of growth for the group of nine East Asian countries (China, Hong Kong, Indonesia, Japan, Malaysia, Singapore, South Korea, Taiwan, and Thailand) that together account for a third of the population of the Third World and that experienced extraordinarily high rates of growth in per capita income since 1980 (ranging between 3.5 and 8.2 percent per year, despite the recent currency crisis).[103] Taiwan, for example, was one of the poorest countries in the world in the 1950s, but today it ranks close to the level of the rich nations. It achieved this remarkable transformation by hitching its wagon to the star of global markets and international technology.

By coupling a high rate of economic growth with rapid increases in the equality of the income distribution, the government of Taiwan and those of the other HPAEs were also able to make achieving economic growth a national mission. The gains in both economic growth and economic equality were achieved by rejecting once-popular theories that poor countries had to protect themselves with high tariffs and other barriers to foreign capital and had to subsidize domestic industry by taxing agriculture and keeping interest rates low. The HPAEs shifted to a policy of promoting exports at market-determined exchange rates and of promoting private saving and the efficient allocation of capital by letting the market set interest rates.

The East Asian Road to Egalitarianism

The governments of HPAEs did intervene to promote more equal income distributions, but they rejected the European and American pattern of imposing high taxes on corporations and prosperous individuals in order to provide revenue for persons at the lower end of the income distribution. HPAE leaders are, of course, well aware of the ideological rationale for the OECD approach but consider it counterproductive. They believe that the most effective way to raise the living standards of the lower end of the income distribution is by encouraging a high rate of growth and that anything that inhibits rapid growth will merely ossify the position of the poor.[104]

The equalization of the income distributions of HPAEs was brought about primarily through educating and upgrading the labor force, through the formation of human capital. In the case of Korea, for example, there was an enormous increase in the proportion of children aged twelve to seventeen receiving a secondary education, from 19 percent in 1960 to 90 percent in 1992. Although Korea and Taiwan have led the way in the investment in human capital, other HPAEs have also made remarkable strides in this direction.

The extent of the dedication to higher education in the HPAEs is demonstrated by the huge investment made in providing advanced training for their students, sending them to study in science, business, and engineering programs in the United States and other countries. In 1991, about 24 percent of all graduate students in the United States were from other countries. The largest single group was the 40,000 students from the People's Republic of China, followed by the 36,600 students from Japan and the 33,500 from Taiwan. The size of the Taiwanese contingent is particularly impressive as it comes from a much smaller population than that of either Japan or China. There are no exact figures on the total annual investment of the Taiwanese on graduate training in the United States, but a rough estimate would be about $1.0 billion, or 0.5 percent of the GDP of Taiwan.[105]

Since this investment in professional training is necessary to meet the increasing demand for a highly skilled labor force as the HPAEs speed along their growth path, welcoming Third World students, and in some cases subsidizing their education, is another way in which the United States can promote international equity. Such programs evoke widespread support among disciples of the Fourth Great Awakening. Building the stock of human capital in advanced mathematics, computer science, engineering, chemistry, and other skills required by the new growth technologies takes more time than putting up a skyscraper. Failure to increase the supply of such technologically trained individuals as rapidly as the demand for them increases may create bottlenecks that slow economic expansion, as recently happened in Thailand. Such a bottleneck also appears to be distorting the earnings structure in the United States.[106]

Another aspect of the progrowth culture of the HPAEs is the emphasis on meritocracy and competitiveness. A recent test of twelve thousand young people from forty-one countries from all continents revealed that those from Asia scored higher on competitiveness than young people from anywhere else in the world. They know that family connections, important as they are, are not by themselves enough to secure one's future. The competition to get into the best universities at home and abroad has become extremely intense in HPAEs.[107]

The absorption of Western technical expertise, the shift from a rural to an urban society, and the creation of new professional classes similar to those that emerged in Europe and America earlier in this century have not led to an abandonment of traditional Asian cultures. Asian political leaders have recently reasserted their religious and national values. The insistence on the primacy of their own culture has been particularly strong in Malaysia and Singapore, but it resonates throughout the HPAEs. It reflects in part a confidence promoted by their economic achievements so far. Asian leaders recognize the threat that rapid industrialization brings to traditional culture, and they are determined to avoid what they believe to be the cultural decay of the United States and Europe.[108]

Asians believe that maintenance of traditional values provides not only the best ethical foundation for the economic transformation of their societies but also the best hope of achieving a good life. In this connection, they stress that an individual must be seen, not as separate from, but as an integral part of the family. Maintenance of the family as the central institution of society requires filial piety, loyalty to the extended family, and respect for scholarship and learning. Asians also believe that, in a society in which children behave reverentially toward their elders, there will be relatively little juvenile delinquency or crime. Such views are compatible with the reform agenda of the Fourth Great Awakening.

A proposition that follows from this line of thought is that the government should not try to provide for a person what the family provides best. As Lee Kuan Yew, the prime minister of Singapore, put it, "We start with self-reliance. In the West today it is the opposite. The government says give me a popular mandate and I will solve all of society's problems."[109] That point of view, Lee contends, has promoted special interest politics and moral sloth. As a consequence, many East Asian nations have rejected the European and American models of the welfare state. Singapore has privatized social security by requiring workers to save for their retirement in approved funds. Once-socialist Vietnam has drastically reduced subsidies for medical care and now relies on the private sector to provide the bulk of outpatient care. Asian leaders increasingly see the principal function of government as providing the political stability required to attract capital, promoting education, developing infrastructure, and instituting policies that facilitate international trade.[110]

As their economies grow, Asian nations look increasingly within their region for models of future economic and social development. China's economic growth appears to have been a major factor in promoting privatization in India, in reducing its tariff barriers, and in reconsidering its attempts to manage the growth of particular industries. HPAEs whose trade was originally largely with Europe and North America are increasingly turning to each other as their primary trading partners.[111]

The emphasis on Asian values does not imply an unwillingness to recognize that industrialization and urbanization require cultural adjustment. Muslim countries have recognized that commercial banking and equity markets are vital in mobilizing the capital needed for economic growth. China has been bolder than many capitalist countries in utilizing techniques advocated by neoclassical economists. It has, for example, instituted a system of charges against firms that pollute the environment, making the penalty proportional to the damage. In Malaysia, Prime Minister Datuk Seri Mahathir Mohamad, who has been in the forefront of the movement for the promotion of Malaysian culture, nevertheless advocated the use of English in the teaching of scientific and technological subjects at universities.[112]

Perhaps the most salient cultural characteristic in the HPAEs is their fusion of old and new cultural imperatives as well as old and new institutions. I have already referred to one example of this kind of fusion: the combination of kin preferences in business appointments with the requirement that the holder of the office meet objective tests of performance, which is a sine qua non of rapid economic growth. The tradition of kin preference does not violate this condition because rates of increase in the demand for labor (especially for highly trained professional labor) are far more rapid than the natural increase in the old elites. Consequently, an increasing share of managerial and technical positions are necessarily being filled outside kin networks. Similarly, the approach to welfare in HPAEs is aimed at reinforcing the traditional family rather than undermining it. Thus, Singapore has sought to house members of extended families close to one another.[113]

Because they see the government welfare programs of Europe and the

United States as destroying values needed to sustain rapid economic growth, Asian countries have designed programs that depend on self-reliance and that are consistent with the obligation of the family to provide for the needs of the elderly and the children. In this respect, these programs mirror some of the reforms promoted in the United States by the Fourth Great Awakening. In Singapore and other Asian nations, the welfare programs are not Western-style redistribution schemes but systems in which employees are forced to save some minimum share of their wages (they can exceed the minimum if they desire). In the case of Singapore, such savings are invested in interest-bearing bank accounts and in approved private pension plans and stocks. Savings above the minimum may be invested in an even wider array of private and government financial instruments. These accumulated savings and earnings, which are not taxed until they are withdrawn, may be used, not only to finance retirement, but also to purchase a home and for health care and education.[114] Despite what appears to be such a different road, the HPAEs have achieved growth with equity—their Gini ratios declined rapidly to levels that are on a par with or in some cases below those achieved by OECD nations. This mystery is explained partly by their heavy investment in education, which has rapidly raised basic levels of knowledge and skill.[115]

Cultural Equity with China

In a world in which immaterial assets are becoming the dominant form of wealth, equity (justice) in the cultural sphere becomes a pressing issue, both domestically and internationally. At home, equity is increasingly equated with ethnic diversity, which often means acknowledging that non-Western cultures are the moral equal of Western cultures. On the international level, equity means not only the rapid economic development of less-developed nations to reach OECD levels but the acknowledgment that Asian and African cultures are on a moral par, if not superior to, American and other Western cultures. Leaders in many rapidly growing Asian nations want to combine what they consider to be the best of modern technology with the traditional values of their societies.

The fusion of old and new institutions is particularly striking in China. Although that country remains a single-party state and lacks certain constitutional, legislative, and judicial protections of property rights, it has taken major strides toward the development of a market economy. It began this process in the late 1970s with a successful reform of agriculture, switching from collectives to a household-based system that more than doubled the growth rate of agriculture and released millions of workers to other sectors of the economy. Industrial reform proceeded more slowly at first. Although individuals were permitted to set up private businesses, at the outset of the reforms state-owned enterprises (SOEs) and collective enterprises accounted for over 90 percent of industrial output. However, important reforms in the operation of SOEs were instituted, giving more control over them to localities, and permitting them to enter into free market production once they had fulfilled state quotas—a move that encouraged SOEs to take on characteristics of profit-making firms. These moves helped build a constituency for reform. They also made the SOEs vehicles of reform and served to weed out the inefficient state enterprises.[116]

The opening of Guangdong Province to world trade, the creation of fourteen coastal cities with released restrictions on foreign investment, and the establishment of five special economic zones with added incentives for foreign investors initiated a boom of unprecedented proportions in a province whose population (63 million) would make it the sixteenth largest country in the world. Huge quantities of foreign capital have poured into China, particularly from Hong Kong, Singapore, and Taiwan, but also from OECD nations. Enterprises in which foreigners have invested, including joint ventures, have gained a substantial share of GDP. All told, it is estimated that private enterprise now accounts for 50 percent of China's GDP. Despite the absence of standard protections for private property against any arbitrary action of the central government, investor confidence is high because of recent government decisions to "corporatize" state-owned enterprises and to privatize some of the smaller state enterprises. China has developed what some analysts refer to as *market-preserving federalism*, by which they mean a decentralization of power, particularly power over economic matters, and its transference to local governments— a move that is difficult to reverse.[117]

How is cultural equity to be achieved between China and the OECD nations, particularly the United States? There is no easy answer to this question, as is demonstrated by a spate of recent attempts to reassess international affairs in the post–cold war era. Some analysts believe that, driven by an aggressive nationalism, a desire to avenge past humiliations, and a lust for international power, China views the United States as the chief obstacle to the realization of its hegemonic ambitions. These analysts see no sign that the prevailing Chinese leadership is likely to move toward political democracy at home or to abandon its use of past national humiliation at the hands of foreigners as a means of consolidating domestic power. To keep China in check, they argue, the United States must build strategic alliances with Japan and the other friendly nations of Southeast Asia aimed at preventing China from achieving its goals.[118]

Samuel P. Huntington, one of Harvard's most esteemed political scientists and an expert in international affairs, worries about new international conflicts based, not on ideological or economic grounds, but on cultural matters embodied in what he calls *civilizations*. Civilizations may include one nation (e.g., Japan) or many nations (e.g., Western civilization or the Latin American or Islamic civilizations). Western civilization—the United States, Canada, and Protestant and Catholic Europe—is not only one of the eight major civilizations that Huntington identifies (the others are Confucian, Japanese, Islamic, Hindu, Slavic-Orthodox, Latin American, and African), but the bearer of Western attitudes and values, such as liberty, equality, constitutionalism, limited government, individual rights, the protection of private property, and the rule of law. These values, derived from Western Christianity as shaped by the Reformation and the Enlightenment, are resisted to one degree or another by all non-Western civilizations, which view the West as the principal obstacle to their own self-realization (their achievement of predominant cultural goals). Huntington foresees the rise of Southeast Asia, not as an economic threat, but as a cultural threat, spreading as it will Confucian and Islamic values that will block the further spread of the democratic and ethical ideals of the West. He fears that, unless the West promotes cooperation and unity within its own civilization and incorporates into the West those societies that are closest to it, Western civilization may decline.[119]

The issue that Huntington ultimately raises is whether the rapid economic growth of the Confucian and Islamic civilizations will check America's three-hundred-year crusade to restructure the world in its own liberal image, a crusade that is reinforced by the Fourth Great Awakening. This possibility, he argues, is the greatest threat to the survival of the fundamental American values and Western civilization because America has defined itself through its persistent struggle to extend its unique values to the rest of the world. The end of the cold war brought such a decisive victory for American principles over those of totalitarianism, he argues, that the United States has lost sight of the uniqueness and special value of its creed. This loss of direction, Huntington continues, is complicated by the simultaneous rise of the ideology of multiculturalism within the United States, which denies the uniqueness and superiority of an American culture based on a secularized evangelical creed. Moreover, with the dramatic rise of non-Western immigration since 1965, the United States stands in danger of losing its national identity because of the absence of the determined effort that prevailed in the past to Americanize immigrants.

Critics of the Huntington thesis have pointed out that both Islamic and Confucian civilizations contain deep rifts and that wars are as likely to break out between the nations of each civilization (between China and Taiwan, e.g., or Iran and Iraq) as between nations of these civilizations and outsiders.[120] Some analysts see communal wars (wars of secession among ethnic groups that were bound together by colonial powers) as the most likely source of military conflict for the foreseeable future. Even critics who admire Huntington's insights believe that he has misinterpreted dynamic debates that reflect an Asian renaissance among elites seeking the best way to cast off centuries of domination by colonial powers. Others note that the Asian critique of cultural decay in the West is similar to critiques expressed by ascending Western denominations, especially those associated with the Fourth Great Awakening.

Huntington's interpretation of American culture has also been challenged. Multiculturalism, which has deep roots in American life, has previously been expressed in the inscription on the Statue of Liberty and in the concept of the melting pot that was so fashionable among scholars half a century ago. What is really at stake for participants in the current debate is the definition of *acceptable* multiculturalism and the ordering of the hierarchy of different values that coexist in the United States. During the eighteenth century and part of the nineteenth, some leaders wanted to limit acceptable multiculturalism to those doctrines advocated by European Protestants and their descendants. The doctrines of Irish and German Catholics were not finally admitted to the circle of acceptable multiculturalism until well into the twentieth century.

The process of expanding the limits of acceptable multiculturalism required concessions on both sides. The Americanization of European Catholicism yielded the most Protestant Catholic Church in the world, just as American Judaism is the most Protestant Judaism in the world, in the sense of accommodating ritual style and theology to Protestant practices (e.g., Reform Jews hold services on Sundays).[121] To some analysts, the new wave of multiculturalism reflects the shift in the locus of free immigration (as opposed to the forced immigration of slaves) from predominantly European nations to predominantly Asian and Latin American nations. Cultural leaders of the new migrants have combined with African American and feminist leaders to demand a far-reaching reconsideration of the prevailing hierarchy of cultural values, which is derived primarily from European experiences and values—a demand that is stoutly resisted by admirers of the old hierarchy.[122]

Whatever one thinks of Huntington's arguments, he has set off the most probing secular debate in more than four decades, not only on the direction of foreign policy, but also on the direction of American culture, on how American culture is perceived in the HPAEs and other modernizing societies, and on how immaterial equity between nations will be achieved during the next half century.[123] That debate is highly relevant to the shaping of a postmodern egalitarian agenda, both domestically and internationally, because it focuses attention on immaterial considerations.

The debate over the Huntington thesis underscores another point: the shift in priority from material to spiritual equity is not just domestic but international. If not entirely gone, the old cry of Third World countries that they are prevented from growing by the economic imperialism of the West has given way to a call for the West to invest more and more heavily in their countries. Despite recent setbacks, the HPAEs and other rapidly growing economies are confident that, in a generation or two, they will overtake the West economically. It is in the realm of culture that emerging market nations in Asia and Latin America now feel most threatened and in which they are most insistently demanding independence and freedom from Western domination.

Finally, the Huntington debate has forcefully raised the issue of whether it is possible for the United States to retain its intellectual vitality if international equity requires that it abandon its three-century-long crusade to spread the American creed of economic, social, and political equality worldwide. Huntington has argued forcefully for retrenchment. He wants to concentrate on the assimilation of non-Western immigrants, on defeating multiculturalist ideology at home and elsewhere in the West, and on shoring up creedal values in other Western countries. He also suggests that we temporarily retreat from attempting to push our ethical values on other countries since that sort of aggressive proselytizing may not be effective now. He proposes instead that we concentrate on educating the children of foreign elites who are eager to study in American universities. Whether such a laid-back approach will be feasible when the influence of the Fourth Great Awakening reaches its height remains to be seen. Its fervor is already influencing foreign policy toward China.

This chapter has shown that, in its material aspects, modern economic growth has pushed the United States onto a plane unforeseen by the most optimistic of the modernist reformers. Food, clothing, and shelter now are abundantly available not only for the typical worker but even for those we designate as poor. Commodities that used to account for 80 percent of household consumption can now be obtained in greater abundance than previously with less than a third of either the market or the household labor once required. Technological change has made the whole range of consumer durables so cheap that even poor households have adequate stocks of appliances that until recently were thought to be luxuries or that were the stuff of science fiction during the first third of the twentieth century.

Leisure—volwork—which used to be available in abundance only for the rich, has been democratized. Today, even ordinary people have the time to be lavish consumers of amenities that broaden the mind, enrich the soul, and relieve the monotony of most earnwork. And so today ordinary people must confront the issue that Socrates put to the rich children of Athens two thousand years ago: What is the nature of the good life?

Self-realization is not something that can be provided to the weak by the strong; rather, it involves individual choice. However, the quality of the choices made and the range of available opportunity depend critically on how well endowed an individual is with spiritual resources. The transfer of spiritual resources begins at very early ages and takes place largely outside the marketplace. It is therefore necessary to develop forms of intervention that make it possible to remedy the maldistribution of spiritual resources early in life as well as among the elderly.

A quintessential element of postmodern egalitarianism is that distributional issues are no longer confined to the domestic arena but have been internationalized. Income levels in many once-poor countries are now increasing at rates far more rapid than those seen in OECD nations, and nations that once lagged far behind the rich nations are now rapidly approaching them, not only in standards of living, but also in military capacity, giving rise to the vastly complicated issues of international cultural equity.

AFTERWORD

Whither Goes Our World?

The egalitarian tradition in the United States is alive and healthy. It is part of the bequest of my generation and my children's generation to our grandchildren. The return to the principle of equality of opportunity as the touchstone of egalitarian progress is not a retreat but a recognition that, at very high average incomes for ordinary people, self-realization becomes the critical issue. Equal opportunity turns less on the command of physical capital now than it did at the close of the nineteenth century. Today, and for the foreseeable future, spiritual capital, especially command of those facets of knowledge that are both heavily rewarded in the marketplace and the key to opportunities of volwork, is the crux of the quest for self-realization.

What is the nature of the world we are bequeathing to the youngsters who will inherit the twenty-first century? On the material side, it is clearly a richer and healthier world than that inherited by my parents, who were born in 1898. Not only is life expectancy thirty years longer today than it was a century ago, but it is still increasing. It is likely that my granddaughters will live into their late eighties or early nineties. It is also likely that the gender gap in life expectancy will continue to close so that my grandson will live nearly as long as his sisters. My grandchildren are also likely to enjoy good health for nearly the whole of their lives.

Lifelong good health for our grandchildren is a reasonable expectation, partly because the average age for the onset of chronic diseases will be delayed by ten or more years, partly because of the increasing effectiveness of medical interventions for those who incur chronic diseases, and partly because an increasing proportion of the population will never become severely disabled. Perhaps the most promising development is the discovery that many chronic conditions that surface at older ages begin in utero or early in childhood. These conditions may be ameliorated or eliminated by improved prenatal and early childhood health care. Moreover, improvements in the physiology of one generation have been shown to result in further improvements in that of the next or even a third generation. Hence, our grandchildren will continue to reap the benefits of the public health investments made during the early and middle decades of the twentieth century.

Despite the continuing rapid increase in the world's population, food is likely to become more abundant. The fact is that advances in agricultural technology have made it possible to increase the food supply fivefold since the start of the twentieth century, with less land in grains than was employed in that manner half a century ago. Even without major breakthroughs in genetic engineering, it is possible to raise worldwide per capita consumption of food to recommended levels merely by extending known agricultural technologies to Third World nations. The spectacular increase in the productivity of Chinese agriculture during the past two decades is a harbinger of what is to come in other developing nations.[1]

Clothing and housing are also likely to become better, and more people are likely to have an adequate supply of both. During the last generation alone, the number of square feet of floor space per new house in the United States has increased by 50 percent, despite the decline in the average number of persons per household. Moreover, major appliances that were luxuries a generation ago not only have become standard but are now larger, more versatile, more durable, and cheaper to buy and run. Technological change will both increase the efficiency of energy-using devices and reduce the cost of energy production. Clothing will become so cheap that, in the future, we may recycle some garments after use rather than clean them.

More people will become more educated, and the education that they receive will continue to increase in quality, despite the bureaucracies that now encumber many primary and secondary school systems, especially in major urban centers, and despite the need for new approaches enabling us to reach the children of the underclass. The promise that lies ahead is shown by the extent to which computers have penetrated the primary and secondary schools (even in many inner-city and rural areas), the fact that children are often more knowledgeable about, and comfortable with, computers than their parents, and the increasing accessibility of the Internet. Novel forms of lifelong education are rapidly expanding. Subjects once taught only at the college level are now routinely taught in the better secondary and even some primary schools. In the sciences, material once available only in advanced college courses is now taught in introductory courses, and topics in advanced courses that used to extend over a whole semester are now compressed into the opening weeks.

Jobs are likely to become better paying and more flexible. Pay will rise because of both the increase in labor productivity and the higher levels of human capital embodied in the labor force. Continued expansion of the services sector and advances in computer technology will make jobs more flexible, with a larger proportion of work performed at home, a larger proportion of the labor force working part-time or compressed-time, and enhanced opportunities to leave and reenter the labor force as circumstances require. Cyclic disturbances of labor markets will become milder than they were in the past as large-scale industries, the most cyclically vulnerable sector of the economy, continue to shrink proportionally. The average length of the workyear will continue to shrink and the average age of retirement continue to decline as more and more workers feel that they can afford to substitute volwork for earnwork.

Opportunities for ethnic and racial minorities are likely to increase, partly because of improved educational attainment, partly because of a reduction in the relative supply of low-skilled workers, and partly because of more effective programs targeting the underclass. Moreover, the responsiveness of political parties to the demands of African Americans, Asians, Hispanics, and other ethnic minorities will increase, spurred by the relatively rapid growth in those population groups. As the combined share of these groups rises toward half or more of the electorate, those now classified as ethnic minorities will emerge as decisive parts of the reigning political coalitions.

Women are likely to break through more and more glass ceilings, partly because of demographic factors. Women in full-time professional and business occupations have become an increasing part of middle management and hence will be a larger part of the pool from which the top echelon is drawn. The rising importance of small businesses in the economy, many of which have been started by women, will also create new opportunities. As working arrangements become more flexible and the possibility of working from home (telecommuting) becomes more feasible, the conflict between occupational attainment and family life will probably diminish.

The traditional family is likely to become stronger. Culture is one engine of change. Business, educational, and government institutions are increasingly accommodating themselves to a labor force that places great emphasis on a life outside work. The cultural effect of the family ethic of the Fourth Great Awakening, which emphasizes the bearing and rearing of children, is already visible in some new media programming that celebrates religion and the family. Technology, which once promoted large-scale enterprise and separated the workplace from home, is now facilitating the reunification of workplace and home.

Major reductions in inequality among nations over the next half century are also likely. Despite temporary setbacks along the way, the emerging market economies in Asia, Latin America, and Eastern Europe, representing half the population of the world, will continue to catch up with those of the OECD nations. Many of these countries, including China, are expected to reach current OECD levels of per capita income in a generation or less, and some may match the OECD nations by the mid-twenty-first century. Such achievements are likely since the economic institutions that must be established to permit poor countries to adapt to the march of modern technology are now understood. Technological progress also promises to diminish the threat to the earth's atmosphere by decarbonizing the energy supply (lowering the carbon content of fuels) and by making energy use more efficient. Current investment in research and development may make the struggle for commensal balance (coexistence among species) in future decades far less costly than it now appears.

Are we delivering to our grandchildren a world without challenge to the nobler side of their nature? Hardly. I have argued only that viable solutions to the current set of divisive issues have already appeared, that some of these solutions will be promoted by new technologies, and that others will be promoted by changes in policies for which winning coalitions are, if not in place, within reach.

Still, our grandchildren will be faced with critical transitions. Although I expect that the impediments that block African Americans, Hispanics, other ethnic minorities, and women from reaching the highest positions in government and educational and business life will be removed, they will not be removed easily. Winning coalitions must be built and firmly dedicated to a smooth transition from a governing minority that is white and Protestant to a governing majority that is nonwhite and non-Protestant, one that does not sacrifice fundamental egalitarian ethical, political, social, and economic principles. These are dangerous passages attended by an array of contingencies, some favorable, some unfavorable, and arrival at the ultimate destination is not assured.

Our grandchildren will discover and implement new scientific principles and technologies that will greatly enhance the capacity of humankind to control its environment and to alter its fundamental genetic makeup. It is likely, however, that not everyone will gain from these technologies. While the majority may be made better off, some will inevitably be made worse off because their skills will be devalued, their opportunities eroded, their desires scorned.

Some discoveries may even threaten the progress of civilization. I have in mind the continuing threat posed to the earth's atmosphere and the ecosystem by the impending doubling of the population in the next half century or so, which some fear may do irreparable damage to the commensal balance among species. However, it is possible, perhaps likely, that progress in science and technology will yield practical and affordable solutions to these problems during the next half century.

More dire is the threat that enhanced scientific capacity may itself become a menace to fundamental human values. Some humanists worry that science may lead to the dehumanization of individuals, to the transformation of people into just another product, into something that can be cloned, transplanted, artificially transformed in external appearance, personality, and intelligence. This power to alter, to improve, and even artificially to produce human beings threatens to undermine the mystery inherent in human consciousness and risks the sanctity of an individual's unique identity. Science is blurring the line between artificial and human intelligence, says Zbigniew Brzezinski, one of the leading architects of recent American foreign policy, who worries about its effects on the international struggle for human rights: "In addition to ideological conflicts over the feasibility of a secular utopia, as in the very recent past, or debates over human rights between advanced democracies and nondemocratic states, ethical conflicts over the definition of the human being will increasingly dominate [international] political life." In this connection, Brzezinski points to the worldwide growth of "religious extremism" as an omen of what is to come.[2]

Danger to our grandchildren also lurks in the demography of aging. Assuming that life expectancy will increase ten to fifteen years and that the fertility rate will continue at current levels, by 2055 the average age of the population will be about forty-five. About a third of the population, including our grandchildren, will be over age sixty, enough to prevent entry into the best jobs if elderly professionals and executives choose to stay at work rather than retire.

Such a lock on the most fulfilling jobs could mean that younger workers will have to wait an extra decade, perhaps more, to get their turn. Moreover, since younger workers are a major source of new ideas, slowing down the rate of entry of the next generation may retard the pace of technological change. It may also slow down the rate at which women and ethnic minorities can advance professionally since native-born white males will form a larger proportion among the elderly holders of top jobs, women and ethnic minorities abounding among the younger workers who seek to replace them.

The solution to this problem will not be easy. Those in my grandchildren's generation who find fulfillment in their work should not be shunted aside merely because they have been on the job for thirty-five years. At age sixty, they will be vital, experienced, and wise and can expect to be in good health for another twenty-five to thirty years. To force early retirement will undermine not only their morale but the morale of those who expect to replace them. The intergenerational conflict could be made more acute if the fertility rate of our grandchildren rises significantly. A new baby-boom generation may find gaining access to spiritually rewarding jobs even harder than postwar boomers who glutted the market for materially rewarding jobs in the 1970s.

Providing incentives to maintain fertility rates at levels close to population replacement is one possible approach to the problem. However, this is not easily accomplished since most adults consider the rearing of children to be one of life's most rewarding, albeit most challenging, tasks. More rapid technological change, which creates new occupations, is another possible solution since younger people are the bearers of new skills and have a competitive advantage over the elderly. Policies that promote research and development and expand training among the young may quicken the pace of technological change, but, as we have seen, rapid technological change brings with it a string of potentially dangerous problems.

How will our grandchildren deal with the search for cultural equity between China, which will probably become the economic monolith of the twenty-first century, and the OECD nations, particularly the United States? The United States has, from the Revolution on, sought to spread its cultural values worldwide. If, as many believe, China (and much of the rest of Southeast Asia) resists and remains wedded to prevailing values (authority, filial obedience, and discipline), will our grandchildren be able to adjust to the end of an international crusade that has been so large a factor in American vitality during the twentieth century? Will they have to prepare for a cataclysmic war or learn to endure a protracted cultural and political stalemate?

Although the world that our grandchildren will inherit will be materially richer and contain fewer environmental risks, its spiritual struggles will be more complex and more intense than those of my generation. Ethical issues will be at the center of intellectual life, and engagement with those issues will form a larger part of the fabric of daily life than is the case today. The democratization of intellectual life will broaden spiritual debates and insinuate spiritual issues more deeply into political life. Clashes between advocates of the old and the new religions may become more acute, but the average age of the population will rise significantly, and with that aging will come, one hopes, a maturity and intellectual vitality that will help our grandchildren find better solutions than we have found.

ACKNOWLEDGMENTS

This book is based on four decades of research on the interrelations among economic growth, technological change, demographic change, and institutional change. Since the mid-1970s, the main focus of that research has been on secular trends in nutritional status, morbidity, mortality, human physiology, and the process of aging. All that I have learned about these matters is reflected in this book. My first debt therefore is to the various individuals with whom I have collaborated over the years—students, research assistants, colleagues, and teachers.

Simon Kuznets, my principal teacher, introduced me to the complex issues in the measurement and study of economic growth and its interrelations, including its effects on the distribution of income and on population growth. It was Kuznets who first called my attention to the tendency of workers in rich countries to take an increasing share of their income capacity in the form of leisure and in other activities beyond the market.

My closest collaborators since the late 1970s have been investigators or consultants in the project Early Indicators of Later Work Levels, Disease, and Death. Dora Costa, Roderick Floud, John Kim, Chulhee Lee, Robert Mittendorf, Louis Nguyen, Clayne Pope, Irwin H. Rosenberg, Nevin S. Scrimshaw, J. M. Tanner, James Trussel, Sven Wilson, and Larry Wimmer have provided criticisms of one or more drafts of the book or of collateral papers. Some of the central ideas in this book, particularly the theory of technophysio evolution, evolved from our collaborative research.

These colleagues also shaped my understanding of anthropometric measures as sensitive indicators of nutritional and health status and as indexes of inequality.

Early Indicators is one of a number of projects launched at the National Bureau of Economic Research (NBER) after 1978, when Martin Feldstein, NBER president, sought to encourage studies that placed current economic policies in a long-term perspective. Other NBER research projects that inform the analysis in this book are Secular Trends in Nutrition, Labor, Welfare, and Labor Productivity and The Economics of Mortality in North America since 1650.

I first became immersed in the interrelation between technological change and the ethical and political crises that it spawns during my work on the economics of slavery. It was in the course of this work that I learned of the powerful, recurrent populist movements led by evangelical reformers and their far-reaching influence on American politics and institutions. Stanley Engerman, who helped shape my views on the economics of slavery and the ideological and political struggle to abolish it, has read and criticized several drafts of this book.

My understanding of the evolution of evangelical theology, the changing agenda of evangelical reforms, and the internal divisions within the movement was aided by Martin E. Marty. He encouraged my work and carefully read and criticized several drafts of the book. Peter J. Hill also criticized several drafts of the book and organized two seminars of faculty members at Wheaton College, one on a 1992 draft of the book, the other on a late draft in 1998. The searching criticisms at these seminars helped redirect my research agenda. Some of the difficulties with the Great Awakenings constructs outlined by Mark A. Noll were particularly helpful. Christopher Gamwell read a late draft and provided criticisms that led me to rewrite parts of the introduction and chapter 1.

Douglass C. North also read both early and late drafts of the book. His criticisms led me to extend my treatment of the disruptive effect of technological change. He emphasized the difficulties in developing adequate institutional adjustments to the changes in economic and social life induced by new technologies.

My understanding of the realignment theory of American politics and my attempt to integrate it into the Great Awakening construct was enriched by the criticisms and suggestions of Walter D. Burnham, Allan G. Bogue, Joseph Cropsey, Seymour Drescher, the late François Furet, and J. Morgan Kousser. Kousser provided pointed criticisms of both the 1996 and the 1998 drafts, criticisms that forced me to reconsider and revise numerous aspects of my argument.

The lens through which I have viewed the bearing of my research on the ethical and political crises of our age was shaped in "A Guide to Business Ethics" (Business 564), a course that I have taught in the Graduate School of Business (GSB) of the University of Chicago since 1988. The course hinges on the question of why ethical standards are changing so rapidly and on approaches to the ethical turbulence confronting economic and business policy makers. Was the cascade of scandals during the mid-1980s due to an increase in immoral behavior among business executives and other public figures, or to an upsurge of concern about long-standing practices, or to both?

Although the answer to that question was unclear to me in the late 1980s, I thought that the ethical crisis could be at least partly attributed to the enormous acceleration in technological change and the difficulty in finding an adequate institutional response to destabilizing changes in everyday life brought about by the new technologies. The reemergence of a zealous religious movement extremely critical of the breakdown in personal standards of behavior contributed to the upsurge in media scrutiny of long-standing corporate practices. The intensification of ideological divisions within Congress and in state legislatures, and the shift from a focus on economic issues to one on social and ethical ones, was still another factor contributing to the sense of ethical and social crisis.

Among the problems debated in Business 564 are the interrelation of technological change and religious-political cycles with the ethics of prohibited products and services; the ethics and politics of income redistribution; ethical aspects of social security and the employment of the aged; changing standards for the employment and compensation of women and racial and ethnic minorities; the conflict between personal rights and public welfare; and agency problems (which cover both behavior in the boardroom and the conflict between management, shareholders, and other stakeholders). The many-sided aspects of these issues that emerged during the course of classroom debates are reflected in this book. My understanding of these issues was advanced by the teaching assistants who helped me design and redesign the course: Ralph Galantine, Jeffrey Martin, Christopher J. Acito, Mark Guglielmo, and Allison M. Garrett. I am also indebted to the numerous students who have taken the course each year for their lively and probing insights.

By 1992, I had proceeded far enough in my thinking on the ethical crisis and its implication for egalitarianism to present my ideas to a professional audience. The occasion was the Eighth Simon Kuznets Memorial Lectures, sponsored by the economics department of Yale University. I presented these lectures under the title "Egalitarianism: The Economic Revolution of the Twentieth Century." The three lectures were entitled "The Foundations of Modern Egalitarianism," "Institutional Paradoxes and Policy Dilemmas," and "The Unfinished Egalitarian Agenda." The intense debate that followed each of these lectures made me aware of how much additional research lay ahead of me and contributed significantly to my research agenda.

After two more years of research, I began presenting papers and addresses on various aspects of the book to scholarly and business audiences that represented a wide range of viewpoints. The feedback from these discussions helped me come to grips with issues that were inadequately developed. Comments from foreign scholars and business executives helped clarify the international aspects of a postmodern egalitarian agenda and gave me a broader perspective on American issues. The meetings from which I benefited included talks to scholars and policy makers at the Universidad Torcuato Di Tella (Buenos Aires), De Paul College of Commerce (Chicago), the World Bank, EDS Management Consulting Services, the American Enterprise Institute (Washington, D.C.), the Islamic Development ment Bank (Jeddah), the 1995 WinConference (sponsored by Winterthur Insurance in Geneva), the Eleventh World Congress of the International Economic Association (Tunis), the Loyola University Baumhart Business Ethics Lectures (Chicago), Osaka Gakuin University (Osaka), the Japan Center for Economic Research (Tokyo), the Kansai Economic Research Center (Osaka), the Chamber of Commerce and Industry of Pusan, Dong-A University (Pusan), the Korea Development Institute (Seoul), Seoul National University, the Royal Society (London), National Taiwan University (Taipei), the International Conference on Economic Aspects of the Demographic Transition (Taipei), Brigham Young University (Provo), the International Council for Global Health Progress, Unesco (Paris), the Calvert House Conference on God and Mammon: A Moral Vision of Economic Life (Chicago), and the DuSable Conference on Business Ethics (Chicago).

I also spoke on issues of business ethics and technophysio evolution to alumni meetings of the GSB in Chicago, New York, Buenos Aires, Pusan, and Seoul and to meetings for middle-management executives organized by the GSB in Paris, Chicago, London, Brussels, Berlin, Frankfurt, Barcelona, and Madrid.

Other colleagues who read one or more drafts of the book and who provided insights and criticisms that led me to reconsider and rewrite sections are John Comaroff, Marilyn Coopersmith, Gerald Friedman, Eugene D. Genovese, James Gilbert, Claudia Goldin, Bernard Harris, Richard Hellie, D. Gale Johnson, Lawrence F. Katz, John Komlos, David Landes, Emmet Larkin, Peter Laslett, Stanley Lebergott, Ralph Lerner, Peter Lindert, Robert Margo, William N. Parker, J. R. Pole, Arthur E. Rasmussen, Joseph Reid, Richard Saller, Lewis C. Solomon, Richard H. Steckel, David Surdam, Jenny B. Wahl, William Julius Wilson, C. Vann Woodward, and Yasukichi Yasuba.

Enid M. Fogel read the manuscript at its various stages. Among her many suggestions was the need to give more attention to the role, present and potential, of voluntary organizations in mentoring alienated youths and in providing outlets for the elderly who seek self-realization by helping others.

I have had the support, both intellectual and material, of a succession of deans at the GSB: Richard N. Rossett, Jack P. Gould, and Robert S. Hamada. Rossett has encouraged and supported my research since we were both assistant professors at the University of Rochester. He persuaded me to return to Chicago in 1981. Hamada's enthusiasm about both my courses and my research began when he first became acquainted with my work and has continued through his stewardship of the GSB. At Harvard, Henry Rosovsky, fellow economic historian and dean of the faculty of arts and sciences, provided insightful criticism and generous research facilities.

Others who have helped with the research on various aspects of the book include Jibum Kim, Mario Sanchez, Max Henderson, Peter Viechnicki, Min-Woong Sohn, Chen Song, Eveline Murphy, and Julene Bassett.

The editorial work on this volume fell mainly on Katherine A. Chavigny, Susan E. Jones, and Katharine J. Hamerton. Chavigny shared with me her own research on the effect of evangelical reformers on American culture during the eighteenth and nineteenth centuries. In addition, our discussions of the various drafts of the book from 1992 until the present helped clarify many of the issues with which I was struggling. She also made a number of helpful suggestions on the reorganization of material within the book. The penultimate draft was extensively edited by Anita Samen. Her suggestions strengthened the argument of the book, helped highlight and integrate its major themes, and improved the movement of the manuscript. The numerous drafts were efficiently typed by Karen

Brobst, Carol J. Bridgeman, and Pat Mackins-Morrow. Ms. Brobst also made numerous helpful editorial suggestions.

The funding of the research on which this book is based came from the National Science Foundation, the National Institutes of Health, the National Bureau of Economic Research, the Walgreen Foundation, and the University of Chicago.

APPENDICES

APPENDIX IA

*Measuring the Partisan Shifts
among Believers in Enthusiastic Religion*

Calculations of recent shifts in voting patterns in the United States are based on the computer tapes containing the data of exit polls available from the Inter-University Consortium for Political and Social Research (ICPSR 1993, 1995b) as well as polls, taken shortly after the relevant elections, containing information on the political attitudes of nonvoters by religious affiliation (ICPSR 1995a, n.d.). Since the questions in the postelection surveys on religion were modified after 1988, it was necessary to work out the following equivalencies in the characterizations of believers in enthusiastic religion: Prior to 1988, they included believers grouped in the category *Protestant Neo-Fundamentalist,* codes 130–49 *(United Missionary/Protestant Missionary; Church of God/Holiness; Nazarene/Free Methodist; Church of God in Christ; Plymouth Brethren; Pentecostal/Assembly of God; Church of Christ; Salvation Army; Primitive/Free Will/Missionary Fundamentalist/Gospel Baptist; Seventh Day Adventist; Southern Baptist; Missouri Synod Lutheran; Other Fundamentalist),* plus the *Mormon Latter-Day Saints* (code 152) and the *Jehovah's Witnesses* (code 154) from the category *Non-Traditional Christian.* After 1988, believers in enthusiastic religion included those who professed affiliation with any church in the categories *Adventist* (codes 100, 102, 109), *Independent-Fundamen-*

The following abbreviations are used throughout the appendices: HS = U.S. Bureau of the Census, *Historical Statistics of the United States, Colonial Times to 1970,* 2 pts. (Washington, D.C.: U.S. Government Printing Office, 1975); and SA = U.S. Bureau of the Census, *Statistical Abstract of the United States* (Washington, D.C.: U.S. Government Printing Office, published annually), the date of which varies according to the *Abstract* cited.

talist (codes 201, 211, 219), and *Pentecostal* (codes 250–58, 260–61, 267–69), plus selected denominations from the categories *Baptist* (codes 120, 124, 127–28, 133) *Holiness* (codes 121–84), *Lutheran* (codes 221–23), *Presbyterian* (codes 271–72), *Reformed* (code 281), and *Non-Traditional Protestants* (codes 301, 304, 306). The polls of the electorate were checked for consistency with the Princeton-Gallup polls for 1982 and 1994. The sampling fraction of the polls was used to convert sample figures to population figures using data from the relevant *Statistical Abstract of the United States* (cf. Kosmin 1991, and Kosmin, Keysar, and Lerer 1992).

APPENDIX 3A

The Calorie Consumption of Ultrapoor and Average
Households and Their Location in the Massie (1759) and
Colquhoun (1801) Distributions of English Income

Estimates of the English distribution of calories circa 1790 and of the American distribution of calories in 1700 and 1840 are reported in Fogel and Floud (1999). These distributions indicate that the calories available to Americans at the tenth centile of calorie consumption exceeded the bottom seven deciles of British calorie consumption circa 1790.

Although the British lower classes were severely malnourished, they were even worse off in other aspects of consumption since calories were more equally distributed than income. Studies of household consumption of agricultural and nonagricultural rural laborers allow us to reconstruct the income of the British lower classes. These studies omitted the very poor and the prosperous. None of the households in these samples had an annual income of less than £15 or of as much as £70 per year. The mean annual expenditure on all items in the Davies study was £27.00 per household circa 1790 (about 72 percent of which went for food) and £39.84 per household in the Eden study circa 1794 (about 74 percent of which went for food) (Stigler 1954). The expenditures in both studies have been converted to 1759 prices to make them comparable (prices rose rapidly over the period covered by the two, especially after the outbreak of the war with France). The annual expenditure figures in 1759 prices are £21.8 in the Davies survey and £29.3 in the Eden. Using the Schumpeter-Gilboy index of consumer prices, the index number is 100 for 1759, 124 for 1790, and 136 for 1794 (Mitchell and Deane 1962, 469).

English political arithmeticians produced estimates of the social distribution of income in England circa 1759 (Massie, in Mathias 1957) and circa 1801 (Col-

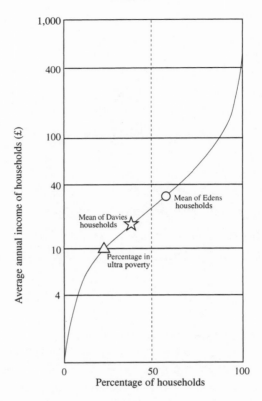

Figure 3A.1 The income distribution of English households in 1759.
SOURCES: See the text of app. 3A.

quhoun 1814). These tables have been revised and converted into size distributions of income by Lindert and Williamson (1982). I have further corrected the revised Massie distribution for an underestimate of the proportion of the population that was ultrapoor. Figure 3A.1 displays the estimated size distribution of income by households for 1759. It also locates the average household income (as measured by expenditures in 1759 pounds) in the Davies and Eden surveys. Figure 3A.1 shows that, in both surveys, average income is close to the median of the estimated English income distribution during the third quarter of the eighteenth century, with one of the means falling slightly above it, the other slightly below it.

Since the median income was only about 53 percent of the mean income, the households selected for the two surveys, on standards that prevailed in the United States during the first two-thirds of the twentieth century (and apparently quite similar to the standard used by the reformers who conducted the surveys [cf. Smolensky 1971]), straddled the poverty line. However, none of the households were so poor that they fell below the ultrapoverty line, which encompassed paupers and

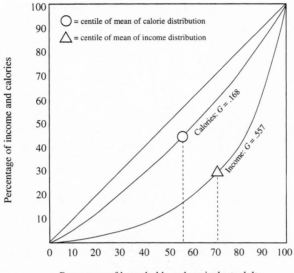

Figure 3A.2   A comparison of the Lorenz curves for calories and for income in England during the second half of the nineteenth century.

SOURCES: See the text of app. 3A; and Fogel and Floud (1999, table A.4).

vagrants. The ultrapoor (the bottom 21 percent) had incomes below £10.0, which was hardly a fifth of the mean. The average income of the ultrapoor in 1759 was about £5.3, almost the same in purchasing power (£9.7 in the prices used by Colquhoun) as the ultrapoor had to spend on average circa 1801 (£10). So the first four decades of the Industrial Revolution did little to change either the proportion of the English ultrapoor or the level of their real earnings.

The finding that households in the two surveys had incomes well below the English national average does not imply that their calorie consumption (twenty-eight hundred calories per consuming unit) was also below the average for England. Since size distributions of calories are generally much more equal than those of income, the centile of the calorie distribution at which average calorie consumption is reached is much lower than the centile of the income distribution at which the average income is reached (see fig. 3A.2). This is because in cross-section (but not longitudinally) very poor households have a high propensity to purchase additional calories as their income increases, which initially leads the consumption of calories to increase more rapidly than income. But, as calorie consumption approaches the societal mean, the propensity to purchase additional calories declines sharply, even though incomes are still quite low. Thus, at average levels of calorie consumption similar to those found in the Davies and Eden surveys, when calories are sufficiently cheap and the distribution of income sufficiently skewed, the mean consumption of calories might well be achieved by households that are below the median of the income distribution. In rural India in 1971–72, for example, the average consumption of calories was achieved by households in the forty-ninth centile of the income distribution. Since calories usually were relatively cheap in England during the last half of the eighteenth century, and England's income distribution was far more skewed than that of rural India in the 1970s, the calorie consumption of median-income families was probably well above the mean calorie consumption of English households in 1790 (estimated from the data in Lipton [1983, 73] by fitting a lognormal curve to the income distribution).

I have corrected the Lindert and Williamson (1982) estimate of the proportion of households that were in the class of paupers and vagrants (the ultrapoor) in 1759. They put the figure at 12.5 percent, although they put the proportion at 24.2 percent in 1688 and 19.9 percent in 1801 (both their 1688 and their 1801 proportions are downward revisions of those estimated by King and Colquhoun). This large implied drop in the English proportion of the ultrapoor during the mid-eighteenth century appears to be an artifact of their estimating procedure. They assumed that the paupers and vagrants omitted by Massie were equal to their estimate of Massie's overstatement of households in manufacturing and agriculture, less Massie's understatement of households in the building trades and mining. However, there is little evidence to support the implication that the proportion of the ultrapoor dropped sharply from 1699 to 1759 and then rose nearly as sharply between 1759 and 1801. Given the large military drain on manpower during 1801, one would expect the proportion of the ultrapoor to have been relatively low. Various studies indicate that the 1750s and 1760s were a troubled period for labor, with the problem of the ultrapoor unabated (Marshall 1968; Lipson 1971; Rose 1961; Barnes 1930; Schwartz 1985; Thompson 1963). Consequently, I have reestimated the proportion of the ultrapoor for 1759 (21.4 percent) by interpolating between the proportions for 1688 and 1801.

The procedure for identifying the parameters of the lognormal distribution that fits the revised Massie table is somewhat different from those fitting procedures employed in the construction of table 4 of Fogel (1993). There, the specification of the coefficient of variation determined σ. And σ, plus Toutain's estimate of mean calorie consumption (2,290) in consuming units, determined μ. The two equations used in Fogel (1993, table 4) were

$$(3A.1) \quad \frac{\sigma^2}{2} + \mu = \ln \overline{X},$$

(3A.2) $\quad \dfrac{s}{\overline{X}} = (e^{\sigma^2} - 1)^{0.5}$.

In the case of the revised Massie social table, $s/\overline{X}$ is not known. However, the finding that 21.4 percent of English households were ultrapoor (paupers and vagrants), and that this class was defined by incomes of £10 or less, takes the place of equation (3A.2), implies equation (3A.3):

$$(3A.3) \quad \dfrac{2.3026 - \mu}{\sigma} = -0.791,$$

where 2.3026 is the natural log of 10, and -0.791 is the Z score corresponding to 21.4 percent. Since $\overline{X}$ is known (£46.37) and its natural log is 3.8367, equations (3A.1) and (3A.3) imply the following quadratic in σ:

$$(3A.4) \quad \sigma^2 + 1.58\sigma - 3.07 = 0.$$

Solving equation (3A.4) gives a value for σ of 1.13, which, when substituted in equation (3A.3), yields $\mu = 3.20$.

This procedure for fitting the lognormal retains the estimates of the mean income and the household count reported by Lindert and Williamson (1982). Under these circumstances, the revised estimate of the proportion who were ultrapoor produces an adjustment in the share of income received by the upper classes.

An alternative procedure is to assume that the 137,066 households added to the ranks of the ultrapoor represent an addition to the population (rather than a redistribution of a fixed total population). The new assumption increases the total of English households by 8.91 percent, not an implausible figure, and changes the variance of the distribution, in a direction that depends on the estimate of the mean and the standard deviation of the income in the previously omitted ultrapoor households. If one assumes that the additional ultrapoor households had the same distribution of income as the ultrapoor originally specified by Lindert and Williamson, the following equations apply:

$$(3A.5) \quad \dfrac{\sigma^2}{2} + \mu = 3.7642,$$

$$(3A.6) \quad \dfrac{2.3026 - \mu}{\sigma} = -0.85.$$

Here, 3.7642 is the log of the mean income (£43.13); it is less than the previous mean because the added households had incomes well below the mean. And the new Z score (-0.85) is further below zero than the score in equation (3A.3) because adding persons to the denominator slightly reduces the share of the population that is ultrapoor. Solving equations (3A.5) and (3A.6) yields

$$\mu = 3.20,$$

$$\sigma = 1.06.$$

The consequence of the alternative procedure is to reduce slightly the inequality of the income distribution, but this change does not affect any of the major points under discussion here. For example, the median of the income distribution (£24.5) is unchanged to three significant places, and the mean income of the ultrapoor is also virtually unchanged (£5.5). Other reasonable alternatives for fitting the distribution demonstrated that the principal points at issue here are robust to the fitting procedure.

The procedure used to compare the real average income of the English ultrapoor circa 1759 and circa 1801 is as follows. The Davies sample indicates that fewer than 0.5 percent of the servants in husbandry, the class that it describes, had household incomes below £10.9 in 1759 prices. Since none of the households in the Davies sample were characterized as ultrapoor (i.e., as paupers or vagrants), the upper-bound income for the ultrapoor is below that figure. So I have chosen £10, the next lower whole number, as the upper income bound of the pauper class.

To compare the mean income of the ultrapoor in 1759 prices with the comparable figure in Colquhoun's table for 1801–3, it was necessary to develop an appropriate price deflator. This deflator was obtained by projecting the mean average income estimated by Lindert and Williamson (1982) for 1759 (£46.37) to 1801 by using Crafts's (1985, 45) estimate of the average annual real rate of growth in per capita income between 1760 and 1801. The procedure yielded a figure of £50.01 for the 1801 per household income in 1759 prices. Lindert and Williamson's revisions of Colquhoun's table yielded a per household income of £91.63 in 1801–3 prices. Consequently, the implied national income deflator is 1.83 (91.63 ÷ 50.01 = 1.83), which makes the mean income of the ultrapoor in 1801–3 pounds about £9.7 (5.3 × 1.83 ≈ 9.7).

It follows that the real rate of increase in the average earnings of the ultrapoor, $(10 \div 9.7)^{1/42} - 1 = 0.00073$, was less than that of society as a whole, $(50.01 \div 46.37)^{1/42} - 1 = 0.00180$.

APPENDIX 5A

The Length of the Workyear circa 1880

There was a considerable change in labor conditions between 1880 and 1900. Between these two dates, the share of labor in agriculture declined from about 51 to 40 percent. Hence, in 1880, manufacturing industries, the main industries covered by the state bureaus of labor, constituted only about 19 percent of the labor force.

The best evidence on working hours in agriculture comes from a series of surveys undertaken by the USDA between 1905 and 1940. These indicate an average workyear of about 3,130 hours. Using 1917 as the midpoint, and assuming a very low income elasticity in the demand for leisure (0.1), the rise in per capita income suggests that working hours in agriculture may have been about 180 hours more in 1880 than circa 1917, or about 3,308 hours. Given a workyear over all non-agricultural occupations of 304 days and 10.25 hours of work per day, the national annual average comes out to about 3,214 hours. Although 10.25 hours is slightly longer than Atack and Bateman (1992) reported, these authors focused on manufacturing and hence did not take account of longer hours in other nonagricultural industries.

The average workweek, after allowing for 25 sick days and holidays, was about 6.25 days per week, which implies 304 equivalent full days of work per year. The USDA surveys circa 1917 indicate that about a third to a half day generally was set aside for work on Sundays. Outside agriculture, iron and steel worked 7 days a week, 24 hours a day (running two 12-hour shifts until 1923) year-round, closing only for about a week a year to reline the furnaces. Other industries that worked a seven-day week included railroads, utilities, lumber, shipping, telegraph, postal service, police, construction, much of retail trade, hospitality, servants, and various professions (clergy, medicine, journalists). Moreover, although blue laws were on the books in many states, they had been resisted in others. Where they existed, they appear to have been poorly enforced before 1880 and often had escape clauses permitting businesses to function. These laws apparently became increasingly effective after the rise of the Social Gospel movement, which worked in conjunction with the labor movement, particularly the AFL and the miners' union, to limit hours of work. Even if Sunday nonagricultural work averaged just one hour a day in 1880 (it was probably more), the weighted average of agricultural and nonagricultural work would yield a workweek of 6.25 days (Vincent 1976; Roth 1973; Pitzer 1968–69). On the workweek of housewives, see Lebergott (1993).

Rees (HS 1975, 154–55, 172) put the manufacturing workyear in 1890 at 2,945 hours. He used state BLS data for interpolating between census years. His figures were 294 days for 1890, 297 for 1891, and 296 for 1892. His two worst years between 1890 and 1914 are 1893 and 1894, which he put at 271 and 272 days, respectively. Rees also estimated average hours worked daily, which declined from 10.2 in 1890 to 9.28 in 1914. His implied annual hours of work in all manufacturing industries are as follows: 2,945 in 1890; 2,973 in 1891; 2,972 in 1892; 2,698 in 1894; 2,882 in 1899; 2,787 in 1904; 2,762 in 1909; and 2,607 in 1914. Rees used reports of manufacturing firms rather than surveys of individuals.

The USDA studies for 1905–30 indicate a seasonal variation similar to those in Engerman and Goldin (1994). The February low was just 76 percent of the August high. However, the variation was mainly in hours worked per day, not in days worked per month. There was also a shift in the composition of activity, from the predominance of fieldwork in the summer to the predominance of chores in the winter. Daylight was substantially shorter during winter in the Northern dairy and spring wheat regions than in the cotton South. However, this was offset by the longer summer workdays in the dairy and spring wheat regions. Consequently, although there may have been more days off in the Northern wheat belt than elsewhere during the winter, the hours were made up during the long summer days and also during the early fall, when harvest work was conducted in twilight (Olson 1992).

Unemployment rates increased sharply between 1890 and World War I, becoming a much more severe problem in both urban and rural areas than they had been in the early 1880s and previously. The change is signaled by the inability of agriculture to absorb its natural increase. Down to 1880, the average annual increase in the agricultural labor force exceeded the natural rate of increase in the population. But, between 1880 and 1910, agriculture was dumping most of the natural increase in its labor force into the cities, and, after 1910, the decline in the agricultural labor force became absolute. The excess supply of labor between 1893 and most of the first decade of the twentieth century was aggravated by the upswing in the long migration cycle. Hence, unemployment rates were relatively high through most of these fifteen years. Thus, Rees reports that, near the peak of the 1899 boom, the manufacturing workyear was six days shorter than it had been near the peak of the 1892 boom and that the average workday for those employed was down by about six minutes. The combined effect is a 3 percent decline in hours of work. The year 1900 suffers from being the trough of a business cycle. Lebergott put the unemployment rate at about 10 percent in 1900.[1]

Both the state labor reports and the 1900 microsample display more days lost to unemployment than was the case in 1880. The 1880s mark a divide on this issue, as is indicated by the rise of the Social Gospel movement and the crisis in agricultural employment. I chose 1880 as the comparison year because of the complexities raised by the subsequent deterioration in labor markets.

Neither involuntary cyclic unemployment nor nutritionally imposed indolence can be considered leisure since leisure requires the choice of doing what you want. On the other hand, if seasonal unemployment is predictable, it may constitute leisure. The figures in table 5.1 in the text indicate a total of 657 hours of leisure in 1880, which, divided by the 14 discretionary hours in a day, yields 47 equivalent full days of leisure. These leisure days were probably allocated disproportionately to slack seasons.

The extra labor needed for harvest came primarily from within the rural areas, where about half the labor force was nonagricultural. The 50 percent premium on harvest labor was enough to induce many common nonagricultural rural laborers temporarily to leave their regular work for harvest work. Schoolchildren were another source of extra labor since, as Lewis Solmon (1968) pointed out in his dissertation, rural schools in the late nineteenth century and the early twentieth were closed during harvest and other times of peak farm labor.

APPENDIX 5B

On the Calculation of the Expected Length of Retirement at Age Fifty and the Proportion of a Cohort That Lives to Retire

The assertion that the enormous increase in per capita incomes of OECD nations has permitted the average length of retirement to increase fivefold, the proportion of a cohort that lives to retire to increase sevenfold, and the amount of leisure time available to those still in the labor force to increase nearly fourfold has been based on computations from data on labor force participation rates by age obtained from the U.S. censuses for 1880 and 1990 and reported by Lee (1996) and Costa (1998b). These were combined with the period life tables for 1900 and 1990 reported by Bell, Wade, and Goss (1992); for further details on the basic methodology, see Lee (1996, chap. 3) and Costa (1998a, chap. 2). I have assumed that the period life tables and labor force participation rates can be used as proxies for the respective cohorts, an assumption that probably minimized the gains experienced by the cohort born in 1940 compared with the cohort born in 1830 (see Pope 1992; Haines 1992).

Before age fifty, the share of a cohort that is retired is estimated to be zero because death preceded retirement before that age. After age fifty, retirement preceded death for an increasing proportion of a cohort. However, in 1880, the percentage of survivors who remained in the labor force did not drop to 50 percent until age eighty-five. Consequently, in 1880, only about 2.60 years of retirement were expected at age fifty, while life expectancy for males at age fifty was 20.54 years (Lee 1996). It follows that, at age fifty, the expected length of retirement in that year was only about 13 percent of life expectancy (2.60 ÷ 20.54 ≈ 0.127).

The calculation is symmetrical for 1990, with retirement again presumed to begin at age fifty. In 1990, however, 50 percent of the survivors are retired by age sixty-three and 90 percent by age seventy-seven. Consequently, the expected period of retirement at age fifty, which is 13.80 years, is now more than half as large as life expectancy (13.80 ÷ 26.08 ≈ 0.53). It follows that the expected length of retirement in 1990 is more than five times as large as the corresponding figure in 1880 (13.80 ÷ 2.60 ≈ 5.3).

The data already described make it possible to compute the proportion of a cohort that lives to retire, which was 10 percent in 1880 and 71 percent in 1990.

Persons too malnourished for work are excluded from the calculations with respect to retirement and leisure since, as discussed in the text, leisure requires the resources needed to do what one desires. Nutritionally dictated indolence is not leisure.

APPENDIX 5C

Procedures for Estimating the Long-Term Income Elasticities of Extended Consumption

ESTIMATE OF THE DISTRIBUTION OF CONSUMPTION EXPANDED TO INCLUDE HEALTH CARE AND EDUCATION

The Current Population Survey reports only out-of-pocket expenditures of households on health care and education (SA 1997, 461). In 1995, however, most expenditures on these items were made by government or employers on behalf of households. Hence, in table 5C.1, for the year 1995, expenditures on medical care were increased from $1,732 to $9,600, and expenditures on education were increased from $471 to $4,910 (SA 1997, 112, 153, 461, 464).

The earliest date for which the government share of health-care expenditures is available is 1929, when total health-care expenditures were 3.5 percent of GNP and one-fifth of that (0.7 percent of GNP) was provided from public sources (HS 1975, 74). The 1929 share, extrapolated geometrically back to 1875 on the basis of the rate of change in the share between 1929 and 1950, yielded a share of 1.89 percent. Since GNP was $7.4 billion circa 1875, population was 45,073 million, average household size was 5.1 persons, and national consumption was about 78 percent of GNP, of which $12 per household was spent on health care ($10 out of pocket) (HS 1975, 8, 74, 224; Kuznets 1952, 30, 59; U.S. Department of Labor 1959, 35).

Solmon (1970, 579) provides the data needed to estimate out-of-pocket and public direct expenditures on education (which exclude the value of forgone earnings) in 1880. The relevant figures per capita (HS 1975, 8) are $0.32 out of pocket and $1.52 from public sources. Multiplied by 5.1 persons per household, these become $1.63 and $7.75 per household, respectively. When the last two figures were

APPENDICES

Table 5C.1   The Distribution of Reported Consumption per Household Corrected for Health Care and Educational Expenditures (in Current Dollars)

Consumption Class	1875 $	1875 %	1995 $	1995 %
Food	427	57.2	5,150	12.2
Clothing	106	14.2	1,700	4.0
Shelter	117	15.7	5,930	14.0
Health care	12	1.6	9,600	22.7
Education	8	1.1	4,900	11.6
Other	77	10.3	15,060	35.6

NOTE: The value of noncash food benefits, including food stamps and free lunches (SA 1997, 375, using 1994 data), has been added to food, but other socially provided consumption not elsewhere indicated (such as public housing subsidies and union benefits) has been omitted since these amount to less than 0.5 percent of household consumption. Expenditures on pensions and social security have been excluded since they are forms of saving rather than consumption. Columns may not add to 100 because of rounding.

deflated by 1.14 (using the average of 1875 and 1876 in the Warren Pearson price index [HS 1975, 201]) to put them in prices circa 1875, they became $1.43 and $6.80 or, rounded to the nearest dollar, 1 and 7.

Table 5C.1 presents the corrected consumption expenditures of households in 1875 and 1995.

THE ESTIMATION OF LEISURE AS A SHARE OF EXTENDED CONSUMPTION

Leisure, whether produced at home or elsewhere, requires not only purchased materials and services but also the time of individuals. The value of the purchased materials for leisure services, which are included in the Consumer Expenditures Survey, averaged about $7,421 in 1995 (SA 1997, 265, 461; items included are entertainment, reading, tobacco, charity and 74 percent of transport), which is about 49 percent of "other" in table 5C.1.

The value of the time of consumers is a far larger item and may be measured by the forgone income of those who consume leisure. Only persons in the labor force or those who have retired will be considered to have forgone income (cf. Kuznets 1952; Nordhaus and Tobin 1972; Zolotas 1981; Jorgenson and Fraumeni 1987; Kendrick 1987; and Eisner 1988). Annual hours of leisure are divided between those of retirees, who are on average age sixty-three or over ($37,595 \times 10^3 \times 5,110 = 192,110 \times 10^6$; from table 5.3 in the text; and SA [1996, 23]); and those of individuals aged twenty to sixty-two, of which 63.5 percent are presumed to be in the

Table 5C.2   The Distribution of Reported Consumption Extended to Include the Consumption of Leisure (in Current Dollars)

Consumption Class	1875		1995	
	$	%	$	%
Food	427	48.6	5,150	4.8
Clothing	106	12.1	1,700	1.6
Shelter	117	13.3	5,930	5.5
Health care	12	1.4	9,600	8.9
Education	8	.9	4,900	4.6
Other	48	5.5	7,640	7.1
Leisure	161	18.3	72,600	67.5

NOTE: For 1875, it was assumed that about three-eighths of expenditures on "other" in table 5C.1 above represented items purchased for leisure. Use of the ratio of hours of leisure to hours of work for males to cover both men and women implies that the leisure pattern by age was the same for both sexes (so that numerator and denominator are multiplied by the same factor). Although women left the labor market at different ages than men, an increased amount of their time was devoted to chores, leaving hours of leisure approximately the same. Columns may not add to 100 because of rounding.

labor force ($149,371 \times 10^3 \times 0.635 \times 2,117 = 200,979 \times 10^6$; from table 5.2 in the text; SA [1996, 22–23]; and SA [1997, 397]).

Hence, total hours of leisure in 1995 was 392,900 million, which, if valued at the average compensation per hour of those in the labor force in 1995, $17.10 (SA 1996, 430), yields an estimated value of total consumption of $6,720 billion, or $65,200 per household ($6,720 \times 10^9 \div 103.0 \times 10^6$ households; for the number of households, see SA [1997, 464]). It follows (see table 5C.2) that average household expenditure on extended consumption in 1995 was about $107,500, of which 67.5 percent ($65,200 + $7,400 = $72,600) was on the consumption of leisure and 32.5 percent was on all other household consumption shown in table 5C.1 above.

The computation of extended consumption in 1875 makes use of the information on the age structure of the population in 1880, which is assumed to be the same as that of the population in 1875. It is also assumed that the average age at which men entered the labor force is seventeen and that, between age seventeen and age fifty, the proportion retired was zero. On the basis of data in Costa (1998b, 12), the proportion retired is estimated to rise from 0.01 at ages fifty to fifty-four to 1.0 at age ninety. The computation yields a total of $29.8 \times 10^6 \times 0.635$ hours of leisure annually and 168.2×10^6 hours of work (including chores and travel to work). The ratio of these numbers is 17.7 percent, which is the share of leisure due to time in extended consumption. Adding $29 for out-of-pocket expenditures raises the leisure share to 18.3 percent. See table 5.3 in the text.

ESTIMATION OF THE GROWTH OF CONSUMPTION BY SEVEN CLASSES BETWEEN 1875 AND 1995 AND OF THE INCOME ELASTICITY OF CONSUMPTION FOR EACH CLASS

The real level of consumption in any consumption class in 1995, in terms of the standardized units of 1875, is equal to the real increase in total consumption between 1875 and 1995, multiplied by the share of that class in total consumption in 1995. Thus,

$$(5C.1) \quad c_{j2} = (c_{j2}/c_{t2})[c_{t1}(1 + r)^{120}],$$

where c_{j2} = consumption in class j in 1995 in standardized units of 1875; c_{j1} = standardized consumption in class j in 1875; c_{t2} = total consumption in 1995 in units of 1875; c_{t1} = total consumption in 1875, which is standardized to equal 1; and r = the average annual rate of increase in total consumption between 1875 and 1995. It follows that the elasticity of consumption in each class with respect to income is given by

$$(5C.2) \quad \epsilon_j = [(c_{j2} \div c_{j1})^{1/120} - 1] \div r,$$

where ϵ_j = the income elasticity of consumption in the jth class. The procedures indicated by equations (5C.1) and (5C.2) are executed in table 5C.3.

Table 5C.3 The Computation of the Income Elasticity of Demand for Each Consumption Class, 1875–1995

Consumption Class	Standardized Level of Extended Consumption, 1875 (1)	Class Share in Extended Consumption, 1995 (2)	Level of Class Consumption in 1995 in Units of 1875 (3)	Annual Rate of Growth in the Level of Consumption, by Class (4)	Income Elasticity of Consumption Class (5)
Food	.486	.048	.909	.00523	.21
Clothing	.121	.016	.303	.00768	.31
Shelter	.133	.055	1.042	.01730	.70
Health care	.014	.089	1.686	.04073	1.64
Education	.009	.046	.871	.03884	1.56
Other	.055	.071	1.345	.02700	1.09
Leisure	.183	.675	12.791	.03602	1.45

NOTES: *Col. 1:* From table 5C.2 above. *Col. 2:* From table 5C.2 above. *Col. 3:* Entries in col. 2 × 18.95, where 18.95 = 1.02482^{120}. Growth in conventional GNP per capita between 1875 and 1994 was computed from data in Maddison (1995, 196–97) and extended to 1995 with data in SA (1997, 452). Standardizing GNP per capita in 1875 at 1, real per capita GNP is 8.778 in 1995. To take account of unmeasured leisure, the last number was multiplied by (2.541 ÷ 1.177 =) 2.159, the ratio of extended consumption to conventional consumption in 1995 (1.177 is the corresponding figure for 1875). Thus, 8.778 × 2.159 = 18.95. *Col. 4:* Computed from [(col. 3 ÷ col. 1)$^{1/120}$ − 1]. It should be noted that, under this procedure, the income elasticities, weighted by a convex combination of class shares in 1875 (45 percent) and 1995 (55 percent), sum to 1.00. *Col. 5:* Entries in col. 4 divided by 0.02482.

APPENDIX 5D

The Amount of Pensions, Education, and Health Care That Can Be Purchased by a New Household with Median Income That Earnworks for Only Thirty-Five Years and Saves 32 Percent of Annual Income during These Years

SAVING CALCULATION

In 1993 dollars (SA 1996, 463), mean money income of household heads ages fifteen to twenty-four was $23,041. The ratio of total compensation to money income in 1995 (SA 1996, 430) was 17.10 ÷ 13.81 = 1.23823; therefore

$$23,041 \times 1.23823 \ = \ 28,530.$$

To shift the base year to 1995, use the ratio of per capita personal income 1995:1993 (SA 1996, 453): 22,788/20,809 = 1.09510; therefore

$$28,530 \times 1.09510 \ = \ 31,243.$$

The life-cycle increase during ages twenty to thirty-five (SA 1996, 463, using linear interpolation) is 1.88757, and the ratio of age-fifty-five to age-thirty-five income (SA 1996, 463, using the interval forty-five to fifty-four) is 1.32831. The annual rate of increase during ages thirty-five to fifty-five is $1.32831^{1/20} = 1.014297$; similarly the annual rate of increase over ages twenty to thirty-five is $1.88757^{1/15} = 1.04326$. Combining the annual rate of growth of the economy at 1.015 and the life-cycle effect, yields income at age thirty-five of 73,728 (31,243 $[1.015 \times 1.04326]^{15}$ = 31,243 × 2.35982 = 73,728). Income at age fifty-five is 131,911 (73,728 × $[1.015 \times 1.01430]^{20}$ = 73,728 × 1.78916 = 131,911). Current consumption at age fifty-five is 89,699 (131,911 × 0.68 = 89,699).

The value of savings at age fifty-five is 1,219,185 ([0.32 × 31,243 {1.12245^{15} − 1} × 1.06^{20}]/0.12245 = 380,147 × 3.20714 = 1,219,185) (where 1.12245 = 1.05891 × 1.06, and where 0.32 = 1 − 0.68). And, since 0.32 × 73,728(1.09129^{20} − 1)/0.09129 = 1,224,634, then 1,219,185 + 1,224,634 = 2,443,819.

PENSION

Income at age fifty-five is 31,243 × $(1.04326 × 1.015)^{15}$ × $(1.015 × 1.01430)^{20}$ = 31,243 × 2.35982 × 1.78916 = 131,911, and the annual pension for twenty-eight years is 131,911 × 0.6 = 79,146. The present value of that pension at age fifty-five for twenty-eight years (using beginning mode) is 1,124,706. The share of the income that must be saved during working years to buy the stipulated pension is 14.7 percent (1,124,706 ÷ 2,443,819 = 0.46022 × 0.32 = 0.147).

EDUCATION

Annual expenditure per pupil in 1995 (SA 1996, 153) was $5,887 ([$298,932 × 10^6]/ [50,776 × 10^3 pupils]) at the elementary and secondary school level and $13,738 ([$195,205 × 10^6]/[14,209 × 10^3 pupils]) at the college and university level.

I am making the following assumptions: Child 1 is born in year 4, enters school in year 10, and enters college in year 22. Child 2 is born in year 8, enters school in year 14, and enters college in year 26. For child 1, the present value of school in year 10 projected to year 35 is 224,538 (52,317.03 × $[1.06]^{25}$ = 224,538), and the present value of college in year 22 projected to year 35 is 107,627 (50,459.84 × $[1.06]^{13}$ = 107,627). For child 2, the present value of school in year 14 projected to year 35 is 177,855 (52,317.03 × $[1.06]^{21}$ = 177,855), and the present value of college in year 26 projected to year 35 is 85,251 (50,459.84 × $[1.06]^9$ = 85,251). Now, 224,538 + 107,627 + 177,855 + 85,251 = 595,271. And 595,271 ÷ 2,443,819 = 0.24358 × 0.32 = 0.07795, or 7.8 percent of income.

MEDICAL INSURANCE

I am making the following assumptions. The second child is born four years after the first child. The discount rate is 1.013 × 1.06 = 1.07378, where 1.013 is the annual rate of decline in the real cost of insurance (i.e., the rate of decline in disabilities computed from Manton, Corder, and Stallard 1997).

Using the age structure of health expenditures shown in table 5D.1, the present value of health-care expenditures on child 1 (born at parents' age twenty-four) is 8,294.98. Therefore, at age fifty-five, present value is 50,500.67 ([8,294.98] ×

Table 5D.1 Age Structure of U.S. Health-Care Expenditures, Using a 1987 Cross Section

	Per Capita Expenditure (1987 $)	Annual Proportion of Lifetime Expenditures	Cumulated Proportion at End of Interval
0–4	900	.00508	.0254
5–9	500	.00282	.0395
10–14	700	.00395	.0593
15–19	900	.00508	.0847
20–24	1,250	.00706	.1200
25–29	1,250	.00706	.1553
30–34	1,250	.00706	.1906
35–39	1,250	.00706	.2259
40–44	1,400	.00791	.2654
45–49	1,500	.00847	.3077
50–54	1,900	.01073	.3614
55–59	2,000	.01129	.4178
60–64	2,900	.01637	.4997
65–69	3,900	.02202	.6098
70–74	4,500	.02541	.7369
75–79	5,300	.02993	.8865
80–82	6,700	.03783	1.0000
Lifetime expenditures	177,100		

SOURCE: Computed from Warshawsky (1994, fig. 1, p. 297).

$[1.06]^{31} = 50,500.67$). The present value of health-care expenditures on child 2 (born at parents' age twenty-eight) is 8,294.98. Therefore, at age fifty-five, present value is 49,001.26 ($8,294.98 \times 1.06^{27} = 49,001.26$). For parents, the present value of health-care expenditures at age twenty over the span from age twenty to age eighty-three is 20,788.12. Therefore, the present value of expenditures for one parent at age fifty-five is 159,779 ($20,727.96 \times 1.06^{35} = 159,779$), that for both parents $159,779 \times 2 = 319,558$. When the figures for parents and children are added, we get a total of 410,060 ($319,558 + 50,501 + 40,001 = 410,060$).

The factor allowing us to convert 1987 dollars to 1995 dollars is 1.82961 (SA 1996, 111; SA 1995, 8, 118). Hence, $410,060 \times 1.82961 = 750,251$, and $750,251 \div 2,443,819 = 0.30700$; thus, $0.30700 \times 0.32 = 0.09824$, or 9.8 percent of income.

APPENDIX 5E

The Relation of the Growth in Income Inequality to the Organization of Work and the Structure of Consumption

CHULHEE LEE

Changes in Employment and Hours and Household Income Inequality, 1969–89

In the late 1960s, the trend among U.S. households toward more equal incomes among wage earners reversed itself. The difference between households at the top and those at the bottom of the annual income distribution as measured by the Current Population Surveys began to increase. This reversal has often been attributed to a structural transformation in the U.S. economy that many fear may further polarize American society and undermine the standard of living of the middle classes.

The primary focus of the recent economic literature has been on earnings inequality, in particular on wage differentials among individual workers. Since annual earnings are determined by annual hours of work and hourly wages, an increase in the earnings inequality may result from the following two sources: changes in the distribution of hourly wages and changes in hours worked. Only a few studies have investigated the potential contribution of changes in hours of work and employment to the earnings inequality. Burtless (1990, 1993) and Moffitt (1990), for example, reported that the growth in annual earnings inequality for male workers during the 1970s and 1980s was primarily due to growing inequality in hourly wage rates. On the other hand, Haveman (1996) suggested that the increase in earnings inequality between 1973 and 1988 among working-age men was largely produced by increased variability in the amount that potential breadwinners worked. Previous studies have focused exclusively on male workers. However, patterns of individual labor force participation and of hours worked need to be understood in the context of joint decisions made by family members.

Table 5E.1 Definitions of the Variables Used

Variable	Definition of Variable
N	Average money income of households in a given income decile
H_h	Mean annual hours worked by employed head of household
H_s	Mean annual hours worked by employed spouse
W_h	Mean hourly wage rate of employed head of household
W_s	Mean hourly wage rate of employed spouse
P_h	Employment rate for heads of households
P_s	Employment rate for spouses
δ	The fraction of households in which both husband and wife are present
Q	The mean income from other sources
*	The difference in the log of an income variable between the top and the bottom income deciles; e.g., $H_h^* = \ln(H_h^{\text{TOP}}) - \ln(H_h^{\text{BOTTOM}})$
Φ_h	The weight of the income earned by the head of household
Φ_s	The weight of the income earned by the spouse
Φ_Q	The weight of the income from other sources

For example, fewer working hours by a family head might be supplemented by increased hours worked by the spouse or other family members. A number of recent studies suggest the direction in which changing patterns of work have affected household income inequality. Declining employment was particularly pronounced among less-educated and low-paid men between 1967 and 1988 (Juhn 1992). The rise in two-earner couples has been more visible among families in which the husband's earnings are higher (Cancian, Danziger, and Gottschalk 1993). Employment and earnings gains have been greatest for wives of midrange and highly paid men (Juhn and Murphy 1997). Each of the changes in employment and earnings patterns of men and women outlined above could have increased family income inequality to some extent. However, the relative importance of each of these factors and their joint effect cannot be derived from a priori arguments.

The purpose of this appendix is to estimate the relative contribution of change in each element of household income, including hours and employment of the head and the spouse, to the rise in income inequality between 1969 and 1989. I begin with a decomposition of total household income into several components (for definitions of variables, see table 5E.1). The average money income of households in a given income decile, denoted N, may be given as

$$(5E.1) \quad N \equiv H_h W_h P_h + H_s W_s P_s \delta + Q,$$

where H_h, H_s, W_h, and W_s stand for the mean annual hours worked and the mean hourly wage rates for employed heads and spouses, respectively; P_h and P_s stand for the employment rates for heads and, if married, spouses; δ is the fraction of households in which both husband and wife are present; and, finally, Q stands for the mean incomes from other sources.

As the measure of income inequality, I use the difference in the log of average household income between the top and the bottom income deciles. This measure is denoted by N^*, where N^* is the difference between the logarithm of the average income in the top decile and the logarithm of the average income in the bottom decile (i.e., $N^* = \ln [N^{\mathrm{TOP}}]) - \ln ([N^{\mathrm{BOTTOM}}])$. Using an approximation, N^* can be decomposed as shown in equation (5E.2), where the asterisk denotes the difference in the logs of a variable in the top and bottom deciles of households. For example, $H_h^* = \ln(H_h^{\mathrm{TOP}}) - \ln(H_h^{\mathrm{BOTTOM}})$. Equation (5E.1) can be rewritten as

$$(5E.2) \quad N^* \approx \Phi_h(H_h^* + W_h^* + P_h^*) + \Phi_s(H_s^* + W_s^* + P_s^* + \delta^*) + \Phi_Q(Q^*),$$

where subscript h denotes the weight of each of the three income sources. For example, $\Phi_h [(H_h, W_h, P_h)/N]$ indicates the earnings of the head as a proportion of the total household income.

It is possible to decompose the change in N^* over time, in this case, between 1969 and 1989, by differentiating equation (5E.2) totally, to obtain

$$(5E.3) \quad \Delta N^* \approx \Phi_h\Delta H_h^* + \Phi_h\Delta W_h^* + \Phi_h\Delta P_h^* + \Delta\Phi_h(H_h^* + W_h^* + P_h^*) +$$
$$\Phi_s\Delta H_s^* + \Phi_s\Delta W_s^* + \Phi_s\Delta P_s^* + \Phi_s\Delta\delta^* + \Delta\Phi_s(H_s^* + W_s^* + P_s^* + \delta^*) +$$
$$\Phi_Q\Delta Q^* + \Delta\Phi_Q Q^*.$$

The first term on the right-hand side of equation (5E.3), for example, represents the annual rate of change in the disparity in average hours worked by household heads in the top and bottom deciles, weighted by the relative share of household income derived from the earnings of the head. The estimate of this term will indicate the relative contribution of the change in average working hours of the head to the rise in the measure of income inequality between 1969 and 1989. Likewise, the second and third terms show the relative contributions of changes in hourly wages and in the employment rate of the head, respectively. On the other hand, the fourth term represents the effect of changing weight, that is, the relative importance of earnings of the household head as a source of income.

Each element of equation (5E.3) is estimated from the Annual Demographic Files of the March Current Population Surveys (Moffitt 1995; CPS hereafter). Although the benchmark years used in this analysis, 1969 and 1989, are fairly comparable in terms of labor market activity, I averaged three years of data centered around these years to further ensure against possible business-cycle effects. Thus, the averages that I report for 1969 and 1989 are actually based on the 1968–70 and 1988–90 CPS data. The sample is limited to households whose head is of working age (between eighteen and sixty-four).

It is also appropriate to look at the pattern of changes in hours and employment between 1969 and 1989 suggested by the data. The overall employment rate of household heads (P_h) fell substantially over the two decades under investigation, particularly during the 1970s. The decline in P_h was much greater for lower-income than for higher-income households. P_h fell 20 percent for the bottom income decile, while it remained nearly unchanged for the top three deciles. Changes in the annual hours worked by the household head (H_h) exhibit a similar pattern. The overall decrease in hours was largely concentrated in the bottom three income deciles. These patterns imply that uneven changes in P_h and H_h should be at least partly responsible for the rise in household income inequality.

The proportion of households with an employed spouse (P_s) rose by more than a third over the two decades. The increase in labor market activity of spouses was most pronounced among middle-income households. On the other hand, there was nearly no gain for spouses in families of the lowest decile. The change in annual hours of employed spouses (H_s) is similar to that of P_s; it was spouses in middle-income households who increased their working hours the most. This finding suggests that the effect on the household income inequality of changes in P_s and H_s, if any, should be small in magnitude.

Table 5E.2 reports the result of the decomposition based on equation (5E.3). The data on which the decomposition is based are presented in table 5E.3. It turns out that changes in the employment rate and hours of the head were the most important factors, accounting for 45 percent of the rise in the inequality between the top and the bottom income deciles between 1969 and 1989. In particular, more than a quarter of the increase in the measure of inequality can be attributed to changing the employment rate of the head. Change in the employment rate of the spouse explains another 9 percent. This result suggests that more than half the rise in inequality can be accounted for by the changing pattern of labor supply. In contrast, wage changes contributed less than 6 percent to the increase in the income gap between rich and poor households.

This result is highly robust to changes in sample selection. For example, the decompositions based on families (excluding single-person households) headed by a working-age person, families headed by a person aged twenty-five to fifty-five, families headed by a male aged between twenty-five and fifty-five, and so on provide remarkably similar results (Lee 1997). If we use a household income per capita or per equivalent prime-aged male, the major implications remain unchanged.

APPENDICES

Table 5E.2 A Decomposition of the Change in Household Income Inequality, 1969–89

Variable	Estimate	Contribution (%)
(1) ΔN^*	.424	100.0
(2) $\phi_b \Delta H_b^*$	.080	18.9
(3) $\phi_b \Delta W_b^*$	.003	1.9
(4) $\phi_b P_b^*$	.111	26.2
(5) $\Delta\phi_b (H_b^* + W_b^* + P_b^*)$	−.257	−60.6
(6) $\phi_s \Delta H_s^*$	−.003	−1.9
(7) $\phi_s \Delta W_s^*$	.022	5.2
(8) $\phi_s \Delta P_s^*$	.040	9.4
(9) $\phi_s \Delta\delta_s^*$	.040	9.4
(10) $\Delta\phi_s (H_s^* + W_s^* + P_s^* + \delta_s^*)$	.216	50.9
(11) $\phi_q \Delta Q^*$	.158	35.4
(12) $\Delta\phi_q Q^*$	.015	3.5
Work of the head: (2) + (4)	.191	45.0
Work of the spouse: (6) + (8)	.037	8.7
Total labor supply	.228	53.8
Total wage: (3) + (7)	.025	5.9
Household structure: (9)	.040	9.4
Other incomes: (11)	.158	37.3
Composition: (5) + (10) + (12)	−.026	−6.1
Sum: (2) − (12)	.425	100.3

NOTE: Columns may not sum exactly owing to rounding errors.

The Structure of Consumption and the Nature of Inequality and Poverty

Annual income is the most widely used measure of the economic well-being of a family in the literature on inequality and poverty, presumably because it is readily available from various data sources. In spite of its popularity, annual income is in many respects an incomplete indicator with which to determine the standard of living of a family. It often fails to capture lifetime or permanent income of a household, which is more relevant for assessing the quality of living of a household. The permanent income hypothesis predicts that, when a household experiences a temporary decrease in income, it will draw on savings or loans to spend more than its current income, thus smoothing consumption. If this is the case, an index of inequality or poverty based on annual income would be misleading.

Table 5E.4 shows that a considerable proportion of households, particularly those in lower income groups, experience a temporary deficit in the family budget. In 1994, for example, four of five households in the bottom income decile spent more than their incomes. On the other hand, the percentage of households experiencing a deficit was lower in richer deciles: only 9 percent of households in the

276

Table 5E.3 Components of the Average Family Income for Three Periods (in Dollars)

Year	All	Bottom	9th	8th	7th	6th	5th	4th	3d	2d	Top
1. Total family income											
1968–70	30,182	6,275	13,502	18,078	21,813	25,252	28,763	32,818	37,966	45,536	71,778
1978–80	32,535	5,372	12,855	18,087	22,871	27,263	31,691	36,615	42,624	51,736	76,230
1988–90	34,522	4,966	12,237	17,900	22,979	27,775	32,756	38,422	45,457	56,185	86,837
2. Annual earnings for employed family heads											
1968–70	23,034	4,106	10,139	14,236	17,583	20,051	22,377	24,495	27,328	31,375	50,427
1978–80	23,376	3,448	9,454	13,240	16,559	20,006	22,800	25,794	28,821	33,504	48,389
1988–90	22,889	3,567	8,283	12,146	15,500	18,219	21,193	24,369	28,155	33,320	51,251
3. Employment rate for family heads											
1968–70	.929	.697	.859	.918	.946	.959	.968	.972	.976	.983	.984
1978–80	.986	.598	.800	.871	.922	.932	.952	.960	.976	.973	.978
1988–90	.888	.552	.806	.871	.908	.932	.945	.956	.962	.972	.975
4. Annual hours worked for employed family heads											
1968–70	2,187	1,685	2,001	2,119	2,159	2,229	2,241	2,245	2,287	2,315	2,418
1978–80	2,117	1,518	1,875	2,013	2,094	2,142	2,179	2,217	2,230	2,260	2,418
1988–90	2,121	1,426	1,877	2,022	2,109	2,149	2,179	2,212	2,238	2,266	2,382
5. Annual earnings for employed spouses											
1968–70	8,319	1,831	3,393	4,303	5,282	5,934	7,198	8,576	10,101	12,261	15,653
1978–80	9,956	2,204	4,050	5,213	6,493	7,526	8,800	10,127	11,812	13,938	17,871
1988–90	12,624	1,523	4,582	6,120	7,794	9,316	10,787	12,763	14,814	18,121	24,844

continued

Table 5E.3 continued

Year	All	Bottom	9th	8th	7th	6th	5th	4th	3d	2d	Top
6. Employment rate for spouses											
1968–70	.542	.413	.451	.463	.464	.517	.555	.601	.632	.659	.589
1978–80	.644	.405	.474	.563	.626	.636	.670	.700	.740	.760	.691
1988–90	.737	.471	.563	.665	.713	.748	.774	.800	.835	.844	.808
7. Annual hours worked for employed spouses											
1968–70	1,411	1,095	1,099	1,167	1,221	1,279	1,409	1,500	1,597	1,672	1,729
1978–80	1,454	1,054	1,091	1,186	1,325	1,369	1,454	1,408	1,599	1,666	1,675
1988–90	1,644	1,194	1,291	1,410	1,545	1,606	1,659	1,718	1,760	1,827	1,842
8. Proportion of husband–wife families											
1968–70	.884	.588	.783	.861	.910	.930	.938	.947	.952	.958	.967
1978–80	.852	.477	.714	.803	.873	.903	.925	.944	.954	.959	.970
1988–90	.868	.481	.774	.851	.890	.920	.931	.946	.954	.960	.968
9. Family size											
1968–70	3.854	3.555	3.729	3.764	3.782	3.847	3.882	3.911	3.967	4.000	4.102
1978–80	3.534	3.388	3.418	3.419	3.469	3.495	3.518	3.544	3.589	3.671	3.823
1988–90	3.435	3.360	3.420	3.414	3.406	3.415	3.446	3.445	3.448	3.467	3.523

Table 5E.4   Percentage of Households with Deficit by Income Decile, 1972–73 and 1994

	Income Decile									
	All	**10**	**9**	**8**	**7**	**6**	**5**	**4**	**3**	**2**	**1**
1972–73	20.4	52.9	50.4	33.0	23.7	16.3	10.7	7.0	4.8	3.0	2.0
1994	37.3	80.5	65.8	56.6	44.9	34.6	30.0	22.6	16.0	13.8	8.8

SOURCES: U.S. Department of Labor, Bureau of Labor Statistics, *Survey of Consumer Expenditures, 1972–1973* (ICPSR 9034); U.S. Department of Labor, Bureau of Labor Statistics, *Consumer Expenditure Survey, Interview Survey, 1994, Public Use Tape.*

richest decile were in deficit in the same year. The first four columns of tables 5E.5 and 5E.6 report the average amounts of income, expenditures, and savings and the savings rates for households in each income decile in 1972–73 and 1994.[1] The average amount of deficit for the lowest income group was nearly $6,000 in 1994. In contrast, the households in the top income decile saved $37,000 on average in the same year.

Because of this difference in patterns of expenditure between high- and low-income households, the degree of inequality measured using expenditure is much lower than that indicated by measures of income inequality. For example, the ratio of the average income of the top- to that of the bottom-decile households was 13.7 in 1972–73 and 19.5 in 1994. The same measure of inequality based on expenditure was 5.4 in 1972–73 and 5.9 in 1994. It is notable that the degree of inequality in expenditure was relatively stable between the early 1970s and the early 1990s, during which time various measures of income inequality rose dramatically.

A puzzle arising from these findings is how such a large fraction of low-income households managed to maintain a substantial annual deficit in their household budget. A possible explanation is that many low-income households that spent more than their incomes are not chronically poor. In face of a temporary decrease in income, a household might maintain its previous consumption level with savings, loans, or liquidation of assets. If this hypothesis is true, the low-income households who have a deficit (denoted DEF, hereafter) should be similar to middle-income households in terms of consumption patterns, earning potential, and household characteristics. Also, they should be distinct from other low-income households who have a surplus (SUR).

The first four columns of tables 5E.5 and 5E.6 present the average amount of income, expenditure, savings, and savings rate of households in each income decile separately for SUR and DEF households. Among lower-income households, the pattern of expenditures and savings is clearly different between SUR and DEF. For the bottom decile of households in 1994, the average amount of expen-

Table 5E.5 Income and Expenditure of Households by Income Decile, 1972–73:
A Comparison between Deficit- (DEF) and Surplus- (SUR) Income Households

Decile	(1) Income			(2) Expenditure			(3) Savings		
	All	SUR	DEF	All	SUR	DEF	All	SUR	DEF
All	11,981	14,489	5,972	8,070	8,019	8,270	3,911	5,500	−2,297
Poorest	2,146	2,133	2,157	2,948	1,478	4,255	−802	656	−2,097
9	3,545	3,600	3,490	3,949	2,629	5,246	−404	971	−1,756
8	5,449	5,490	5,366	5,085	3,839	7,611	364	1,651	−2,245
7	7,484	7,510	7,399	6,177	5,084	9,699	1,307	2,426	−2,299
6	9,546	9,569	9,431	7,210	6,343	11,674	2,336	3,225	−2,244
5	11,637	11,651	11,519	8,149	7,433	14,146	3,488	4,218	−2,628
4	13,891	13,901	13,757	9,163	8,579	16,943	4,728	5,322	−3,187
3	16,552	16,556	16,472	10,473	9,981	20,158	6,079	6,575	−3,686
2	20,214	20,215	20,187	11,766	11,417	23,182	8,448	8,798	−2,995
Richest	29,336	29,304	30,901	15,775	15,190	43,985	13,561	14,114	−13,084

	(4) Savings Rate (%)[a]			(5) Predicted Income			(6) Residual Income		
	All	SUR	DEF	All	SUR	DEF	All	SUR	DEF
All	18.5	37.1	−53.9	11,981	12,662	9,318	0	856	−3,346
Poorest	−37.9	31.0	−99.1	5,092	3,796	6,244	−2,946	−1,662	−4,086
9	−12.6	26.8	−51.4	6,719	6,055	7,371	−3,174	−2,455	−3,881
8	6.1	29.9	−42.3	8,699	8,239	9,634	−3,250	−2,749	−4,268
7	17.2	32.2	−31.3	10,293	10,041	11,107	−2,809	−2,530	−3,708
6	24.3	33.7	−23.8	11,899	11,740	12,719	−2,354	−2,172	−3,288
5	29.9	36.2	−23.0	13,157	13,153	13,194	−1,520	−1,502	−1,676
4	34.0	38.3	−23.3	14,226	14,207	14,480	−335	−306	−724
3	36.7	39.6	−22.3	15,191	15,158	15,845	1,361	1,398	627
2	41.7	43.5	−14.9	16,409	16,377	17,457	3,806	3,839	2,730
Richest	46.1	47.9	−39.4	18,116	18,097	19,033	11,220	11,206	11,868

SOURCE: U.S. Department of Labor, Bureau of Labor Statistics, *Survey of Consumer Expenditures, 1972–1973* (ICPSR 9034).

[a]Not weighted by income.

diture by DEF households ($12,792) was more than twice the average income of
SUR households ($5,040). In the early 1970s, the average expenditure of the lowest decile of households was three times greater for DEF than for SUR households. The average expenditure of DEF households in the lowest decile was comparable to the amount spent by a household in the lower tail of the middle-income group. The size of negative savings (defined as the reduction in savings or increase in debt) among DEF households was substantial. In 1994, it was nearly $8,000 for households in the bottom decile, which was even greater than their average income of $5,000. The average savings rate for DEF households in the bottom decile was −99 percent in 1972–73 and −344 percent in 1994.

Table 5E.6   Income and Expenditure of Households by Income Decile, 1994:
A Comparison between DEF and SUR

Decile	(1) Income			(2) Expenditure			(3) Savings		
	All	SUR	DEF	All	SUR	DEF	All	SUR	DEF
All	36,981	46,028	21,802	30,993	30,448	31,907	5,987	15,581	−10,105
Poorest	5,302	6,340	5,051	11,281	5,040	12,792	−5,978	1,300	−7,741
9	10,189	10,148	10,210	14,297	8,135	17,506	−4,109	2,012	−7,296
8	14,797	15,052	14,601	18,575	11,659	23,876	−3,778	3,393	−9,274
7	19,997	20,147	19,812	22,470	15,267	31,293	−2,473	4,879	−11,481
6	26,050	26,091	25,974	25,649	19,180	37,858	402	6,910	−11,885
5	32,678	32,746	32,520	29,369	23,614	42,785	3,309	9,131	−10,264
4	40,853	40,921	40,619	34,584	28,887	54,130	6,269	12,034	−13,511
3	51,154	51,130	51,280	39,492	34,430	66,159	11,662	16,699	−14,879
2	65,082	65,223	64,205	47,547	43,030	75,734	17,535	22,193	−11,529
Richest	103,638	104,226	97,081	66,626	61,411	120,969	37,012	42,855	−23,888

	(4) Savings Rate (%)[a]			(5) Predicted Income			(6) Residual Income		
	All	SUR	DEF	All	SUR	DEF	All	SUR	DEF
All	−24.2	29.8	−114.7	36,981	40,725	30,700	0	5,305	−8,899
Poorest	−272.9	20.5	−343.9	16,443	11,133	17,729	−11,141	−4,793	−12,678
9	−40.8	19.7	−72.3	19,633	15,459	21,806	−9,445	−5,312	−11,597
8	−26.4	22.5	−63.9	26,319	22,458	29,277	−11,522	−7,407	−14,676
7	−13.0	24.2	−58.6	29,849	27,754	32,417	−9,853	−7,606	−12,605
6	1.6	26.6	−45.6	33,061	31,923	35,208	−7,010	−5,832	−9,234
5	10.0	27.8	−31.8	39,624	39,139	40,753	−6,945	−6,393	−8,233
4	15.3	29.4	−33.0	43,567	43,678	43,185	−2,714	−2,757	−2,567
3	22.7	32.6	−29.5	46,682	46,084	49,836	4,471	5,046	1,444
2	26.8	34.0	−17.9	54,160	54,144	54,259	10,922	11,079	9,946
Richest	34.4	40.0	−23.4	60,436	60,429	60,509	43,201	43,838	36,572

SOURCE: U.S. Department of Labor, Bureau of Labor Statistics, *Consumer Expenditure Survey, Interview Survey, 1994, Public Use Tape.*

[a]Not weighted by income.

If the permanent income hypothesis presented here is correct, DEF households should have a greater earning potential than do SUR households with a similar amount of actual income. As a measure of potential earning power, I estimated the household income predicted by gender, race, age, education, occupation, and marital status of the head of the household and interaction terms between marital status and labor force status of the spouse.[2] The variables included in the regression explain nearly half the variations in income across households in the sample. The predicted income and residual for each income decile are reported in columns 5 and 6 of tables 5E.5 and 5E.6.

As expected, the potential income predicted by household characteristics is much greater for DEF than for SUR households in the lowest two deciles. The predicted income for DEF households in the bottom income decile is 65 percent greater than that for SUR households in both 1972–73 and 1994. For these households (DEF in the bottom decile), the potential income ($6,244 for 1972–73 and $17,729 for 1994) is three times as great as the actual income ($2,157 for 1972–73 and $5,051 for 1994). This result indicates that DEF households have considerably greater earning power than do SUR households. Many low-income DEF families are poor presumably because they earn lower incomes than they could potentially earn. For example, had DEF households in the bottom decile earned as much as predicted by their characteristics, they would have been as well off as middle-income households in 1972–73 and 1994. And if so, their incomes would have been more than half of the mean income of all households.

A comparison of various demographic and economic characteristics between DEF and SUR households in the lowest two income deciles leads to similar conclusions. DEF household heads are younger on average than those in SUR households. Such a difference in the age structure is reflected in the much higher retirement rate of SUR heads of households as compared with DEF. It appears that the majority of SUR households in the lower-income groups are the retired elderly. For many DEF poor households, age is probably not the major reason for their lower incomes. In terms of household structure, race, and occupation, DEF households are less typical of the poor than SUR households. DEF households are more likely to be male headed, to be white, and to have married couples than are SUR. The percentage of the household heads who are professionals or managers is considerably higher for DEF households than for SUR. DEF households are superior to SUR households in terms of educational attainment, too.

Compared to low-income households, the family characteristics and the predicted incomes are generally similar between DEF middle- and high-income and SUR middle- and high-income households. The only notable systematic difference between DEF and SUR households is that the percentage of the self-employed is considerably higher for DEF than for SUR in every income decile. This result could be explained by the fact that the volatility in income is generally greater for the self-employed than for wage and salary-earners.

The result of this analysis suggests that a large fraction of low-income households probably experience poverty-level incomes only temporarily. These households had a much greater normal earning capability than their actual incomes in 1972–73 and in 1994. Faced with a temporary decrease in income, they maintain their consumption level by spending more than their income. (The chronically poor appear to be much more frugal in their consumption than usually thought, and many manage to squeeze out some small savings despite their low incomes).

As far as the degree of well-being of people is concerned, the proportion of the population seriously damaged by poverty could be considerably smaller than the official poverty rate suggests. Also, the measures of income inequality seem to overstate the real state of inequality in material well-being.

NOTES

INTRODUCTION

1. HS (1975, 139); SA (1998, table 672); cf. n. 68, chap. 2.

2. Smith ([1776] 1937, 364).

3. Lincoln, speech in Independence Hall, Philadelphia, 22 February 1861.

4. *Economic Report of the President* (1992). The ascendancy of equality of condition as the touchstone of egalitarianism is described in chap. 3. Measures of the redistribution of income during the past century are presented in chaps. 4–5 (cf. Pole 1993; and Sen 1996).

5. As both historians and sociologists of religion have pointed out, this distinction between state churches and evangelical churches is critical in understanding the emergence and evolution of American democracy (see, e.g., Lipset 1996; Wood 1992a, 1992b). As Emmet Larkin (personal communication, 14 October 1998) has called to my attention, the Irish Roman Catholic Church is an exception to this generalization. Because of the political situation between the Irish and the English, Irish Roman Catholics endorsed separation of church and state even before immigration to the United States. Since the Irish already stood for the

The following abbreviations are used throughout the notes: HS = U.S. Bureau of the Census, *Historical Statistics of the United States, Colonial Times to 1970*, 2 pts. (Washington, D.C.: U.S. Government Printing Office, 1975); and SA = U.S. Bureau of the Census, *Statistical Abstract of the United States* (Washington, D.C.: U.S. Government Printing Office, published annually), the date of which varies according to the *Abstract* cited.

principle of voluntary association independent of the state, unlike the German, Italian, and French Roman Catholics, who were dependent on state protection and financial support, the Irish Catholic clergy in America held views that were similar to those increasingly held by Protestants, especially after 1830 (see also Burdenski and Dunson 1999; National Conference of Catholic Bishops 1986).

6. See Ahlstrom (1972, chaps. 18–20); Bailyn (1967); Hall (1994); and Lambert (1994). Evangelical Protestant churches were not the only contributors to popular democracy and individualism. Other churches and religions, such as German pietism and Judaism, also had structures and theologies that emphasized the individual. Also important was the presence of the frontier, which the historian Frederick Jackson Turner elaborated into a theory of American character and society (see Turner 1920) and the doctrine of laisser-faire.

7. Nor should *the disciples of the Fourth Great Awakening* be taken to mean only those highly publicized political conservatives who want to push the agenda of the Awakening in a particular direction. The black churches are also disciples of the current Awakening, but they interpret the agenda of spiritual inequality in the light of their own historical experience.

CHAPTER ONE

1. See app. 1A below. The largest Republican gains between 1982 and 1994 were in the North Central, Southern, and Mountain regions (SA 1983, 254; SA 1995, 275).

2. Silbey (1967, 1991a); HS (1975, 1083); cf. Brady (1988); Howe (1990); Jensen (1984); Lichtman (1983); Swierenga (1990).

3. See Fogel, Galantine, and Manning (1992, entries 59–60) and Fogel and Galantine (1992, entry 69, and the sources cited there); cf. Bailyn (1986a, 1986b); Fischer (1989); and Fogel (1992f).

4. According to Albanese (1981, 290; cf. Albanese 1976), fifty-two of the fifty-six signers of the Declaration of Independence and the majority of the members of the Continental Congress were Freemasons, the main organization of deists in the colonies at that time.

5. Methodism was the chief vehicle through which Arminianism (the rejection of predestination and of the doctrine of human inability effectively to strive for grace) was propagated in the United States, although this form of Protestant-

ism was also embraced by liberal Congregationalists, who eventually became Unitarians (Ahlstrom 1972, chap. 24; Reid 1990).

6. For a more complete analysis, see Fogel (1989, chap. 10) and Fogel and Galantine (1992).

7. For examples of economic and conspiratorial arguments against slavery, see Fehrenbacher (1962) and Fogel (1989, 342–54). Lincoln, e.g., feared that, by 1858, only one element was missing from the conspiracy to nationalize slavery: a Supreme Court decision "declaring the Constitution of the United States does not permit a *state* to exclude slavery from its limits." And such a decision "will be soon upon us," he warned, "unless the power of the present political dynasty shall be met and overthrown." Otherwise, "We shall *lie down* pleasantly dreaming the people of *Missouri* are on the verge of making their state *free;* and we shall awake to the reality, instead, that the *Supreme* Court had made *Illinois* a *slave* state" (Angle 1958, 6–7).

8. The legacy of the antislavery struggle did not die easily. On the residual vitality of civil rights sentiment among Republicans during the post–Civil War period and its congressional and judicial expressions, see Kousser (1999).

9. Although these doctrines have indigenous roots in America, they were articulated in Europe as well.

10. Although non-Protestant religions have played an increasingly important role in shaping American institutions, including participation in government at the state and federal levels, the role of these groups was greatly constrained prior to World War II. As is pointed out in chap. 3 below, the principal reform programs of the nineteenth century and the early twentieth emanated from Northern evangelical reformers. Moreover, although the non-Protestants are now a large and rapidly growing portion of the population, Protestants still dominate American political life, often forming strong coalitions on particular issues that cut across religion and ethnicity. For an elaboration of these points, see chaps. 3, 5 below.

11. Data on the rates of growth in the membership of the mainline and enthusiastic denominations are from Ostling et al. (1989) and private communications with denominational authorities; see also Ajemian (1985) and Ostling (1985). It is important to keep in mind that, although the mainline denominations abandoned enthusiasm, preferring to emphasize ethics over spiritual intensity, this transformation was not completed. There remain important minorities within the mainline denominations that embrace enthusiastic religion and seek to expand its influence within their churches.

12. The data in this paragraph were obtained from the Princeton-Gallup religion polls for 1988, applying the sampling fraction in the poll to the population data for 1988 that can be found in the *U.S. Statistical Abstract* for 1991 (Princeton Religion Research Center 1978, 1982, 1988; cf. *Religion in America* 1987; see also app. 1A below; and Barrett (1988, 810–30). The Fourth Great Awakening is the American expression of an international revolt against modernism and its corruptions that finds reflection in Islam, Buddhism, Judaism, and other religious movements that are described in Marty and Appleby (1991–95). The theology of the Mormon Church differs significantly from that of evangelical denominations, as is reflected in the Book of Mormon. The Mormon Church also differs from the mainline churches on a series of issues, including the centrality of the conversion experience in Mormon doctrine and practice, which Mormons, along with evangelicals and Pentecostals, endorse.

13. Henderson (1995); "Abortion Foes Differ on Tactics" (1996).

14. On political realignment theory, see Key (1955), Burnham (1967, 1970, 1981, 1986a, 1986b, 1991), Riker (1982), and Clubb, Flanigan, and Zingale (1980); cf. Benson (1961), Formisano (1971), Jensen (1971, 1984), Kleppner (1970, 1979), Kousser (1976), Lichtman (1976, 1982), Bogue (1983a, 1983b), and McCormick (1986). On polymetric analysis of congressional and popular voting behavior, see Silbey (1967), Alexander (1967), Bogue (1982, 1989), Kousser (1974, 1976), Holt (1969, 1978, 1992), Campbell et al. (1960, 1966), and Gienapp (1987); cf. Fogel and Galantine (1992) and Fogel (1989, 1992f, 1994c). On the history of technological change and its effect on economic growth, institutional change, and cultural change, see Schumpeter ([1934] 1961), Kuznets (1966, 1979), Landes (1969, 1998), Mokyr (1990), North (1990), Rosenberg and Birdzell (1986), and Wrigley (1987). On demographic history, see Easterlin (1972, 1996), Higgs (1979), and Fogel, Galantine, and Manning (1992, esp. pts. 8, 9).

15. In Fogel (1992f), I have sought to spell out more fully than is possible here the complex set of problems encountered in explaining past political realignments and to indicate the limits of using such models for purposes of forecasting. In that paper, I argued that, even when simultaneous equation models, such as rational expectations, include stochastic terms, they cannot adequately capture the relative importance of intergenerational, generational, and period processes in setting the context for a political realignment. Moreover, simultaneous equation models do poorly in representing the critical role of contingent circumstances in determining the outcome of given realignments. I also argued that models of sequential choice are more useful than rational expectation models in characterizing political realignments because they make it possible to identify critical transition points.

The paper indicated how ecological and other regression techniques can be employed to estimate the relative importance of various factors that determined outcomes at particular transition points and that various transitions could be integrated into a dynamic model with simulation techniques. The complexity of the path diagram presented there indicates the extent of vital detail omitted in table 1.1. Table 1.1 is meant to provide only a very general framework. Important details needed to make the framework useful are elaborated in the balance of the book.

16. Bailyn et al. (1992, 1:66); see also Bailyn (1967).

17. Bushman (1967, 220, 286).

18. Wood (1992a, 51); Wood (1992b). Other scholars who have linked this Awakening to the Revolution include Isaac (1974, 1982), Nash (1979), Lockridge (1981), Heimert (1966), Stout (1977), Pole (1993), Noll (1993), and Sweet (1952).

19. Barnes (1964); Cross ([1950] 1982); Davis (1975, 1984); Ahlstrom (1972); McLoughlin (1978); Foster (1960); Pole (1993); McKivigan (1984); Marty (1970); cf. Howe (1991) and the sources cited therein.

20. McLoughlin (1978, 143–44); cf. Smith (1983). Others who, in one degree or another, recognize a Third Great Awakening include Cauthen (1962), Mulder (1978), Gordon-McCutchan (1981, 1983), and Johnson (1995). For a fuller discussion of the issues raised by the Third Great Awakening concept, see the sources cited there.

21. For more on Dwight Moody, see n. 62, chap. 3 below, and pp. 121–22.

22. McLoughlin (1978).

23. Albanese (1990); McLoughlin (1978).

24. Ajemian (1985); Ostling (1985); Ostling et al. (1989); Woodward (1989); Woodward and Joseph (1991); Woodward (1992); Marty (1987); Cromartie (1992); Cox (1995); cf. Wuthnow (1988).

25. Escobar (1992); Martin (1990); McClory (1991).

26. Smith (1983).

27. McLoughlin (1978, 141–45).

28. Cross (1950); Foster (1960); Barnes (1933).

29. Compare Fogel (1989). The Burned-Over District encompassed those areas in western New York State, Ohio, and Pennsylvania that were heavily proselytized (burned over) by itinerant Congregational and Presbyterian ministers.

30. Ely (1938); Rader (1966); Dorfman (1959, 3:276–94); La Follette (1960); Thelen (1976); Bryan (1925); Cherny (1985).

31. Butler (1982, 1990); Noll (1993); Hall (1994); Lambert (1994).

32. Wood (1992a, 1992b).

33. Niebuhr ([1937] 1988, 197).

34. The discussion in this and the next three paragraphs draws on Brady (1988), Burnham (1967, 1970, 1981, 1986a, 1986b, 1991), Jensen (1971, 1984, 1986), Kleppner (1970, 1979, 1982), Lichtman (1976, 1982, 1983), Keller (1977, 1990), McCormick (1986), Clubb, Flanigan, and Zingale (1980), Silbey (1967, 1991a, 1991b), Sundquist (1983), Shafer (1991), Wattenberg (1991), Ladd (1991, 1995, 1997), Nardulli (1995), Abramovitz and Saunders (1998), Orren and Skowronek (1998), and Brunell and Grofman (1998).

35. See Burnham (1991).

36. This and the next paragraph are from Ladd (1991, 1995, 1997).

37. Compare Jensen (1984), Howe (1990), Swierenga (1990), Jensen (1971), Kleppner (1979), Silbey (1991a, 1991b), Kellstedt and Noll (1991), and Abramovitz and Saunders (1998).

38. Compare Clubb, Flanigan, and Zingale (1980), Lichtman (1983), and McCormick (1986).

39. Jones (1997); Maxwell (1995); Morgan (1995); Grady (1994); Olsen (1997).

40. The real per capita income of the United States in 1890 and 1990 is from Maddison (1995, 196–97). Comparison of the gains of the lower fifth and the upper four-fifths were based on the assumption that the income distributions were approximately lognormal and that the standard deviation of the logs was approximately 1.2 in 1890 and 0.7 in 1990 (see Soltow 1989, 1992; table 5E.3 below; SA 1992, 462; and SA 1993, 475; cf. chaps. 3, 4 below). Although the economy was severely depressed in the mid-1890s, 1890, on which the real income comparison with 1990 was based, was a fairly normal year.

41. Comparing prevalence rates over a century for behavior considered immoral by Social Gospelers is fraught with difficulty. Not only are statistics very patchy during the late nineteenth and early twentieth centuries, but standards have changed. Few if any Social Gospelers would have considered sex within marriage as ever constituting rape, while birth to unwed mothers, teenage or not, was always considered a moral and social problem. However, available mortality statistics show that nonaccidental violent deaths are far more frequent among teenagers and young adults today than they were in the 1890s. The same can be said about divorce rates, drug addiction, and births to single teenage girls. The prevalence rates of the physical abuse of women and children are particularly susceptible to changing cultural norms. The abuse that concerned reformers a century ago was associated particularly with male drunkenness. In the case of chil-

dren, judicious corporal punishment was widely accepted as a legitimate method of child rearing. On the decreasing incidence of violence against women, particularly wives, over the course of the nineteenth century and in comparison to the late twentieth century, see Del Mar (1996, 227). On drug abuse, cf. Courtwright (1982) and SA (1996, 144). On births to single teenage girls and the incidence of broken families, see Himmelfarb (1995, 229). On violent teenage deaths, compare the mortality rates in U.S. Bureau of the Census (1896) and those in U.S. Department of Health and Human Services (1992).

42. Alter (1997); Sloan (1997).

43. In the case of social security, the aging of the system is a major complication. When the system was new, the ratio of payees to recipients was quite high, and rates of return on the investment of recipients were also very high. As the system matured, the ratio of payees to recipients and the rate of return declined to low levels. For a further discussion of these issues, see chap. 5 below.

44. McLoughlin (1978), drawing on Wallace (1956), attributed the initiation of Great Awakenings to "revitalization movements." According to Wallace, such movements stem from a set of factors including hostility to the intrusion of alien persons and customs, gripping visions, myths, and dreams, and cultural distortions. These analytic categories have virtue, particularly in explaining premodern phenomena. However, the pace of technological change has accelerated so much and control of the environment has increased so much during the past three hundred years that humankind has been transformed both physiologically and culturally.

45. Bailyn et al. (1992, 1:241); Williamson (1960); cf. Wood (1992b).

46. Wood (1992b, chaps. 11, 13).

47. Barrett (1988); Cox (1995).

48. Lindholm (1996); Marty and Appleby (1991–95); Burdenski and Dunson (1999); National Conference of Catholic Bishops (1986).

CHAPTER TWO

1. David Landes, personal communication, 30 April 1996.

2. The average annual figure for unemployment was 25 percent; in some months of the depression, unemployment reached 33 percent (Nathan 1936; cf. Hopkins 1936).

3. Rostow (1960); SA (1955, 846); SA (1967, 729); SA (1982–83, 758).

4. Goldin (1990); Robinson and Godbey (1997); Wallace (1945).

5. Shils (1974, 11).

6. Gerald Holton, quoted in Graubard (1974, vi).

7. Shils (1974, 12).

8. SA (1984, 583). However, by 1988, the proportion of the power produced in the United States by nuclear energy had risen to one-fifth of the total (SA 1992, table 943). The antinuclear movement had substantial influence even before the incidents at Three Mile Island and Chernobyl; those incidents accelerated its growth.

9. Francis (1851, 119–20); cf. Knowles (1926).

10. Denault (1993) reports that there were in all 303 boiler explosions on U.S. steamboats between 1816 and 1860, resulting in 3,187 deaths. He stresses that this listing is incomplete for steamboats and that it does not include boiler explosions on moving trains and stationary engines. An extensive compilation of deaths associated with collisions and stationary engines is not yet available for the antebellum era.

11. Dickson (1989); Rothman and Lichter (1983); Szatmary (1987).

12. Piggott (1965); Trewartha (1969); UN (1973, 12); cf. Sahlins (1972, chap. 1). The adult life span in Neolithic times was a small fraction of the prevailing adult life span in OECD nations today.

13. On the horse collar, see White (1962). The first two ploughs on the left side of the figure were pulled by humans.

14. Malthus ([1798] 1926); Kuznets (1966). In the second edition of *An Essay on the Principle of Population* ([1803] 1992, chap. 14), Malthus acknowledged that the food supply could grow indefinitely with sufficient rapidity for the population to expand without precipitating crises.

15. Kuznets (1971).

16. Kuznets (1971); Fogel and Engerman (1974); Maddison (1982, 1995); Rostow (1963); World Bank (1993).

17. Kuznets (1971, table 1).

18. Fogel and Floud (1999); Bairoch (1973); Wrigley (1987, esp. chaps. 4–5).

19. Allen (1992); Bairoch (1973); Braudel (1979); Lindert (1994); Crafts (1994, 1984); Wrigley (1986, 1985); Mathias (1983); Mokyr (1993); cf. Hammond and Hammond (1975, [1911] 1978); Hobsbawm (1964); Mayhew (1851–61); Himmelfarb (1991); and Perkin (1969). Gregory King estimated that, in 1688 over 24.2 percent of English households consisted of paupers, vagrants, and cottagers who could not provide for themselves (see Laslett 1973, in which is included "'The LCC Burns Journal,' A manuscript notebook containing workings for several projected works [composed c. 1695–1700]" by Gregory King). Colquhoun (1814) put

the figure at 19.9 percent in ca. 1801. In ca. 1790, the bottom 20 percent of house-holds consumed only about seventeen hundred calories per equivalent adult male, which was not enough to sustain regular work in agriculture or in the manual trades (cf. Fogel 1992g).

20.   Bairoch (1988); Chandler and Fox (1974).

21.   Bairoch (1988); Chandler and Fox (1974); Bairoch (1988) defines a city as containing five thousand or more people.

22.   Wrigley (1987a); Allen (1988, 1992, 1994); Fogel (1989).

23.   North (1968); Fogel et al. (1978); Klein (1978); Gemery (1980, 1984); Kapp (1870); Galenson (1981, 1986a); Eltis (1987); Taylor ([1951] 1957); Grubb (1984).

24.   Haites, Mak, and Walton (1975); Taylor ([1951] 1957), Fogel (1964).

25.   Fishlow (1965); Fogel (1964); HS (1975, chap. Q).

26.   Field (1978). On migration patterns, see Fogel, Galantine, and Manning (1992, entries 35, 59, 60) and Steckel (1983). The migration also had a major effect on the election of 1860 (see Burnham 1955; Foner 1970; McPherson 1982; see also Fogel and Galantine 1992, esp. 512–513, table 69.9, and the sources cited therein; Atack and Bateman 1987; Bidwell and Falconer 1941). On the development of the canal system in the Midwest, see Cranmer (1960) and Ransom (1963) as well as Taylor ([1951] 1957), Hunter (1964), and Fogel (1964).

27.   Fogel (1994c). It is likely that Northeastern farmers pushed out of agri-culture by the shipment of Midwestern grains were largely native born, while common laborers in the nonfarm sector of the North were predominantly foreign born. During relatively prosperous years such as 1850 and 1860, the gap in real wages between comparable farm- and nonfarmworkers may have been relatively small (see Margo 2000, chap. 4).

28.   Meyers (1960, 239–40); cf. Brock (1975, chap. 11).

29.   Franklin quoted in Field (1978, 146).

30.   Hamilton quoted in Goldin and Sokoloff (1984, 461).

31.   On the relatively low productivity of women and children in Northern agriculture, see Goldin and Sokoloff (1982). On the surplus of agricultural labor in the Northeast, see Field (1978). On the factors affecting the relative rates of growth in agricultural and nonagricultural sectors in the North between 1840 and 1860, see McCutcheon (1992). It is sometimes argued that the widespread use of women in field labor on Caribbean sugar plantations undermines the proposition that men generally had a comparative advantage in heavy agricultural labor. But, even there, men were still predominant in the heaviest aspects of production,

which were the boiling of sugar, artisanal crafts, and the cutting of cane (see Fogel, Galantine, and Manning 1992, entry 12). The occasional use of women in plowing does not contradict the fact that the overwhelming majority of plowing was done not only by men but by men at the peak of physical strength (ages eighteen to thirty-six) (see Olson 1983, 1992).

32. Taylor ([1951] 1957); Handlin (1979).

33. The belief that cities were threats to health, morality, and political stability was widely held, not just among reformers. In addition to Tocqueville (1969), see also Boyer (1978), Bremner (1956), Brock (1975), and Weber ([1899] 1967).

34. Howe (1979); Nye (1974); Rothman (1971); Richardson (1970).

35. Richardson (1970, 27, 52).

36. Parrington (1930a, 347, 173). Life expectancy at age ten in the North declined from 56.7 years during the period 1790–94 to 47.9 years during the period 1850–54 (Fogel 1986a, table 9.A.1). In the 1790s, there was little difference between urban and rural mortality rates. The much sharper decline in life expectancy in New York, Philadelphia, and Boston than in other places appears to have resulted partly from the inability of public health agencies to keep up with the extraordinary increases in population density and partly from diseases brought into the cities by new immigrants (see Yasuba 1962; Higgs 1979; cf. Jaffe and Lourie 1942; Vinovskis 1972; Ernst 1949, 48; Warner 1968; Glaab 1963; Chudacoff 1975; and Fogel, Galantine, and Manning 1992, entry 41). Infant death rates in tenement areas were far higher than in the less-dense, high-income wards in all three cities. The experience in England was similar (Ashby 1915).

37. Newspapers, welfare agencies, and government documents reported severe and unprecedented overcrowding and skyrocketing rental charges from the mid-1840s to the mid-1850s in New York, Boston, Brooklyn, Philadelphia, Buffalo, Cincinnati, Chicago, and St. Louis (see Handlin 1979; Ernst 1949; Commons et al. 1910, vol. 7; Commons et al. 1918, vol. 1; Abbott 1926; Griscom [1845] 1970; and New York State Legislature 1857; cf. Martin 1942).

38. Tocqueville (1969, 278). For the views of Thomas Jefferson and Benjamin Rush on cities, see Glaab (1963, 52–54). On the creation of an armed, uniformed police, see Monkkonen (1981) and Lane (1967).

39. Van Deusen (1963, 97).

40. HS (1975, 105–7); SA (1995, 10); SA (1987, 11).

41. Those nine Northern states were California, Connecticut, Iowa, Min-

nesota, New Hampshire, New Jersey, Rhode Island, Vermont, and Wisconsin (HS 1975, 1–6; U.S. Census Bureau 1854, 40).

42.   There has been a long and still unresolved debate as to the causes of these huge waves in immigration. For commentaries on this debate, see Easterlin (1961), Williamson (1974), and Gould (1979, 1980).

43.   Howe (1979, 18). See also Van Deusen (1963); Pessen (1978); and Silbey (1967).

44.   This paragraph and the next are based on Fogel (1989, chaps. 9, 10).

45.   At the federal level, the Whigs won the presidential elections in 1840 and 1848, and the Democrats won in 1836 and 1844. Of the eight Congresses between 1837 and 1851, the Democrats controlled the House of Representatives six times, and the Whigs controlled the Senate five times (HS 1975, chap. Y).

46.   Holt (1973); Gienapp (1985, 1987); Sewell (1976); Cooper (1978); Fogel (1989).

47.   A shift of just 25,069 votes from Lincoln to Stephen A. Douglas in New York, or an even smaller shift of 18,234 votes in four other states (California, Illinois, Indiana, and New Jersey), would have thrown the vote on the presidency into Congress, where either Douglas or Breckinridge, the candidate of the slaveholding Southerners, would have been elected in 1860 (Fogel and Galantine 1992).

48.   Fogel and Galantine (1992). The Northern vote went from a combined Free Soilers and Whig share of 50.2 percent in 1852 to a Republican share of 51.9 percent in 1860 (Fogel and Galantine 1992).

49.   In 1860, the Republicans received 70 percent of the Old American vote, the Democrats only 30 percent (computed from Fogel 1994c, table 9.5; cf. Fogel and Galantine 1992, pt. 2 and appendix, pt. A; and Fogel 1992f).

50.   Fogel (1992f, 1994c); Fogel and Galantine (1992). In this section, I have emphasized the effect of waves of foreign immigration on political alignments. Internal migration was also important and took place in waves, which, although much smaller than those of foreign migration, played a critical role in Lincoln's victory. The last wave of the New England exodus into the Middle Atlantic and Midwestern states was a crucial factor in the political realignment of the 1850s. That wave began about 1840, after the sharp decline in New England's natural rate of increase. It was precipitated by a massive upsurge in shipments of grain and animal products from the Midwest to the East. This competition devastated farmers up and down the Connecticut River Valley, and they left Vermont, Massachusetts, and Connecticut in droves. The relative number of these new migrants was not very large. New Englanders who moved West after 1840 represented

hardly 3 percent of the population in the nine-state region that formed the Yankee diaspora. Nevertheless, because they voted overwhelmingly Republican (on the order of nine to one) in the elections of 1856 and 1860, they would merely have added to the lopsided Republican majority in New England had they not migrated. But the same votes cast in the diaspora provided the margin of victory for Lincoln in New York, Illinois, and Wisconsin (Fogel and Galantine 1992, table 69.9, pp. 512–13).

51.   During the 1896 election, the Democrats were able to lure back a significant section of Northern evangelicals, particularly in the Midwest. After the rise of the Social Gospel movement, the Democrats under Franklin D. Roosevelt were able to bring many of the new lights of the Third Great Awakening into the Democratic fold.

52.   U.S. Bureau of the Census (1864, 656–80); Burritt (1912, table 68, p. 143), Barber (1988).

53.   Singer ([1941] 1959, chap. 5); Marsden (1994).

54.   Wills (1936); Thwing (1906); Burritt (1912, 143); Tewkesbury (1932); cf. Barber (1988).

55.   Wills (1936, chap. 3); Barber (1988, chap. 1); Thwing (1906, chap. 13).

56.   Wills (1936, chap. 4).

57.   Wills (1936, chap. 2); Bowman (1962); cf. Veysey (1965, chap. 2).

58.   Predecessors of the elective system were established at the University of Virginia when it opened in 1825 and at Brown University as a reform in 1850 (Wills 1936, 176–80; Veysey 1965, chaps. 2–3; Marsden 1994, chaps. 5–11).

59.   Veysey (1965, chap. 4); Marsden (1994, pt. 2). Woodrow Wilson, who came from a line of ministers and a stern Presbyterian tradition, was prominent in church affairs.

60.   Burritt (1912).

61.   Goldin and Katz (1996); HS (1975, 379); SA (1977, 368–69); cf. Wiebe (1967) and Chandler (1977).

62.   Emery and Emery (1996, chaps. 8–9); HS (1975, 80, 81); Tebbel and Zuckerman (1991, chap. 12).

63.   Emery and Emery (1996, chaps. 8–10); Burritt (1912).

64.   Taylor (1991, passim); Faulkner (1931, chap. 5); Tebbel and Zuckerman (1991, chap. 10); Emery and Emery (1996, chap. 10). For additional recent scholarship on the practices of the Standard Oil Co., see McGee (1958), Mariger (1978), and Granitz and Klein (1996).

65.   Statistical studies of the standard of living are described in Williams and Zimmerman (1935) and Dorfman (1959, chap. 4).

66.   For an example of the new skills required, see the discussion on the change in the chemical industry in Landes (1969, chaps. 3, 5); cf. Chandler (1990).

67.   Chandler (1977); Wills (1936).

68.   HS (1975, 383); SA (1992, 166).

69.   SA (1998, table 672). In this *Statistical Abstract* table, professionals are defined to include those listed under "managerial and professional specialty" and those fields under "technical, sales, and administrative support" that normally require college training as well as "health service occupations" and "supervisors, protective service."

70.   *World Almanac* 1991, 377–81. The information on the education of cabinet members is from *Who's Who in America*, 1980–81 ed.

71.   For a further discussion of the role of the Social Gospel movement in shaping the ethos of the social sciences, see chap. 3 below (cf. Ross 1991).

72.   On the basis of the data in SA (1991, 393, 435, 417), it was estimated that there were 107,355 million full-time equivalent employees with average annual earnings of $48,445 in 1989 (based on annual year-round employment). The full-time income of nonhousehold service workers averaged out to $15,589, rounded down to $15,000 (to allow a small component of human capital in the labor of ordinary service workers). The difference between $15,000 and $48,445 is $33,445, which, when multiplied by the number of full-time-equivalent workers, yields $3.590 trillion as the income of human capital. This increase was converted into a capital stock using a multiplication factor of 13.76, which yielded a figure of $49.4 trillion dollars as the capitalized value of payments to human capital. The value of all reproducible tangible wealth in the United States in 1989 was $23.8 trillion (SA 1991, 470). On this calculation, two-thirds of all capital in the United States is human capital [49.4/(49.4 + 23.8) ≈ 0.67]; cf. Becker (1993).

73.   For a more skeptical view of professionals, see Genovese (1995).

74.   On this paragraph and the next, see Fogel and Costa (1997).

75.   Fogel (1986a).

76.   The procedures used to create table 2.1 are described in Fogel and Floud (1999).

77.   Fogel (1997a). For data on heights in Great Britain, see Floud, Wachter, and Gregory (1990). For Norway, see Kiil (1939), cited in Floud (1983). For Sweden, see Sandberg and Steckel (1988a, table 1). On France, see Meerton (1989), as amended by Weir (1993), with 0.9 centimeters added to allow for additional

growth between age twenty and maturity (Gould 1869, 104–5; cf. Friedman 1982, 510, n. 14). For Hungary, see Komlos (1989, table 2.1, p. 57). For a fuller discussion of these estimates, consult Fogel (1987, table 7 and the source notes) and Fogel (1997b).

78. Tanner (1990, 1993); cf. *Economist* (1995a); and Vaupel (1997).

79. Scrimshaw and Gordon (1968); Martorell, Rivera, and Kaplowitz (1990); Lozoff, Jimenez, and Wolf (1991); Czeizel and Dudás (1992); Rosenberg (1992); Scrimshaw (1998); Chavez, Martinez, and Soberanes (1995); cf. Scrimshaw, Taylor, and Gordon (1968).

80. Barker (1992); Barker (1994, 1998).

81. McMahon and Bistrian (1990).

82. Fogel (1994a).

83. There were some exceptions to this rule. As the classical historian Richard Saller pointed out to me (personal communication, 15 April 1996), the Roman paterfamilias was considered responsible for increasing the family estate that he bequeathed to his son.

84. "The Rights of Frozen Embryos" (1989); "Tempest in a Test Tube" (1989).

85. Kolata (1988); "It's a Tall Tall World" (1994).

86. On this paragraph and the next, see Larson (1996), Pellegrino (1993), and Silver and Pellegrino (1993).

87. Wilson (1995); see also Wickelgren (1989).

88. Schneider (1989); Brooks (1989); Levidow (1995).

89. Toufexis (1989).

90. Koshland (1989).

91. In some respects, science promotes anxieties similar to those spawned by Calvinist doctrine, which left the adequacy of individual efforts to achieve salvation in doubt. Science promises ever more control over the environment but cannot guarantee that an individual will be safe from risks associated with new technologies.

CHAPTER THREE

1. Gras (1915); cf. Slack (1990, 1998).

2. For an elaboration of these points, see the next section of this chapter and pp. 152–53 of chap. 4 (cf. Fogel 1992g; and Slack 1998).

3.   Malthus ([1803] 1992).

4.   For further details, see Fogel (1992g). For England, the earliest annual observations for individuals are recorded for 1541 (Wrigley and Schofield 1981). For France, the earliest national observation is recorded for 1740 and the earliest observation for an eleven-year moving average is 1745. However, mortality rates for the region around Paris go back to 1676 (INED 1977; cf. Rebaudo 1979).

5.   On this and the next two paragraphs, see Everitt (1967, 578–79, 581, 583–85).

6.   Gras (1915, 236–46); Everitt (1967, 581–85).

7.   Everitt (1967, 585–86); Lipson (1971, 444–53); Supple (1964, 244–45). For evidence that bears on these claims and those of the next two paragraphs, see Fogel (1992g, 1997b).

8.   Lipson (1971, 457–67); Rose (1961).

9.   Hufton (1974, 176, 193).

10.   Crafts (1985, 45); Rose (1971, 40–41); Marshall (1968, 26); Mitchell and Deane (1962, 469); cf. Slack (1990).

11.   Henretta (1965); Kulikoff (1971); Pessen (1973, 1978); Main (1982); Jones (1980); Soltow (1989); cf. Williamson and Lindert (1980).

12.   Calhoun (1960); Soltow (1981, 1989); Lindert and Williamson (1982); Tocqueville (1969).

13.   See Fogel (1992g, esp. table 9.5 and the corresponding section of the appendix).

14.   Fogel and Floud (1999). For evidence bearing on levels and distributions of food consumption and income in America and Britain in the eighteenth century and the early nineteenth, see chap. 4 and app. 3A.

15.   Coll (1972); Schneider and Deutsch (1941).

16.   Coll (1972); Trattner (1994); Katz (1986).

17.   Trattner (1994); Foster (1960).

18.   Ahlstrom (1972, 420; see also chaps. 26, 28); Fogel (1989, chap. 8). Although the New Divinity was dominant among the Congregationalists, the Unitarians, the Northern Baptists, the Northern Methodists, and the Northern Presbyterians, orthodox Calvinism continued to reign in the Southern branches of the evangelical denominations (see Mathews 1977; Genovese 1994, 1995).

19.   Fogel (1989, chap. 8).

20.   Ahlstrom (1972, 326). On the democratization of American evangelical religions, see Hatch (1989).

21. Cross and Livingstone (1983, 1063). See also Smith (1957, 114–18).

22. Perfectionism, or the doctrine that man was capable of achieving a sinless state, was more prevalent before the Civil War in the North than in the South. It received its strongest support from two strains of Protestantism, churches of liberal theology, such as the Unitarian Church, led by men like William Ellery Channing, and the millennial reform perfectionism associated with Methodism and the revivalism of Charles Grandison Finney. In both strains, the injunction to labor to banish sin from the world, also known in Jonathan Edwards's theology as *benevolence,* became a prominent feature of pious practice that led men and women into reform movements to abolish slavery and intemperance. In the 1840s, the religious doctrine of perfectionism found expression in the Methodist Holiness movement, whose adherents strove to achieve a second conversion, which entailed complete "sanctification" or sinlessness (see Ahlstrom 1972, 308–11, 474–78, 397–400; and Schneider 1993).

23. Mathews (1977, 24). See also Gaustad (1962, 4, 10–13, 57); Ahlstrom (1972, 318–20, 375–76); and McLoughlin (1978, 89–94).

24. Ahlstrom (1972, 408, 472, 422). Old light Presbyterianism predominated in the South, and its doctrines were fashioned by Princeton theologians (ibid., chap. 38).

25. McLoughlin (1978, 128, 129; see generally 128–30).

26. Cross ([1950] 1982, 198; see generally 198–99, 268).

27. For a still unsurpassed discussion of ultraism, see Cross ([1950] 1982, chaps. 10–12). Antislavery sentiment within the Methodist Episcopal Church, e.g., led to a schism in the early 1840s. Those members believing in the ultraist disciplines of total abstinence from alcohol and abolition separated to form the Wesleyan Methodist Church (ibid., 264–67).

28. Foster (1960).

29. Although *Native American* is the current term of choice for indigenous Americans, during the nineteenth century *native American* referred to American-born whites of European ancestry. *Nativists* were evangelicals who organized to limit the entry, voting rights, and economic opportunities of European Catholics and orthodox Lutherans.

30. Bodo (1954). Jedidiah Morse is an example of how orthodox theology can sometimes inform radical social policy.

31. Quoted in Bodo (1954, 97).

32. Cross ([1950] 1982); Reid (1990).

33. Ahlstrom (1972); Griffin (1960); Reid (1990).

34. Reid (1990); *Encyclopedia Britannica,* 1962 ed., s.v. "United States of America."

35. Rorabough (1979, 23); see also Tyrell (1979, 16).

36. Rorabaugh (1979, 7–12).

37. Bodo (1954); Foster (1960); Rorabaugh (1979); Lender and Martin (1982); Gusfield ([1963] 1986); Cross ([1950] 1982).

38. Lender and Martin (1982); Ahlstrom (1972).

39. Lender and Martin (1982); Schlesinger (1933); Ahlstrom (1972); Reid (1990).

40. Ahlstrom (1972); Lender and Martin (1982).

41. New Jersey had granted women the vote in its state constitution (1776–1807). Wyoming Territory gave women the vote in 1869 and became the second state with woman suffrage in 1890, when it joined the Union on 23 July. The vote was gained for women in Colorado in 1893 and in Utah and Idaho in 1896 (see Schlesinger 1933; cf. "A Few Important Dates from the Woman Suffrage Movement," at http://www.inform.umd.edu:8080/EdRes/Topic/WomensStudies/ReadingRoom/History/Vote.html).

42. Faulkner (1931); Cochran and Andrews (1962, s.v. "education"); Schlesinger (1933).

43. There is a general consensus that literacy rates in America rose from between 65 and 76 percent in 1700 to about 90 percent in 1900 and that they rose more rapidly in most parts of the United States than they did in England, France, and other Continental countries. Where dissenting reformed churches dominated, however, such as in Scotland and Geneva, literacy rates were as high as they were in the United States. Not all issues of measurement have been resolved, especially those pertaining to the literacy of women, the effect of new waves of migration on literacy rates, and the intergenerational transmission of literacy (see, e.g., Lockridge 1974; Grubb 1990; and Perlmann and Shirley 1991). In states like Illinois, the literacy rates were much higher for migrants from New England than for migrants from the South (Fishlow 1966a).

44. Bailyn et al. (1992, 1: chap. 4).

45. Cochran and Andrews (1962, 314). On this paragraph and the next, see, generally, ibid., s.v. "education"; Bailyn et al. (1992, 1: chap. 13).

46. Bodo (1954, chaps. 2 and 6).

47. The statute is quoted in Stokes (1950, 2:53).

48. It is important to keep in mind that, while the most significant purvey-

ors of nativism, the Know-Nothings, were a product of the 1850s, the ideological offensive against Catholicism began in the 1830s, when uneasiness about the rise of the Catholic Church turned into an organized attack. The politicization of anti-Catholicism also traces back to the 1830s, when a series of newspaper articles by Samuel F. B. Morse (Morse 1835) led to the formation in New York City of a nativist party, which won the mayoral election in 1837. Lyman Beecher's 1835 tract *A Plea for the West* also fanned the flames of anti-Catholicism (see Bodo 1954; Billington 1964; Ahlstrom 1972; Benson 1961).

49. Holt (1969, 1973); Gienapp (1987); Fogel (1989); Fogel and Galantine (1992); cf. Holt (1992). The quotations are from Stokes (1950, 2:56, 57).

50. The quotation is from Bremner (1970, 1:83). See also Bodo (1954, 165); Reid (1990, 689); and Albanese (1981).

51. Mann is quoted in Bailyn et al. (1992, 1:416). See also Landes and Solmon (1972); Fishlow (1966b); Wilentz (1984); Cochran and Andrews (1962, s.v. "education"); Higham (1963); Hennessey (1981); Commons et al. (1918, vol. 1); Billington (1964). As Landes and Solmon (1972) point out, compulsory education laws usually followed high enrollment, codifying an already existing situation rather than creating it.

52. In New York in 1850, the cordwainers, painters, bricklayers and plasterers, sashmakers and blindmakers, carpenters, plumbers, jewelers, printers, cabinetmakers, boilermakers, and tailors each had their independent benevolent organization (cf. Wilentz 1984). Some of the benevolent and fraternal organizations cut across trade lines, and these often had an ethnic and religious orientation. This was true of the Order of United Americans, formed in New York in 1844, and the Order of United American Mechanics, formed in Philadelphia in 1845. Both, reflecting the nativist upsurge of the mid-1840s, limited membership to "American-born laborers" (Billington 1964; cf. Higham 1963; May 1949).

53. Pessen (1977, 1978); Chudacoff (1975); Wiebe (1967); Warner (1968); Feldberg (1975); Ernst (1949); Jones ([1960] 1992); Laurie (1980).

54. Warner (1968); Ernst (1949); Feldberg (1975); Fogel (1989); Billington (1964); Jones ([1960] 1992); Higham (1963).

55. Wiebe (1967); Strong (1885); Jones ([1960] 1992); Chudacoff (1975); May (1949).

56. Chudacoff (1975); Bailyn et al. (1992, 1: chaps. 24–25).

57. Chudacoff (1975); May (1949); Bailyn et al. (1992, 1: chap. 25).

58. The quotations are from Davis (1984, 114) and Davis (1966, 306).

59. For discussions of the relation between federal power in the U.S. Con-

stitution and the institution of slavery, see Robinson (1979, chaps. 6–7) and Wiecek (1977).

60. Some of the abolitionists also turned out to be brilliant political tacticians. Chief among them was Salmon P. Chase, who was instrumental in creating a much broader antislavery party in 1848 (the Free Soil Party) by combining the Liberty Party with dissident factions from the Democrats and Whigs. His most brilliant move (in which he was aided by other key political abolitionists) was his recognition of the opportunity that the Know-Nothing Party offered to create a new coalition on a minimalist antislavery program that united the Free Soilers, large portions of the Northern Whigs, the Northern Know-Nothings, and some Northern ex-Democrats. As a result, the Republican Party emerged as the principal opposition to the Democrats in the election of 1856. Although the Republicans lost their bid for the presidency in that year, they made a strong showing in the House of Representatives and gained control of it in the 1858 elections. In 1860, they not only retained their control of the House but also elected Abraham Lincoln, the first antislavery president, who set in course the train of events that led to the freeing of the slaves (Fogel 1989, chap. 10; cf. Foner 1970; Gienapp 1987).

61. Channing (1848, 81).

62. It is of course possible to have a religious awakening, even one with political implications, that does not demarcate a new political phase, as occurred with the urban revivals of 1857 and 1858 and those led by Dwight Moody and Ira Sankey after the Civil War (Long 1998).

63. Landes and Solmon (1972).

64. Dorfman (1946, 2:761, 759–60).

65. Ibid., 763–64.

66. Ibid., 764.

67. Ibid., 967.

68. Dorfman (1959, 3:178–79); Hoeveler (1976).

69. Charles Grandison Finney as quoted and paraphrased in McLoughlin (1978, 128–29).

70. Hannon (1985); Coll (1972); Katz (1986); Trattner (1994).

71. Hannon (1985); Coll (1972); Katz (1986); Trattner (1994); Taylor ([1951] 1957).

72. Lebergott (1964). The recession hit the nonagricultural sector much more sharply than the agricultural sector and was heavily concentrated in those manufacturing industries competing with British exports. Lebergott estimates that, within manufacturing, employment might have fallen by as much as two-

thirds, but then relatively few people were engaged in manufacturing. Agricultural prices were affected but not agricultural employment; nor was unemployment a problem in the hand trades or in navigation. For the nonagricultural labor force as a whole, Lebergott puts the rate of unemployment at about one-sixth.

73. Pessen (1978).

74. Gates (1934); Swierenga (1968); Bogue (1963); Fogel and Rutner (1972).

75. Hannon (1984a, 1984b, 1985).

76. Robbins (1962, 108).

77. Fishlow (1966c); Gallman (1966).

78. Lesley (1859); Temin (1964); Poulson (1981); U.S. Bureau of the Census (1883, 126).

79. Chandler (1977, 1990); Ratner, Soltow, and Sylla (1979).

80. Chandler (1977, 1990); Ratner, Soltow, and Sylla (1979); Hughes (1991); Benson (1955).

81. Ratner, Soltow, and Sylla (1979, 289); Faulkner (1960, chap. 23).

82. Hughes (1991, chap. 4).

83. Taft (1964); Dulles (1949); May (1949, pt. 3, chap. 1); Faulkner (1960, chap. 22); Cochran and Andrews (1962, s.v. "Pullman strike").

84. Keller (1977); Nye (1959); Lebergott (1964); Weir (1992); Hannon (1984a).

85. Lebergott (1964); Weber ([1899] 1967); Keller (1977); Wiebe (1967); Faulkner (1959).

86. For this paragraph and the previous two, see Gallman (1966), Lebergott (1966), Ratner, Soltow, and Sylla (1979), and Taft (1964).

87. Beard and Beard (1927); Parrington (1930); Higgs (1979).

88. Dorfman (1959, 3:280–81).

89. Hoeveler (1976, 196); Dorfman (1959, 3:281).

90. Reid et al. (1990, 1088). For a social history of sin in early Christianity, see Pagels (1995).

91. Reid et al. (1990, 1088–89).

92. Ibid., 1089. For a survey of denominational differences on this issue, see ibid., s.v. "sin."

93. Tarbell (1939, 27).

94. Ibid., 28–29.

95. *Encyclopedia Britannica,* 1962 ed., s.v. "history."

96. Ahlstrom (1972, 779).

97. Rauschenbusch quoted in Ahlstrom (1972, 785–86).

98. On temperance, prohibition, and the Social Gospel, see Bordin (1981), Gusfield ([1963] 1986), Ahlstrom (1972, chap. 51), and Hopkins (1940).

99. Reid et al. (1990, s.v. "conversion").

100. Reid et al. (1990, 647); Hutchison ([1976] 1992); see also Hutchison (1989).

101. Reid et al. (1990, 648); see also Ahlstrom (1972, chap. 51); Hopkins (1940); Handy (1991); Muller (1959).

102. Szasz (1982).

103. Cox (1995); Ahlstrom (1972, chap. 48); Reid et al. (1990, s.v. "Pentecostalism"). On Latin America, see Martin (1990). The worldwide growth in membership during the twentieth century is reported in Barrett (1988).

104. Hutchison ([1976] 1992); Marsden (1994).

105. Marsden (1980); Reid et al. (1990, s.v. "Harry Emerson Fosdick").

106. *Dictionary of American Biography,* 1929 ed., s.v. "William Jennings Bryan"; Reid et al. (1990, s.v. "Scopes trial").

107. Marsden (1980); Reid et al. (1990, s.v. "fundamentalism"); Marty (1986, chap. 22); Balmer (1993); Carpenter (1997).

108. Hopkins (1940, 290–91). See also Reid et al. (1990, s.v. "Federal Council of Churches").

109. Rader (1966); Crunden (1982); cf. Haskell (1977); Ross (1991); Coats (1960, 1964).

110. On this and the next paragraph, see Rayback (1966).

111. Brownlee (1979).

112. Higham (1963); Goldin (1994b).

113. Bain (1951); Faulkner (1960, chap. 21).

114. Hughes (1991); Stigler (1975); Kolko ([1963] 1977).

115. HS (1975, 1106).

116. Ratner (1942); Faulkner (1960); Brownlee (1979).

117. Ratner (1942); Brownlee (1979); Faulkner (1960); HS (1975); Ratner, Soltow, and Sylla (1979).

118. For unemployment figures, see Hopkins (1936); cf. Nathan (1936), HS

(1975, 135), Ahlstrom (1972, chaps. 53–55), Reid et al. (1990, s.vv. "neo-orthodoxy" and "H. Richard Niebuhr"), and Marty (1986, chap. 12).

119.   *Dictionary of American Biography,* 1973 ed., s.v. "John R. Commons." An example of direct connection between scholarship at the University of Wisconsin and legislation at the statehouse is the case of Dr. Stewart Scrimshaw and his work on apprenticeship. Scrimshaw, who had completed an apprenticeship in England as a mason before college, began graduate work in labor economics at Wisconsin in 1912 with John R. Commons, who became his thesis advisor, and Richard T. Ely. Scrimshaw was appointed state supervisor of apprenticeship from 1915 to 1920, administering the 1915 apprenticeship law (personal communication from Dr. Nevin Scrimshaw, 24 December, 1999). Scrimshaw went on to write a Ph.D. thesis on apprenticeship (Scrimshaw 1926) and a book on apprenticeship (Scrimshaw 1932).

120.   HS (1975, 386); Brownlee (1979); Mitchell (1947); Schlesinger (1957).

121.   Salant (1990); Stein (1969, 1986, 1988).

122.   Duncan and Shelton (1978); Stein (1969, 1986).

123.   Samuelson (1944); Nathan (1990); Salant (1990); Friedman and Friedman (1991, 1992); Stein (1969, 1986); Kindleberger (1991); Rostow (1981).

124.   HS (1975, 164, 178–79); Brownlee (1979); Mitchell (1947); Lewis (1986); Freeman (1976); Goldin and Margo (1992).

125.   Stein (1988).

126.   HS (1975, 382–83); Olson (1974).

127.   Burner, Genovese, and McDonald (1980); Bailyn et al. (1992, 2: chap. 32).

128.   Burner, Genovese, and McDonald (1980, 695).

CHAPTER FOUR

1.   Federal government employment reached a peak in 1990 and has declined slightly since then. This trend, however, has been offset by the rise in state and local government employment (SA 1998, 331).

2.   Sen (1996).

3.   Marx stressed the absolute decline in the standard of living because the weight of the evidence at the time he completed *Das Kapital* seemed consistent with that conclusion. By the beginning of the twentieth century, evidence began to accumulate that standards of living had risen in recent decades, but not as fast for the working class as for the upper classes. As a result, the heirs of Marx began to stress the relative decline in working-class conditions.

4. Floud, Gregory, and Wachter (1985); Rowntree (1901); Bowley and Burnett-Hurst (1915).

5. Douglas (1930); Rees (1961); Coale and Demeny (1966).

6. Floud (1985).

7. Fogel (1986a, 467); cf. Pope (1992).

8. For data on heights, see n. 77, chap. 2 above.

9. Maddison (1982); Crafts (1985); Gallman (1966, 1972).

10. Stature and Gini ratios are significantly correlated, but, as the discussion of height and body mass index below indicates, the anthropometric measures reveal important aspects of welfare that are not as apparent in the movement of Gini ratios.

11. There has been a subsequent rise in the Gini ratio since 1973 in virtually all the rich nations for which such information is available. The reasons for this reversal and its significance for the future of egalitarianism are discussed in chap. 5 and in app. 5E below.

12. On trends in the Gini ratio between ca. 1690 and 1973 and the debate over this trend, see Soltow (1968), Sawyer (1976), Feinstein (1988), Williamson (1981b, 1985), Lindert and Williamson (1982, 1983a), Floud, Wachter, and Gregory (1990), and Atkinson, Rainwater, and Smedling (1994).

13. On this paragraph and the previous one, see Steckel (1995), Wrigley and Schofield (1981), and Rona et al. (1978).

14. Fogel (1992g); Fogel and Costa (1997); cf. van Wieringen (1986); Drukker and Tassenaar (1997); Schmidt, Jorgensen, and Michaelsen (1995).

15. Cipolla (1980); Laslett ([1965] 1984); Himmelfarb (1984); Soltow (1968); Lindert and Williamson (1982); Fogel (1987, 1989, 1993); Colquhoun (1814); Hannon (1984a, 1984b, 1985); Jencks (1994).

16. It is sometimes argued that the left side of the U curve between BMI and mortality is due primarily to smoking, which depresses appetite. However, various studies have found a significant negative relation between BMI and mortality at low BMIs after controlling for smoking (see Mansson et al. 1996; Ross, Langer, and Barrett-Connor 1997; Rabkin et al. 1997; Chyou et al. 1997; Bonora et al. 1998; and Brown, Dobson, and Mishra 1998).

17. Factors that relate stature to the risk of dying include not only current malnutrition and malnutrition during infancy and early childhood but also nutritional factors that undermine the development of the fetus in utero. Animal experiments indicate that nutritional insults in one generation may affect several generations. These effects are environmental rather than genetic. These studies

do not rule out genetic effects; what they show is that environmental effects can be more long lasting than many investigators had hitherto assumed (see Chandra 1975; Fraker et al. 1986; Meinhold et al. 1993; cf. Barker 1998).

18. Kim (1996).

19. Fogel (1994a); Barker (1998).

20. At the present stage of knowledge, discussion of the relative importance of these factors in temporarily offsetting the benefits of increased productivity is provisional and may be revised by ongoing research.

21. Wrigley (1969); Bairoch (1988).

22. On the United States, see Vinovskis (1972) and Fogel et al. (1978). On Europe, see Weber ([1899] 1967); Woods (1984); Bairoch (1988).

23. See Fogel (1986a, 1986b) on the link between city size, stature, and mortality in America. On the relation between mortality and stature in eight European countries during the nineteenth century, see Floud (1983) and Floud, Wachter, and Gregory (1990). On similar regression analyses for Trinidad, see John (1984, 1988).

24. U.S. Surgeon General's Office (1875).

25. Boyd (1941); Ackernecht (1945, [1952] 1965); Drake (1850, [1850] 1854); Coolidge (1856).

26. Ackernecht (1945); Boyd (1941).

27. Landes (1969). Recent studies have revealed that, in addition to providing a stream of permanent migrants to the city, the countryside provided a large stream of temporary laborers. Perhaps two or three times as many rural residents rotated work between the city and the countryside as left the countryside permanently. Thus, trade and labor rotation carried such diseases as typhoid, typhus, dysentery, cholera, and other major killers of the nineteenth century from the city to the countryside (see Goubert 1973; de Vries 1984).

28. Komlos (1985, 1989).

29. Komlos (1989).

30. Fogel and Floud (1999); cf. FAO, WHO, and UNU (1985, 71, 77, 79). These levels are in excess of current recommended daily allowances for males engaged in heavy work for ten hours a day.

31. Ackernecht (1945); Boyd (1941); Smillie (1955). Increases in the prevalence of such diseases could have reduced nutrients available for growth because of the diversion of nutrients to fighting the diseases, the decreased absorption of nutrients, reduced appetite, and the poorer-quality diets that are often fed to the sick (cf. Scrimshaw and Gordon 1968; Scrimshaw, Taylor, and Gordon 1968).

32. On permanent stunting, see Tanner (1982); Billewicz and McGregor (1982); Horton (1984, 1985, 1986); Martorell (1985); and Martorell and Habicht (1986); cf. Strauss (1986).

33. As Roderick Floud pointed out to me, "A very potent example of the problems of infant nutrition is the failure of infant mortality to fall in Britain until the first decade of the twentieth century, although child, youth, and adult mortalities were falling from several decades earlier" (personal communication, 6 June 1996).

34. The discovery that the children of prosperous farmers were stunted shows how data on height can reveal subtle processes in the degradation of health and other aspects of standards of living that real wages or incomes do not capture. Real-wage indices rarely adjust adequately for changes in environmental circumstances. Very often, rises in wages that reflect compensation for hazards are treated as if they were net gains to welfare (see Fogel 1992g).

35. N. Scrimshaw, personal communication; Whitehead (1977).

36. Martorell (1985); Barker (1998). Increases in the inequality of the distribution of income (and hence of the consumption of nutrients) could also explain the periodic declines in average stature during the nineteenth century. This factor could have been at work, particularly during depressions that sharply increased unemployment among manual workers and reduced their real wages. The fact that the heights of the British upper classes did not exhibit the same cycling in stature as found among the laboring classes and the correlation between the real wages of urban workers and stature suggest that there may have been cyclic surges in inequality, even if there was no marked secular increase in inequality in Britain between 1775 and 1875 (Floud, Wachter, and Gregory 1990; Lindert and Williamson 1982, 1983a, 1983b; Williamson 1985, Feinstein 1988). Sharp declines in the real wages of nonagricultural manual workers appear to have been a factor in the American case as well (Williamson 1976; Margo and Villaflor 1987; Fogel and Engerman 1992; Fogel, Galantine, and Manning 1992). However, even those who prospered during the period 1840–60, such as farmers, experienced sharp decreases in stature. In the American case, about four-fifths of the decline in average stature between 1830 and 1860 took place among rural populations that prospered (Fogel 1986a).

37. This and the next paragraph are based on research reported in Fogel (1992g) and on unpublished research by Chris Acito at the Center for Population Economics of the University of Chicago ca. 1992 (cf. Slack 1998).

38. Crop failures caused by natural factors that were sufficient to create a famine were relatively rare (see Fogel 1992g). Even in the case of the Irish potato blight of the 1840s, where the failure of the potato crop was substantial, the famine

could have been avoided. In that instance, English authorities were reluctant to expend the resources required to replace the failed potato crop (see Mokyr 1985).

39. The term *excessive growth* is a reference to the effect on public health conditions. In commenting on an earlier draft of the book, Seymour Drescher made the point that the lower rate of immigration and population growth in the North might have undermined the capacity to build a Northern antislavery coalition with enough electoral clout to undermine the dominant proslavery coalitions (personal communication, 20 May 1996).

40. Foreign immigration was the major factor in urban growth prior to 1860 (see Fogel, Galantine, and Manning 1992, esp. entries 60, 63).

41. Goldin (1994b); Higham (1963); cf. chap. 2 above.

42. Reluctance to prevent urban growth was also probably related to an inadequate grasp of the mechanisms of disease transmission.

43. See Fogel (1993) and Kim (1996).

44. Toutain (1971); Holmes (1907); Bennett and Pierce (1961). During the eighteenth and nineteenth centuries, meat was a luxury that only the rich could afford to eat regularly in substantial quantities. One recent study indicates that, near the beginning of the eighteenth century, the Gini ratio for the distribution of meat was 0.65 (Stone 1988). Figures here and in the text are net of refuse, which is calculated at 15 percent of dressed weight. Currently, the World Health Organization recommends that persons about the size of the French in 1880 and using about the same level of energy as the French did at that time consume about 50 percent more high-quality protein than the French consumed during the 1880s (FAO, WHO, and UNU 1985; Toutain 1971).

45. Holmes (1907); Fogel (1989).

46. SA (1967, 874); U.S. Intelligence Agency (1978); Peach and Constantin (1972).

47. Fogel (1986a); National Center for Health Statistics, Najjar, and Rowland (1987).

48. For an elaboration of the point, see Fogel (1986a, 1992g, 1994b) and Fogel and Floud (1999).

The apparent final height of the London ultrapoor ca. 1800, which was about 62 inches, may be taken as representing the combined effect of exceedingly poor diet and exposure to exceedingly severe disease environments. On the other hand, the combined effects of a relatively good diet and a mild disease environment produce average heights of about 72 inches (as observed in Holland today). These figures, and the fact that final heights of American farmers born about 1860 averaged just 67.2 inches, suggest that, even with good diets, continuous exposure to a severe disease environment will lead to stunting in males of about 5 inches.

Such stunting, by itself, increases the risk of death by about 31 percent. However, Americans born before the Civil War were not only stunted but somewhat "wasted." With average BMIs of 22, they were about three points below the optimal BMI for their stature (Fogel, Costa, and Kim 1993; Costa and Steckel 1997). The joint effect of stunting and wasting increased their odds of dying by about 52 percent. Relative risks are computed from Fogel (1993, table A.2).

49.   The word *primarily* in this sentence should be emphasized since the government did contribute to some of the increase in productivity by subsidizing research and development, including education and the dissemination of information. Government also provided social overhead capital, an important input into economic growth.

50.   Soltow (1989, 1992); Sawyer (1976).

51.   Computed on the assumption that the overall Gini ratio is a convex combination of the component Gini ratios and that the approximate Gini ratio for physical and financial capital is 0.9 while that for wages is 0.3 (cf. Fei, Ranis, and Kuo 1978; Williamson and Lindert 1980; Soltow 1992; Wilcox 1992; app. 5E below; Fogel 1994a, 1994b, 1997b, and the sources cited therein).

52.   The evidence underlying this section is presented in Fogel (1994a, 1994b, 1997b) and the sources cited therein.

53.   On the rise of real wages in England, see Mitchell and Deane (1962); Matthews, Feinstein, and Odling-Smee (1982); Crafts (1985); Williamson (1985, 1987a, 1987b, 1994); Floud, Wachter, and Gregory (1990); and Feinstein (1988, 1990, 1991); cf. MacKinnon (1994).

54.   On the rapid rise of real wages in the United States, see Williamson (1976); David and Solar (1977); and Gallman and Wallis (1992).

55.   Barker (1994); Costa (1993b, 1993c); Kim (1993); Steckel and Floud (1997).

56.   On the effect of internal migration on measured per capita income, see Fogel and Engerman (1971); Gallman (1972); Easterlin (1975); McCutcheon (1992). On its effect on the spread of disease, see Boyd (1941); Ackerknecht (1945, [1952] 1965); Smillie (1955); May (1958); Kunitz (1983); New York State Board of Health (1867).

57.   See Fogel (1992g).

58.   Kuznets (1952).

59.   Floud, Wachter, and Gregory (1990).

60.   Consider, e.g., the food that gave the upper classes their superior diet

and the housing that reduced their exposure to disease. If the nutrients were sold to them by a perfectly discriminating monopolist, the benefits that they derived in improved health would have been incorporated in the price of the nutrients. However, food was sold in a competitive market. Similarly, the value of the extra health benefits that accrued to the rich because of the nature of their housing could not be captured by the laborers who built the houses or by the brickmakers who sold their wares competitively, nor could they be fully captured by the land owners. Since there was an excess supply of land with the quality called *separated from reservoirs of disease,* land owners could usually capture only conventional benefits of proximity.

61.   Not only are measures of height, weight, and BMI proving to be useful measures of aggregate differences between populations at a moment of time, and changes in these aggregates over time, but they are also providing much information about differences in distributions of health, nutrition, and conditions of life at various points in time. The implications of these data for assessing the socioeconomic status of particular individuals are more complex. Shortness, e.g., may, at a particular point in time, reflect primarily genetic or primarily environmental influences. If, however, there is information available about parents' stature, or if a record exists of annual measurements of height during growing ages, the independent influence of environmental conditions may be discerned. Studies of twins can also be used to partition genetic and environmental factors (cf. Vaupel 1993).

62.   Case, Harley, and Pearson (1962); Haines (1979, 1992); U.S. Public Health Service (1963).

63.   Williamson and Lindert (1980); Phelps Brown (1988); Perkin (1990).

64.   U.S. Bureau of the Census (1975); Karpinos (1958). For somewhat different views on these issues, see Preston (1975), Preston and van de Walle (1978), and McKeown (1976).

65.   See chap. 5 and app. 5A below.

66.   Kuznets (1952); apps. 5C and 5E below; Robinson and Godbey (1997). For a discussion of changes in the use of time, including household chores, a variety of leisure activities, and commuting, see chap. 5 below. It is worth noting that not all extra leisure time has been constructively employed. The twentieth century, particularly the last few decades, has experienced sharp increases in such unmeasured costs as crime, drug use, and threats to safety that significantly offset unmeasured benefits.

Another implication of this line of argument is that the inequality of the international distribution of income is greater than is indicated by current conventions for comparing the income of nations. The human development index (UN 1990) may overcome some of these deficiencies by giving explicit recognition to life expectancy (but not to the level of morbidity) and by including a measure of education. However, there is room to doubt whether schooling by itself adequately captures the wide disparities in both the quantity and the quality of leisure.

67. The computations assume an instantaneous and sustained decline to zero in the rate of growth of per capita income from 2.5 percent per annum. It was also assumed that the distribution of income was lognormal with a Gini ratio of 0.35 in the egalitarian case and 0.40 in the progrowth case.

68. Computed from World Bank (1989, table 30) for OECD countries. Compare Putterman, Romer, and Silvestre (1998).

69. Weeks et al. (1994); compare Becker (1993).

70. AMA (1992, 134–41); SA (1990, 411, 412, 407, 386); cf. AMA (1999). I used the median earnings of service workers (except private household) in 1988 ($18,670) as the standard for common labor (full-time, male). I assumed that full-time male laborers worked an average of 1,786 hours per year ($38 \times 47.0 \approx 1,786$). The number of weeks worked is equal to 52×1 minus the ratio of expenditures on paid leave to wages $[52 \{1 - (0.97 \div 10.02)\} \approx 47.0]$ (SA 1990, 413). Manufacturing workers in Germany during 1990 averaged 36 hours per week for about 44 weeks per year, while those in the United States averaged 38 hours per week for about 47 weeks (see Bell and Freeman 1995).

71. I have not taken account of the fact that, whereas the typical manual worker receives fringe benefits equal to about 38 percent of his or her pay, the bulk of physicians (76 percent), who are engaged in independent practice, do not (SA 1990, 413; AMA 1992, 24). An adjustment for fringe benefits (assuming that the employed physicians also receive fringe benefits equal to 38 percent of their pay and excluding paid leave from the compensation package of service workers) reduced the ratio of surgeons' to ordinary laborers' hourly compensation from 6.4 to 5.4. If account were taken of overtime pay for more than 40 hours per week, the ratio would be lower.

72. This discussion is based partly on my own involvement in policy making at Harvard and on my work at the Mathematical Social Science Board, which attempted to work out relocation programs for new and recent Ph.D.'s who were having difficulty finding jobs in mathematics and the physical sciences. However, this excess supply of the late 1970s turned out to be temporary and diminished much more rapidly than anticipated in some fields, but other markets (such as

mathematics) remain sluggish. For further discussion of this issue, see chap. 5 below (cf. Bowen and Rudenstine 1991; Bound and Johnson 1992; Katz and Murphy 1992; Levine 1997; Barkume 1996–97; app. 5E below).

73. Estimated from data in AMA (1992).

74. HS (1975, 55); SA (1998, 94); Bell, Wade, and Goss (1992, 16, 36).

75. Annual earnings are from HS (1975, 425) and SA (1998, 434). Nominal earnings were deflated by the wholesale price index to avoid the upward bias in the consumer price index (CPI), combining the series from HS (1975, 199 [all items]) for 1890–1960 with the series from SA (1998, 497 [crude materials]) for 1960–96. On the bias in the CPI, see Boskin et al. (1998). For the discussion of the decline in working hours, see chap. 5 below.

76. Blau (1998); Hecker (1998); Goldin (1990, 1995). The on-line database of the 46th ed. of Marquis's *Who's Who in America* permits analysis of the trend in occupations among prominent women. This analysis reveals that the share of women among prominent professionals increased from 5 percent among individuals born before 1911 to 20 percent among individuals born since 1951. The greatest gains were made in journalism, business, law, and the social sciences. However, so far, only a third of these highly successful women have been able to combine careers with marriages that included children.

77. Goldin (1994a); Smith and Welch (1989); Heckman (1990, 1991); Donohue and Heckman (1991); Alexis (1998); Bound and Freeman (1992).

78. Goldin (1994a); Freeman (1990, 1994, 1995); Blanchflower and Freeman (1990).

79. Goldin (1994a); HS (1975, 15, 368–70); Margo (1990).

80. Goldin (1994a, 1995, 1997); HS (1975, 379); Goldin and Katz (1996).

81. Goldin (1990, 1994a).

82. Goldin (1995, 34). See also Goldin (1994a).

83. Goldin (1994a); Weir (1992); SA (1997, 556); Zarnowitz (1992); Zarnowitz and Moore (1986).

84. *Economic Report of the President* (1992).

85. Niebuhr ([1937] 1988, 193). See also Ahlstrom (1972).

86. For sources bearing on these shifts, see n. 41, chap. 1 above. Compare Fukuyama and Berman (1999), who argue that the moral decay has begun to abate.

87. Himmelfarb (1995); Moynihan (1993); cf. Burnham (1993).

CHAPTER FIVE

1. Fogel (1992c).

2. Even in New England, where the largest cotton mills were located, most textile firms operated with fewer than one hundred workers. Some of the iron-works, particularly rolling mills and anthracite blast furnaces, were very large enterprises. The New Jersey Iron Works, headed by Abraham Hewitt, who was also a prominent reformer and mayor of New York City toward the end of the century, employed two hundred people and had a capitalization of several hundred thousand dollars. By far the biggest enterprises before the Civil War were the railroads. The numerous small railroads built in the 1830s and 1840s were integrated into trunk lines by such entrepreneurs as Commodore Vanderbilt, who created the New York Central Railroad, and Jay Gould, the archetype of the rapacious financier, who created the Erie system. In 1860, the New York Central was worth about $35 million (equivalent to over $3 billion today) and employed about four thousand workers.

Even the very large cotton textile mills, which were based mainly on the labor of children and young women recruited from farm families over a wide region, did not lead to a large separation between living space and workplace. In Lowell, the factory operators were housed in dormitories adjacent to the factories and supervised by matrons pledged to maintain the chastity and good reputation of the young women in their charge. In other large-scale nonagricultural enterprises that were based mainly on the labor of adult males, the unity of the home and the workplace was often maintained by employers who built homes for their employees in villages adjacent to the factories, often at subsidized prices (Lebergott 1964). Down to the end of the Civil War, the typical nonagricultural enterprise consisted of a master who worked alongside a score of journeymen and apprentices.

3. Zunz (1990).

4. Thorp and Crowder (1941); U.S. National Resources Committee (1939).

5. Rosenman (1941, 633–44); Lynch (1946); cf. Wilcox (1940).

6. Schumpeter (1942).

7. SA (1996, 405–11); cf. HS (1975, 240); Kuznets (1952, 1966, 1971). See also Bell (1973, 1999), whose prescient analysis of the changing structure of industry and consumption led him to reconsider the cultural, sociological, and economic implications of the decline of industrial society.

8. Although it is widely presumed that most of the increase in jobs has been at very low incomes, the reverse is actually true (see app. 5E below).

9. For a discussion of the methods and sources used in estimating the length

of the workyear ca. 1880, see app. 5A below (cf. Lebergott 1993; Vanek 1984). Although cyclic unemployment was severe during the last third of the nineteenth century, it had little effect on the average length of the workday. During the 1890s, e.g., cyclic unemployment averaged about 4 percent of the workyear, which amounts to about a third of an hour per day. However, lost work time during recession years was offset by the extra hours worked during boom years. Similarly, short workdays and layoffs during the winter were offset by long workdays during the summer.

10. Measurement procedures were as follows (figures reported in the text have been rounded):

Chores. Chores include chopping firewood; shoveling coal; repairs in home, fences, etc.; maintaining tools; gardening; carting; weaving and sewing; caring for children and the aged.

Travel to and from work. In the case of farm laborers, travel is the time spent walking from their cottages to the fields in which their work was conducted.

Work. Work ca. 1880 was calculated on the basis of a 3,109-hour workyear, which assumes a 64-hour workweek, 7 holidays, and 18 sick days. Work ca. 1995 was calculated on the basis of a 1,730-hour workyear, which assumes a 37.5-hour workweek, 28 holidays, and 14 sick days. Work ca. 2040 was calculated on the basis of a 1,400-hour workyear, which assumes a 30-hour workweek, 30 holidays, and 12 sick days.

Illness. Sick days ca. 1880 and ca. 1995 are based on U.S. data and are applied to the 14 discretionary hours.

Residual for leisure activities. This includes travel time to and from leisure-time activities. Seven holidays, given 14 hours per day discretionary time over 365 days, provide 0.3 hours of leisure per day ca. 1880. The corresponding figures are 1.1 hours per day ca. 1995 and 1.2 hours per day ca. 2040.

11. It is worth noting how little time leisure occupied in 1880, despite the emergence of such public entertainment as circuses, spectator and participatory sports, theaters of various types, political rallies, public lectures, entertainment of the type associated with the Fourth of July and other major holidays, and such summer programs as those held at Chautauqua, in upstate New York. Although historians have recently paid a great deal of attention to the rise of these institutions, they did not occupy much of the time of the typical worker, who had a paltry 1.8 hours per day for leisure-time activities in 1880. Most of that meager budget was spent in church on Sundays and in local saloons during other days of the week.

12. For a discussion of the method of estimating the length of the workyear ca. 1880, see app. 5A below.

13. Robinson (1988); cf. Robinson and Godbey (1997) and Moffitt (1995).

14. Bell and Freeman (1995); Dawkins and Simpson (1994); Levine (1997).

15. Hunnicutt (1988); Roediger and Foner (1989); Nyland (1989).

16. See app. 5A below; cf. Cross (1989) and Costa (1998b).

17. Lebergott (1993); Roberts ([1988] 1995); Goldin (1990); Vanek (1984).

18. Robinson (1988); cf. Robinson and Godbey (1997).

19. Shaw ([1928], 1931, 91).

20. On anxiety about declining hours of work in the late twentieth century, see, e.g., Rifkin (1995) and Aronowitz and DiFazio (1994). They, along with numerous writers in the popular press, attribute reduced work hours to a malfunctioning of technology. Workers are being displaced by machines. The anxiety is fed by politicians and commentators who looked to the revenue from increased employment as the solution to pension and health-care problems.

21. Lee (1996); Costa (1998a).

22. Discretionary time excludes time required for sleep, eating, and vital hygiene, which is taken to require an average of 10 hours per day, and total earnwork includes chores, travel to and from earnwork, and earnwork. The availability of discretionary time is taken to commence with entry into the labor force. Expected years of life after entering the labor force is 50.1 in 1880, 58.4 in 1995, and 63 in 2040. Expected years in the labor force at time of entry is 42.3 in 1880, 43 in 1995, and 33 in 2040. Twenty percent of lifetime illness is charged against earnwork in 1995. See Vaupel (1997) for a summary of research on long-term trends in the length of the lifespan; cf. Wilmoth (1998) and Kannisto et al. (1994).

23. Among households above the poverty line in 1995, about 94 percent owned cars (SA 1998, 634). On other consumer durables, see SA (1996, 723, 838, 839). The market for consumer durables is expanding rapidly in the emerging market countries. Over the next two or three decades, these markets will absorb far more consumer durables than was true of OECD nations between World War II and the present. Although firms in the United States and Europe are positioning themselves to capture a share of those markets, it remains to be seen how successful they will be. Even if they are successful, they may make far more use of labor in the developing nations than in OECD nations. These issues are discussed far more fully below (cf. U.S. Department of Labor, Bureau of Labor Statistics 1994).

24. SA (1996, 623, 889).

25. Cox and Alm (1998); app. 5C below; cf. U.S. Department of Labor (1959) and Lebergott (1993).

26. For the method of computation, see app. 5C below. For a review of proposals to redesign the national income accounts, extending them to include uncovered sectors of the economy, see Eisner (1988).

27. For the method of computation, see app. 5C below. As noted previously, households in the top 20 percent of the income distribution work about twice as many hours as those at the bottom end. Some do so, not so much because of the additional income generated, as because of the satisfaction derived from work. Others are accumulating the income that they will need to finance an early retirement and so are trading leisure now for leisure in the future (cf. the discussion on p. 218; see also Lee 1997 and app. 5E).

28. Kirkland (1951, chap. 20); Ratner, Soltow, and Sylla (1979, chap. 21).

29. See app. 5E.

30. For data on the share of earned income contributed by spouses, see app. 5E.

31. Quotation in Laabs (1996, 66); see also Marks (1995); Shellenbarger (1997). Surveys of large companies indicate that most prorate fringe benefits according to hours worked (see, e.g., "'Work/life' Programs on the Rise, Survey Finds" 1998; "The Benefits of Part-Time Work" 1996; Zinkewicz 1996; Brotherton 1997).

32. Scott (1996); Peak (1996); Zinkiewicz (1996).

33. York (1990); Dannhauser (1999); cf. Hamblen (1999).

34. See app. 5E; cf. Ausubel and Grübler (1995); Costa (1998b).

35. See app. 5B.

36. Maddison (1995); SA (1996, 448); Boskin et al. (1998). I have chosen a low average real rate of growth for a long-term forecast in order to bias the computation against my argument. Between 1870 and 1995, it is possible to compute eighty-six average annual growth rates for forty-year periods. Average annual growth rates exceeded 1.5 percent in 78 percent of these periods; they exceeded 1.7 percent in 63 percent of the periods. The average annual growth rate over all eighty-six periods was 1.82 percent (Maddison 1995).

37. For the calculations behind the figures reported in this paragraph and the next, see app. 5D.

38. Iyer (1993); Poortvliet and Laine (1995).

39. U.S. Social Security Administration (1997).

40. Birch (1974).

41. On the argument in this and the next five paragraphs, see apps. 5C and

5D and the sources cited there (cf. Wildansky 1998; Blöndal and Scarpetta 1998; Eisner 1998; Slusher 1998; Burtless and Bosworth 1999; *Economist* (1998); McGrattan and Rogerson 1998).

42.　About a quarter of the loss is due to a four-year reduction in the length of the stream of payments as a result of lower life expectancy at age seventy than at age sixty-five. The balance of the loss is due to the diminished present value of the stream of payments delayed by five years because of an earlier age of retirement. A discount of 6 percent was employed in the calculation.

43.　A transparent system is one in which it is evident that individuals are basically saving for their own retirement and the rates of return and risks to savings under different systems of intermediation are also evident.

44.　Shigehara (1998); Hicks (1998); Vanston (1998); Blöndal and Scarpetta (1998); Blommestein (1998); cf. Feldstein and Samwick (1998); Eisner (1998); Kotlikoff, Smetters, and Walliser (1998); Diamond (1996).

45.　Diamond (1996); Murphy and Welch (1998).

46.　Prevalence rates of Union army veterans are based on examinations by physicians. Those for the 1980s are based on self-reporting. Comparison of the National Health Interview Survey (NHIS) rates with those obtained from physicians' examinations in the National Health and Nutrition Examination Survey II (NHANES II) indicates that the use of self-reported health conditions does not introduce a significant bias into the comparison. For a more detailed discussion of possible biases and their magnitudes, and for sources for this table, see Fogel, Costa, and Kim (1993).

47.　Manton, Corder, and Stallard (1993). On the renewed rise in the demand for health care, see *Economist* (1999).

48.　Parrington (1930, 81).

49.　Bailyn et al. (1992, 2: pt. 6); Fox (1993); Fox and Lears (1983); Lears (1983); cf. Stearns (1997) and Burnham (1993).

50.　Laslett (1991); Lenk (1994).

51.　Weinstein (1993); Shusterman (1994); Marty (1991); cf. Elster (1986) and Chan and Miller (1991).

52.　Shusterman (1994, 396–97).

53.　Wilson (1987, [1996] 1997); see also Rowe and Kahn (1997, 1998); Miller (1999).

54.　Wilson ([1996] 1997, 135).

55.　Stern (1996). The article reporting the survey indicated that the comparison was controlled for "percent minority" but not whether it was controlled for income and immaterial resources.

56. Some leaders of religious colleges may feel that dependence on government subsidies inevitably involves state interference and curbs their academic freedom. Of course, all peer review involves some interference with individual creativity. Those who find such limitations too constraining are not obliged to accept grants from either the state or private foundations, or they may accept peer review of some activities but not others.

57. The median income (money income plus Medicare) of elderly households is about 77 percent of the median income of nonelderly households, which is roughly in proportion to need (computed from data in SA [1997, 115, 470, 471] and Fogel [1993]). The proportion of elderly families below the poverty line is slightly less than the proportion of the nonelderly (SA 1997, 476).

58. SA (1997, 476).

59. SA (1967, 339).

60. HS (1975, 379).

61. Samuels (1997).

62. Fletcher and Hansson (1991); Yamashita et al. (1993); Pahkala, Kivelea, and Laippala (1992); cf. Rowe and Khan (1998).

63. Mutchler et al. (1997); Henretta (1997).

64. Rowe and Kahn (1997, 1998).

65. SA (1997, 160).

66. Laslett (1991, 171–72).

67. Boling (1998).

68. Rowe and Kahn (1997, 1998); Glass et al. (1995); Okwumabua et al. (1997); Kington and Smith (1997); cf. Wachter and Finch (1997); Johnson (1999).

69. Rowe and Kahn (1997).

70. SA (1997, 391); Hodgkinson, Weitzman, and Gallup Organization (1996); cf. Hayghe (1991).

71. SA (1997, 168). Annual income was divided by 1,750 hours to obtain an hourly rate.

72. Winter (1997); Rabey (1996); Tapia (1996); Freeman (1996).

73. Glass et al. (1995); Rowe and Kahn (1997); Bernstein (1999).

74. McFadden (1995, 1996); Levin (1994).

75. Moberg (1990); McFadden (1995); cf. Spiegler (1996); Markwood (1994); Hoge et al. (1996).

76. Freudenheim (1998); cf. Lublin (1998).

77. SA (1997, 416, 424); app. 5C below.

78. SA (1997, 153, 448).

79. Markwood (1994).

80. In the balance of this section, I use the term *Gini ratio* to cover measures closely correlated with it, such as the difference in the logarithms of the income in the highest decile and that in the lowest decile of the income distribution, the log variance, and the share of income going to the top 10 percent of the income distribution.

81. SA (1997, 470).

82. The calculations reported in the text are based on the assumption that both Harry and John started work at age twenty and worked 1,800 hours per year for $20.00 per hour, earning an annual money income of $36,000 per year, of which each saved $1,099.34 per year in a mutual fund that returned 6 percent interest per year. Such saving for forty-five years permits John to retire at age sixty-five with an annuity of $21,600 per year, or 60 percent of his preretirement income, for the rest of his life (eighteen years). Until his forty-fifth birthday, Harry pursued the same pattern but decided to retire at age fifty-five. Given that he has the same temporal income pattern in later life as John ($21,600 per year from age sixty-five until death), Harry has had to save $38,205 per year between his forty-fifth and fifty-fifth birthdays. He does so by working an extra 1,400 hours per year, with 1,021 hours paid at time and a half. To do so, he gives up 3.8 hours per day of leisure, which he will recoup after retiring. His extra annual savings ($37,106) between age forty-five and age fifty-five are invested in a mutual fund earning 6 percent per year. Harry's consumption during ages forty-five to sixty-five exceeds John's by about $1,100 per year. John's cumulative lifetime wages are $1,620,000, Harry's $1,642,000.

83. See app. 5E.

84. Costa (1998b).

85. These percentages are based on the Public Use Micro-Sample of the 1980 and 1990 censuses, which is available at http://www.ciesin.org/datasets/pums/pums-home.html.

86. On the chronically poor, see Shea (1995, table 3), who defines the chronically poor as those persistently below the poverty line for twenty-four consecutive months during 1992 and 1993 (cf. app. 5E). In my computation, the chronically

poor were distributed between the two bottom deciles in proportion to the number of households whose expenditures did not exceed their income.

87. Wilson ([1996] 1997).

88. See chap. 4 above; cf. Soltow (1989, 1992).

89. Compare Freeman (1976).

90. SA (1991, 167–69).

91. SA (1991, 166, 434); AMA (1992).

92. Computed from data in SOI (1981–82, 8) and SOI (1990, 15). The consumer price index was used to convert 1980 dollars to 1988 dollars (SA 1991, 473). The proportion of returns between $50,000 and $71,800 was estimated on the assumption that income in this range was lognormally distributed. The implied values of μ and σ were estimated from $(X_i - \mu)/\sigma = Z_i$, using the natural logs of 50,000 and 75,000 for the X_i and estimating Z_i at those values from the distribution of returns reported in SOI (1990).

93. See n. 92 above.

94. See n. 72, chap. 4 above.

95. See chaps. 2–3 above; cf. Fishlow (1966a).

96. For a calculation of the proportion of human capital in 1989, see chap. 2, n. 72 above.

97. Computed from the UN International Comparison Program (ICP) estimates of GDP and the population estimates for 1990 in World Bank (1992, 276–77, 218–19). Using GDP estimates based on exchange rates yields a Gini ratio of 0.72. For a further discussion of the Gini ratio, see chap. 4.

98. The observations in this paragraph are based on Bairoch (1977, compare 1981) and Maddison (1995). Bairoch put European per capita income at about $180 (in 1960 dollars) in 1750 and estimated that Chinese per capita income in that year was about $225. Chinese per capita income in 1995 (in 1960 dollars) was about $926.

99. Compare Landes (1998).

100. The computations are based on Bairoch (1997, compare 1981) and Maddison (1995); cf. Landes (1998).

101. Fogel and Floud (1999); Abramovitz (1986); Baumol (1986); World Bank (1992). On malnutrition in the Third World, see United Nations (1993); compare FAO (1996); FAO and WHO (1992); Fogel (1996, 1997b).

102. North (1961); Davis and Huttenback (1986); Kravis (1970).

103. World Bank (1995, 162–63); SA (1997, 838).

104. Bradley (1994a, 1994b); Campbell and Bradley (1994); Massaro and Wong (1995).

105. Wolff (1993); SA (1998, 190, 202).

106. East Asian Executive Reports (1993); app. 5E.

107. Scalberg (1993); Zakaria (1994).

108. This and the next paragraph are drawn from Zakaria (1994), *Economist* (1994a), Funabashi (1993), Blackburn (1994), and Mahbubani (1995); cf. *Economist* (1994b, 1994c).

109. Yew quoted in Zakaria (1994, 114).

110. Zakaria (1994); Gellert (1995); Bradley (1994a, 1994b); Campbell and Bradley (1994); Massaro and Wong (1995).

111. *Economist* (1995b).

112. Ching (1994); Potier (1995); El-Erian and Kumar (1995).

113. Zakaria (1994).

114. Zakaria (1994); Abdoolcarim (1994).

115. World Bank (1993).

116. Liew (1995); Zhu (1995); Jacob (1995a, 1995b); Kraar (1994); Curran (1994); Loeb (1995); Hiebert (1995); Karp (1994).

117. Montinola, Qian, and Weingast (1995).

118. Bernstein and Munro (1997a).

119. On this and the next paragraph, see Huntington (1993, 1996a, 1996b).

120. The discussion in this and the next two paragraphs draws on McNeill (1997), Moody (1996), Yamazaki (1996), Halloran (1996), Tu (1996), Raines (1996), and Nye (1996).

121. Herberg (1960).

122. Some adversaries find common cause in the critique of consumerism (the fetishism of commodities, in the language of the Marxism), which has been such an overpowering feature of American culture during the twentieth century.

123. The dimensions of that debate are described in *Economist* (1996) and McNeill (1997).

AFTERWORD

1. Ausubel (1996); Lin (1998).

2. Brzezinski (1996, 31).

APPENDIX 5A

1.   Lebergott's results are implied in HS (1975, 164, ser. 723–24).

APPENDIX 5E

1.   The shift in dates in table 5E.4 from those listed in table 5E.2 is due to the different starting dates for the Consumer Expenditure Survey and the Current Population Survey.

2.   The regression result can be obtained from the author on request.

REFERENCES

Abbott, E., ed. 1926. *Historical aspects of the immigration problem: Selected documents*. Chicago: University of Chicago Press.

Abdoolcarim, Z. 1994. How to make welfare work. *Asian Business* 330, no. 8: 36–39.

Abel, W. 1980. *Agricultural fluctuations in Europe from the thirteenth to the twentieth centuries*. New York. St. Martin's.

Abortion foes differ on tactics. 1996. *The Christian Century*, 22 May, 566–67.

Abramovitz, A. I., and K. L. Saunders. 1998. Ideological realignment in the U.S. electorate. *Journal of Politics* 60:634–52.

Abramovitz, M. 1986. Catching up, forging ahead, and falling behind. *Journal of Economic History* 46:385–406.

Ackernecht, E. H. 1945. *Malaria in the upper Mississippi Valley, 1760–1900*. Baltimore: Johns Hopkins University Press.

———. [1952] 1965. Diseases in the Middle West. In *Essays in the history of medicine in honor of David J. Davis, M.D., Ph.D.: The first ten lectures of the Davis Memorial Lecture Series, University of Illinois College of Medicine*. Chicago: University of Illinois Press.

Ahlstrom, S. E. 1972. *A religious history of the American people*. New Haven, Conn.: Yale University Press.

Ajemian, R. 1985. Jerry Falwell spreads the word: The fundamentalist leader wages political war on immorality. *Time*, 2 September, 58–61.

Albanese, C. L. 1976. *Sons of the fathers: The civil religion of the American Revolution*. Philadelphia: Temple University Press.

————. 1981. *America: Religion and religions.* Belmont, Calif.: Wadsworth.

————. 1990. *Nature religion in America from the Algonkian Indians to the New Age.* Chicago: University of Chicago Press.

Alexander, T. B. 1967. *Sectional stress and party strength: A study of roll-call voting patterns in the United States House of Representatives, 1836–1860.* Nashville: Vanderbilt University Press.

Alexis, M. 1998. Assessing 50 years of African American economic status, 1940–1990. *American Economic Review* 88, no. 2:368–75.

Allen, R. C. 1988. The growth of labor productivity. *Explorations in Economic History* 25:117–46.

————. 1992. *Enclosure and the yeoman: The agricultural development of the South Midlands, 1450–1850.* Oxford: Oxford University Press.

————. 1994. Agriculture during the Industrial Revolution. In *The economic history of Britain since 1700*, ed. R. Floud and D. McCloskey. Cambridge: Cambridge University Press.

Alter, J. 1997. Powell's new war. *Newsweek*, 28 April, 28–34.

American Medical Association (AMA). 1992. *Socioeconomic characteristics of medical practice, 1989.* Chicago.

————. 1999. *Physician socioeconomic statistics, 1999 edition.* Chicago.

Angle, P. M., ed. 1958. *Created equal? The complete Lincoln-Douglas debates of 1858.* Chicago: University of Chicago Press.

Aronowitz, S., and W. DiFazio. 1994. *The jobless future: Sci-tech and the dogma of work.* Minneapolis: University of Minnesota Press.

Ashby, Hugh T. 1915. *Infant mortality.* Cambridge: Cambridge University Press.

Atack, J., and F. Bateman. 1987. *To their own soil: Agriculture in the antebellum North.* Ames: Iowa State University.

————. 1992. How long was the workday in 1880? *Journal of Economic History* 52:129–60.

Atkinson, A. B., L. Rainwater, and T. Smedling. 1994. *Income distribution in OECD countries: Evidence from the Luxembourg Income Study.* Luxembourg: Luxembourg Income Study.

Ausubel, J. H. 1996. Can technology spare the earth? *American Scientist* 84 (March–April): 166–78.

Ausubel, J. H., and A. Grübler. 1995. Working less and living longer: Long-term trends in working time and time budgets. *Technological Forecasting and Social Change* 50:113–31.

Bailyn, B. 1967. *The ideological origins of the American Revolution.* Cambridge, Mass.: Harvard University Press.

————. 1986a. *The peopling of British North America: An introduction.* New York: Knopf.

————. 1986b. *Voyagers to the West: A passage in the peopling of America on the eve of the Revolution.* New York: Knopf.

Bailyn, B., et al. 1992. *The great republic: A history of the American people.* 4th ed. Lexington, Mass.: D.C. Heath.

Bain, J. S. 1951. Industrial concentration and anti-trust policy. In *The growth of the American economy,* ed. H. F. Williamson. Englewood Cliffs, N.J.: Prentice-Hall.

Bairoch, P. 1973. Agriculture and the Industrial Revolution. In *The Fontana economic history of Europe,* ed. C. M. Cipolla. London: Collins/Fontana.

————. 1977. Historical evolution of inequality of levels of income among developed and underdeveloped countries, 1800–1975. Report no. 7778-3. Harvard University, Workshop in Economic History, Economics 4045, 14 October.

————. 1981. The main trends in national economic disparities since the Industrial Revolution. In *Disparities in economic development since the Industrial Revolution,* ed. P. Bairoch and M. Léboyer. New York: St. Martin's.

————. 1988. *Cities and economic development: From the dawn of history to the present.* Chicago: University of Chicago Press.

Balmer, R. 1993. *Mine eyes have seen the glory: A journey into evangelical subculture.* New York: Oxford University Press.

Barber, W. J., ed. 1988. *Breaking the academic mould: Economists and American higher learning in the nineteenth century.* Middletown, Conn.: Wesleyan University Press.

Barker, D. J. P., ed. 1992. *Fetal and infant origins of adult disease: Papers.* London: British Medical Journal.

————. 1994. *Mothers, babies, and disease in later life.* London: BMJ Publishing Group.

————. 1998. *Mothers, babies, and disease in later life.* 2d ed. Edinburgh: Churchhill Livingstone.

Barkume, M. 1996–97. The job market for Ph.D.'s: Two views. *Occupational Outlook Quarterly* 40, no. 4 (winter): 2–15.

Barnes, D. G. 1930. *A history of the English corn laws from 1660 to 1846.* London: George Routledge & Sons.

Barnes, G. H. [1933] 1964. *The anti-slavery impulse, 1830–1844.* New York: Harcourt, Brace, & World.

Barrett, D. B. 1988. Global statistics. In *Dictionary of Pentecostal and charismatic movements,* ed. S. M. Burgess and G. B. McGee. Grand Rapids, Mich.: Zondervan.

Baumol, W. J. 1986. Productivity growth, convergence, and welfare: What the long-run data show. *American Economic Review* 76:1072–85.

Beard, C. A., and M. R. Beard. 1927. *The rise of American civilization.* New York: Macmillan.

Becker, G. S. 1993. *Human capital: A theoretical and empirical analysis, with special reference to education.* 3d ed. Chicago: University of Chicago Press.

Beecher, L. 1835. *A plea for the West.* Cincinnati: Truman & Smith.

Bell, A., H. Wade, and S. C. Goss. 1992. Life tables for the United States social security area: 1900–2080. Actuarial Studies, no. 107. Washington, D.C.: U.S. Department of Health and Human Services, August.

Bell, D. 1973. *The coming of post-industrial society: A venture in social forecasting.* New York: Basic.

———. 1999. *The coming of post-industrial society.* Rev. ed. New York: Basic.

Bell, L., and R. Freeman. 1995. Why do Americans and Germans work different hours? Working Paper no. 4808. Cambridge, Mass.: National Bureau of Economic Research.

The benefits of part-time work. 1996. *HR Focus* 73, no. 9:7–14.

Bennett, M. K., and R. H. Pierce. 1961. Change in the American national diet, 1879–1959. *Food Research Institute Studies* 2:95–119.

Benson, L. 1955. *Merchants, farmers, and railroads: Railroads regulation and New York politics, 1850–1887.* Cambridge, Mass.: Harvard University Press.

———. 1961. *The concept of Jacksonian democracy: New York as a test case.* Princeton, N.J.: Princeton University Press.

Bernstein, N. 1999. Old pattern cited in missed signs of child abuse. *New York Times,* 22 July, A1, A19.

Bernstein, R., and R. H. Munro. 1997a. China I: The coming conflict with America. *Foreign Affairs* 76, no. 2:18–32.

———. 1997b. Clash of the titans. *Transpacifica* 49 (May): 46–48.

Bidwell, P. W., and J. I. Falconer. 1941. *History of agriculture in the Northern United States, 1620–1860.* New York: Peter Smith.

Billewicz, W. Z., and I. A. McGregor. 1982. A birth to maturity longitudinal study of heights in two West African (Gambian) villages, 1951–1975. *Annals of Human Biology* 9:309–20.

Billington, R. A. 1964. *The Protestant crusade, 1800–1860: A study of the origins of American nativism.* Chicago: Quadrangle.

Birch, R. C. 1974. *The shaping of the welfare state.* Seminar Studies in History. [London:] Longman.

Bishop, C. W. 1936. Origin and early diffusion of the traction plow. *Antiquities* 10:261–81.

Blackburn, K. 1994. Does the West need to learn "Asian values"? *IPA Review* 47, no. 2:35–36.

Blanchflower, D. G., and R. B. Freeman. 1990. Going different ways: Unionism in the U.S. and other advanced OECD countries. Discussion paper. London School of Economics, Centre for Economics.

Blau, F. D. 1998. Trends in the well-being of American women, 1970–1995. *Journal of Economic Literature* 36:112–65.

Blommestein, H. J. 1998. Pension funds and financial markets. *OECD Observer*, no. 212 (June/July): 24–28.

Blöndal, S., and S. Scarpetta. 1998. Retire early, stay at work? *OECD Observer*, no. 212 (June/July): 15–19.

Bodo, J. R. 1954. *The Protestant clergy and public issues, 1812–1848.* Philadelphia: Porcupine.

Bogue, A. G. 1963. *From prairie to farm belt: Farming on the Illinois and Iowa prairie in the nineteenth century.* Chicago: University of Chicago Press.

———. 1982. *The earnest men: Republicans of the Civil War Senate.* Ithaca, N.Y.: Cornell University Press.

———, ed. 1983a. *Clio and the bitch goddess: Quantification in American political history.* Beverly Hills, Calif.: Sage.

———. 1983b. United States. The "new" political history. In *Clio and the bitch goddess: Quantification in American political history,* ed. A. G. Bogue. Beverly Hills, Calif.: Sage.

———. 1989. *The congressmen's Civil War.* Cambridge: Cambridge University Press.

Boling, R. 1998. America's dirty little secret. *Modern Maturity* 41, no. 2:86–89.

Bonora, E., J. Willeit, S. Kiechl, F. Oberhollenzer, G. Egger, R. Bonadonna, and M. Muggeo. 1998. U-shaped and J-shaped relationships between serum insulin and coronary heart disease in the general population. *Diabetes Care* 21: 221–30.

Bordin, R. B. A. 1981. *Woman and temperance: The quest for power and liberty, 1873–1900.* Philadelphia: Temple University Press.

Boskin, M. J., et al. 1998. Consumer prices, the consumer price index, and the cost of living. *Journal of Economic Perspectives* 12:3–26.

Bound, J., and R. B. Freeman. 1992. What went wrong: The erosion of relative earnings and employment among young black men in the 1980s. *Quarterly Journal of Economics* 7:201–32.

Bound, J., and G. Johnson. 1992. Changes in the structure of wages in the 1980s: An evaluation of alternative explanations. *American Medical Review* 82: 371–92.

Bowen, W. G., and N. Rudenstine. 1991. *In pursuit of the Ph.D.* Princeton, N.J.: Princeton University Press.

Bowley, A. L., and A. R. Burnett-Hurst. 1915. *Livelihood and poverty.* London: Ratan Tan Foundation.

Bowman, M. J. 1962. The land-grant colleges and universities in human resource development. *Journal of Economic History* 22:523–46.

Boyd, M. F. 1941. An historical sketch of the prevalence of malaria in North America. *American Journal of Tropical Medicine* 21:223–44.

Boyer, P. S. 1978. *Urban masses and moral order in America, 1820–1920.* Cambridge, Mass.: Harvard University Press.

Bradley, H. L. 1994a. Hong Kong's new rules on private retirement plans and planned retirement pension system. *Social Security Bulletin* 57, no. 2:82.

———. 1994b. New pension improvements and supplements in Singapore. *Social Security Bulletin* 57, no. 2:85–86.

Brady, D. W. 1988. *Critical elections and congressional policy making.* Stanford, Calif.: Stanford University Press.

Braudel, F. 1979. *The wheels of commerce: Civilization and capitalism, 15th–18th century.* Vol. 2. New York: Harper & Row.

Bremner, R. H. 1956. *From the depths: The discovery of poverty in the United States.* New York: New York University Press.

———. 1970. *Children and youth in America: A documentary history.* 3 vols. in 5. Cambridge, Mass.: Harvard University Press.

Brock, W. R. 1975. *The United States, 1789–1890.* Ithaca, N.Y.: Cornell University Press.

Bronowski, J. 1973. *The ascent of man.* Boston: Little, Brown.

Brooks, W. T. 1989. The global warming panic: A classic case of overreaction. *Forbes,* 25 December, 97–102.

Brotherton, P. 1997. For many part-timers, less is more. *HR Magazine* 42, no. 6:102–6.

Brown, W. J., A. J. Dobson, and G. Mishra. 1998. What is a healthy weight for middle-aged women? *International Journal of Obesity and Related Metabolic Disorders* 22:520–28.

Brownlee, W. E. 1979. *Dynamics of ascent: A history of the American economy.* New York: Knopf.

Brunell, T. L., and B. Grofman. 1998. Explaining divided U.S. Senate delegations, 1788–1996: A realignment approach. *American Political Science Review* 92, no. 2:391–400.

Bryan, W. J. 1925. *The memoirs of William Jennings Bryan by himself and his wife, Mary Baird Bryan.* Philadelphia: John C. Winston.

Brzezinski, Z. 1996. New dimensions: Foreign policy and human rights. *Current,* no. 385 (1 September): 29–33.

Burdenski, H. M. and D. H. Dunson. 1999. Acquiring economic justice for all: An ongoing struggle. *Journal of Business Ethics* 20, no. 2:93–99.

Burner, D., E. D. Genovese, and F. McDonald. 1980. *The American people.* St. James, N.Y.: Revisionary.

Burnham, J. 1993. *Bad habits: Drinking, smoking, taking drugs, gambling, sexual misbehavior, and swearing in American history.* New York: New York University Press.

Burnham, W. D. 1955. *Presidential ballots, 1836–1892.* Baltimore: Johns Hopkins University Press.

———. 1967. Party systems and the political process. In *The American party system: Stages of political development,* ed. W. D. Burnham and W. N. Chambers. New York: Oxford University Press.

———. 1970. *Critical elections and mainsprings of American politics.* New York: Oxford University Press.

———. 1981. The 1980 earthquake: Realignment, reactions, or what? In *The hidden election: Politics and economics in the 1980 presidential campaign,* ed. T. Ferguson and J. Roger. New York: Pantheon.

———. 1986a. Periodization schemes and "party systems": The "system of 1896" as a case in point. *Social Science History* 10:254–314.

———. 1986b. Those high nineteenth-century American voting turnouts. Fact or fiction? *Journal of Interdisciplinary History* 16:574–644.

———. 1991. Critical realignment: Dead or alive? In *The end of realignment? Interpreting American electoral eras,* ed. B. E. Shafer. Madison: University of Wisconsin Press.

Burritt, B. B. 1912. *Professional distribution of college and university graduates.* Washington, D.C.: U.S. Government Printing Office.

Burtless, G. 1990. Earnings inequality over the business and demographic cycles. In *A future of lousy jobs? The changing structure of U.S. wages,* ed. G. Burtless. Washington, D.C.: Brookings.

———. 1993. The contribution of employment and hours changes to family income inequality. *American Economic Review Papers and Proceedings* 83:131–35.

Burtless, G., and B. Bosworth. 1999. Privatizing social security: The troubling trade-offs. *Washington Quarterly,* 22:205–15.

Bushman, R. 1967. *From Puritan into Yankee: Character and the social order in Connecticut, 1690–1765.* Cambridge, Mass.: Harvard University Press.

Butler, J. 1982. Enthusiasm denied and decried: The Great Awakening as interpretive fiction. *Journal of American History* 69:305–25.

———. 1990. *Awash in a sea of faith: Christianizing the American people.* Cambridge, Mass.: Harvard University Press.

Calhoun, A. 1960. *A social history of the American family from colonial times to the present.* New York: Barnes & Noble.

Campbell, G. R., and H. Bradley. 1994. Hong Kong proposes a first-time pensions scheme. *Social Security Bulletin* 57, no. 4:75–76.

Campbell, A., P. E. Converse, W. E. Miller, and D. E. Stokes. 1960. *The American voter.* Chicago: University of Chicago Press.

———. *Elections and the political order.* New York: Wiley.

Cancian, M., S. Danziger, and P. Gottschalk. 1993. Working wives and family income inequality among married couples. In *Uneven tides,* ed. S. Danziger and P. Gottschalk. New York: Russell Sage.

Carpenter, J. A. 1997. *Revive us again: The reawakening of American fundamentalism.* New York: Oxford University Press.

Case, R. A. M., J. L. Harley, and J. T. Pearson. 1962. *Chester Beatty Research Institute abridged serial life tables, England and Wales, 1841–1960, Part 1.* London: Chester Beatty Research Institute.

Cauthen, K. 1962. *The impact of American religious liberalism.* New York: Harper & Row.

Chamla, M. Cl. 1983. L'évolution récent de la stature en Europe occidentale (période 1960–1980). *Bulletin et Memoire de la Société d'Anthropologie de Paris* 13, no. 10:195–224.

Chan, J., and D. Miller. 1991. Elster on self-realization in politics: A critical note. *Ethics* 102:96–102.

Chandler, A. D., Jr. 1977. *The visible hand: The managerial revolution in American business.* Cambridge, Mass.: Harvard University Press.

———. 1990. *Scale and scope: The dynamics of industrial capitalism.* Cambridge: Harvard University Press.

Chandler, T., and G. Fox. 1974. *Three thousand years of urban growth.* New York: Academic.

Chandra, R. K. 1975. Antibody formation in first and second generation offspring of nutritionally deprived rats. *Science* 190:289–90.

Channing, W. E. 1848. *The works of William E. Channing, D.D.* 8th ed. 6 vols. Boston: James Munroe.

Chartres, J. A. 1985. The marketing of agricultural produce. In *The agrarian history of England and Wales,* ed. J. Thirsk. Cambridge: Cambridge University Press.

Chavez, A., C. Martinez, and B. Soberanes. 1995. The effect of malnutrition on human development: A 24-year study of well-nourished children living in a poor Mexican village. In *Community-based longitudinal studies of the impact of early malnutrition on child health and development: Classical examples from Guatemala, Haiti, and Mexico,* ed. N. S. Scrimshaw. Boston: International Nutritional Foundation for Developing Countries.

Cherny, R. W. 1985. *A righteous cause: The life of William Jennings Bryan.* Boston: Little, Brown.

Ching, F. 1994. Mahathir grasps a nettle. *Far Eastern Economic Review* 157, no. 13:32.

Chudacoff, H. P. 1975. *The evolution of American urban society.* Englewood Cliffs, N.J.: Prentice-Hall.

Chyou, P. H., C. M. Burchfiel, K. Yano, D. S. Sharp, B. L. Rodriguez, J. D. Curb, and A. M. Nomura. 1997. Obesity, alcohol consumption, smoking, and mortality. *Annals of Epidemiology* 7:311–17.

Cipolla, C. M. 1974. *The economic history of world population.* Harmondsworth: Penguin.

———. 1980. *Before the Industrial Revolution: European society and economy, 1000–1700.* New York: Norton.

Clark, J. G. 1971. *World prehistory: An outline.* Cambridge: Cambridge University Press.

Clubb, J. M., W. H. Flanigan, and N. H. Zingale. 1980. *Partisan realignment: Voters, parties, and government in American history.* Beverly Hills, Calif.: Sage.

Coale, A. J., and P. Demeny. 1966. *Regional model life tables and stable populations.* Princeton, N.J.: Princeton University Press.

Coats, A. W. 1960. The first two decades of the American Economic Association. *American Economic Review* 50:555–75.

———. 1964. The American Economic Association, 1904–29. *American Economic Review* 54:261–85.

Cochran, T. C., and W. Andrews, eds. 1962. *Concise dictionary of American history.* New York: Scribner.

Coll, B. D. 1972. Public assistance in the United States. In *Comparative development in social welfare,* ed. E. W. Martin. London: Allen & Unwin.

Colquhoun, P. 1814. *Treatise on the wealth, power, and resources of the British Empire.* London: Joseph Mawmay.

Commons, J. R., U. B. Phillips, E. A. Gilmore, H. L. Simner, and J. B. Andrew, eds. 1910. *History of labour in the United States.* 10 vols. Vol. 7. New York: Macmillan.

Commons, J. R., D. J. Saposs, H. J. Sumner, E. B. Mittlemen, H. E. Hoagland, J. B. Andrews, and S. Perlman, eds. 1918. *History of labour in the United States.* 2 vols. Vol. 1. New York: Macmillan.

Coolidge, R. H. 1856. *Statistical report on sickness and mortality in the Army of the United States.* Washington, D.C.: A. O. P. Nicholson.

Cooper, G., and P. Scherer. 1998. Can we afford to grow old? *OECD Observer,* no. 212 (June/July): 20–22.

Cooper, W. J., Jr. 1978. *The South and the politics of slavery, 1828–1856*. Baton Rouge: Louisiana State University Press.

Costa, D. L. 1993a. Health, income, and retirement: Evidence from nineteenth century America. Ph.D. diss., University of Chicago.

———. 1993b. Height, wealth, and disease among the native-born in the rural, antebellum North. *Social Science History* 17:355–83.

———. 1993c. Height, weight, wartime stress, and older age mortality: Evidence from the Union army records. *Explorations in Economic History* 30:424–49.

———. 1998a. *The evolution of retirement: An American economic history, 1880–1990*. Chicago: University of Chicago Press.

———. 1998b. The unequal work day: A long-term view. Working Paper no. 6419. Cambridge, Mass.: National Bureau of Economic Research.

Costa, D. L., and R. H. Steckel. 1997. Long-term trends in health, welfare, and economic growth in the United States. In *Health and welfare during industrialization,* ed. R. H. Steckel and R. Floud. Chicago: University of Chicago Press.

Courtwright, D. 1982. *Dark paradise: Opiate addiction in America before 1940*. Cambridge, Mass.: Harvard University Press.

Cox, H. G. 1995. *Fire from heaven: The rise of Pentecostal spirituality and the reshaping of religion in the twenty-first century*. Reading, Mass.: Addison-Wesley.

Cox, W. M., and R. Alm. 1998. Time well spent: The declining real cost of living in the United States. In *Annual report, 1997*. Dallas: Dallas Federal Reserve Bank.

Crafts, N. F. R. 1984. Patterns of development in nineteenth-century Europe. *Oxford Economic Papers* 36:438–58.

———. 1985. *British economic growth during the Industrial Revolution*. Oxford: Clarendon.

———. 1994. The Industrial Revolution. In *The economic history of Britain since 1700,* ed. R. Floud and D. McCloskey. Cambridge: Cambridge University Press.

———. 1997. Economic growth in East Asia and Western Europe since 1950: Implications for living standards. *National Institute Economic Review,* no. 162 (October): 75–84.

Cranmer, H. J. 1960. Canal investment, 1815–1860. In *Trends in the American economy in the nineteenth century* (Studies in Income and Wealth, vol. 24). Princeton, N.J.: Princeton University Press.

Cromartie, M. 1992. Fixing the world: From nonplayers to radicals to New Right conservatives. *Christianity Today,* 27 April, 23–25.

Cross, F. L., and E. P. Livingstone. 1983. *The Oxford dictionary of the Christian church*. Oxford: Oxford University Press.

Cross, Gary. 1989. *A quest for time: The reduction of work in Britain and France, 1840–1940*. Berkeley and Los Angeles: University of California Press.

Cross, W. R. [1950] 1982. *The burned-over district: The social and intellectual history of enthusiastic religion in western New York*. Ithaca, N.Y.: Cornell University Press.

Crunden, R. M. 1982. *Ministers of reform: The Progressives' achievement in American civilization, 1889–1920*. New York: Basic.

Curran, J. J. 1994. China's investment boom. *Fortune*, 7 March, 116–24.

Curwen, E. C. 1953. *Plough and pasture, part I: The early history of farming*. New York: Henry Schuman.

Czeizel, A. E., and I. Dudás. 1992. Prevention of the first occurrence of neural-tube defects by periconceptional vitamin supplementation. *New England Journal of Medicine* 327:1832–35.

Dannhauser, C. L. 1999. Who's in the home office? *American Demographics* 21, no. 6:50–56.

Dasgupta, P. 1993. *An inquiry into well-being and destitution*. Oxford: Clarendon.

David, P. A., and P. Solar. 1977. A bicentenary contribution to the history of the cost of living in America. *Research in Economic History* 2:1–80.

Davis, D. B. 1966. *The problem of slavery in Western culture*. Ithaca, N.Y.: Cornell University Press.

———. 1975. *The problem of slavery in the Age of Revolution*. New York: Oxford University Press.

———. 1984. *Slavery and human progress*. New York: Oxford University Press.

Davis, L. E., and R. A. Huttenback. 1986. *Mammon and the pursuit of empire: The economics of British imperialism*. Cambridge: Cambridge University Press.

Dawkins, P., and M. Simpson. 1994. Work, leisure, and the competitiveness of Australian industry. *International Journal of Manpower* 15, nos. 9–10: 38–76.

Del Mar, D. P. 1996. *What trouble I have seen: A history of violence against wives*. Cambridge, Mass.: Harvard University Press.

Denault, D. J. 1993. An economic analysis of steam boiler explosions in the nineteenth-century United States. Ph.D. diss., University of Connecticut.

Derry, T. K., and T I. William. 1960. *A short history of technology*. London: Oxford University Press.

de Vries, J. 1984. *European urbanization, 1500–1800*. London: Methuen.

Diamond, P. A. 1996. Proposals to restructure social security. *Journal of Economic Perspectives* 10, no. 3:67–88.

Dickson, D. 1989. France weighs benefits, risks of nuclear gamble. *Science* 233: 930–32.

Donohue, J. J., III, and J. Heckman. 1991. Continuous versus episodic change:

The impact of civil rights policy on the economic status of blacks. *Journal of Economic Literature* 29:1603–43.

Dorfman, J. 1946. *The economic mind in American civilization*. Vol. 2, *1790–1865*. New York: Viking.

———. 1959. *The economic mind in American civilization*. Vol. 3, *1865–1918*. New York: Viking.

Douglas, P. H. 1930. *Real wages in the United States, 1890–1926*. Boston: Houghton Mifflin.

Drake, D. 1850. *A systematic treatise, historical, etiological, and practical, on the principal diseases of the interior valley of North America as they appear in the Caucasian, African, Indian, and Esquimaux varieties of its population*. Cincinnati: W. B. Smith.

———. [1850] 1854. *A systematic treatise, historical, etiological, and practical, on the principal diseases of the interior valley of North America as they appear in the Caucasian, African, Indian, and Esquimaux varieties of its population*. Philadelphia: Lippincott, Grambo.

Drukker, J. W., and V. Tassenaar. 1997. Paradoxes of modernization and material well-being in the Netherlands during the nineteenth century. In *Health and welfare during industrialization*, ed. R. H. Steckel and R. Floud. Chicago: University of Chicago Press.

Dulles, F. R. 1949. *Labor in America: A history*. New York: Thomas Y. Crowell.

Duncan, J. W., and W. C. Shelton. 1978. *Revolution in United States government statistics, issued by the U.S. Department of Commerce*. Washington, D.C.: U.S. Government Printing Office.

East Asian Executive Reports. 1993. Thailand: Coping with economic success— Shortage of workers threatens economic growth. *East Asian Executive Reports* 15, no. 2:16.

Easterlin, R. A. 1961. Regional income trends, 1840–1950. In *American economic history*, ed. S. Harris. New York: McGraw-Hill.

———. 1972. The American population. In *American economic growth: An economist's history of the United States*, by L. E. Davis, R. A. Easterlin, W. N. Parker, D. S. Brady, A. Fishlow, R. E. Gallman, S. Lebergott, R. E. Lipsey, D.C. North, N. Rosenberg, E. Smolensky, and P. Temin. New York: Harper & Row.

———. 1975. Farm production and income in old and new areas at mid-century. In *Essays in nineteenth-century economic history: The old Northwest*, ed. D.C. Kingaman and R. K. Vedder. Athens: Ohio University Press.

———. 1996. *Growth triumphant: The twenty-first century in historical perspective*. Ann Arbor: University of Michigan Press.

Economic report of the president. 1992. Washington, D.C.: U.S. Government Printing Office.

REFERENCES

Economist. 1991. Asia's emerging economies. 16 November, S3–S18.

Economist. 1994a. Asian values. 28 May, 13–14.

Economist. 1994b. Fings ain't wot they used to be. 28 May, 31–32.

Economist. 1994c. Teaching Asia to stay Asian. 8 October, 39.

Economist. 1995a. Forward to Methuselah. 7 January, 65–68.

Economist. 1995b. The revolution yet to come. 21 January, 116–18.

Economist. 1996. The man in the Baghdad café. 9 November, 23–26.

Economist. 1998. Can America's workforce grow old gainfully? 25 July, 59–60.

Economist. 1999. Health care costs: On the critical list. 13 February, 65–66.

Eisner, R. 1988. Extended accounts for national income and product. *Journal of Economic Literature* 26:65–66.

———. 1998. *Social security: More, not less.* Century Foundation/Twentieth Century Fund Report. New York: Century Foundation Press.

El-Erian, M. A., and M. S. Kumar. 1995. Emerging equity markets in Middle Eastern countries. *IMF Staff Papers* 42:313–43.

Elster, J. 1986. Self-realization in work and politics: The Marxist conception of the good life. *Social Philosophy and Policy* 3:97–126.

Eltis, D. 1987. *Economic growth and the ending of the transatlantic slave trade.* New York: Oxford University Press.

Ely, R. T. 1938. *Ground under our feet: An autobiography.* New York: Macmillan.

Emery, M., and E. Emery. 1996. *The press and America: An interpretive history of the mass media.* Boston: Allyn & Bacon.

Engerman, S., and C. Goldin. 1994. Seasonality in nineteenth-century labor markets. In *American economic development in historical perspective,* ed. T. Weiss and D. Schaefer. Stanford, Calif.: Stanford University Press.

Ernst, R. 1949. *Immigrant life in New York City, 1825–1863.* New York: Columbia University, King's Crown Press.

Escobar, S. 1992. A new Reformation. *Christianity Today,* 6 April, 30–34.

Eveleth, P. B., and J. M. Tanner. 1976. *Worldwide variation in human growth.* Cambridge: Cambridge University Press.

Everitt, A. 1967. Farm labourers. In *The agrarian history of England and Wales,* ed. J. Thirsk. Cambridge: Cambridge University Press.

Fagan, B. M. 1977. *People of the earth.* 2d ed. Boston: Little, Brown.

Food and Agriculture Organization (FAO). 1996. *The sixth world food survey.* Rome.

FAO and World Health Organization (WHO). 1992. *International Conference of Nutrition: Nutrition and development—a global assessment.* Rome, December.

FAO, WHO, and United Nations University (UNU). 1985. *Energy and protein requirements: Report of a joint FAO/WHO/UNU expert committee.* Technical Report no. 724. Geneva: WHO.

Faulkner, H. U. 1931. *The quest for social justice, 1898–1914.* New York: Macmillan.

———. 1959. *Politics, reform, and expansion, 1890–1900.* New York: Harper & Bros.

———. 1960. *American economic history.* New York: Harper & Bros.

Fehrenbacher, D. H. 1962. *Prelude to greatness: Lincoln in the 1850s.* Stanford, Calif.: Stanford University Press.

Fei, J. C. H., G. Ranis, and S. W. Y. Kuo, 1978. Growth and the family distribution of income by factor components. *Quarterly Journal of Economics* 92: 17–53.

Feinstein, C. H. 1988. The rise and fall of the Williamson curve. *Journal of Economic History* 48:699–729.

———. 1990. What really happened to real wages? Trends in wages, prices, and productivity in the United Kingdom, 1880–1913. *Economic History Review* 43:329–55.

———. 1991. A new look at the cost of living, 1870–1914. In *New perspectives on the late Victorian economy: Essays in quantitative economic history, 1860–1914,* ed. J. S. Foreman-Peck. Cambridge: Cambridge University Press.

Feldberg, M. 1975. *The Philadelphia riots of 1844: A study of ethnic conflict.* Westport, Conn.: Greenwood.

Feldstein, M. S., and A. A. Samwick. 1998. The transition path in privatizing social security. In *Privatizing social security,* ed. M. S. Feldstein. Chicago: University of Chicago Press.

Field, A. J. 1978. Sectoral shift in antebellum Massachusetts: A reconsideration. *Explorations in Economic History* 15:146–71.

Fischer, D. H. 1989. *Albion's seed: Four British folkways in America.* New York: Oxford University Press.

Fishlow, A. 1965. *American railroads and the transformation of the antebellum economy.* Cambridge, Mass.: Harvard University Press.

———. 1966a. The American common school revival: Fact or fancy? In *Industrialization in two systems: Essays in honor of Alexander Gershenkron,* ed. H. Rosovsky. New York: Wiley.

———. 1966b. Antebellum interregional trade reconsidered. In *New views on American economic development,* ed. R. Andreano. Cambridge, Mass.: Schenkman.

———. 1966c. Productivity and technological change in the railroad sector, 1840–1910. In *Output, employment, and productivity in the United States after 1800* (Studies in Income and Wealth, vol. 30). New York: Columbia University Press.

Fletcher, W. L., and R. O. Hansson. 1991. Assessing the social components of retirement anxiety. *Psychology of Aging* 6:76–85.

Floud, R. 1983. The heights of Europeans since 1750: A new source for European economic history. Cambridge, Mass.: National Bureau of Economic Research. Mimeo.

———. 1984. Measuring the transformation of European economies: Income, health, and welfare. University of London, Birkbeck College. Mimeo.

———. 1985. Two cultures? British and American heights in the nineteenth century. University of London, Birkbeck College. Mimeo.

Floud, R., A. Gregory, and K. W. Wachter. 1985. The physical state of the British working class, 1870–1914: Evidence from army recruits. Working Paper no. 1661. Cambridge, Mass.: National Bureau of Economic Research.

Floud, R., K. W. Wachter, and A. Gregory. 1990. *Height, health, and history: Nutritional status in the United Kingdom, 1750–1980.* Cambridge: Cambridge University Press.

Fogel, R. W. 1964. *Railroads and American economic growth: Essays in econometric history.* Baltimore: Johns Hopkins University Press.

———. 1986a. Nutrition and the decline in mortality since 1700: Some preliminary findings. In *Long-term factors in American economic growth,* ed. S. L. Engerman and R. E. Gallman. Chicago: University of Chicago Press.

———. 1986b. Physical growth as a measure of the economic well-being of populations: The eighteenth and nineteenth centuries. In *Human growth: A comprehensive treatise* (2d ed.), vol. 3, *Methodology,* ed. F. Falkner and J. M. Tanner. New York: Plenum.

———. 1987. Biomedical approaches to the estimation and interpretation of secular trends in equity, morbidity, mortality, and labor productivity in Europe, 1750–1980. University of Chicago, Center for Population Economics. Typescript.

———. 1989. *Without consent or contract.* Vol. 1. New York: Norton.

———. 1992a. An analysis of the growth of the Northern population. In *Without consent or contract: Evidence and methods,* ed. R. W. Fogel, R. A. Galantine, and R. L. Manning. New York: Norton.

———. 1992b. The body mass index of adult male slaves in the U. S. c. 1863 and its bearing on mortality rates. In *Without consent or contract: Evidence and methods,* ed. R. W. Fogel, R. A. Galantine, and R. L. Manning. New York: Norton.

———. 1992c. The distribution of U.S. slaves by size of slaveholding in 1850 and 1860. In *Without consent or contract: Evidence and methods,* ed. R. W. Fogel, R. A. Galantine, and R. L. Manning. New York: Norton.

———. 1992d. An estimate of the proportion of the Northern population outside of New England in 1820 that was Yankee or of Yankee origin. In *Without consent or contract: Evidence and methods,* ed. R. W. Fogel, R. A. Galantine, and R. L. Manning. New York: Norton.

————. 1992e. The life expectation of U.S. slaves c. 1830. In *Without consent or contract: Evidence and methods,* ed. R. W. Fogel, R. A. Galantine, and R. L. Manning. New York: Norton.

————. 1992f. Problems in modeling complex dynamic interactions: The political realignment of the 1850s. *Economics and Politics* 4:215–54.

————. 1992g. Second thoughts on the European escape from hunger: Famines, chronic malnutrition, and mortality rates. In *Nutrition and poverty,* ed. S. R. Osmani. Oxford: Clarendon.

————. 1993. New sources and new techniques for the study of secular trends in nutritional status, health, mortality, and the process of aging. *Historical Methods* 26:5–43.

————. 1994a. Economic growth, population theory, and physiology: The bearing of long-term processes on the making of economic policy. *American Economic Review* 84:369–95.

————. 1994b. The relevance of Malthus for the study of mortality today: Long-run influences on health, mortality, labour force participation, and population growth. In *Population, economic development, and the environment,* ed. P. Dasgupta. Oxford: Oxford University Press.

————. 1994c. Toward a new synthesis on the role of economic issues in the political realignment of the 1850s. In *American economic development in historical perspective,* ed. T. Weiss and D. Schaefer. Stanford, Calif.: Stanford University Press.

————. 1996. Economic growth and cultural change: Lessons from the early leaders and the high-performing Asian economies. Paper presented to the Islamic Research and Training Institute of the Islamic Development Bank, Jeddah, Saudi Arabia, 16 January.

————. 1997a. Economic and social structure for an ageing population. *Philosophical Transactions of the Royal Society,* ser. B, 352:1905–17.

————. 1997b. New findings on secular trends in nutrition and mortality: Some implications for population theory. In *Handbook of population and family economics,* ed. M. R. Rosenzweig and O. Stark. Amsterdam: Elsevier.

Fogel, R. W., and D. L. Costa. 1997. A theory of technophysio evolution, with some implications for forecasting populations, health care costs, and pension costs. *Demography* 34:49–66.

Fogel, R. W., D. L. Costa, and J. M. Kim. 1993. Secular trends in the distribution of chronic conditions and disabilities at young adult and later ages, 1860–1988: Some preliminary findings. University of Chicago, Center for Population Economics. Typescript.

Fogel, R. W., and S. L. Engerman. 1971. The economics of slavery. In *The reinter-*

pretation of American economic history, ed. R. W. Fogel and S. L. Engerman. New York: Harper & Row.

———. 1974. *Time on the cross.* Boston: Little, Brown.

———. 1992. The slave diet on large plantations in 1860. In *Without consent or contract: Evidence and methods,* ed. R. W. Fogel, R. A. Galantine, and R. L. Manning. New York: Norton.

Fogel, R. W., S. L. Engerman, J. Trussell, R. Floud, C. L. Pope, and L. T. Wimmer. 1978. The economics of mortality in North America, 1650–1910: A description of a research project. *Historical Methods* 11:75–109.

Fogel, R. W., and R. Floud. 1999. A theory of multiple equilibria between populations and food supplies: Nutrition, mortality, and economic growth in France, Britain, and the United States, 1700–1980. University of Chicago, Center for Population Economics. Typescript.

Fogel, R. W., and R. A. Galantine. 1992. The change in voter alignment in the North between 1850 and 1869: An exploratory analysis. In *Without consent or contract: Evidence and methods,* ed. R. W. Fogel, R. A. Galantine, and R. L. Manning. New York: Norton.

Fogel, R. W., R. Galantine, and R. L. Manning, eds. 1992. *Without consent or contract: Evidence and methods.* New York: Norton.

Fogel, R. W., C. L. Pope, S. H. Preston, N. Scrimshaw, P. Temin, and L. T. Wimmer. 1986. The aging of Union army men: A longitudinal study, 1830–1940. University of Chicago, Center for Population Economics. Mimeo.

Fogel, R. W., and J. L. Rutner. 1972. The efficiency effects of federal land policy, 1850–1900: Some provisional findings. In *The dimensions of quantitative research in history,* ed. W. O. Aydelotte, A. G. Bogue, and R. W. Fogel. Princeton, N.J.: Princeton University Press.

Foner, E. 1970. *Free labor, free soil, free men: The ideology of the Republican Party before the Civil War.* New York: Oxford University Press.

Formisano, R. P. 1971. *The birth of mass political parties: Michigan, 1827–1861.* Princeton, N.J.: Princeton University Press.

Foster, C. I. 1960. *An errand of mercy: The evangelical united front, 1790–1837.* Chapel Hill: University of North Carolina Press.

Fox, R. W. 1993. The culture of liberal Protestant progressivism, 1875–1925. *Journal of Interdisciplinary Studies* 23:639–60.

Fox, R. W., and T. J. Lears. 1983. *The culture of consumption: Critical essays in American history, 1880–1980.* New York: Pantheon.

Fraker, P. J., M. E. Gershwin, R. A. Good, and A. Prasad. 1986. Interrelationships between zinc and immune function. *Federation Proceedings* 45: 1474–79.

Francis, J. 1851. *A history of the English railway: Its social relations and revelations, 1820–1845.* London: Longman, Brown, Green, & Longmans.

Freeman, R. 1976. *The over-educated American.* New York: Academic.

———. 1994. H. G. Lewis and the study of union wage effects. *Journal of Labor Economics* 12:143–49.

———. 1995. Longitudinal analyses of the effects of trade unions. In *Labor economics*, vol. 3, *Unemployment, trade unions, and dispute resolution*, ed. O. C. Ashenfelter and K. F. Hallock. Aldershot: Elgar.

———. 1996. Working for nothing: The supply of volunteer labor. Working Paper no. 5435. Cambridge, Mass.: National Bureau of Economic Research.

Freudenheim, M. 1998. Health insurers seek big increases in their premiums. *New York Times,* 24 April, A1.

Friedman, G. C. 1982. The heights of slaves in Trinidad. *Social Science History* 6:482–515.

Friedman, M., and R. Friedman. 1991. Interview by R. W. Fogel and E. M. Fogel. San Francisco, 21 March.

———. 1992. Interview by R. W. Fogel and E. M. Fogel. San Francisco, 16 March.

Fukuyama, F., and P. Berman. 1999. Reconstructing America's moral order. *Wilson Quarterly* 23, no. 3:32–44.

Funabashi, Y. 1993. The Asianization of Asia. *Foreign Affairs* 72, no. 5:75–85.

Galenson, D. W. 1981. *White servitude in colonial America: An economic analysis.* New Rochelle, N.Y.: Cambridge University Press.

———. 1986. *Traders, planters, and slaves: Market behavior in early English America.* New York: Cambridge University Press.

Gallman, R. E. 1966. Gross national product in the United States. In *Output, employment, and productivity in the United States after 1800* (Studies in Income and Wealth, vol. 30). New York: Columbia University Press.

———. 1972. The pace and pattern of American economic growth. In *American economic growth: An economist's history of the United States,* by L. E. Davis et al. New York: Harper & Row.

Gallman, R. E., and J. J. Wallis, eds. 1992. *American economic growth and standards of living before the Civil War.* Chicago: University of Chicago Press.

Gallup Report. See *Religion in America.*

Gates, P. W. 1934. *The Illinois Central Railroad and its colonization work.* Cambridge, Mass.: Harvard University Press.

Gaustad, E. S. 1962. *Historical atlas of religion in America.* New York: Harper & Row.

Gellert, G. A. 1995. The influence of market economics on primary health care in Vietnam. *Journal of the American Medical Association* 273:1498–1502.

Gemery, H. A. 1980. Emigration from the British Isles to the New World, 1630–1700: Inferences from colonial populations. *Research in Economic History* 5:179–231.

———. 1984. European emigration to North America, 1700–1820: Numbers and quasi numbers. *Perspectives in American History* 1:283–342.

Genovese, E. D. 1994. *The Southern tradition: The achievement and limitations of an American conservatism.* Cambridge, Mass.: Harvard University Press.

———. 1995. *The Southern front: History and politics in the cultural war.* Columbia: University of Missouri Press.

———. 1998. *A consuming fire: The fall of the Confederacy in the mind of the white Christian South.* Mercer University, Lamar Memorial Lectures, no. 41. Athens: University of Georgia Press.

Gienapp, W. E. 1985. Nativism and the creation of a Republican majority in the North before the Civil War. *Journal of American History* 72:529–59.

———. 1987. *The origins of the Republican Party, 1852–1856.* New York: Oxford University Press.

Glaab, C. N. 1963. *The American city: A documentary history.* Homewood, Ill.: Dorsey.

Glass, T. A., T. E. Seeman, A. R. Herzog, R. L. Kahn, and L. F. Berkman. 1995. Change in productive activity in late adulthood: MacArthur studies of successful aging. *Journal of Gerontology: Social Sciences* 50B:S65–S76.

Goldin, C. 1990. *Understanding the gender gap: An economic history of American women.* New York: Oxford University Press.

———. 1994a. How America graduated from high school: 1910 to 1960. Working Paper no. 4762. Cambridge, Mass.: National Bureau of Economic Research.

———. 1994b. The political economy of immigration restriction in the United States, 1890–1921. In *The regulated economy: A historical approach to political economy,* ed. C. Goldin and G. D. Libecap. Chicago: University of Chicago Press.

———. 1995. Career and family: College women look to the past. Working Paper no. 5188. Cambridge, Mass.: National Bureau of Economic Research.

———. 1997. Exploring the "present through the past": Career and family across the last century. *American Economic Review* 87:396–99.

Goldin, C., and L. F. Katz. 1996. The origins of technology-skill complementarity. Working Paper no. 5657. Cambridge, Mass.: National Bureau of Economic Research.

Goldin, C., and R. A. Margo. 1992. The great compression: The wage structure in the United States at mid-century. *Quarterly Journal of Economics* 107 (February 1992): 1–33.

Goldin, C., and K. Sokoloff. 1982. Women, children, and industrialization in the early Republic: Evidence from the manufacturing censuses. *Journal of Economic History* 42:741–74.

———. 1984. The relative productivity hypothesis of industrialization: The American case, 1820–1850. *Quarterly Journal of Economics* 99:461–87.

Gordon-McCutchan, R. C. 1981. The irony of evangelical history. *Journal for the Scientific Study of Religion* 20:309–26.

———. 1983. Great Awakenings? *Sociological Analysis* 44:83–97.

Gottschalk, P., and R. Moffitt. 1994. The growth of earnings instability in the U.S. labor market. *Brookings Papers on Economic Activity*, no. 2:217–72.

Goubert, P. 1973. *The ancien régime.* New York: Harper.

Gould, B. A. 1869. *Investigations in the military and anthropological statistics of American soldiers.* Cambridge, Mass.: Riverside.

Gould, J. D. 1979. European inter-continental emigration, 1815–1914: Patterns and causes. *Journal of European Economic History* 8, no. 3 (Winter): 593–679.

———. 1980. European inter-continental emigration: The road home: Return migration from the USA. *Journal of European Economic History* 9, no. 1 (Spring): 41–112.

Grady, J. L. 1994. Pentecostals renounce racism: Memphis gathering begins mending historic rift. *Christianity Today*, 12 December, 58.

Granitz, E., and B. Klein. 1996. Monopolization by "raising rivals' costs": The Standard Oil case. *Journal of Law and Economics* 39:1–48.

Gras, N. S. C. 1915. *The evolution of the corn market from the twelfth to the eighteenth century.* Cambridge, Mass.: Harvard University Press.

Graubard, S. R. 1974. Preface [to the issue *Science and its public: The changing relationship*]. *Daedalus* 103 (summer):v–vii.

Greenbaum, F. 1975. *Robert Marion La Follette.* Boston: Twayne.

Griffin, C. S. 1960. *Their brothers' keepers: Moral stewardship in the United States, 1800–1865.* New Brunswick, N.J.: Rutgers University Press.

Griscom, J. H. [1845] 1970. *The sanitary condition of the laboring class of New York, with suggestions for its improvement.* New York: Arno.

Grubb, F. W. 1984. Immigration and servitude in the colony and commonwealth of Pennsylvania: A quantitative and economic analysis. Ph.D. diss., University of Chicago.

———. 1990. Growth of literacy in colonial America: Longitudinal patterns, economic models, and the direction of future research. *Social Science History* 14:451–82.

Gusfield, J. R. [1963] 1986. *Symbolic crusade: Status politics and the American temperance movement.* Urbana: University of Illinois Press.

Haines, M. R. 1979. The use of model life tables to estimate mortality for the United States in the late nineteenth century. *Demography* 16:289–312.

———. 1992. Estimated life tables for the United States, 1850–1900. Working Paper: Series on Historical Factors in Long-Run Growth, Historical Paper no. 59. Cambridge, Mass.: National Bureau of Economic Research.

Haites, E. F., J. Mak, and G. M. Walton. 1975. *Western river transportation: The era of early internal development, 1810–1860.* Baltimore: Johns Hopkins University Press.

Hall, T. D. 1994. *Contested boundaries: Itinerancy and the reshaping of the colonial American religious world.* Durham, N.C.: Duke University Press.

Halloran, R. 1996. The rising East. *Foreign Policy,* no. 112:3–22.

Hamblen, M. 1999. Merrill trains staff to work at home. *Computerworld* 33, no. 17:50.

Hammond, J. L., and B. Hammond. [1911] 1978. *The village labourer.* London: Longman.

———. 1975. *The town labourer: The new civilisation, 1760–1832.* Gloucester, Mass.: Peter Smith.

Handlin, O. 1979. *Boston's immigrants, 1790–1880: A study in acculturation.* Cambridge, Mass.: Harvard University Press.

Handy, R. T. 1991. *Undermined establishment: Church-state relations in America, 1880–1920.* Princeton, N.J.: Princeton University Press.

Hannon, J. U. 1984a. The generosity of antebellum poor relief. *Journal of Economic History* 44:810–21.

———. 1984b. Poverty in the antebellum Northeast: The view from New York State's poor relief rolls. *Journal of Economic History* 44:1007–32.

———. 1985. Poor relief policy in antebellum New York State: The rise and decline of the poorhouse. *Explorations in Economic History* 22:233–56.

Haskell, T. L. 1977. *The emergence of professional social science: The American Social Science Association and the nineteenth-century crisis of authority.* Urbana: University of Illinois Press.

Hatch, N. O. 1989. *The democratization of American Christianity.* New Haven, Conn.: Yale University Press.

Haveman, R. 1996. *Earnings inequality: The influence of changing opportunities and choices.* Washington, D.C.: American Enterprise Institute Press.

Hayghe, H. V. 1991. Volunteers in the U.S.: Who donates the time? *Monthly Labor Review* 114, no. 2:17–24.

Hecker, D. E. 1998. Earnings of college graduates: Women compared with men. *Monthly Labor Review* 121, no. 3:62–71.

Heckman, J. J. 1990. The central role of the South in accounting for the economic progress of black Americans. *American Economic Review* 80:242–246.

———. 1991. Accounting for the economic progress of black Americans. In *New approaches to economic and social analyses of discrimination*, ed. R. R. Cornwall and P. V. Wunnava. Westport, Conn.: Greenwood, Praeger.

Heimert, A. 1966. *Religion and the American mind: From the Great Awakening to the Revolution.* Cambridge, Mass.: Harvard University Press.

Henderson, S. 1995. Family weekend. *Christian Century,* 22–29 November, 1102–4.

Hennessey, J. J. 1981. *American Catholics: A history of the Roman Catholic community in the United States.* Oxford: Oxford University Press.

Henretta, J. A. 1965. Economic development and social structure in colonial Boston. *William and Mary Quarterly,* 3d ser., 22, no. 1 (January): 75–92.

———. 1997. Changing perspective on retirement. *Journal of Gerontology: Psychological Sciences and Social Sciences* 52, no. 1 (January): S1–S3.

Herberg, W. 1960. *Protestant, Catholic, Jew: An essay in American religious sociology.* Rev. ed. Garden City, N.Y.: Anchor.

Hicks, P. 1998. The policy challenge of ageing populations. *OECD Observer,* no. 212 (June/July): 7–10.

Hiebert, M. 1995. Singapore: Close to you. *Far Eastern Economic Review* 158, no. 41:662–63.

Higgs, R. W. 1979. Cycles and trends of mortality in eighteen large American cities, 1871–1900. *Explorations in Economic History* 16:381–408.

Higham, J. 1963. *Strangers in the land: Patterns of American nativism, 1860–1925.* New York: Atheneum.

Himmelfarb, G. [1983] 1984. *The idea of poverty: England in the early industrial age.* New York: Knopf.

———. 1991. *Poverty and compassion: The moral imagination of the late Victorians.* New York: Knopf.

———. 1995. *The de-moralization of society: From Victorian virtues to modern values.* New York: Knopf.

Hobsbawm, E. 1964. *Laboring men: Studies in the history of labor.* New York: Basic.

Hodgkinson, V., M. Weitzman, and the Gallup Organization. 1996. *Giving and volunteering in the United States, 1996 edition.* Washington, D.C.: Independent Section.

Hoeveler, J. D. 1976. The university and the Social Gospel: The intellectual origins of the "Wisconsin Idea." *Wisconsin Magazine of History* 59:283–98.

Hoge, D. R., C. E. Zech, P. H. McNamara, and M. J. Donahue. 1996. Who gives to the church and why. *Christian Century,* 4 December, 1194–96, 1198–99.

Holmes, G. K. 1907. *Meat supply and surplus.* Washington, D.C.: U.S. Government Printing Office.

Holt, M. F. 1969. *Forging a majority: The formation of the Republican Party in Pittsburgh, 1848–1860.* New Haven, Conn.: Yale University Press.

———. 1973. The politics of impatience: The origins of Know Nothingism. *Journal of American History* 60:309–31.

———. 1978. *The political crisis of the 1850s.* New York: Wiley.

———. 1992. *Political parties and American political development from the age of Jackson to the age of Lincoln.* Baton Rouge: Louisiana State University Press.

Hopkins, C. 1940. *The rise of the Social Gospel in American Protestantism, 1865–1915.* New York: AMS.

Hopkins, H. 1936. *Spending to save: The complete story of relief.* New York: Norton.

Horton, S. 1984. Nutritional status and living standards measurement. Washington, D.C.: World Bank. Mimeo.

———. 1985. The determinants of nutrient intake: Results from western India. *Journal of Development Economics* 19:147–62.

———. 1986. Child nutrition and family size in the Philippines. *Journal of Development Economics* 23:161–76.

Hoskins, W. G. 1964. Harvest fluctuations and English economic history, 1480–1619. *Agricultural History Review* 12, pt. 1:28–46.

———. 1968. Harvest fluctuations and English economic history, 1620–1759. *Agricultural History Review* 16, pt. 1:15–31.

Howe, D. W. 1979. *The political culture of the American Whigs.* Chicago: University of Chicago Press.

———. 1990. Religion and politics in the antebellum North. In *Religion and American politics from the colonial period to the 1980s,* ed. M. A. Noll. New York: Oxford University Press.

———. 1991. The evangelical movement and political culture in the North during the second party system. *Journal of American History* 77:1216–39.

Hufton, O. W. 1974. *The poor of eighteenth-century France.* Oxford: Clarendon.

Hughes, J. R. T. 1991. *The governmental habit redux: Economic controls from colonial times to the present.* Princeton, N.J.: Princeton University Press.

Hunnicutt, B. K. 1988. *Work without end: Abandoning shorter hours for the right to work.* Philadelphia: Temple University Press.

Hunter, L. C. 1964. *Steamboats on the western rivers.* Cambridge, Mass.: Harvard University Press.

Huntington, S. P. 1993. The clash of civilizations? *Foreign Affairs* 72, no. 3 (summer): 22–49.

———. 1996a. *The clash of civilizations and the remaking of world order.* New York: Simon & Schuster.

———. 1996b. The West: Unique, not universal. *Foreign Affairs* 75, no. 6:28–46.

Hutchison, W. R. [1976] 1992. *The modernist impulse in American Protestantism.* Oxford: Oxford University Press.

———. 1989. *Between the times: The travail of the Protestant establishment in America, 1900–1960.* Cambridge: Cambridge University Press.

Institut National d'Études Démographiques (INED). 1977. Sixième rapport sur la situation démographique de la France. *Population* 32, no. 2:253–338.

Inter-University Consortium for Political and Social Research (ICPSR). 1993. CBS News/*New York Times* election day surveys, 1982. ICPSR no. 8168. Ann Arbor, Mich.

———. 1995a. American national election study, 1994: Postelection survey, ICPSR no. 6507.

———. 1995b. Voter News Service general election poll, 1994. ICPSR no. 6520.

———. n.d. American national election studies cumulative data file, 1952–1992. ICPSR no. 8475.

Isaac, R. 1974. Evangelical revolt: The nature of the Baptists' challenge to the traditional order in Virginia, 1765–1775. *William and Mary Quarterly*, 3d ser., 31:345–68.

———. 1982. *The transformation of Virginia, 1740–1798.* Chapel Hill: University of North Carolina Press.

It's a tall, tall world. 1994. *Discover*, January, 83–84.

Iyer, S. N. 1993. Pension reform in developing countries. *International Labour Review* 132:187–207.

Jablonski, M., L. Rosenblum, and K. Kunze. 1988. Productivity, age, and labor composition changes in the U.S. *Monthly Labor Review* 111:202–29.

Jacob, R. 1995a. China: A growth beast's rough ride. *Fortune* 132 (30 October): 182.

———. 1995b. Where to invest in Asia. *Fortune* 132 (30 October): 182.

Jaffe, A. J., and W. I. Lourie Jr. 1942. An abridged life table for the white population of the United States in 1830. *Human Biology* 14:352–71.

Jencks, C. 1994. *The homeless.* Cambridge, Mass.: Harvard University Press.

Jensen, R. 1971. *The winning of the Midwest: Social and political conflict, 1888–1896.* Chicago: University of Chicago Press.

———. 1984. Historiography of American political history. In *Encyclopedia of American political history: Studies of the principal movements and ideas*, vol. 1, ed. J. P. Greene. New York: Scribner's.

———. 1986. The changing shape of Burnham's political universe. *Social Science History* 10:209–20.

John, A. M. 1984. The demography of slavery in nineteenth-century Trinidad. Ph.D. diss., Princeton University.

———. 1988. *The plantation slaves of Trinidad, 1783–1816: A mathematical and demographic enquiry.* Cambridge: Cambridge University Press.

Johnson, G. 1999. Think again: How much give can the brain take? *New York Times*, 24 October, section 4:1, 6.

Johnson, P. 1995. God and the Americans. *Commentary* 99, no. 1 (January): 25–45.

Jones, A. H. 1980. *Wealth of a nation to be: The American colonies on the eve of the Revolution*. New York: Columbia University Press.

Jones, J. 1997. Still playing catch-up. *Christianity Today*, 19 May, 56.

Jones, M. A. [1960] 1992. *American immigration*. Chicago: University of Chicago Press.

Jordan, W. K. 1959. *Philanthropy in England, 1480–1660*. London: Allen & Unwin.

Jorgenson, D. W., and B. M. Fraumeni. 1987. The accumulation of human and non-human capital, 1848–1984. Harvard University. Typescript.

Juhn, C. 1992. Decline of male labor market participation: The role of declining market opportunities. *Quarterly Journal of Economics* 107:79–121.

Juhn, C., and K. M. Murphy. 1997. Wage inequality and family labor supply. *Journal of Labor Economics* 15:72–97.

Juster, F. T., and F. P. Stafford, eds. 1985. *Time, goods, and well-being*. Ann Arbor: University of Michigan, Institute for Social Research, Survey Research Center.

Kannisto, V., et al. 1994. Reductions in mortality at advanced ages: Several decades of evidence from 27 countries. *Population and Development Review* 20, no. 4 (December): 793–810.

Kapp, F. 1870. *Immigration and the commissioners of emigration of the state of New York*. New York: n.p.

Karp, J. 1994. Media: Cast of thousands. *Far Eastern Economic Review* 157, no. 4:46–50.

Karpinos, B. D. 1958. Height and weight of selective service registrants processed for military service during WWII. *Human Biology* 30:292–321.

Katz, L. F., and K. M. Murphy. 1992. Changes in relative wages, 1963–1987. Supply and demand factors. *Quarterly Journal of Economics* 107:35–78.

Katz, M. B. 1986. *In the shadow of the poorhouse: A social history of welfare in the United States*. New York: Basic.

Keller, M. 1977. *Affairs of state: Public life in late nineteenth-century America*. Cambridge, Mass.: Harvard University Press.

———. 1990. *Regulating a new economy: Public policy and economic change in America, 1900–1933*. Cambridge, Mass.: Harvard University Press.

Kellstedt, L. A., and M. A. Noll. 1991. Religion, voting for president, and party identification. In *The end of realignment? Interpreting American electoral eras*, ed. B. E. Shafer. Madison: University of Wisconsin Press.

Kendrick, J. W. 1987. Happiness is personal productivity growth. *Challenge* 13, no. 2:37–44.

Key, V. O., Jr. 1955. A theory of critical elections. *Journal of Politics* 17:3–18.

Kiil, V. 1939. *Stature and growth of Norwegian men during the past two hundred years.* Oslo: I kommison hos J. Dybwad.

Kim, J. M. 1993. Waaler surfaces: A new perspective on height, weight, morbidity, and mortality. University of Chicago, Center for Population Economics. Typescript.

———. 1996. Waaler surfaces: The economics of nutrition, body build, and health. Ph.D. diss., University of Chicago.

Kindleberger, C. P. 1991. *The life of an economist: An autobiography.* Cambridge, Mass.: Basil Blackwell.

Kington, R. S., and J. P. Smith. 1997. Socioeconomic status and racial and ethnic differences in functional status associated with chronic disease. *American Journal of Public Health* 87:805–10.

Kirkland, E. C. 1951. *A history of American economic life.* 3d ed. New York: Appleton-Century-Crofts.

Klein, H. 1978. *The middle passage: Comparative studies in the Atlantic slave trade.* Princeton, N.J.: Princeton University Press.

Kleppner, P. 1970. *The cross of culture: A social analysis of Midwestern politics, 1850–1900.* New York: Free Press.

———. 1979. *The third electoral system, 1853–1892: Parties, voters, and political cultures.* Chapel Hill: University of North Carolina Press.

———. 1982. *Who voted? The dynamics of election turnout, 1870–1980.* New York: Praeger.

Knowles, L. C. A. 1926. *The Industrial and Commercial Revolutions in Great Britain during the nineteenth century.* London: Routledge & Kegan Paul.

Koenig, L. W. 1971. *Bryan: A political biography of William Jennings Bryan.* New York: Putnam.

Kolata, G. 1988. Multiple fetuses raise new issues tied to abortion. *New York Times,* 25 January, 1.

Kolko, G. [1963] 1977. *The triumph of conservatism: A reinterpretation of American history.* New York: Free Press.

Komlos, J. 1985. Stature and nutrition in the Hapsburg monarchy: The standard of living and economic development in the eighteenth century. *American Historical Review* 90:1149–61.

———. 1989. *Nutrition and economic development in the eighteenth-century Habsburg monarchy: An anthropometric history.* Princeton, N.J.: Princeton University Press.

Koshland, D. E. 1989. Scare of the week. *Science* 244:9.

Kosmin, B. A. 1991. Research report: The National Survey of Religious Identification, 1989–90: Selected tabulations. CUNY Graduate School and University Center, March.

Kosmin, B. A., A. Keysar, and N. Lerer. 1992. Secular education and the religious profile of contemporary black and white Americans. *Journal for the Scientific Study of Religion* 31:523–32.

Kotlikoff, L. J., K. A. Smetters, and J. Walliser. 1998. Social security: Privatization and progressivity. *American Economic Review* 88:137–42.

Kousser, J. M. 1974. *The shaping of Southern politics: Suffrage restriction and the establishment of the one-party South.* New Haven, Conn.: Yale University Press.

———. 1976. The "new history": A methodological critique. *Reviews in American History* 4:1–14.

———. 1999. *"Colorblind" injustice: Race, election law, and the undoing of the Second Reconstruction.* Chapel Hill: University of North Carolina Press.

Kraar, L. 1994. The new power in Asia. *Fortune,* 31 October, 80–88.

Kravis, I. B. 1970. Trade as a handmaiden of growth: Similarities between the nineteenth and twentieth centuries. *Economic Journal* 80, no. 323:850–72. Reprinted in *Development economics,* vol. 3, ed. D. Lal. Brookfield, Vt.: Elgar.

Kulikoff, A. 1971. The progress of inequality in revolutionary Boston. *William and Mary Quarterly,* 3d ser., 28:375–412.

Kunitz, S. J. 1983. Speculation on the European mortality decline. *Economic History Review* 36:349–64.

Kuznets, S. 1952. Long-term changes in the national income of the United States of America since 1870. In *Income and wealth of the United States: Trends and structure,* ed. S. Kuznets. Cambridge: Bowes & Bowes.

———. 1966. *Modern economic growth: Rate, structure, and spread.* New Haven, Conn.: Yale University Press.

———. 1971. *Economic growth of nations: Total output and production structure.* Cambridge, Mass.: Harvard University Press.

———. 1979. *Growth, population, and income distribution: Selected essays.* New York: Norton.

Laabs, J. J. 1996. Downshifters: Workers are scaling back; are you ready? *Personnel Journal* 75, no. 3:62–76.

Ladd, E. C. 1991. Like waiting for Godot: The uselessness of "realignment" for understanding change in contemporary American politics. In *The end of realignment? Interpreting American electoral eras,* ed. B. E. Shafer. Madison: University of Wisconsin Press.

———. 1995. The 1994 congressional elections: The postindustrial realignment continues. *Political Science Quarterly* 110:1–23.

———. 1997. 1996 vote: The "no majority" realignment continues. *Political Science Quarterly* 112:1–29.

La Follette, R. M. 1960. *La Follette's autobiography: A personal narrative of political experiences.* Madison: University of Wisconsin Press.

Lambert, F. 1994. *"Peddlar in divinity": George Whitefield and the transatlantic revivals.* Princeton, N.J.: Princeton University Press.

Landes, D. S. 1969. *The unbound Prometheus.* Cambridge: Cambridge University Press.

———. 1998. *The wealth and poverty of nations: Why some are so rich and some so poor.* New York: Norton.

Landes, W. M., and L. C. Solmon. 1972. Compulsory schooling legislation: An economic analysis of law and social change in the nineteenth century. *Journal of Economic History* 22:54–92.

Lane, R. 1967. *Policing the city: Boston, 1822–1885.* Cambridge, Mass.: Harvard University Press.

Larson, E. 1996. The soul of an HMO. *Time,* 22 January, 44–52.

Laslett, P. [1965] 1984. *The world we have lost: England before the industrial age.* New York: Scribner's.

———, comp. 1973. *The earliest classics.* Farnborough: Gregg International.

———. 1991. *A fresh map of life.* Cambridge, Mass.: Harvard University Press.

Laurie, Bruce. 1980. *Working people of Philadelphia, 1800–1850.* Philadelphia: Temple University Press.

Lears, T. J. J. 1983. From salvation to self-realization: Advertising the therapeutic roots of the consumer culture, 1880. In *The culture of consumption: Critical essays in American history, 1880–1980,* ed. T. J. J. Lears and R. W. Fox. New York: Pantheon.

———. 1994. *Fables of abundance: A cultural history of advertising in America.* New York: Basic.

Lebergott, S. 1964. *Manpower in economic growth: The American record since 1800.* New York: McGraw-Hill.

———. 1966. Labor force and employment, 1800–1969. In *Output, employment, and productivity in the United States after 1800.* New York: Columbia University Press.

———. 1993. *Pursuing happiness: American consumers in the twentieth century.* Princeton, N.J.: Princeton University Press.

Lee, C. 1996. *Essays on retirement and wealth accumulation in the United States, 1850–1990.* Ph.D. diss., University of Chicago.

———. 1997. Changes in employment and hours, and family income inequality, 1969–1989. University of Chicago, Center for Population Economics. Mimeo.

Lemann, N. 1997. The limits of charity. *Newsweek,* 28 April, 37.

Lender, M. E., and J. K. Martin. 1982. *Drinking in America: A history*. New York: Free Press.

Lenk, H. 1994. Value changes and the achieving society: A social-philosophical perspective. In *OECD societies in transition: The future of work and leisure*. Paris: OECD.

Leonard, E. M. 1965. *The early history of English poor relief*. New York: Barnes & Noble.

Lesley, J. P. 1859. *The iron manufacturer's guide to the furnaces, forges, and rolling mills of the United States*. New York: J. Wiley.

Levidow, L. 1995. The Oxford baculovirus controversy—safety testing safety. *BioScience* 45:545–52.

Levin, J. S. 1994. Religion and health: Is there an association, is it valid, and is it causal? *Social Science Medicine* 38:1475–82.

Levine, A. 1997. How the academic profession is changing. *Daedalus* 126:1–21.

Levine, R. 1997. The pace of life in 31 countries. *American Demographics* 19, no. 11:20–29.

Lewis, H. G. 1986. *Union relative wage effects: A survey*. Chicago: University of Chicago Press.

Lichtman, A. J. 1976. Critical election theory and the reality of American presidential politics, 1916–40. *American History Review* 81, no. 2 (April):317–51.

———. 1982. The end of realignment theory? Toward a new research program for American political history. *Historical Methods* 15, no. 4 (fall): 170–88.

———. 1983. Political realignment and "ethnocultural" voting in late nineteenth-century America. *Journal of Social History* 16, no. 3:55–82.

Liew, L. H. 1995. Gradualism in China's economic reform and the role for a strong central state. *Journal of Economic Issues* 29:883–95.

Lin, J. Y. 1998. *How did China feed itself in the past? How will China feed itself in the future?* Second Distinguished Economist Lecture. Mexico, D.F.: CIMMYT.

Lindert, P. H. 1986. Comment. In *Long-term factors in American economic growth*, ed. S. L. Engerman and R. E. Gallman. Chicago: University of Chicago Press.

———. 1994. Unequal living standards. In *The economic history of Britain since 1700*, ed. R. Floud and D. McCloskey. Cambridge: Cambridge University Press.

Lindert, P. H., and J. G. Williamson. 1982. Revising England's social tables, 1688–1812. *Explorations in Economic History* 19:385–408.

———. 1983a. English workers' living standards during the Industrial Revolution: A new look. *Economic History Review* 36:1–25.

———. 1983b. Reinterpreting Britain's social tables, 1688–1913. *Explorations in Economic History* 20:94–109.

Lindholm, C. 1996. *The Islamic Middle East: An historical anthropology*. London: Blackwell.

Lipset, S. M. 1996. *American exceptionalism: A double-edged sword.* New York: Doubleday.

Lipson, E. 1971. *The economic history of England.* Vol. 3, *The age of mercantilism.* London: Adam & Charles Black.

Lipton, M. 1983. Poverty, undernutrition, and hunger. Staff Working Paper no. 597. Washington, D.C.: World Bank.

Lockridge, K. 1974. *Literacy in colonial New England: An enquiry into the social context of literacy in the early modern West.* New York: Norton.

———. 1981. *Settlement and unsettlement in early America: The crisis of political legitimacy before the Revolution.* Cambridge, Mass.: Harvard University Press.

Loeb, M. 1995. China: A time for caution. *Fortune,* 20 February, 129–30.

Long, K. 1998. *The revival of 1857–58.* New York: Oxford University Press.

Lozoff, B., E. Jimenez, and A. W. Wolf. 1991. Long-term developmental outcome of infants with iron deficiency. *New England Journal of Medicine* 325:687–95.

Lublin, J. S. 1998. Pay for no performance. *Wall Street Journal,* 9 April, 4R1, R4.

Lynch, D. 1946. *The concentration of economic power.* New York: Columbia University Press.

MacKinnon, M. 1994. Living standards, 1870–1914. In *The economic history of Britain since 1700,* ed. R. Floud and D. McCloskey. Cambridge: Cambridge University Press.

Maddison, A. 1982. *Phases of capitalist development.* Oxford: Oxford University Press.

———. 1995. *Monitoring the world economy, 1820–1992.* Paris: OECD, Development Centre.

———. 1998. *Chinese economic performance in the long run.* Paris: OECD, Development Centre.

Mahbubani, K. 1995. The Pacific way. *Foreign Affairs* 74, no. 1:100–11.

Main, G. L. 1982. *Tobacco colony: Life in early Maryland, 1650–1720.* Princeton, N.J.: Princeton University Press.

Malthus, T. R. [1798] 1926. *An essay on the principle of population.* London: J. Johnson.

———. [1803] 1992. *An essay on the principle of population.* Cambridge: Cambridge University Press.

Mansson, N. O., K. F. Eriksson, B. Israelsson, J. Ranstam, A. Melander, and L. Ranstam. 1996. Body mass index and disability pension in middle-aged men—non-linear relations. *International Journal of Epidemiology* 25, no. 1:80–85.

Manton, K. G. 1993. Biomedical research and changing concepts of disease and aging: Implications for long-term forecasts for elderly populations. In *Forecasting the health of elderly populations,* ed. K. G. Manton, B. H. Singer, and R. M. Suzman. New York: Springer.

Manton, K. G., L. S. Corder, and E. Stallard. 1993. Estimates of change in chronic disability and institutional incidence and prevalence rates in the U.S. elderly population from the 1982, 1984, and 1989 National Long Term Care Survey. *Journal of Gerontology* 48, no. 4 (July): S153–S166.

———. 1997. Chronic disability trends in elderly United States populations, 1982–1994. *Proceedings of the National Academy of Science, USA* 96:2593–98.

Margo, R. A. 1990. *Race and schooling in the South, 1880–1950: An economic history.* Chicago: University of Chicago Press.

———. 2000. *Wages and labor markets before the Civil War.* Chicago: University of Chicago Press.

Margo, R. A., and R. H. Steckel. 1992. The heights of American slaves: New evidence on slave nutrition and health. *Social Science History* 6(4): 516–38.

Margo, R. A., and G. C. Villaflor. 1987. The growth of wages in antebellum America: New evidence. *Journal of Economic History* 47:873–95.

Mariger, R. 1978. Predatory price cutting: The Standard Oil of New Jersey case revisited. *Explorations in Economic History* 15:341–67.

Marks, J. 1995. Time out. *U.S. News and World Report,* 11 December, 85–96.

Markwood, S. R. 1994. Volunteers in local government: Partners in service. *Public Management* 76:6–10.

Marsden, G. M. 1980. *Fundamentalism and American culture: The shaping of twentieth-century evangelism, 1870–1925.* New York: Oxford University Press.

———. 1994. *The soul of the American university: From Protestant establishment to established non-belief.* New York: Oxford University Press.

Marshall, J. D. 1968. *The old poor law, 1795–1834.* London: Macmillan.

Martin, D. 1990. *Tongues of fire: The explosion of Protestantism in Latin America.* Oxford: Basil Blackwell.

Martin, E. W. 1942. *The standard of living in 1860: American consumption levels on the eve of the Civil War.* Chicago: University of Chicago Press.

Martorell, R. 1985. Child growth retardation: A discussion of its causes and its relationship to health. In *Nutritional adaptation in man,* ed. K. Blaxter and J. C. Waterlow. London: John Libby.

Martorell, R., and J.-P. Habicht. 1986. Growth in early childhood in developing countries. In *Human growth: A comprehensive treatise* (3 vols.), ed. F. Falkner and J. M. Tanner. New York: Plenum.

Martorell, R., J. Rivera, and H. Kaplowitz. 1990. Consequences of stunting in early childhood for adult body size in rural Guatemala. *Annales Nestlé* 48:85–92.

Marty, M. E. 1970. *Righteous empire: The Protestant experience in America.* New York: Dial.

———. 1986. *Protestantism in the United States: Righteous empire.* New York: Scribner's.

———. 1987. *Religion and republic: The American circumstance.* Boston: Beacon.

———. 1991. *Modern American religion: The noise of conflict, 1919–1941.* Chicago: University of Chicago Press.

Marty, M. E., and R. S. Appleby, eds. 1991–95. *The Fundamentalism Project.* 5 vols. Chicago: University of Chicago Press.

Massaro, T. A., and Y. N. Wong. 1995. Positive experience with medical savings accounts in Singapore. *Health Affairs* 14:267–72.

Mathews, D. G. 1977. *Religion in the old South.* Chicago: University of Chicago Press.

Mathias, P. 1957. The social structure in the eighteenth century: A calculation by Joseph Massie. *Economic History Review,* 2d ser., 10:30–45.

———. 1983. *The first industrial nation: An economic history of Britain, 1700–1914.* 2d ed. London: Methuen.

Matthews, R. C. O., C. H. Feinstein, and J. C. Odling-Smee. 1982. *British economic growth, 1856–1973.* Stanford, Calif.: Stanford University Press.

Maxwell, J. 1995. Black Southern Baptists: The SBC's valiant efforts to overcome its racist past. *Christianity Today,* 15 May, 26–32.

May, H. F. 1949. *Protestant churches and industrial America.* New York: Harper.

May, J. M. 1958. *The ecology of human disease.* New York: MD Publishing.

Mayhew, H. 1851–61. *London labour and London poor: Encyclopedia of the condition and earnings of those that will work, those that cannot work, and those that will not work.* London: G. Woodfall.

McClory, R. J. 1991. Why did the Catholic cross the road? *U.S. Catholic,* January, 6–12.

McCormick, R. L. 1986. *The party period and public policy: American politics from the age of Jackson to the Progressive Era.* New York: Oxford University Press.

McCutcheon, B. J. 1992. An exploration into the courses of the growth of per capita income in the North, 1840–1860. In *Without consent or contract: Evidence and methods,* ed. R. W. Fogel, R. A. Galantine, and R. L. Manning. New York: Norton.

McFadden, S. H. 1995. Religion and well-being in aging persons in an aging society. *Journal of Social Issues* 51:161–75.

———. 1996. Religion, spirituality, and aging. In *Handbook of the psychology of aging,* 4th ed., ed. J. E. Birren and K. W. Schaie. San Diego: Academic.

McGee, J. S. 1958. Predatory price cutting: The Standard Oil (N.J.) case. *Journal of Law and Economics* 1:136–69.

McGrattan, E. R., and R. Rogerson. 1998. Changes in hours worked since 1950. *Federal Reserve Bank of Minneapolis* 22, no. 1:2–19.

McKeown, T. 1976. *The modern rise of population.* New York: Academic.

McKivigan, J. K. 1984. *The war against proslavery religion: Abolitionism and the Northern churches, 1830–1865.* Ithaca, N.Y.: Cornell University Press.

McLoughlin, W. G. 1978. *Revivals, awakenings, and reform: An essay on religion and social change in America, 1607–1977.* Chicago: University of Chicago Press.

McMahon, M. M., and B. R. Bistrian. 1990. The physiology of nutritional assessment and therapy in protein-calorie malnutrition. *Disease-a-Month* 36:373–417.

McNeill, W. H. 1971. *A world history.* New York: Oxford University Press.

———. 1997. Decline of the West? Review of *The clash of civilizations and the remaking of world order,* by S. P. Huntington. *New York Review of Books,* 9 January, 18–22.

McPherson, J. M. 1982. *Ordeal by fire: The Civil War and Reconstruction.* New York: Knopf.

Meerton, M. A. von. 1989. Croissance économique en France et accroissement des français: Une analyse "Villermetrique." Center voor Economische Studiën, Louvain. Typescript.

Meinhold, H., A. Compos-Barros, B. Walzog, R. Kohler, F. Muller, D. Behne, and K. Steglitz. 1993. Effects of selenium and iodine deficiency on Type I, Type II, and Type III iodothyronine deiodinases and circulating thyroid hormones in the rat. *Experimental and Clinical Endocrinology* 101:87–93.

Meyers, M. 1960. *The Jacksonian persuasion: Politics and belief.* Stanford, Calif.: Stanford University Press.

Miller, L. 1999. Today, it's reading, writing, and "diligence" in elementary schools. *Wall Street Journal,* 25 October, A1, A8.

Mitchell, B. 1947. *Depression decade: From New Era through New Deal, 1929–1941.* Vol. 9 of *The economic history of the United States.* New York: Rinehart.

Mitchell, B. R., and P. Deane. 1962. *Abstract of British historical statistics.* Cambridge: Cambridge University Press.

Moberg, D. O. 1990. Religion and aging. In *Gerontology: Perspectives and issues,* ed. K. F. Ferraro. New York: Springer.

Moffitt, R. 1990. The distribution of earnings and the welfare states. In *A future of lousy jobs? The changing structure of U.S. wages,* ed. Gary Burtless. Washington, D.C.: Brookings.

———. 1995. *Current population surveys: March individual-level extracts, 1968–1992.* ICPSR no. 6171. Ann Arbor, Mich.: Inter-University Consortium for Political and Social Research.

Mokyr, J. 1985. *Why Ireland starved: A quantitative and analytical history of the Irish economy, 1800–1850.* London: Allen & Unwin.

―――. 1990. *The lever of riches: Technological creativity and economic progress.* New York: Oxford University Press.

―――, ed. 1993. *The British Industrial Revolution: An economic perspective.* Boulder, Colo.: Westview.

Monkkonen, E. H. 1981. *Police in urban America, 1860–1920.* Cambridge: Cambridge University Press.

Montinola, G., Y. Qian, and B. R. Weingast. 1995. Federalism, Chinese style: The political basis for economic success in China. *World Politics* 48:50–81.

Moody, P. R., Jr. 1996. Asian values. *Journal of International Affairs* 50:166–92.

Morgan, T. C. 1995. Racist no more? Black leaders ask. *Christianity Today,* 14 August, 53.

Morse, S. F. B. 1835. *Foreign conspiracy against the liberties of the United States.* New York.

Moynihan, D. P. 1993. Defining deviancy down. *American Scholar* 62:17–31.

Mulder, J. M. 1978. The heavenly cities and human cities: Washington Gladden and urban reform. *Ohio History* 87:151–74.

Muller, D. R. 1959. The social philosophy of Josiah Strong: Social Christianity and American Progressivism. *Church History* 28:183–201.

Murphy, K. M., and F. Welch. 1990. Empirical age-earnings profiles. *Journal of Labor Economics* 8:202–29.

―――. 1998. Perspectives on the social security crisis and proposed solution. *American Economic Review* 88:142–50.

Mutchler, J. E., J. A. Burr, A. M. Pienta, and M. P. Massagli. 1997. Pathways to labor force exit: Work transitions and work instability. *Journal of Gerontology: Psychological Sciences and Social Sciences* 52B:S4–S13.

Nardulli, P. F. 1995. The concept of a critical realignment, electoral behavior, and political change. *American Political Science Review* 89:10–23.

Nash, G. B. 1979. *The urban crucible: Social change, political consciousness, and the origins of the American Revolution.* Cambridge, Mass.: Harvard University Press.

Nash, R. F. 1989. *The rights of nature: A history of environmental ethics.* Madison: University of Wisconsin Press.

Nathan, R. R. 1936. Estimates of unemployment in the United States, 1929–1935. *International Labour Review* 33, no. 1:49–82.

―――. 1990. Interview by R. W. Fogel and E. M. Fogel. Arlington, Va., 26 December.

National Center for Health Statistics, M. F. Najjar, and M. Rowland. 1987. *Anthropometric reference data and prevalence of overweight, United States, 1976–80.* Vital Health and Statistics, ser. 11, no. 238. Washington, D.C.: Public Health Service, U.S. Government Printing Office.

National Conference of Catholic Bishops. 1986. *Economic justice for all: Catholic social teaching and the U.S. economy.* Washington, D.C.: U.S. Catholic Conference.

New York State Board of Health. 1867. *Annual report.* Albany, N.Y.: Van Benthuysen.

New York State Legislature. Assembly. 1857. *Report of the select committee appointed to examine into the condition of tenement houses in New York and Brooklyn.* 80th sess., vol. 3, no. 205. Albany.

Niebuhr, H. R. [1937] 1988. *The kingdom of God in America.* Middletown, Conn.: Wesleyan University Press.

Noll, M. A. 1993. The American Revolution and Protestant evangelicalism. *Journal of Interdisciplinary History* 23:615–38.

Nordhaus, W. D., and J. Tobin. 1972. Is growth obsolete? In *Economic growth.* New York: National Bureau of Economic Research.

North, D.C. 1961. *The economic growth of the United States, 1790–1860.* New York: Norton.

———. 1968. Sources of productivity change in ocean shipping, 1600–1850. *Journal of Political Economy* 76:953–70.

———. 1990. *Institutions, institutional change, and economic performance.* Cambridge: Cambridge University Press.

Nye, J. S., Jr. 1996. Future wars: Conflicts after the cold war. *Current,* no. 381:31–41.

Nye, R. B. 1959. *Midwestern Progressive politics.* East Lansing: Michigan State University Press.

———. 1974. *Society and culture in America, 1830–1860.* New York: Harper & Row.

Nyland, C. 1989. *Reduced worktime and the management of production.* New York: Cambridge University Press.

Oates, D., and J. Oates. 1976. *The rise of civilization: The making of the past.* New York: Elsevier Phaidon.

Okwumabua, J. O., F. M. Baker, S. P. Wong, and B. O. Pilgram. 1997. Characteristics of depressive symptoms in elderly urban and rural African Americans. *Journals of Gerontology: Biological and Medical Sciences* 52, no. 4:M241–M246.

Olsen, K. A. 1995. Privatizing social security: The troubling trade-offs. *Washington Quarterly* 22:205–15.

Olsen, T. 1997. Racial reconciliation emphasis intensified: Promise Keepers. *Christianity Today,* 6 January, 67.

Olson, J. F. 1983. The occupational structure of plantation slave labor in the late antebellum era. Ph.D. diss., University of Rochester.

———. 1992. The occupational structure of southern plantations during the late antebellum era. In *Without consent or contract: Markets and production: Technical Papers,* vol. 1, ed. R. W. Fogel and S. L. Engerman. New York: Norton.

Olson, K. W. 1974. *The G. I. Bill, the veterans, and the colleges.* Lexington: University of Kentucky Press.

Orren, K., and S. Skowronek. 1998. Regimes and regime building in American government: A review of literature on the 1940s. *Political Science Quarterly* 113, no. 4:689–702.

Ostling, R. N. 1985. Jerry Falwell's crusade: Fundamentalist legions seek to remake church and society. *Time,* 2 September, 48–57.

Ostling, R. N., et al. 1989. Those mainline blues. *Time,* 22 May, 94–96.

Pagels, E. 1995. *The origin of Satan.* New York: Random House.

Pakhala, K., S. L. Kivelea, and P. Laippala. 1992. Social and environmental factors and dysthymic disorders in old age. *Journal of Clinical Epidemiology* 45, no. 7 (July): 775–83.

Parrington, V. L. 1930. *Main currents in American thought: An interpretation of American literature from the beginnings to 1920.* 2 vols. New York: Harcourt, Brace.

Peach, W. N., and J. A. Constantin. 1972. *Zimmerman's world resources and industries.* New York: Harper & Row.

Peak, M. 1996. Face-time follies. *Management Review* 85:1.

Pellegrino, E. D. 1993. The metamorphosis of medical ethics: A 30-year retrospective. *Journal of the American Medical Association* 269:1158–62.

Perkin, H. J. 1969. *The origins of modern English society, 1780–1880.* London: Routledge & Kegan Paul.

———. 1990. *The rise of professional society: England since 1880.* London: Routledge.

Perlmann, J., and D. Shirley. 1991. When did New England women acquire literacy? *William and Mary Quarterly* 48:50–67.

Pessen, E. 1973. *Riches, class, and power before the Civil War.* Lexington, Mass.: D.C. Heath.

———. 1977. Who governed the nation's cities in the "era of the common man"? In *The many faceted Jacksonian era: New interpretations,* ed. E. Pessen. Westport, Conn.: Greenwood.

———. 1978. *Jacksonian America: Society, personality, and politics.* Homewood, Ill.: Dorsey.

Phelps Brown, H. 1988. *Egalitarianism and the generation of inequality.* New York: Oxford University Press.

Piggott, S. 1965. *Ancient Europe from the beginnings of agriculture to classical antiquity.* Chicago: Aldine.

Pitzer, D. 1968–69. Revivalism and politics in Toledo. *Northwest Ohio Quarterly* 41:13–24.

Pole, J. R. 1993. *The pursuit of equality in American history.* Berkeley and Los Angeles: University of California Press.

Pollard, S. 1981. Sheffield and sweet Auburn—amenities and living standards in the British Industrial Revolution. *Journal of Economic History* 41:902–4.

Poortvliet, W. G., and T. P. Laine. 1995. A global trend: Privatization and reform of social security pension plans. *Benefits Quarterly* 1, no. 3:63–84.

Pope, C. L. 1992. Adult mortality in America before 1900: A view from family histories. In *Strategic factors in nineteenth-century American economic history: A volume to honor Robert W. Fogel*, ed. C. Goldin and H. Rockoff. Chicago: University of Chicago Press.

Potier, M. 1995. China charges for pollution. *OECD Observer*, no. 192:18–22.

Poulson, B. W. 1981. *Economic history of the United States.* New York: Macmillan.

Preston, S. H. 1975. The changing relation between mortality and level of economic development. *Population Studies* 29:231–48.

Preston, S. H., and E. van de Walle. 1978. Urban French mortality in the nineteenth century. *Population Studies* 32:275–97.

Princeton Religion Research Center. 1978. *The unchurched America.* Princeton, N.J.

———. 1982. *Religion in America, 1982, with commentary by George Gallup Jr.* Princeton, N.J.

———. 1988. *The unchurched America—ten years later.* Princeton, N.J.

Putterman, L., J. E. Romer, and J. Silvestre. 1998. Does egalitarianism have a future? *Journal of Economic Literature* 36:861–902.

Rabey, S. 1996. Where is the Christian men's movement headed? Burgeoning Promise Keepers inspires look-alikes. *Christianity Today,* 29 April, 46–50.

Rabkin, S. W., Y. Chen, L. Leiter, L. Liu, and B. A. Reeder. 1997. Risk factor correlates of body mass index: Canadian Heart Health Surveys Research Group. *Canadian Medical Association Journal* 157, suppl. 1:S26–S31.

Rader, B. G. 1966. *The academic mind and reform: The influence of Richard T. Ely in American life.* Lexington: University of Kentucky Press.

Raines, J. C. 1996. The politics of religious correctness: Islam and the West. *Cross Currents* 46:39–49.

Ransom, R. L. 1963. Government investment in canals: A study of the Ohio Canal. Ph.D. diss., University of Washington.

Ratner, S. 1942. *A political and social history of federal taxation, 1789–1913, with special reference to the income tax and the inheritance tax.* New York: Norton.

Ratner, S., J. H. Soltow, and R. Sylla. 1979. *The evolution of the American economy: Growth, welfare, and decision making.* New York: Basic.

Rayback, J. G. 1966. *A history of American labor.* New York: Free Press.

Rebaudo, D. 1979. Le mouvement annual de la population française rurale de 1670 à 1740. *Population* 34:589–606.

Rees, A. 1961. *Real wages in manufacturing, 1890–1914.* Princeton, N.J.: Princeton University Press.

Reid, D. G., ed. 1990. *Dictionary of Christianity in America*. Downer's Grove, Ill.: Inter-Varsity.

Religion in America. 1987. Report no. 259. Princeton, N.J.: Gallup Organization.

Richardson, J. F. 1970. *The New York police: Colonial times to 1901*. New York: Oxford University Press.

Rifkin, J. 1995. *The end of work: The decline of the global labor force and the dawn of the post-market era*. New York: Putnam's.

The rights of frozen embryos. 1989. *Time*, 24 July, 63.

Riker, W. H. 1982. *Liberalism against populism: A confrontation between the theory of democracy and the theory of social choice*. San Francisco: W. H. Freeman.

Robbins, R. M. 1962. *Our landed heritage: The public domain, 1776–1936*. Lincoln: University of Nebraska Press.

Roberts, E. M. [1988] 1995. *Women's work, 1840–1940*. Cambridge: Cambridge University Press.

Robinson, D. 1979. *Slavery in the structure of American politics, 1765–1920*. New York: Norton.

Robinson, J. P. 1988. Who's doing the housework? *American Demographics* 10, no. 12:24–28, 63.

Robinson, J. P., and G. Godbey. 1997. *Time for life: The surprising ways Americans use their time*. University Park: Pennsylvania State University.

Roediger, D. R., and P. S. Foner. 1989. *Our own time: A history of American labor and the working day*. New York: Greenwood.

Rona, R. J., et al. 1978. Social factors and height of primary school children in England and Scotland. *Journal of Epidemiology and Community Health* 32: 147–54.

Rorabaugh, W. J. 1979. *Alcoholic republic: An American tradition*. New York: Oxford University Press.

Rose, M. E. 1971. *The relief of poverty, 1834–1914*. London: Macmillan.

Rose, R. B. 1961. Eighteenth century price riots and public policy in England. *International Review of Social History* 6:277–92.

Rosenberg, I. H. 1992. Folic acid and neural-tube defects—time for action? *New England Journal of Medicine* 327:1875–77.

Rosenberg, N., and L. E. Birdzell Jr. 1986. *How the West grew rich: The economic transformation of the industrial world*. New York: Basic.

Rosenman, S. I. 1941. *The public papers and addresses of Franklin D. Roosevelt*. Vol. 9, *1940, war—and aid to democracies*. New York: Macmillan.

Ross, C., R. D. Langer, and E. Barrett-Connor. 1997. Given diabetes, is fat better than thin? *Diabetes Care* 20, no. 4:650–52.

Ross, D. 1991. *The origins of American social science*. Cambridge: Cambridge University Press.

Rostow, W. W. 1960. *The stages of economic growth: A non-Communist manifesto.* Cambridge: Cambridge University Press.

———, ed. 1963. *The economics of take-off into sustained growth: Proceedings of a conference held by the International Economic Association.* London: Macmillan.

———. 1981. *Pre-invasion bombing strategy: General Eisenhower's decision of March 25, 1944.* Austin: University of Texas Press.

Roth, A. 1973. Sunday "blue laws" and the California state Supreme Court. *Southern California Quarterly* 55:43–47.

Rothman, D. J. 1971. *The discovery of the asylum: Social order and disorder in the new republic.* Boston: Little, Brown.

Rothman, S., and S. R. Lichter. 1983. *Nuclear electricity: Who stands where?* Washington, D.C.: U.S. Committee for Energy Awareness.

Rowe, J. W., and R. L. Kahn. 1997. Successful aging. *Gerontologist* 37:433–40.

———. 1998. *Successful aging.* New York: Pantheon.

Rowntree, B. S. 1901. *Poverty: A study of town life.* London: Macmillan.

Ruggles, S., and M. Sobek. 1997. Integrated public use micro data series: Version 2.0. Minneapolis: University of Minnesota, Historical Census Project.

Sahlins, M. D. 1972. *Stone age economics.* Chicago: Aldine-Atherton.

Salant, W. 1990. Interview by R. W. Fogel and E. M. Fogel. Washington, D.C., 27 December.

Samuels, S. C. 1997. Midlife crisis: Helping patients cope with stress, anxiety, and depression. *Geriatrics* 52, no. 7:55–56, 59–63.

Samuelson, P. A. 1944. Unemployment ahead. *New Republic* 111, no. 11 (11 September): 297–99, and no. 12 (18 September): 333–35.

———. 1990. Interview by R. W. Fogel and E. M. Fogel. Cambridge, Mass., 26 December.

Sandberg, L. G., and R. H. Steckel. 1988a. Heights and economic history: The Swedish case. *Annals of Human Biology* 14:101–10.

———. 1988b. Overpopulation and malnutrition rediscovered: Hard times in nineteenth-century Sweden. *Explorations in Economic History* 25:1–19.

Sawyer, M. C. 1976. *Income distribution in OECD countries.* OECD Economic Outlook: Occasional Studies. Paris: OECD.

Scalberg, E. J. 1993. The expanding market for business education in Pacific Asia. *Selections* 10, no. 1:36–39.

Schlesinger, A. M. 1933. *The rise of the city, 1878–1898.* New York: Macmillan.

———. 1957. *The age of Roosevelt.* Vol. 1, *The coming of the New Deal.* Vol. 2, *The politics of upheaval.* Boston: Houghton Mifflin.

Schmidt, I. M., M. H. Jorgensen, and K. F. Michaelsen. 1995. Height of conscripts in Europe: Is postneonatal mortality a predictor? *Annals of Human Biology* 22:57–67.

Schneider, A. M. 1993. *The way of the cross leads home: The domestication of American Methodism.* Bloomington: Indiana University Press.

Schneider, D. M., and A. Deutsch. 1941. *The history of public welfare in New York State, 1867–1940.* Chicago: University of Chicago Press.

Schneider, S. H. 1989. The changing climate. *Scientific American* 261, no. 3:70–79.

Schumpeter, J. [1934] 1961. *The theory of economic development.* New York: Oxford University Press.

———. 1942. *Capitalism, socialism, and democracy.* New York.

Schwartz, D. 1985. The standard of living in the long run: London, 1700–1860. *Economic History Review* 38:24–41.

Scott, M. B. 1996. Work/life programs encompass a broad range of benefit offerings. *Employee Benefit Plan Review* 51:26–27.

Scrimshaw, S. 1926. Apprenticeship: Principles, relationships, procedures. Ph.D. diss., University of Wisconsin.

———. 1932. *Apprenticeship: Principles, relationships, procedures.* New York: McGraw-Hill.

———. 1998. Malnutrition, brain development, learning, and behavior. *Nutrition Research* 18, no. 2 (February): 351–79.

Scrimshaw, N. S., and J. S. Gordon, eds. 1968. *Malnutrition, learning, and behavior.* Cambridge, Mass.: MIT Press.

Scrimshaw, N. S., C. E. Taylor, and J. E. Gordon. 1968. *Interactions of nutrition and infection.* Geneva: World Health Organization.

Sen, A. K. 1996. *Inequality reexamined.* New York: Russell Sage.

Sewell, R. H. 1976. *Ballots for freedom: Antislavery politics in the United States, 1837–1860.* Cambridge, Mass.: Harvard University Press.

Shafer, B., ed. 1991. *The end of realignment? Interpreting American electoral eras.* Madison: University of Wisconsin Press.

Shaw, G. B. [1928] 1931. *The intelligent woman's guide to socialism and capitalism.* Vol. 20 of *The collected works of Bernard Shaw,* ed. Ayot St. Lawrence. New York: Wm. H. Wise.

Shea, Martina. 1995. *Dynamics of economic well-being: Poverty, 1990–1992.* U.S. Bureau of the Census, Current Population Reports. Washington, D.C.: U.S. Government Printing Office.

Shellenbarger, M. 1997. New job hunters ask recruiters, "Is there life after work?" *Wall Street Journal,* 29 January, B2.

Shigehara, K. 1998. New policies for dealing with ageing. *OECD Observer,* no. 212 (June/July): 5–6.

Shils, E. 1974. Faith, utility, and legitimacy of science. *Daedalus* 103 (summer):1–17.

Shorter, E. 1987. *The health century.* New York: Doubleday.

Shusterman, R. 1994. Pragmatism and liberalism between Dewey and Rorty. *Political Theory* 22:391–413.

Silbey, J. 1967. *The shrine of party: Congressional voting behavior, 1841–1852.* Pittsburgh: University of Pittsburgh Press.

———. 1991a. *The American political nation, 1838–1893.* Stanford, Calif.: Stanford University Press.

———. 1991b. Beyond realignment and realignment theory: American political eras, 1789–1989. In *The end of realignment? Interpreting American electoral eras,* ed. B. E. Shafer. Madison: University of Wisconsin Press.

Silver, S. E., and E. D. Pellegrino. 1993. Physician self-interest and medical ethics. *Journal of the American Medical Association* 270: 577–78.

Singer, C. J. [1941] 1959. *A short history of scientific ideas to 1900.* Oxford: Clarendon.

Slack, P. 1990. *The English poor law, 1531–1782.* Houndmills: Macmillan.

———. 1998. *From reformation to improvement: Public welfare in early modern England.* New York: Clarendon.

Slicher von Bath, B. H. 1963. *The agrarian history of Western Europe, A. D. 500–1850.* London: Edward Arnold.

Sloan, A. 1997. Can need trump greed? *Newsweek,* 28 April, 34–36.

Slusher, C. 1998. Pension integration and social security reform. *Social Security Bulletin* 61:20–27.

Smillie, W. G. 1955. *Public health: Its promise for the future.* New York: Macmillan.

Smith, A. [1776] 1937. *An inquiry into the nature and causes of the wealth of nations.* New York: Modern Library.

Smith, J. P., and F. R. Welch. 1989. Black economic progress after Myrdal. *Journal of Economic Literature* 27:519–65.

Smith, T. L. 1957. *Revivalism and social reform in mid-nineteenth-century America.* New York: Abingdon.

———. 1983. My rejection of a cyclical view of "Great Awakenings" in American religious history. *Sociological Analysis* 44:97–103.

Smolensky, E. 1971. The past and present poor. In *The reinterpretation of American economic history,* ed. R. W. Fogel and S. L. Engerman. New York: Harper & Row.

Solmon, L. 1968. Capital formation by expenditures on formal education, 1880 and 1890. Ph.D. diss., University of Chicago.

———. 1970. Estimates of the costs of schooling in 1880 and 1890. *Explorations in Economic History* 7, suppl. 4:531–81.

Soltow, L. 1968. Long-run changes in British income inequality. *Economic History Review* 21:17–29.

———. 1981. Wealth distribution in England and Wales in 1798. *Economic History Review* 34:60–70.

———. 1989. *Distribution of wealth and income in the United States in 1798.* Pittsburgh: University of Pittsburgh Press.

———. 1992. Inequalities in the standard of living in the United States, 1798–1875. In *American economic growth and standards of living before the Civil War,* ed. R. Gallman and J. J. Wallis. Chicago: University of Chicago Press.

Spiegler, M. 1996. Scouting for souls. *American Demographics* 18 (March): 41–49.

Statistics of Income (SOI). 1981–82. Preliminary income and tax statistics from 1980 individual income tax returns. *SOI Bulletin* 1, no. 3:5–11.

———. 1990. Individual income tax returns, preliminary data, 1988. *SOI Bulletin* 9, no. 4:5–25.

Stearns, P. N. 1997. Stages of consumerism: Recent work on the issues of periodization. *Journal of Modern History* 69:102–17.

Steckel, R. H. 1983. The economic foundations of East-West migration during the 19th century. *Explorations in Economic History* 20:14–36.

———. 1995. Stature and the standard of living. *Journal of Economic Literature* 33:1903–40.

Steckel, R. H., and R. Floud, eds. 1997. *Health and welfare during industrialization.* Chicago: University of Chicago Press.

Stein, H. 1969. *The fiscal revolution in America.* Chicago: University of Chicago Press.

———. 1986. The Washington economics industry. *American Economic Review* 72:1–9.

———. 1988. *Presidential economics: The making of economic policy from Roosevelt to Reagan and beyond.* Washington, D.C.: American Enterprise Institute.

Stern, S. 1996. Why the Catholic school model is taboo. *Wall Street Journal,* 17 July, A14.

Stigler, G. 1954. The early history of empirical studies of consumer behavior. *Journal of Political Economy* 52:95–113.

———. 1975. *The citizen and the state.* Chicago: University of Chicago Press.

Stokes, A. P. 1950. *The church and the state in the United States.* 3 vols. New York: Harper & Bros.

Stone, R. 1988. Some seventeenth-century econometrics: Consumers' behaviour. *Revue Européenne des Sciences Sociales* 26:19–41.

Stout, H. S. 1977. Religion, communication, and the ideological origins of the American Revolution. *William and Mary Quarterly,* 3d ser., 34:519–41.

Strauss, J. 1986. Does better nutrition raise farm productivity? *Journal of Political Economy* 94:297–320.

Strong, J. 1885. *Our country: Its possible future and its present crisis.* New York: Baker & Tyler.

Sundquist, J. L. 1983. *Dynamics of the party system: Alignment and realignment of political parties in the United States.* Rev. ed. Washington, D.C.: Brookings.

Supple, B. E. 1964. *Commercial crisis and change in England, 1600–1642.* Cambridge: Cambridge University Press.

Sweet, W. 1952. *Religion in the development of American culture, 1765–1840.* New York: Scribner.

Swierenga, R. P. 1968. *Pioneers and profits: Land speculation on the Iowa frontier.* Ames: Iowa State University Press.

———. 1990. Ethnoreligious political behavior in the mid-nineteenth century: Voting, values, cultures. In *Religion and American politics from the colonial period to the 1980s,* ed. M. A. Noll. New York: Oxford University Press.

Szasz, F. M. 1982. *The divided mind of Protestant America, 1880–1930.* University: University of Alabama Press.

Szatmary, Z. 1987. The health hazard of not using nuclear power. *Medicine and War* 3:211–22.

Taft, P. 1964. *Organized labor in American history.* New York: Harper & Row.

Tanner, J. M. 1982. The potential of auxological data for monitoring economic and social well-being. *Social Science History* 6:571–81.

———. 1990. *Foetus into man: Physical growth from conception to maturity.* Rev. ed. Cambridge, Mass.: Harvard University Press.

———. 1993. Review of D. J. P. Barker, *Fetal and infant origins of adult disease. Annals of Human Biology* 20:508–9.

Tapia, A. 1996. Soul searching: How is the black church responding to the urban crisis? *Christianity Today,* 4 March, 26–29.

Tarbell, I. M. 1939. *All in the day's work: An autobiography.* New York: Macmillan.

Taylor, G. R. [1951] 1957. *The transportation revolution, 1815–1860.* New York: Rinehart.

Taylor, W. R., ed. 1991. *Inventing Times Square: Commerce and culture at the crossroads of the world.* New York: Russell Sage.

Tebbel, J. W., and M. E. Zuckerman. 1991. *The magazine in America, 1741–1990.* New York: Oxford University Press.

Temin, P. 1964. *Iron and steel in nineteenth-century America.* Cambridge, Mass.: MIT Press.

Tempest in a test tube. 1989. *Newsweek,* 21 August, 66–67.

Tewkesbury, D. G. 1932. *The founding of American colleges and universities before the Civil War: With particular reference to the religious influences bearing upon the college movement.* New York: Teachers College, Columbia University.

Thelen, D. P. 1976. *Robert M. La Follette and the insurgent spirit.* Boston: Little, Brown.

Thirsk, J. 1985. Agricultural policy: Public debate and legislation. In *The agrarian history of England and Wales,* ed. J. Thirsk. Cambridge: Cambridge University Press.

Thompson, E. P. 1963. *The making of the English working class.* New York: Vintage.

———. 1967. Time, work-discipline, and industrial capitalism. *Past and Present* 38:57–97.

Thorp, W. L., and W. F. Crowder. 1941. *The structure of industry.* Washington, D.C.: U.S. Government Printing Office.

Thwing, C. F. 1906. *A history of higher education in America.* New York: D. Appleton.

Tocqueville, A. de. 1969. *Democracy in America.* Garden City, N.Y.: Doubleday.

Toufexis, A. 1989. Panic over power lines. *Time,* 17 July, 71.

Toutain, J. 1971. La consommation alimentaire en France de 1789 à 1964. *Economies et Sociétés: Cahiers de l'ISEA* 5:1909–2049.

Trattner, W. I. 1994. *From poor law to welfare state: A history of social welfare in America.* 5th ed. New York: Free Press.

Trewartha, G. T. 1969. *A geography of populations: World patterns.* New York: Wiley.

Tu, W. 1996. Beyond the Enlightenment mentality: A Confucian perspective of ethics, migration, and global stewardship. *International Migration Review* 30:58–75.

Turner, F. J. 1920. The frontier in American history. New York: H. Holt.

Tyrrell, I. R. 1979. *Sobering up: From temperance to prohibition in antebellum America, 1800–1860.* Contributions in American History, no. 82. Westport, Conn.: Greenwood.

United Nations (UN). 1973. *Determinants and consequences of population trends: New summary of findings on interaction of demographic, economic, and social factors.* Vol. 1. New York.

———. 1990. *Human development report, 1990.* New York: Oxford University Press.

———. 1993. *Human development report, 1993.* New York: Oxford University Press.

U.S. Bureau of the Census. 1854. *Statistical view of the United States . . . Seventh Census.* Washington, D.C.

———. 1864. *Report . . . Eighth Census.* Washington, D.C.

———. 1883. *Report on the manufactures of the United States at the Tenth Census . . . 1880.* Washington, D.C.: U.S. Government Printing Office.

———. 1896. *Report on vital and social statistics in the United States at the Eleventh*

Census, 1890: Part I—analysis and rate tables. Washington, D.C.: U.S. Government Printing Office.

————. 1955, 1967, 1982–83, 1984, 1990, 1991, 1992, 1995, 1996, 1997, 1998. *Statistical abstract of the United States.* Washington, D.C.: U.S. Government Printing Office.

————. 1975. *Historical statistics of the United States, colonial times to 1970.* 2 vols. Bicentennial ed. Washington, D.C.: U.S. Government Printing Office.

————. 1992. Health United States 1991 and prevention profile. PHS 92-1232. Hyattsville, Md.

U.S. Department of Labor. 1959. *How American buying habits change.* Washington, D.C.: U.S. Government Printing Office.

————. Bureau of Labor Statistics. 1994. *Consumer Expenditure Survey, Interview Survey, 1994, public use tape.* Washington, D.C.

U.S. Intelligence Agency. 1978. *National basic intelligence factbook.* Washington, D.C.: U.S. Government Printing Office.

U.S. National Resources Committee. 1939. *The structure of the American economy.* Pt. 1, *Basic characteristics.* Washington, D.C.: U.S. Government Printing Office.

U.S. Public Health Service. 1963. *Vital statistics of the United States, 1960.* Vol. 2, *Mortality.* Washington, D.C.: U.S. Government Printing Office.

U.S. Social Security Administration. 1997. *Annual report.* Washington, D.C.: U.S. Government Printing Office.

U.S. Surgeon General's Office. 1875. *The cholera epidemic of 1873 in the United States.* Washington, D.C.: U.S. Government Printing Office.

Usher, D. 1973. An imputation to the measure of economic growth for changes in life expectancy. In *The measurement of economic and social performance,* ed. M. Moss. New York: Columbia University Press.

————. 1980. *The measurement of economic growth.* New York: Columbia University Press.

Van Deusen, G. G. 1947. *Thurlow Weed: Wizard of the lobby.* Boston: Little, Brown.

————. 1963. *The Jacksonian era, 1828–1848.* New York: Harper & Row.

Vanek, J. 1984. Housewives as workers. In *Work and family: Changing roles of men and women,* ed. P. Voydanoff. Palo Alto, Calif.: Mayfield.

Vanston, N. 1998. The economic impacts of ageing. *OECD Observer,* no. 212 (June/July): 10–15.

van Wieringen, J. C. 1986. Secular growth changes. In *Human growth: A comprehensive treatise* (3 vols.), ed. F. T. Falkner and J. M. Tanner. New York: Plenum.

Vaupel, J. W. 1993. Longevity is moderately heritable in a sample of Danish twins born 1870–1880. *Journal of Gerontology* 48:237–44.

————. 1997. Trajectories of mortality at advanced ages. In *Between Zeus and the salmon,* ed. K. W. Wachter and C. E. Finch. Washington, D.C.: National Academy Press.

Veysey, L. R. 1965. *The emergence of the American university.* Chicago: University of Chicago Press.

Vinovskis, M. A. 1972. Mortality rates and trends in Massachusetts before 1860. *Journal of Economic History* 32:184–213.

Waaler, H. T. 1984. Height, weight, and mortality: The Norwegian experience. *Acta Medica Scandinavica,* suppl. 679:1–51.

Wachter, K. W., and C. E. Finch, eds. 1997. *Between Zeus and the Salmon.* Washington, D.C.: National Academy Press.

Wallace, A. F. 1956. Revitalization movements. *American Anthropologist* 58:264–81.

Wallace, H. A. 1945. *Sixty million jobs.* New York: Simon & Schuster.

Warner, S. B., Jr. 1968. *The private city: Philadelphia in three periods of its growth.* Philadelphia: University of Pennsylvania Press.

Wattenberg, M. P. 1991. *The rise of candidate-centered politics: Presidential elections of the 1980s.* Cambridge, Mass.: Harvard University Press.

Weber, A. F. [1899] 1967. The growth of cities in the nineteenth century: A study in statistics. Ithaca, N.Y.: Cornell University Press.

Weeks, W. B., et al. 1994. A comparison of the educational costs and incomes of physicians and other professionals. *The New England Journal of Medicine* 330, no. 18 (5 May): 1280–86.

Weinstein, D. 1993. Between Kantianism and consequentialism in T. H. Green's moral philosophy. *Political Studies* 41:618–35.

Weir, D. R. 1992. A century of U.S. unemployment, 1890–1990: Revised estimates and evidence for stabilization. *Research in Economic History* 14:301–46.

————. 1993. Parental consumption decisions and child health during the early French fertility decline, 1790–1914. *Journal of Economic History* 53:259–74.

Weiss, T., and D. Schaefer. 1994. *American economic development in historical perspective.* Stanford, Calif.: Stanford University Press.

White, L., Jr. 1962. *Medieval technology and social change.* Oxford: Clarendon.

Whitehead, R. G. 1977. Protein and energy requirements of young children living in the developing countries to allow for catch-up growth after infections. *American Journal of Clinical Nutrition* 30:1545–47.

Wickelgren, I. 1989. Please pass the genes: Experts weigh worries of engineered ills in new food crops. *Science News,* 19 August, 120–24.

Wiebe, R. H. 1967. *The search for order, 1877–1920.* New York: Hill & Wang.

Wiecek, W. M. 1977. *The sources of antislavery constitutionalism in America, 1760–1848.* Ithaca, N.Y.: Cornell University Press.

Wilcox, C. 1940. *Competition and monopoly in American industry.* Washington, D.C.: U.S. Government Printing Office.

Wilcox, N. T. 1992. Understanding the distribution of urban wealth: The United States in 1860. In *Without consent or contract: Evidence and methods*, ed. R. W. Fogel, R. A. Galantine, and R. L. Manning. New York: Norton.

Wildansky, B. 1998. Working solutions. *National Journal* 30, no. 7:1560–62.

Wilentz, S. 1984. *Chants democratic: New York City and the rise of the American working class*. New York: Oxford University Press.

Williams, F. M., and C. C. Zimmerman. 1935. *Studies of family living in the United States and other countries: An analysis of material and method.* Washington, D.C.: U.S. Government Printing Office.

Williamson, C. 1960. *American suffrage: From property to democracy, 1760–1860.* Princeton, N.J.: Princeton University Press.

Williamson, J. G. 1974. Migration to the New World: Long-term influences and impact. *Explorations in Economic History* 11, no. 4 (summer): 357–89.

———. 1976. American prices and urban inequality since 1820. *Journal of Economic History* 36:303–33.

———. 1981a. Some myths die hard—urban disamenities one more time: A reply. *Journal of Economic History* 41:905–7.

———. 1981b. Urban disamenities, dark satanic mills, and the British standard of living debate. *Journal of Economic History* 41:75–83.

———. 1982. Was the Industrial Revolution worth it? Disamenities and death in 19th-century British towns. *Explorations in Economic History* 19:221–45.

———. 1984. British mortality and the value of life, 1781–1931. *Population Studies* 38:157–72.

———. 1985. *Did British capitalism breed inequality?* Boston: Allen & Unwin.

———. 1987a. Debating the British Industrial Revolution. *Explorations in Economic History* 24:269–92.

———. 1987b. Did English factor markets fail during the Industrial Revolution? *Oxford Economic Papers* 39:641–78.

———. 1994. Coping with city growth. In *The economic history of Britain since 1700*, ed. R. Floud and D. McCloskey. Cambridge: Cambridge University Press.

Williamson, J. G., and P. H. Lindert. 1980. *American inequality: A microeconomic history.* New York: Academic.

Wills, E. V. 1936. *Growth of American higher education, liberal, professional, and technical.* Philadelphia: Dorrance.

Wilmoth, J. R. 1998. The future of human longevity: A demographer's perspective. *Science* 280 (17 April): 395–97.

Wilson, E. O. 1993. Is humanity suicidal? If *Homo sapiens* goes the way of the dinosaur, we have only ourselves to blame. *New York Times Magazine*, 30 May, 24–29.

Wilson, W. J. 1978. *The declining significance of race: Blacks and changing American institutions.* Chicago: University of Chicago Press.

——. 1987. *The truly disadvantaged: The inner city, the underclass, and public policy.* Chicago: University of Chicago Press.

——. [1996] 1997. *When work disappears: The world of the new urban poor.* New York: Vintage.

Winter, A. 1997. A legacy of learning. *Modern Maturity* 40, no. 5:24B.

Wolff, M. F. 1993. Asian graduates still flocking in U.S. *Research-Technology Management* 36, no. 6:5–6.

Wood, G. S. 1992a. The radical revolution [interview by Fredrick Smoler]. *American Heritage,* 43, no. 8 (December): 51–58.

——. 1992b. *The radicalism of the American Revolution.* New York: Knopf.

Woods, R. I. 1984. Mortality patterns in the nineteenth century. In *Urban disease and mortality in nineteenth-century England,* ed. R. I. Woods and J. H. Woodward. London: Batsford.

Woodward, K. L. 1989. Heaven: This is the season to search for new meaning in old familiar places. *Newsweek,* 27 March, 52–55.

——. 1992. Talking to God. *Newsweek,* 6 January, 39–44.

Woodward, K. L., and N. Joseph. 1991. The return of the fourth R. *Newsweek,* 10 June, 56–57.

World almanac and book of facts. 1991. New York: World Almanac.

"Work/life" programs on the rise, survey finds. 1998. *National Underwriter (Property and Casualty Risk and Benefits Management)* 100, no. 34:9–10.

World Bank. 1989. *World development report, 1989.* New York: Oxford University Press.

——. 1992. *World development report, 1992.* New York: Oxford University Press.

——. 1993. *The East Asian miracle: Economic growth and public policy.* New York: Oxford University Press.

——. 1995. *World development report, 1995.* New York: Oxford University Press.

Wrigley, E. A. 1969. *Population and history.* London: Weidenfeldt & Nicolson.

——. 1985. Urban growth and agricultural change: England and the Continent in the early modern period. *Journal of Interdisciplinary History* 15:683–728.

——. 1986. Men on the land and men on the countryside: Employment in agriculture in early nineteenth-century England. In *The world we have gained: Histories of population and social structure,* ed. L. Bonfield, R. M. Smith, and K. Wrightson. Oxford: Blackwell.

——. 1987. *People, cities, and wealth: The transformation of traditional society.* Oxford: Blackwell.

Wrigley, E. A., and R. S. Schofield. 1981. *The population history of England, 1541–1871.* London: Edward Arnold.

Wuthnow, R. 1988. *The restructuring of American religion: Society and faith since World War II.* Princeton, N.J.: Princeton University Press.

Yamashita, K., et al. 1993. Feelings of well-being and depression in relation to social activity in normal elderly people. *Nippon Ronen Igakkai Zasshi* 30, no. 8 (August): 693–97.

Yamazaki, M. 1996. Asia, a civilization in the making. *Foreign Affairs* 75 (July/August): 106–18.

Yang, D., and G. Friedman. 1992. Some economic aspects of the Southern interregional migration, 1850–1860. In *Without consent or contract: Evidence and methods,* ed. R. W. Fogel, R. A. Galantine, and R. L. Manning. New York: Norton.

Yasuba, Y. 1962. *Birth rates of the white population in the United States, 1800–1860.* Baltimore: Johns Hopkins University Press.

York, T. 1999. Telecommuting trials. *InfoWorld* 21, no. 22:87–88.

Zakaria, F. 1994. Culture is destiny: A conversation with Lee Kuan Yew. *Foreign Affairs* 73, no. 2:109–26.

Zarnowitz, V. 1992. *Business cycles: Theory, history, indicators, and forecasting.* Chicago: University of Chicago Press.

Zarnowitz, V., and G. H. Moore. 1986. Major changes in cyclical behavior. In *The American business cycle: Continuity and change,* ed. R. J. Gordon. Chicago: University of Chicago Press.

Zhu, Y. 1995. Major changes under way in China's industrial relations. *International Labour Review* 134:37–49.

Zinkiewicz, P. 1996. Helping employees balance work and family duties. *Rough Notes* 139, no. 8:16–17.

Zolotas, X. 1981. *Economic growth and declining social welfare.* Athens: Bank of Greece.

Zunz, O. 1990. *Making America corporate, 1970–1920.* Chicago: University of Chicago Press.

INDEX

Fourth Great Awakening (*continued*)
Christian Coalition, 26; employment
of both spouses, 193–95; evolution of,
84; family ethic of, 239; Moral Majority, 26; political processes of, 83; reform
agenda of, 177, 228, 230; relgious-
political cycles, 213; religiosity associated with, 180; religious revival phase,
25–26, 28t, 30–31; spiritual equity as
goal of, 12–13; spiritual matters of, 180;
technological breakthroughs during,
44; in United States, 18
Franklin, Benjamin, 57
Free Soil Party, 64
Frémont, John C., 65
Friedan, Betty, 133
Fundamentalists: during Third Great Awakening, 23

Garrison, William Lloyd, 22, 26, 96–97
Gini ratio: across European countries in
eighteenth century, 224–25; and high-
performing Asian economies, 230; for
international income distribution, 224;
showing inequality of income distribu-
tion, 217–22
Gladden, Washington, 33, 122, 151, 173, 203
Globalization problems, 13
Gompers, Samuel, 126
Gore, Albert A., 27
Government intervention: in high-powered
Asian economies, 226–30; regulation in
England during grain shortages, 87–88
Government role: conception of post–World
War II social scientists, 133–35; as envi-
sioned by Social Gospelers, 151; in
equalization of income, 157
Grange, the, 114
Great Awakenings: criticism of constructs of,
31; defined, 9; in United States, 18;
value of constructs of, 31–32. *See also*
First Great Awakening (1730–60); Sec-
ond Great Awakening (1800–1920);
Third Great Awakening (1890–?);
Fourth Great Awakening (1960–?)
Great Depression: education and experience
of designers of New Deal reforms, 134;
Roosevelt's brain trust, 129–30; Social
Gospel philosophy during, 129
Great Society, 8, 135
Greeley, Horace, 64, 112, 115
Grimké, Angelina, 106
Grimké, Sarah, 106

Hamilton, Alexander, 57
Health: improvements during Third Great
Awakening, 166–67; lifelong good,
236–37; measure to assess, 146; nine-
teenth-century state and local public
programs, 154–56. *See also* Life expec-
tancy; Malnutrition; Morbidity; Mor-
tality
Health-care systems: current crises in, 195–96
Height: cycles in, 148–51, 153; predictive capac-
ity of, 146–48; relevance to chronic mal-
nutrition and well-being, 145–46
Henry VIII (king of England), 85
Homelessness: in England, 158–59; as indica-
tor of reduced inequality, 144–45
Hoover, Herbert, 45
Hoteling, 193
Howe, D. W., 61
Human capital: increasing importance of, 157;
as main form of capital, 2; of profes-
sional class, 73
Huntington, Samuel P., 232–34

Immigrants: antebellum attitudes toward, 62;
attractions in America for, 111
Immigration: antebellum waves of, 60–62;
effect on antebellum American politics, 61–62; latter part of nineteenth
century, 115–16; legislation limiting,
126; regulation to curb urban growth,
154; rise in United States of non-
Western, 232–33
Income distribution: in colonial America and
early Republic, 89–90; comparison of
English and American (1759, 1790,
1794), 253–58; Gini or concentration ratio, 143–45; Gini ratio in England (eighteenth, nineteenth, and twentieth centuries), 143; government role in decline
of Gini ratio, 156–58; in high-powered
Asian economies, 226–30; inequality of
international, 13, 223–35; postwar fiscal
policy to redistribute, 132; reduction in
inequality of (1700–1973), 143; role of
education in, 157; transfers in doctrine
of modern egalitarianism, 84–85. *See
also* Gini ratio
Incomes: growth in Third World countries,
225; of people in Bangladesh, 225; post-
1970s increase in inequality, 218–22; rise
in professional (1980s), 220; stagnation
of high-school graduates', 220
Industrial sector: change in structure of organi-

INDEX

Mortality: BMI and height as predictors of, 146–48; crises for three centuries preceding twentieth century, 86–87; cycles in, 148–51, 153; nineteenth-century rates in large cities, 116

Mott, Lucretia, 96–97

Multiculturalism: acceptable, 233; new wave, 233–34; rise in United States of, 232

Nathan, Robert, 130–31

National Bureau of Economic Research (NBER), 130

National Organization for Women (NOW), 133–34

National Woman Suffrage Association, 99

Native Americans: reforms for, 95–96

Nativist movement: antebellum urban politics, 60; defined, 62; discrimination against immigrants, 112; to limit immigration, 154; as political force during nineteenth century, 21, 63, 102; of Second Great Awakening, 21; urban reform associated with, 102–3

Natural rights doctrine, 105

New Deal, 8, 134

New Divinity: of Second Great Awakening, 92–93

New England Tract Society, 94

New Theology: of Social Gospelers, 120, 121; theological objections to, 123–24

Niebuhr, H. Richard, 33, 172

Northwest Ordinance (1787), colonial America, 100

Nuclear energy: post-1975 emergence of movement against, 47–48

Nutritional status: defined, 145; distinct from diet, 145; policy as factor in income distribution, 138; of a population, 145–46

Original sin doctrine, 117–19

Pankhurst, Emmeline, 99

Parrington, Vernon, 203

Pension systems: current crises in, 195–96

Pentecostal churches: emergence in twentieth century, 122–23; umbrella organization, 36–37

Perfectionism, 300n22

Physical capital: human capital as substitute for, 157

Political parties: postindustrial party system, 35; system in antebellum American, 61–62. See also Democratic Party; Popu-

list Party; Realignments, political; Republican Party; Whig Party

Politics: effect of technological change on, 59–67; of immigration, 154; political realignments of eras of, 35; realignment synthesis, 8; of urban areas in antebellum era, 59–60. See also Realignments, political

Poor relief: in colonial America, 90–91; English system of, 89, 158; in nineteenth-century America, 111–12

Population: anthropometric measures used to assess health of, 146; effect of heterosis on human, 144; increase in world population, 8, 74–75; Malthus's theory of growth of, 86. See also Elderly population

Populist Party: monetary policy demands of, 114; tariff and excise tax demands of, 128. See also Bryan, William Jennings

Porter, Ebenezer, 32

Poverty: changes during Third Great Awakening in levels of, 170–71; increase in nineteenth century, 111–12; meaning before World War I, 1–2; self-realization requirements for poor people, 181; shift of responsibility from individual to society, 137; of spirit, 3. See also Poor relief

Professional class: in American history, 67–74; HPAE investment in training for, 227–28; as political foundation for egalitarianism, 73; rise of, 2, 67–74; role in egalitarian state, 72–73

Progressive movement: as advocate of women's suffrage, 99; reforms, 127

Promise Keepers, 180

Protestantism: beliefs related to original sin, 117–18; egalitarian ideals, 42. See also Baptist church; Methodist church; Pentecostal church

Provident Fund, 197

Railroads: effect of technological change, 55; interest groups influencing regulation of, 114; labor unions and strikes, 114; as targets of small producers, 113–14. See also Robber barons

Rauschenbusch, Walter, 33, 119–20, 128, 173

Reagan, Ronald, 16, 31, 35

Realignments, political: associated with Democratic Party, 8, 16–17; associated with Republican Party, 8, 16–17; catalysts

for, 9; link between religious movements and, 39–40; during 1850s and 1860s, 15–16, 65–66; during 1990s, 16–17, 66; theory of, 34–36; during Third Great Awakening, 27
Realignment synthesis, 8
Religion: associated with Fourth Great Awakening, 180; doctrine of perfectionism, 300n22; enthusiastic religion, 6, 36–37, 251–52; as issue in public schools, 101–2; non-Protestant, 287; religious ultraism, 94; response to technological change, 9; during Second Great Awakening, 91–92
Religious movements: link between political realignments and, 39–43; revival of Fourth Great Awakening, 18; revival phase, 18–19, 93–94; role of evangelical churches, 6–7; of 1990s, 16; of Second Great Awakening (1800–1920), 15–16; of Third Great Awakening, 121–23
Religious-political cycles, 6–7, 17–19, 41–2; egalitarian doctrine during, 39–43; theories of, 28–36. See also Great Awakenings
Religious Right: reform agenda, 180; during 1990s, 16
Republican Party: alignments in (1860–1932), 66; antislavery program of, 65; circumstances for formation of, 22, 65–66; political realignment associated with, 8; predicted role during Fourth Great Awakening, 27; shift of support during Third Great Awakening from, 27
Resources, material and immaterial: redistribution of, 214–15
Resources, spiritual: acquiring, 214; for egalitarian progress, 203–15; identified, 178; individual's endowment, 205–7; inequality in distribution of, 179; intergenerational equity as barrier to, 179; redistribution of, 207–9; redistribution to the elderly, 209–14; transfer of, 235
Retirement: expected length at age fifty of, 262–63; proportion of age fifty cohort living to retire, 262–63
Revolution, American: egalitarian influence on leaders of, 42
Ricardo, David, 109
Robber barons, 113–15
Roe v. Wade (1973), 133–34
Roosevelt, Franklin D., 8, 27, 129–30

Roosevelt, Theodore: antitrust position of, 126–27; endorsement of women's suffrage, 99
Rorty, Richard, 205
Rostow, W. W., 45

Salant, Walter, 130
Samuelson, Paul A., 131
Sankey, Ira, 32
Schumpeter, Joseph, 183
Science: disenchantment with (1960s), 46–47; in higher education, 68–69
Scopes, John T., 123–24
Scrimshaw, Nevin S., 145
Second Great Awakening (1800–1920): beginning of, 10; Darwinian and urban crises, 28t; disruptive new technologies during, 82; economic theory during, 108–10; ethic of benevolence in, 91; ideological base for modern egalitarianism, 85; overlap with Third Great Awakening, 107–8; reform agenda of, 11, 21, 30, 95–107; religiousness of, 91–92; religious revival phase, 21, 28t; social and political effects, 21–22, 28t
Segregation: effect of school segregation, 158
Self-education, 206
Self-esteem: defined, 207; effect of lost, 212; transfer of, 207
Self-realization: achieved through an occupation, 206; in America, 3; development of, 3–4; individual choice in, 235; meaning of, 204–7; obstacles for non-Western civilizations to, 232; opportunities for, 178; prediction of future, 192; problem of and struggle for, 2, 178; requirements for, 181, 203–4; spiritual capital in quest for, 236; technophysio evolution in quest for, 3
Sen, Amartya, 138
Services sector: continued expansion of, 238; growth of, 183
Shaw, George Bernard, 187
Sherman Antitrust Act (1890), 114, 182
Shils, Edward, 46
Slave-power conspiracy theory, 106–7
Slavery: abolition during Second Great Awakening, 104–7; antebellum political opposition to, 62; as dilemma, 105. See also Abolitionist movement
Smith, Adam, 2–3
Social Gospel movement: actions to gain support for egalitarian legislation, 125; con-

149–50; in eighteenth and nineteenth centuries, 53–56, 153–54; emerging crisis, 22–23; increase in poor people with, 111; problems of, 56–59; regulation of, 154

Urban reform: during Second Great Awakening (1800–1920), 102–4; during Third Great Awakening, 103–4

Van Buren, Martin, 63
Veblen, Thorstein, 187
Volwork: defined, 187; desire for, 189; distribution of lifetime (1875–1995), 191; gains from, 212; hours per week and duration by 2040, 196
Voting Rights Act (1965), 133

Waaler, Hans, 146–48
Wallace, Henry A., 45–46
War on Poverty, 132, 135
Wayland, Francis, 108
Weight: as measure of inequality, 144
Weld, Theodore, 32, 62, 106

Welfare state: Asian nations' perception of, 228–29; basis for, 25; installation (1930–1970), 129; transfers of income under, 6
Whig Party, 61–62
Whitefield, George, 19
Willard, Frances, 98
Wilson, Henry, 64
Wilson, William Julius, 205, 209, 220
Wilson, Woodrow, 70, 126–27
Woman's Christian Temperance Union (WCTU), 98
Women: entry into labor force of married, 193; self-realization requirements for, 181; women's movement (1960s), 133
Women's rights: role of temperance movement in development of, 97; role of WCTU in movement for, 98; during Second Great Awakening, 96–99. *See also* Feminist movement
Women's suffrage movement: of Second Great Awakening, 21
Wood, Gordon, 29, 33
Work ethic, 206